Understanding GENDER, CRIME, and JUSTICE

SAGE Titles of Related Interest

The Female Offender, Second Edition by Meda Chesney-Lind and Lisa Pasko

Girls, Women, and Crime: Selected Readings by Meda Chesney-Lind and Lisa Pasko

Doing Gender, Doing Justice by Susan Martin and Nancy Jurik

Race, Ethnicity, Gender, and Class, Fourth Edition by Joseph Healey (a Pine Forge Press title)

About Criminals by Mark Pogrebin

Family Violence Across the Lifespan, Second Edition by Ola Barnett, Cindy Miller-Perrin, and Robin Perrin

Current Controversies on Family Violence, Second Edition by Donileen Loseke, Richard Gelles, and Mary Cavanaugh

Family Violence in the United States by Denise Hines

Family Violence in a Cultural Perspective by Kathleen Malley-Morrison

Sex Crimes, Second Edition by Ronald Holmes and Stephen Holmes

Current Perspectives on Sex Crimes by Ronald Holmes and Stephen Holmes

Ironies of Imprisonment by Michael Welch

Juvenile Justice: Redeeming Our Children by Barry Krisberg

Juvenile Justice: Process and Systems by Gus Martin

Crime and Everyday Life, Third Edition by Marcus Felson

Career Criminals in Society by Matt DeLisi

Crime Waves by Vincent Sacco

Understanding GENDER, CRIME, and JUSTICE

170101

Merry Morash
Michigan State University

SAGE Publications
Thousand Oaks ▪ London ▪ New Delhi

For information:

Sage Publications, Inc.
2455 Teller Road
Thousand Oaks, California 91320
E-mail: order@sagepub.com

SAGE Publications Ltd
1 Oliver's Yard
55 City Road
London EC1Y 1SP
United Kingdom

Sage Publications India Pvt. Ltd.
B-42, Panchsheel Enclave
Post Box 4109
New Delhi 110 017 India

Printed in the United States of America

Library of Congress Cataloging-in-Publication Data

Morash, Merry, 1946-
Understanding gender, crime, and justice / Merry Morash.
    p. cm.
Includes bibliographical references and index.
ISBN 0-7619-2630-5 (pbk.)
    1. Criminal justice, Administration of. 2. Sex discrimination in criminal justice administration. 3. Women—Crimes against. 4. Gays—Crimes against. 5. Female offenders. 6. Women prisoners. 7. Sex and law. 8. Sex role. I. Title.
HV7419.M67 2006
364.3'7—dc22   2005006694

This book is printed on acid-free paper.

05 06 07 08 09 10 9 8 7 6 5 4 3 2 1

Acquisitions Editor:	Jerry Westby
Editorial Assistant:	Laura Shigemitsu
Production Editor:	Kristen Gibson
Copy Editor:	A. J. Sobczak
Typesetter:	C&M Digitals (P.) Ltd.
Cover Designer:	Janet Foulger

Contents

Preface

*U*nderstanding *Gender, Crime, and Justice* emphasizes contemporary knowledge needed to answer several questions: Why are there pronounced gender differences in rates of criminal victimization? Does gender influence the response of the criminal justice system and other parts of the community to offenders and to crime victims? What part does gender play in the etiology of illegal activities of both males and females? In addressing these questions, the book considers some areas that often are neglected. For example, there is considerable information on males' gender identity as an influence on their illegal activity, but little has been written about females' gender identity and their illegal activity. Also, a full chapter is devoted to the role of social movements in shaping laws and programs as well as practices of the justice system.

Much of the early work on crime, victimization, and the justice system ignored girls, women, and the broader concept of gender. Some of it reinforced stereotypes of males and females or provided support for practices that blamed women and girls for their own victimization or punished them for their sexuality. Chapter 1, "Tackling Key Questions About Gender, Crime, and Justice," includes materials on the early theoretical work to explain wife abuse, rape, and incest against females, and to explain the illegal activity of females. The materials in Chapter 1 provide a backdrop for assessing new knowledge, that is, for seeing the advances in understanding. Chapter 2, "Gender and the Law," explains how contemporary law has developed in ways that have significant effects on women and girls. After the first two chapters, the focus is on new discoveries about people who violate the criminal law, who experience criminal victimization, and who respond to both offenders and victims.

Three types of influences on victimization, offending, and justice system responses are systematically considered in Chapters 3 through 7. One is the broad context—for example, economic conditions. A second is the local context, like the nature of the organization, the community, and the family. A final type of influence is located in a person's identity and psychological makeup. The most powerful explanations of human behavior look at the intertwining of both context and individual.

Unique Features of the Book

Throughout the book, there are numerous quotations from the people who are the characters. The comments of women engaged in prostitution, crime victims, workers in the justice system, and men who break the law are included to give insight into a diversity of experiences and standpoints. The persistent emphasis on context makes it clear that people and their individual traits and characteristics do not exist in a vacuum. The words of offenders, victims, and justice system workers shows the degree of agency that these individuals have, but the information on context shows the constraints that they face.

There are parallels in the effects of gender and sexual orientation in laws, in patterns and causes of victimization, and in the responses of the justice system and other community agencies to both victims and offenders. These parallels are considered throughout the book.

The book uses international examples and information to place U.S. experiences in perspective and to show the way that gender inequities on a worldwide scale contribute to patterns of criminal victimization of women and children. Forms of victimization that occur primarily outside the United States, such as female genital mutilation, are described. Countries that do not routinely separate incarcerated mothers from their children are described. Across countries, there are similar circumstances that result in women's involvement in prostitution, including the exploitation of women and children at tourist destinations. These sorts of information show the ways that gender arrangements influence crime and victimization throughout the world, and they also spotlight unique characteristics of crime, victimization, and justice system response in the United States.

Incorporation Into Courses

This book is intended for use in courses that focus on women and criminal justice, and more broadly that consider criminology, gender and the law, women's studies, or social problems. The book could be used as the primary text in a course on women and criminal justice, or as one of a set of texts in courses that have a greater range in focus. For example, in a criminology course, the book would be a useful supplement to traditional texts that often provide very limited attention to the influence of gender in interaction with race, class, and ethnicity on crime causation and on the response of the justice system. For women's studies course, there is full attention to theories and research that use a feminist perspective to examine crime and justice.

The book is written for undergraduates and for graduate students. To make the book accessible to people with limited familiarity with the justice system or with research and theory pertinent to gender, Chapter 1 develops vocabulary and theoretical frameworks for making sense of what we know about gender, crime, and justice. Key terms, like *gender arrangements* and *gender ideologies*, are defined and explained. Alternative theoretical perspectives and related research methods are noted. Criteria are provided for assessing contributions to knowledge. For more advanced students, this chapter might serve as a review. For less advanced students, instructors would take more time to ensure a solid understanding of key concepts and theoretical perspectives.

Pedagogical Tools

Unique for a book of this type are the numerous photos interspersed throughout. The set of photos accurately conveys the degree to which any consideration of justice in the United States must consider people of different racial and ethnic groups, and the potential that justice is distributed differently between these groups. Included are images from both inside and outside the United States. The pictures stir thought about the impact of social arrangements and justice system processing on the human soul and condition. They are a reminder that this is a book about people of all sorts in many different places, but who all share the quality of humanness.

At the end of every chapter, key terms are listed. These terms are introduced in the text and then defined in a glossary that is integrated with the index for the book. Also, review and discussion topics are provided at the end of each chapter. Beginning with Chapter 2, Web sites are listed for further exploration of chapter topics. These Web sites lead to dynamic sources of information on such areas as current social movements, the perspectives of sex workers in the United States, and alternative explanations and remedies for gender-related injustices.

The Dynamics of Understanding and Action

A key theme of postmodern theorists is that the discourses of experts influence the behavior of practitioners and the public. How we explain crime, victimization, and the justice system response can have a profound effect on the laws that are enacted and on the programs and procedures that we put into place as a part of the justice system. The final chapter of the book summarizes the importance of an international perspective on criminal justice, the intersections of gender with race and ethnicity, and both agency and constraints. This chapter can launch discussion of public policy and individual responsibility, and it can serve as a springboard for new research ideas to fill gaps in knowledge.

Acknowledgments

N
o book of this magnitude can be written in isolation. I'd like to thank Dian P. Gonyea, my able graduate assistant, who retrieved numerous books and articles from the library, negotiated lower fines when I failed to return materials, located missing materials in both my office and the library, and generally brought order to the chaos of materials that grew in my office. Even more important, she shared her personal insights into Native American history and culture that helped me to seek and find answers to questions about high levels of violence and variation between tribes. Other graduate assistants who helped me with various tasks were Soek Jin Jeong and Dae Hoon Kwak.

The book is much more than it would have been because of the detailed suggestions and guidance provided by the academic reviewers who were commissioned by Sage Publications to read and comment on the original book proposal and the various drafts of manuscript chapters. To the extent that I have been able to transgress narrow and traditional sources of theory and research, the reviewers were critical influences. These individuals include Elaine Gunnison, University of Nevada, Las Vegas; Emily Gaarder, Arizona State University; Jo-Ann Della-Giustina, John Jay College of Criminal Justice, The City University of New York; Dawn Beichner, Illinois State University; Karin Dudash, Cameron University; and Frances Coles, California State University, San Bernardino. Additionally, from Sage, Jerry Westby was an extraordinary editor, Denise Simon provided help in finding the reviewers, A.J. Sobczak was of tremendous help as copyeditor, and the Sage group was always a pleasure to work with. They seem to do everything quickly and with excellence.

At home, my family of course provided their usual tolerance of late, take-out, or no dinners; weekend and late-night absences to finish one or another bit of the book; and inconsistent though enthusiastic attention. My husband, Ed, and my children, Valerie and SooJin, have always been supportive in this way, because there has never been a time when I have not been engrossed in some demanding work activity. I would not say they sacrificed or suffered, but we have fashioned a unique family, each of us pursuing our own dreams but enjoying important moments together. Our family very much made this book become a reality.

CHAPTER 1

Tackling Key Questions About Gender, Crime, and Justice

I n the past two decades, there has been a tremendous increase in theory and related research that pertains to gender, crime, and justice. Theory has been developed to answer several key questions, such as the following:

- Why are there different patterns of victimization for women and men, girls and boys, and people who are and are not heterosexual?
- How does gender affect the way that the criminal justice system, medical personnel, and others respond to victimization?
- How do laws affect people in different gender groups, and how do laws with differential effect come to be written and implemented?
- Why do the patterns and types of illegal behavior differ by gender group?
- How does the gender of people who break the law influence their treatment by police, prosecutors, courts, and correctional programs?

More broadly, theory has tried to explain the influence of the division of resources and opportunities according to people's gender and beliefs about gender on crime and justice. Theories to provide answers to these questions have been developed primarily in the disciplines of psychology, sociology, and history, as well as in the interdisciplinary fields of criminal justice and criminology and of women's studies. Much of the work has contributed to what is called **feminist theory**,[1] which is actually not one but several theories that consider the disadvantages and oppression faced by girls and women and that emphasize research that will reduce this oppression. The primary objective of this book is to draw widely from the fields of social science and to present promising and innovative contemporary theories relevant to gender, crime, and justice.

The theories that are developed within the various disciplines emphasize different **levels of explanation**. At the *macro* level, explanatory factors include widespread economic conditions and arrangements, public health and illness, type of government and legal system, heritage, and culture. At an *intermediate* level, organizational, community, and family characteristics explain illegal behavior and responses to it. At the *micro* level, human behavior and social life are affected by people's interactions and their ideas and characteristics. Either working within a discipline or integrating across disciplines, many theorists have explained how context, individual interactions, and individual characteristics come together to explain crime and justice. Culture, national policies, and economic conditions can influence both the nature of communities and organizations and the behavior and experiences of individuals. Reciprocally, individual actions and characteristics influence the nature of communities, organizations, and social conditions. Also, influences at one level can either enhance or dampen influences at other levels. For example, individual characteristics can have greater effects in certain community or organizational contexts. Chapter 2 will discuss gender and the law, and the remaining chapters of this book are organized to provide an exposure to theory that is useful in showing macro-, intermediate-, and microlevel influences on victimization, on crime, and on responses to both victimization and crime.

The selection of theory to be presented is based on several criteria pertinent to determining the validity and utility of an explanation. Not all theories presented in the book meet all criteria, but each advances knowledge by meeting some of the criteria. The criteria are that (a) empirical evidence supports the theory; (b) research supporting the theoretical explanation is contemporaneous; (c) the theory situates human behavior in some realistic setting; (d) the theory considers the intersections between gender, race, ethnicity, and social class; and (e) the theory recognizes that people have agency. Theories that recognize patterns of globalization, specifically the influence of population movements and the economic and other interdependencies between nations, also are highlighted. Aside from meeting criteria for good theory, some explanations in the remaining chapters of the book touch on selected postmodern themes, including the complexity of causation and the influence of discourse on human actions.

Working back and forth between theoretical explanations and *empirical evidence* is integral to developing social science theory. Research is a part of the theory development process, and in a sense, unless researchers haphazardly select variables to include in their study, they all are theorists. They are trying to develop or improve explanations of social phenomena.

The criticality of *contemporaneous* research to support theory stems from the pace of reform and change that is occurring on a global scale. Although new theoretical explanations are not necessarily better than old ones, changes in contemporary society provide reason to carefully examine old theories and to update or alter them in response to current conditions. Social movements have redefined violence against women, legislators have changed the behaviors that are criminalized, and justice system employees have been trained and confronted regarding their ideas about gender and race. New groups have immigrated to the United States and to other countries, and economies have grown stronger or weaker. How people think

Consistent with the idea of intersections, people identify themselves as holding a number of statuses, including their racial group membership, sexual orientation, political orientation, and others.
© Bettmann/CORBIS

things through, how they develop and justify decisions, and the contexts in which they live and interact can change. Theory developed in prior decades may or may not still be valid.

The criticality of *situated* explanations stems from the recognition that context makes a difference. The problem is compounded in a country like the United States, which has very different mixes of indigenous and immigrant racial, and ethnic groups in different regions, and which has decentralized systems of justice, social services, and health care. Throughout this book, care is taken to specify the setting to which research applies, and to try to tease out the influence of that setting on the phenomena that the theory explains.

Intersections is an important concept in feminist theory, and therefore in many of the theories considered in the book. Gender can have a powerful influence on one's personhood and one's location within a broad social structure, but race, social class, and other status markers also have a significant influence. Bell hooks's *Ain't I a Woman* (1981) is a milestone in recognizing and stamping into collective memory the invalidity of a sole focus on gender. Hooks wrote about the attempted systematic exclusion of herself and other black women from the human race, accomplished by arguments to keep women out of politics because all women were frail and delicate. Hooks pointed to the evidence that women like herself had fully contradicted this imagery, in part because of the hard labor and the severe living conditions imposed on slaves. The problem of understanding the realities of the lives of women who differ in their combinations of age, color, class, ethnicity, and sexual orientation pervades both legal decisions and contemporary theory.

Two court cases related to discrimination illustrate the importance of intersections and the inadequacy of laws to address discrimination against people who are multiply disadvantaged (Crenshaw, 1989). Five black women sued General Motors on the basis that they were disadvantaged when the people with the least seniority were laid off. They argued that General Motors did not hire black women until 1964, making it impossible for a black woman to have achieved much seniority. The court ruled against them, reasoning that they were not disadvantaged due to sex, because white women had been hired, and they were not disadvantaged due to race, because black men had been hired.[2] In a second case, a black woman alleged that her employer, Hughes Helicopter, discriminated in making promotions.[3] The court again ruled against the plaintiff, on the basis that statistics on all women in the company (most of whom were white) were inconsistent with sex discrimination. The two cases illustrate that the laws against discrimination do not recognize that people with two or more characteristics that may result in discrimination can have experiences different from people with any one of the characteristics. The laws as implemented did not recognize the influence of intersections.

Similarly, many theories have not taken into account that all females or all males do not have similar resource levels or experiences and are not viewed by other people in the same way. Bias and prejudice against lesbian women, for example, may be different from bias against gay men. Also, biases and prejudices against people in a minority group may be different depending on whether those people are female or male. In many cases, there is inadequate empirical research to look at intersections, with the result that theory is erroneously set forth as though it applies to more people than is the case.

Agency is a person's capacity to act in a self-directed and purposeful way. When people come together and challenge stereotypes, exert pressures to have legislation enacted or repealed, press for reform of the criminal justice system, or take steps to reshape a broad cultural context and structural arrangements, they are acting with agency. When people who experience criminal victimization interact with police and prosecutors and make decisions about how much they will cooperate with justice system personnel, they also are self-directed and purposeful. Incarcerated women who have prison jobs for which they deliver HIV/AIDS education to other people and incarcerated women who seek, use, or reject correctional services similarly have agency.

People vary considerably in the constraints on their agency, and observations about a person's agency tell us not only about that individual but also about her or his access to resources and freedom to act as desired. People with little power or experience may be limited to passive resistance and muffled expression of their feelings, and those with more influence can bring about desired changes, either in their own lives, as part of an organization, or even throughout society. Although no groups or individuals can totally control their actions and life courses, very few people, if any, give up individually and collectively to the extent that they do not try to exert influence at all, at least by expressing themselves or by engaging in silent protest.

The concept of agency keeps the human spirit in social science. Some social science theories ignore agency and portray people as pawns that are moved about by external forces or internal pressures and traits. Theorists have sometimes depicted all women offenders as victims who have been led astray by their male partners, and who therefore have no agency (Maher, 1997). Crime victims similarly are sometimes described as completely helpless and needy. Individuals who work in the justice system differ from each other in the labels they attach to victims and offenders, victims and offenders sometimes resist labels placed on them, people work to change social arrangements, and justice system workers vary in their interpretation and application of legal statutes. Therefore, for victims, offenders, and people who work in the criminal justice system, it is misleading to overemphasize lack of agency.

Agency is not static or an all-or-nothing characteristic. It varies depending on the situation and the context. People have different levels of agency in particular places, at particular times, and in particular situations. Some people, for example those who are incarcerated or who have very limited financial resources, may have limited agency at most times and places.

Empowerment is the process of increasing agency. Social movements try to empower groups of people. The women's and the gay and lesbian rights movements have specifically tried to empower people who are victimized by gender-related crimes. Similarly, gender-responsive correctional programs for women were developed to empower them. Empowerment can be achieved by increasing people's financial and other material resources, lending the power of the courts to their cases, meeting needs that include but are not restricted to mental health, and promoting insight and understanding. Given the growth in the law and its intrusions into family and organizational life in the United States, a tough question is whether existing laws increase empowerment across gender, racial, ethnic, and cultural groups, or whether instead particular laws take away individual choice and direction, at least for some people and groups.

Globalization, which refers to the impact of cross-national economic dependencies, multinational firms, and multiple cultures on urban, metropolitan, town, and rural settings, makes it essential to get beyond a singular focus on the United States. Culturally rooted ideas about masculinity and femininity are related to expectations regarding appropriate behaviors and to differential job opportunities and immigration patterns for women and men (Freeman, 2001, p. 1011). One result of gender inequalities is that women and children are trafficked from poor countries and regions of countries and forced into sex work. Prostitutes at tourist destinations around the world come from economically unstable or destitute areas. Another result of gender inequity and the movement of people between countries is that abuse within marriage can result when a couple's exposure to new ideas about how husbands and wives should act erupts into conflict. Both international sexual exploitation and domestic conflict require creative policy and programs in

In the United States and many other countries, the population is increasingly diverse in racial and ethnic characteristics.
© Chuck Savage/CORBIS

order to promote justice for individuals who are economically disadvantaged or who are immigrants in a country where they do not understand the justice system or do not have resources to handle conflicts effectively.

Because of the concentration of wealth and resources in the United States, it has been able to have quite a bit of effect on other nations. The U.S. government has promulgated policies of criminalization and incarceration of drug offenders worldwide, with the result that there has been an influx of women into U.S. prisons for trafficking. Women also have been incarcerated at an increasing rate in their home countries. The U.S. government also has affected women and girls worldwide by refusing to fund overseas agencies that provide information or services related to abortion.

Although the interdependencies and mixtures of people and ideas from different nations and cultures are a fact of life, it is greatly beyond the scope of this book to provide a systematic assessment of gender, crime, and justice worldwide. It would be a daunting if not impossible task, given the number of understudied and undertheorized parts of the world and the limited access to literature and languages relevant to many countries and subgroups within those countries. Also, there are markedly different systems of law in different countries, with roots in different traditions and unique features that have developed because of mixing and adapting of more than one system of law (Fairchild & Dammer, 2001, pp. 42–63). Throughout the book, though, there are examples that illustrate similarities and differences in the interplay of gender, crime, and justice in the United States and other countries, or between cultural, immigrant, indigenous, and ethnic groups within a country. These examples provide reminders that the United States is not representative of a very large part of the world either geographically or in population, and that many countries, like the United States, have a very diverse population. A number of the examples are taken from Australia, New Zealand, Great Britain, and Canada, countries that have both legal and scholarly traditions that are similar to those in the United States. Other examples compare the United States and other countries on the status of women and the related causes of gender-related crime and victimization, and on responses to crime and victimization. Comparison highlights the ways in which the United States is unique and can lead to questions about the justness of unique features. Alternatively, comparison can show commonality in the influence of gender.

Postmodern Themes

One contribution of what is called postmodernism in social science is the consideration of themes that have not been highlighted in prior theories, at least to the extent they are highlighted in postmodern theories. **Postmodern themes** are the impact of the media on shaping different versions of reality, the themes of war and inequity that dominate global politics, and the emergence and power of multinational firms. In relation to crime, postmodern theorists spotlight the U.S. practice of incarcerating large numbers of people who have been defined as dispensable and irredeemable. They also stress the influence of what they call *discourses* on how people in the criminal justice system act.

Discourses are collections of ideas, concepts, explanations, and categorizations that are communicated in bodies of writing and discussion. Discourses can influence social life. Three particular types of discourse are important to understanding the interconnections of gender, crime, and justice. First, there is discourse within formal social control agencies such as police departments, prosecutors' offices, courtrooms, and victim assistance programs. Communication often crosses organizational boundaries, for example when prosecutor, judge, legal defense, and probation officials are present in a courtroom setting. The discourse of criminal justice officials tells us about how they perceive and reason about the events of alleged crime and victimization. Discourse also makes certain actions seem reasonable, fair, and just, and makes others seem out of the question.

As a second type, the discourses of medical, legal, social science, and other experts can alter how people are understood, treated, and managed. For example, according to psychological discourse, a woman who has murdered her husband after he beat her might be viewed as failing to use more appropriate coping responses or as precipitating the beating due to her own psychological problems. Contradictory discourse would emphasize that the greater power and threat of the abusive husband led to murder in self-defense. The psychological discourse suggests the victim's guilt and the need for punishment, and the contradictory discourse suggests that the victim is not guilty, but that there is need to empower potential victims. Alternative discourses have contradictory influences not only on how individuals are treated by the justice system, but also on criminal justice policy and laws.

A third type of discourse occurs in a larger political arena when various interest groups and representatives from particular agencies, along with members of the general public, talk and write about what should and what should not be considered criminal, and how victims and offenders should be understood and treated. Political discourse tells us about the thinking of social activists and citizens who advocate for or who resist change, and it influences people to support particular responses to crime and victimization.

Discourse can be analyzed to reveal the ideas that go into a person's thinking and reasoning. Although there is not an invariable connection between discourse and action, discourse certainly is connected to action. The connection may be after the fact, for example when a person draws on discourse to provide a justification for action. It can also precede and influence or allow certain responses to people considered to be criminal, delinquent, or victims. Thus, discourse is relevant to understanding gender, crime, and justice.

Remaining Contents of Chapter 1

The next section of this chapter provides definitions of key terms relevant to gender and to crime and justice. Much of the contemporary theory and research summarized in this book, and indeed the development of the key theoretical concepts defined below, is a response and a corrective to problematic work that went before. Therefore, this chapter also includes a review of historical and problematic theory, followed by a section on historical and problematic policies and practices in the justice system. Misleading and flawed theories are presented as a backdrop against which to assess contemporary work that is presented in subsequent chapters. Prior policies and practices have perpetuated gender-related injustice, in some cases because they rest on misleading theories. Finally, this chapter considers how empirical evidence can be used to advance theory. In essence, this last section departs from the focus on theories about crime or responses to it, and it considers whether and how it is possible to develop valid theory about social life.

Key Terms Related to Gender, Crime, and Justice

Gender

Macrolevel Conceptualization of Gender

Consistent with the recognition that theory identifies macro to micro influences on social life and behavior, gender can be conceptualized at different levels. At the macro level—that is, within the global system, a country, or a society—whether people are women or men, girls or boys, affects social and economic status and opportunities and expectations in relation to education, work, family, and leisure. Specifically, there are gender differences in monetary and other resources, in power, and in access to different kinds of jobs. The patterns of differences are referred to with different terms, including *gender organization,* the *sex gender system, gender arrangements,* and *gender stratification.* **Patriarchy** is a gender arrangement that is characterized by males' domination of females. There is not one universal form of gender organization that exists through all cultures or historical periods, and within a historical period or a particular setting, gender inequalities are not experienced to the same extent by all groups and individuals (Aker, 1989). Gender organization varies from relatively egalitarian systems to hierarchies marked by extreme inequality, and it has differential effects on people depending on social class, race, ethnicity, and other characteristics.

The notion of gender organization was absent from most social science writing and research until recent decades, though it is currently a central concept in the theoretical work of a number of people. Feminist theorists have focused on patriarchy and how it influences social arrangements, thoughts, and behaviors of both females and males (Heimer & DeCoster, 1999, p. 282; also see Ferree & Hess, 1987; Lorber, 1994). There is a strong presence of feminist theorists in criminology, though still some criminologists do theorize about social structure, context, and identity without attention to gender.

A person's **social location** is her or his place within existing social arrangements, including the existing gender organization. Therefore, social location is related to gender as well as other statuses that differentiate people's access to resources and opportunities.

Individual-Level Conceptualization of Gender

Sex is a physical, biological characteristic, with a more or less fixed state (less when people have genitals that are ambiguous or when they undergo sex-change operations or drug therapies). *Gender* at the individual level involves a dynamic process of definition of appropriate characteristics and actions associated with being feminine or masculine (Kessler & McKenna, 1978; C. West & Zimmerman, 1987). Beliefs about masculinity and femininity differ between cultural, national, religious, social class, and other groups (Anderson, 1988; Vance, 1984). One person's beliefs about gender can vary over the course of her or his life, too. Ideas about gender depend heavily on interactions with other people, but they also are influenced by education, experience, and self-reflection.

Beliefs about characteristics and behaviors considered to be masculine or feminine are referred to as **gender ideologies** or **gender definitions**. Ideologies consist of images, concepts, and assumptions (Patai & Koertge, 1994). A person's gender ideology is her or his image of and assumptions about manhood, womanhood, and marital roles of men and women (Hochschild & Manchung, 1989). A person's gender ideology is not fixed, and with experience and reflection it can change over a person's life course (Mac An Ghaill, 1994). Gender ideologies tend to emphasize differences rather than similarities. Gender ideologies are important because they affect beliefs about inappropriate and appropriate behavior and expectations about how people should act.

Some beliefs about gender are reflected in **gender stereotypes.** In the United States, majority race women are stereotyped as weak, overly emotional, and child-like; black women are stereotyped as promiscuous, dominant, and aggressive; and gay men are stereotyped as sexual predators or as promiscuous. Stereotypes are oversimplified opinions, prejudiced attitudes, and uncritical judgments about groups of people. They often are directed at groups whose members have less power and advantage than others in at least some of life's arenas.

Both gender ideologies and gender stereotypes influence the actions and reactions of people. At the level of the individual, they are incorporated into a sense of self and motivate people to act in a certain way. Neither gender ideologies nor gender stereotypes are accepted uncritically by all people, and thus individual identities, behaviors, and reactions are unique. At the core of human behavior, however, is a sense of self and self-direction, and some notion of gender is a key part of each person's sense of self. **Gender identity** is a person's sense of self as a person of a certain gender.

Gendered Aspects of Social Life

Some theorists write about the *gendered self*, *gendered interactions*, the *gendered organization*, or *gendered law*. What they mean is that the self, people interacting with each other, organizations, and the law cannot be understood adequately without considering gender arrangements and ideologies. It is possible, however, to be so attuned to the importance of gender in understanding some phenomenon that one's thinking becomes reductionist, that is, it explains all of social life as a result of gender. As already noted, often it is the combined effect of different statuses, the intersections, that are important (Anderson & Hill Collins, 1998, p. 3). Also, gender is not consistently a salient influence on every aspect of social life, and a sole focus on gender would obscure the importance of those other influences that are salient. However, for most of the history of criminological theory and research, the neglect of gender, not its overemphasis, has been a shortcoming (Daly & Chesney-Lind, 1988).

Crime and Justice

Crime is activity that is prohibited by criminal law and that makes the offender liable to punishment under that law. Because laws can vary and can be applied with some discretion, certain actions may differentially be classified as crime or not crime. *Justice* requires fairly addressing conflicts and inequities between people. Justice is served when people who are victimized are in some ways protected from additional victimization and compensated for their suffering, and the perpetrators are fairly punished. The term **criminal justice** refers to the laws that define and prohibit criminal behavior as well as the police, court, and corrections agencies that implement the laws. *Criminal justice* is not necessarily just. For example, Amnesty International (Amnesty International, 1999), a human rights watchdog group, and the U.S. General Accounting Office (General Accounting Office, 1999) have documented the sexual abuse of women in prisons in several countries, including the United States. Historically, the lynching of black men in the United States was based on false claims that they had raped white women (Davis, 1978). There are sentencing practices and courtroom dramas that provide powerful examples of how gender disadvantages some people while it advantages others. Laws themselves may unjustly criminalize behaviors, and in some cases the result is that a particular group experiences disproportionately harsh punishment. Laws and the criminal justice agencies that implement them also can fail to protect and compensate crime victims. A great deal of theory is designed to explain when and why laws are just in their form and application, and to document how justice is or is not delivered in spite of the law.

Early Theoretical Work

Many of the advances in theory considered in this book resulted from creative refashioning or outright rejection and replacement of prior theoretical work that did not even consider gender, that ignored women and girls, or that incorporated and perpetuated gender stereotypes. Several excellent articles and books (Belknap, 2001; Leonard, 1982; Naffine, 1987; Scraton, 1990; Smart, 1976) have criticized and analyzed the failures of prior theory about criminology and criminal justice. Dorie Klein's 1973 classic article established that many traditional theories about the causes of crime and delinquency incorporated and disseminated sexist stereotypes about girls and women. In 1988, Daly and Chesney-Lind reviewed the state of criminological knowledge, and they concluded that despite a burst of research attention to women and girls, theory about gender organization was quite limited, and criminology as a field of study had not fully incorporated the understandings that were coming out of feminist theory developed in other disciplines. More recently, Belknap's (Belknap, 2001) book-length assessment of both historical and contemporary theory and research pointed to the invisibility of women and girls both in the justice system and in the theories about them and in policies and procedures that would result in addressing their needs and promoting their empowerment. To provide a point for comparison with theories and practices described in the next chapters, some of the inadequacies of prior work are described.

Theories to Explain Victimization

Wife Abuse

Until the 1970s, scholars who studied crime in the United States paid little or no attention to female victims of abuse by their husbands (Klein, 1973; Rasche, 1974).

From 1939 to 1969, for example, the indexes of the *Journal of Marriage and the Family* did not contain any references to spousal violence (Schechter, 1982). However, by the end of the 1970s in the United States, there was an emerging body of literature on wife abuse. With the growth of the professions of psychoanalysis and social work in the 1980s, Freudian theory directed attention to a host of problems that were cast as manifestations of wife abuse victims' psychological disturbance (R. E. Dobash & Dobash, 1992). For example, a book based on the author's clinical practice, *Sweet Suffering: Woman as Victim* (Shainess, 1984), explained women's victimization as the result of their own masochism. According to the book, some women who grew up in abusive homes learned that their pain and suffering was normal, and therefore they became masochistic and sought out abusive relationships. Other therapeutically oriented explanations were that abused women suffered from a very varied set of personality problems that made them susceptible to violence; these problems included "reserve and caution in emotional expression, low ego strength, inability to cope, shyness and difficulty in self-expression, self destructiveness, skill deficits, problems communicating with others . . . and poor 'locus of control'" (R. E. Dobash & Dobash, 1992, p. 225). The early psychological theories were deficient because they did not provide valid documentation that abused women indeed suffered from psychological problems more than did other women, indicators of these problems were suspect, and there was no evidence that these problems were causally linked to some dynamic that would lead women to seek abusive partners or incite their partners to be abusive.

Early theories about wife abuse also claimed that women stayed in abusive relationships because of their personal failings and weakness (Loseke & Cahil, 1984). L.E.A. Walker (1984) transported the concept of **learned helplessness** from research on rats that responded to electric shocks with passive, helpless behavior. She postulated that abused women, like the rats, gave up and became helpless to the point that they could not stop the abuse or leave the relationship. Over time, the learned helplessness explanation for staying in an abusive relationship became an explanation for being in an abusive relationship in the first place (R. E. Dobash & Dobash, 1992). The range of women's characteristics that were set forth as reasons for their preferences for abusive men included "rigid sex role socialization, . . . a benign, paternalistic, 'Dresden doll' kind of upbringing, and early slavish characteristics" (R. E. Dobash & Dobash, 1992, p. 225). Abused women's characteristics were presented as exasperating to police and therapists, because a condition called **battered women's syndrome** (L.E.A. Walker, 1984) prevented women from leaving abusive relationships. The abused woman's fear of being beaten again rendered her incapable of resisting. Early theory to explain wife abuse ignored the centrality of the abusive male in perpetrating violence. It was reductionist in its sole emphasis on women's state of mind as the reason for being battered and staying in an abusive relationship, and because it ignored cultural, financial, and safety considerations that could explain why rational women would not leave an abusive relationship.

Family conflict theory offered yet another explanation for women's abuse. According to family conflict theory, a man hitting his wife or her hitting him are manifestations of discordant relationships and poor approaches to handling conflict. Family conflict theory was supported by 1975 and 1985 survey findings that in married and cohabitating couples, men and women were equally violent, and indeed men were somewhat more likely to be victims of the most severe incidents of violence (Steinmetz & Lucca, 1988; Straus, 1980; Straus & Gelles, 1990). The data to support family conflict theory consisted of counts of reported instances of hitting, throwing objects, and completing other physically and emotionally aggressive sorts of acts against one's partner. The approach to documenting abuse is invalid, because it does not show whether acts are equally injurious, whether one party is afraid of the other, whether violence by one person is escalating, or whether acts are in self-defense. Family conflict theory and the research that supported it are misleading because they examine acts outside the context of other family dynamics, including whether there is an imbalance of power (Loseke & Cahil, 1984; Pleck, 1987).

One limitation of early theories to explain intimate partner violence is that they rested on the assumption that any incident was part of a similar pattern of abuse. Johnson and Ferraro (2000) examined prior research and identified five types of domestically violent relationships. *Common couple violence* involves one or two incidents but no pattern of abuse and rarely sexual or emotional abuse. *Intimate terrorism* is one tactic in a pattern of control and manipulation, and it is often accompanied by emotional abuse. *Violent resistance* involves violence in self-defense, and in many cases it is a one-time event. *Mutual violent combat* involves each partner using manipulative or controlling violence against the other, though often the male is more active against the female. Finally, there are instances of *dysphoric-borderline violence* by batterers who are very needy and dependent and who strike out to keep their partners with them. The early theories of intimate partner violence did not rest on detailed data on the dynamics and the patterns of abuse.

Rape

Early social science theories also fell far short of adequately explaining rape. One theory, referred to as **victim precipitation** theory, rested on the premise that the psychological makeup of rape victims differentiated them from other women (Amir, 1971), and therefore the victims' psychology precipitated rape. According to victim precipitation theory, the victim's abnormal psychology resulted in unusual behavior—for example, acceptance of a ride in a car or entering an apartment alone with a man—and this behavior could easily be misinterpreted by men to signal willingness to have sexual intercourse. In some cases, according to the theory, the abnormal women actually did agree to sexual activity, but later claimed rape. The theory accepted the rapists' judgments of "She was asking for it" or "She did not resist strongly enough," along with their rationalizations, "Her behavior was provocative" or "She changed her mind too late," and used them for a causal explanation of rape (Schwendinger & Schwendinger, 1983, p. 66). An elaboration of the victim precipitation theory of rape is that rape occurs because the victim failed to confront the rapist's assumption of the right to dominate and, furthermore, failed to communicate that she did not want to have sexual intercourse (Goode, 1969). Victim precipitation theory places responsibility for rape on the victim, suggesting that she acted in a way that was contrary to expectations for the appropriate behavior of a woman, with the result that she incited the violence against herself or left her desires open to misinterpretation (Smart, 1976, p. 100).

Some psychoanalytic theory located the cause of rape in the psyche of the offending male rather than in the psyche of the victim. The key idea was that men who committed rape were psychologically disturbed, and as a result they acted with hatred and aggression toward women. For example, one theory provided the explanation that mother-dominated black families stimulated homosexual tendencies in male children, and the resulting problems of masculinity and sexual identity led them to rape women (Amir, 1971, p. 73). A central part of the logic is that when women's status creates men's sexual anxieties, men will be driven to violence. A key criticism of the psychoanalytic theories is that the "emphasis on irrational and unconscious personality processes implicitly minimizes" the influence of society-wide beliefs that support men's sexual violence against women (Schwendinger & Schwendinger, 1983, p. 74). Also, there is no evidence that homosexual tendencies or mother-dominated family structures are connected to rape.

Some psychological theories have not considered the unconscious but still have emphasized the offender's abnormal personality as the cause of rape (Groth & Burgess, 1977). For example, one explanation was that men who committed rape had personality disorders. A personality disorder is indicated by inflexible and maladaptive patterns of perceiving people and situations, relating to them, and thinking about oneself and the environment. These patterns of thinking and behaving may harm other people and may not even meet an individual's own needs in the long run. Attributing rape to offenders' psychological makeup did correct the problem of blaming rape victims for being attacked; however, a primary criticism of psychological explanations of offenders' behavior is that there would need to be considerable undiagnosed psychological disturbance throughout the population in order to account for the prevalence of rape within marriage, rape in the context of a dating relationship, and rape by acquaintances. This assumption is untenable.

Incest

Early social science theories to explain incest echoed familiar themes. Although Freud initially accepted women's descriptions of incest as valid, he later believed they were fantasies. He reasoned that the fantasies were sparked by neurotic mothers who, because they were not sexually satisfied by their husbands, were overly tender and overly anxious in their interactions with their children. The mothers' behavior awakened sexual precocity, which led to the children's fantasies about being subjected to incestuous acts (Freud, 1966, p. 38). Subsequent to Freud's work, theories based on numerous pieces of research with small samples of women who were undergoing therapy posited that mothers colluded with their husbands to allow incest to continue (Wattenberg, 1985). The typical family context, in which women had little influence over husbands who were committing incest, was ignored by these theories.

Family systems theory also was extended to explain incest. The idea was that incest occurred when families became dysfunctional, for example when the mother was ill and could not carry out her typical activities to support the family. Mothers were sometimes described as providing the primary impetus for incest when they withdrew emotionally and sexually from their husbands (Gavey, Florence, Pezaro, & Tan, 1990; Gutheil & Avery, 1977, p. 113; Swanson & Biaggio, 1985). Each family member was seen as having a part in causing incestuous behavior. The implication of this theory is that women and children are responsible for incest within the family, and that if they can improve the functioning of the family, the incest will stop (Butler, 1982, p. 325). Again, the assumption is that each family member has equal power to control the family and, therefore, each has equal responsibility for incest. As with all of the earliest theories about girls' and women's victimization, victims and/or their mothers explain men's violence, and women (in this case, mothers) are blamed for not fitting **gender role stereotypes,** which are exaggerated oversimplified beliefs about appropriate behavior for females and for males.

Except for theories that linked men's psychological disturbance to rape, the victim's or her mother's psychological inadequacies or inabilities to perform expected roles were seen as the primary causes of violence against women. The idea that men who rape were disturbed because of their mothers' behaviors similarly gave women the ultimate responsibility for the victimization of other women and girls. Notably absent is any indication that beliefs of men and activities of fathers are central in promoting victimization of women and girls. Also absent is any recognition of how macrolevel influences might result in violence against women.

Theories to Explain the Behavior of Offenders

The first theoretical developments relevant to offenders also were limited in their treatment of the sex and gender concepts. By the 1980s, numerous studies had been published on the delinquency of boys, and no apology was offered for omitting girls from the theories or the samples. In the years of relative neglect of females who broke the law, there were some exceptions, but these exceptions did not produce well-founded theories. In a critical essay that exposed questionable assumptions that theorists made about the inherent nature of women, Klein (1973) identified theorists who had had a major impact on thinking about women's criminality (Freud, 1933; Lombroso, 1920; Pollak, 1950; Thomas, 1923) or who represented the contemporary work at the time she was writing (Cowie, Cowie, & Slater, 1968; Konopka, 1966; Vedder & Sommerville, 1970). Her analysis showed that prior theorists had categorized girls and women as good women who are "normal" and bad women who are criminals. Normalcy depended on whether the girl fulfilled traditional gender roles (Klein, 1973, p. 4). The division of women into good and bad based on fulfilling traditional gender roles is sometimes referred to as the **madonna/whore duality** (Feinman, 1986, p. 4).

Psychological theories to explain why girls and women broke the law were based on assumptions about universal psychological traits, and crime was viewed as "a *perversion of* or *rebellion against* [females'] *natural feminine roles*" (Klein, 1973, p. 5). Most theories that linked gangs to delinquency portrayed girls as auxiliaries to the central male members, and/or they emphasized the sexual availability and activities of the girls. In some cases, girls were described as promiscuous when male gang members pressured or forced them into sexual activity (Chesney-Lind & Hagedorn, 1999). Early theories also ignored the family and community context, the larger social structure that might contribute to lawbreaking, and diversity in **gender role prescriptions** for different racial and ethnic groups (Rice, 1990). They were flawed because they emphasized girls' and women's sexuality and femininity (or lack thereof) as explanations for their illegal behavior, and they therefore assumed that desistance from illegal behavior depended on the women's and girls' assumption of traditional roles of females and curtailment of sexual activity outside marriage.

Beginning in the 1960s and increasing through the 1970s, some theories about delinquent girls departed from the pattern of providing psychological or biological explanations. However, girls usually were given much less attention than were boys, and they were portrayed as relatively dull and passive, even when they were delinquent. In contrast, boy delinquents were portrayed as being active and exciting (Belknap, 2001). An exception was a study of a Chicana gang in East Los Angeles, which had considerable independence even though it was an auxiliary to a male group. The girls were loyal to each other, made decisions democratically, and provided each other both with practical help, including protection, and with the emotional support that normally comes from close family or friends (Quicker, 1999). With few such rare exceptions, however, scholarly attention to gangs through the 1970s paid little or no attention to the everyday lives of girls and women.

In contrast to the tendency to ignore or pay short shrift to girls' and women's illegal activity were two books published in the mid-1970s, *Sisters in Crime* (Adler, 1975) and *Women and Crime* (Simon, 1975). These books advanced the **liberation thesis:** The women's movement had loosened gender role prescriptions, and as a result women were becoming more like men in their penchant for competition and therefore in their criminality. Adler specified that women's violent crime rate would be affected. Simon opined that only the property crime rate would increase. Both theories have been criticized because there is no empirical evidence or sound theoretical rational to support the notion that holding a feminist ideology, whether this means believing in gender equality or wanting to rearrange the distribution of resources in society, increases women's competitiveness. There was evidence neither that the women's movement had provided women with tremendously increased opportunities by 1975 nor that women wanted to behave more like men in various spheres of life, including criminal activity (Naffine, 1987). Other serious problems with the theories were that they assumed that criminal activity was masculine, women's rates of violence had not increased, and women's increased rates of property crimes were better explained by financial troubles than by emancipation (Naffine, 1987, p. 88). Finally, the women who were most involved in the Feminist Movement were not the women who were contributing to increased rates of property crime, and property offenders usually were not among the ranks of feminists.

The historical examples of flawed theory to explain girls' and women's criminality demonstrate the importance of grounding theory in information on the details and the realities of women's individual characteristics and lives, in the immediate contexts in which they find themselves, and in some larger social structure. The shortcomings of prior theory also call attention to the need to consider diversity among girls and women. The early theories did not pay attention to immigrant group differences or to racial group differences, but instead presented girls and women as unrelated to any particular context and as having rather homogeneous identities.

Injustices in Prior Policies and Practices

Policies and practices in the criminal justice system have perpetuated a number of different sorts of injustices. In some cases, the flawed theories and expert discourses that incorporated them supported and provided rationale for injustices.

Policies and Practices Pertaining to Victims

Wife Abuse

In the British common law tradition that has influenced U.S. law, women were defined as men's property, so wife battering was not taken seriously, and rape in marriage was considered to be an oxymoron (Klein, 1982; Weis & Borges, 1977). Neither abuse nor rape by a spouse was defined as a crime. The remnants of the view that the state should not intervene in any but the most egregious forms of men's abuse of their wives existed in criminal justice system practices in the United States in the 19th and 20th centuries. Although legislators repealed the ruling in 1894, a Mississippi Supreme Court ruling from 1824 held that wife beating was legal as long as it was not extreme, and this ruling set a precedent (*Bradley v. State*; 1 Miss. (1 Walker) 156, 158 (1824)). States varied in their laws and in implementation of the laws, but in some periods and places violence against a female spouse was legal or tolerated.

Most police officers in the United States (and elsewhere) believed that they should not be involved in personal affairs of the family, and thus violence between family members typically was treated as a private matter (Belknap, 1990, 2001). When police went to a home where there had been domestic violence, a common tactic was to try to calm people down and leave as quickly as possible (Petersilia, 1993). An early study compared police encounters with the parties involved in domestic violence to encounters with people involved in other kinds of disputes (Oppenlander, 1982). Dispatchers describing a call to police were less likely to depict domestic cases as assaults, though when police arrived on the scene of a domestic assault, they more often found upset and agitated people than in other dispute cases. Although police officers were more likely to make an arrest in domestic than in other types of disputes, the severity of the assaults suggested that even more arrests were warranted. The officers seemed to be "victim aversive"; that is, they spent more time in private discussion with the male offenders than in questioning and offering assistance to the victims. In the United States, this type of police non-intervention into acquaintance and intimate partner rape fueled the Feminist Movement to push for more police and prosecutor involvement in domestic violence cases.

In the 1980s, police tended to interact with men whose partners had called the police to complain of domestic violence, but not to interact with the complainants.

© Shepard Sherbell/CORBIS SABA

Research conducted in the 1980s showed that police officers endorsed stereotypes of African American culture and families as being characterized by violence (Edwards, 1989). African American women were viewed as providing provocation for abuse and being more accepting of it than European American women. The myth that African American families are matriarchal, and that therefore women in them have control over men, resulted in criminal justice professionals' lower levels of activity to protect African American women (P. H. Collins, 1990; Hampton, 1987). There is contradictory evidence in other jurisdictions that police handle abuse in upper-class, white families informally (D. A. Smith & Klein, 1984). In the United States, it was only in the last part of the 20th century that domestic violence came to be seen as a crime that, like other crimes, should be treated as an offense against the state. Similarly, not until late in the 20th century was there growing attention to the problem of racially and class biased responses.

The application of early theories in some cases made responses to domestic violence less just. In the field of mental health, wife beating was seen as the result of victim provocation or instigation (D. Martin, 1982, p. 273). Battered women's syndrome and learned helplessness theory were used as a defense in the U.S. courts to explain why abused women would kill offenders. Although this defense saved some women from harsh sentences, the ideas that all abused women had innate incapacities; that by virtue of staying with abusive husbands, they were psychologically abnormal; and that their killing a husband was not self-defense, but a manifestation of this disorder, ultimately did a disservice to many women (R. E. Dobash & Dobash, 1992, p. 229). Also, the assumption that battered women suffered from learned helplessness has been the basis for the argument that children should be taken from their abused mothers because the mothers cannot and will not protect them (Williams, 2003, p. 528). The theories and the defense stances they supported shifted attention away from the danger that the woman was in, to her psychological deficiencies and her inability to be a fit mother, and women's own reasoning and feelings about abuse were not heard in court.

After social movement activists achieved some success in drawing attention to the harm done by domestic violence and the need for battered women's shelters in the 1970s, family violence theorists provided a new rationale for diverting attention and resources to conflict resolution approaches that could be used by police and the courts (R. E. Dobash & Dobash, 1992). Similarly, specialists in alcohol abuse promoted the idea that neurotic wives contributed to their own abuse by encouraging their husbands' drinking, which then resulted in abuse (Klein, 1982, p. 101). This explanation served the interests of alcoholism treatment programs by delineating a new group of clients to treat. In some places, there was a temporary reversion to treating violence in the family as a private matter to be handled by counseling all the family members, or as an alcohol problem supported by family dynamics, rather than as a criminal assault to be handled through apprehension and punishment. The early theories to explain the abuse of women by intimate partners focused on marital relationships and individual- and family-level influences, to the exclusion of broader community and sociological factors that might have had an influence both within and outside marriage.

Rape

English common law defined rape as "carnal knowledge of a woman forcibly and against her will" and specified that married women could not be raped by their spouse within the constraints of the law (Fusilli, 2002, p. 603). The victim's physical resistance to the forced sexual activity of intercourse was necessary for a rape to occur, and this was indicated by her use of a level of force commensurate with the force being used against her. Corroboration that the rape had occurred was important. Strict rules were established to guard against false accusations by women claiming men had raped them (Schulhofer, 1998, pp. 18–19). The vestiges of English law persisted in U.S. law and beliefs about sexual assault (Posner & Silbaugh, 1996), and although laws have been reformed, beliefs have not been fully changed.

Numerous examples in the literature point to the dismissive or hostile treatment of rape victims. The most negative treatment has been directed against black victims. Historically, courts in the United States have instructed juries that black women should be assumed to be unchaste, and therefore suspect as true rape victims (Crenshaw, 1989, p. 158). In more recent times, there is evidence of unsupportive responses to rape victims, and these responses are not restricted to women of color. In 1975, California Supreme Court justices found that when a man misunderstands the intentions of a woman claiming rape, "his actions are legal as long as he 'reasonably and genuinely' believes that she desires intercourse" (Schwendinger & Schwendinger, 1983, p. 69; *People v. Mayberry*, 15 Cal. 3rd 143). Based on the possibility that women claiming rape might have invited sexual intercourse, police routinely questioned rape victims about their sexual history, the clothes they were wearing at the time of the incident, and their actions, in an effort to determine whether they had invited the rape (M. French, 1977, pp. 607–620; Holmstrom & Burgess, 1978, pp. 221–222; Rafter & Stanko, 1982, p. 9). The criminal justice system was not the only perpetrator of injustice. Between 1880 and 1960, the medical profession's literature highlighted the importance of physicians' care in their examinations of girls and women claiming rape, because women and children were prone to making false accusations (Mills, 1982). Also, in the 1950s, political liberals criticized laws against rape as ignoring that women who were raped shared predisposing characteristics (Freedman, 1987, p. 102). Based on the assumption that women potentially were responsible for their rapes, legislators and those with influence on them pressed for laws that would solidify requirements of corroboration of rape charges by witnesses, investigation of victims' prior sexual behavior, and proof of complete sexual penetration. In each of these examples, as was true for victim precipitation theory, the victim was held responsible for her rape by virtue of not having clearly signaled a lack of desire to have intercourse or because of her tendency to desire sexual involvement, and then later claim rape.

The psychological theories that placed the cause of rape in the minds of offenders also created injustices. In the United States during the 1930s, psychologists became more interested in male sexual deviants, whom they viewed as inadequately masculine effeminate homosexuals or as hypermasculine sexual psychopaths (Freedman, 1987, p. 89). Homosexuals were suspected and investigated as potential child molesters, and sexual psychopath laws were passed to allow sex offenders to be sent to secure hospital settings for indefinite periods. The new sexual psychopath laws were used differently for white and black offenders. White men predominated in the group of offenders convicted of sexual relations with children, and they were sent for hospital treatment. Black men were overrepresented among those convicted of rape, and they were sent to prisons or were executed. The result was the treatment of white sex offenders as mentally ill, and the treatment of black offenders as violent (Freedman, 1987, p. 98). The racial inequity could result in two sorts of injustice: for black offenders not diagnosed as psychopaths, lengthy confinement in prisons or execution; and for white offenders, sometimes lengthy confinement for those who served indeterminate periods, or questionable interventions (castration or electroshock therapy). Beginning in the 1970s, sexual psychopath laws were challenged and repealed. A major difficulty was that the term *sexual psychopath* was vague and the condition was not objectively defined. The psychological and psychiatric theories that shaped thinking about crime and justice resulted in many unfair practices for decades during the 20th century.

Incest

Theories proposing that incest victims fantasized the incidents made victims invisible and denied their experience. Theories that located the cause of incest in family dynamics presented the victim as partly responsible for the victimization, which is questionable given the tremendous power imbalance between parent and child. Therapies buttressed by family systems theory diverted attention away from holding the offender responsible for his actions and keeping the child out of harm's way, and blamed victim and wives for the offender's acts.

Policies and Practices Pertaining to Offenders

Control of Sexually Active Girls

Both early and contemporary studies of delinquency show that parents exert more controls over girls than over boys (Cernkovich, 1987, p. 307; Simmons & Blyth, 1987; Thrasher, 1927, p. 228). For example, boys in junior high school are allowed more often than their female peers to go places without parental permission, go out after dark, and stay home alone (Simmons & Blyth, 1987, pp. 73–74). Historically, a major reason for the greater control of girls has been to limit their sexual activity (Chesney-Lind, 1989; Gorham, 1978; Odem, 1995; Schlossman & Wallach, 1978).

The United States' long history of using the criminal law to control girls' and young women's sexual behavior is consistent with the importance that has been attached to girls' virginity. During the Progressive Era (1896–1920), high levels of concern about divorce, illegitimate birth, and prostitution spilled over to a more general condemnation of immoral behavior and a specific concern about sexually active girls. Typical of the times, social workers at Hull House in Chicago, which offered neighborhood-based social services to assist immigrants adapting to their new country, acted as "guardians of virtue" by trying to discourage working-class young women's sexuality (L. S. Abrams, 2000). As working-class women moved into the paid labor force, there was a punitive response to female independence and sexuality (Schlossman & Wallach, 1978; also see Rafter, 1990; Rosen, 1982). This response was manifested in the institutionalization of girls and women deemed to be feebleminded and in danger of immoral behavior, specifically out-of-wedlock sex and reproduction. Institutionalization would both protect the unwed girls and women and prevent the birth of what were assumed to be mentally deficient offspring (Hahn, 1980).

After the Progressive Era and into the 1980s, concern with promiscuity and pregnancy superseded the emphasis on preventing the birth of deficient children, with the result that girls continued to be institutionalized when they were suspected of being sexually active (Conway & Bogdan, 1977; Datesman & Scarpitti, 1980, p. 168; Odem, 1995; Sarri, 1976). In the 1970s, police were more likely to release a girl than a boy who had committed a delinquent act, but were more likely to arrest a girl than a boy for sexual activity (Milton, Pierce, Lyons, & Hippenstead, 1977, p. 7). An early study of juvenile courts found that for criminal offenses, girls were treated more leniently than were boys, but for status offenses, many of which involved sexual behavior or risk of being sexually active (for example, being runaway), girls were treated more harshly (Datesman & Scarpitti, 1977).[4] Girls were punished more severely for actual and expected sexual behavior than were boys for violent acts and serious property crimes, sometimes even more severely than were boys with long criminal histories (Chesney-Lind, 1977; Cohn, 1970; Terry, 1970). As a result of the criminalization of girls' sexual activity, a much higher proportion of girls than of boys was institutionalized for status offenses such as running away, being out of control, or being in need of supervision (Gibbons, 1970, p. 16; Selo, 1976). Black girls were especially likely to be put on probation and were repeatedly incarcerated for suspected or known sexual activity (Chesney-Lind, 1973, p. 58). Not only were status offender girls more likely to be incarcerated, but they also were incarcerated for a longer period than were boys who had committed delinquent acts (Gibbons, 1970, p. 16). The perception that girls needed controls to prevent or stop their sexual activity for their own protection motivated court intervention and incarceration.

The harsh treatment of female status offenders had serious ramifications for girls who were being sexually abused in their homes. A high proportion of sexual and other child abuse is concentrated on girls, many of whom use the survival strategy of running away from home. Parents or guardians, who are sometimes the abusers, were able to enlist the courts' help to force the girls to return home. The statutes meant to protect girls in fact "criminalized their survival strategies" (Chesney-Lind, 1989, p. 24) and supported their return to the homes where they were at risk for continued victimization. The questionable efficacy of mixing status offenders with youth who had committed serious property and violent offenses, coupled with the overrepresentation of female status offenders in institutions, resulted in federal efforts to encourage states to deinstitutionalize status offenders and to house them in separate facilities. In the aftermath of this reform, there are lingering concerns that girls are charged with delinquency offenses that result in more controls not just because of those offenses, but because they are sexually active. Alternatively, girls who are sexually active may be channeled into mental health settings with strict controls, but their psychiatric label will not reflect decision makers' and parents' concerns about their sexual activity. Unfortunately, there is a limited contemporary research to confirm or discredit concerns that the historical legacy of using the justice system to control sexually active girls is currently widespread.

Regulation and Criminalization of Prostitution

At various periods and places, prostitution has been regulated or criminalized. Regulation has focused on handling prostitution as a public health issue, and the emphasis typically is on ensuring that women who engage in prostitution are not spreading infection through sexually transmitted diseases. For example, Britain in 1864 passed the Contagious Diseases Act to curb the spread of venereal diseases to members of the British army and navy who frequented ports (Vicinus, 1973; Walkowitz, 1980). Members of a special enforcement unit and registered doctors could obtain an order from a justice of the peace to physically examine suspected prostitutes to determine whether they were infected with disease. Healthy women would be registered and provided with a certificate. Infected women were confined in hospitals and forced to accept treatment. Women activists and selected politicians vigorously opposed the law on the grounds that there was not evidence to support the need for the intervention, forced medical examination and detention interfered with civil liberties and were conducted in a cruel and callous manner, and prostitution is a vice that involved trafficking in women, and therefore should not be tolerated by the state but should be criminalized. Women activists argued that it was not fair to punish only the women, whom they saw as the victims of vice, and not to punish men. As a result of opposition, the Contagious Diseases Act was repealed in 1869.

In the United States, federal and local laws have criminalized prostitution. At the federal level, the Mann Act, which was passed in 1910, forbade the interstate and international transportation of women for immoral purposes. By 1915, most states had passed laws against profiting from the earnings of people involved in prostitution. Although the early laws focused on people who profited from prostitution, later laws were passed against soliciting for the purpose of engaging a person in paying for sex, and practices of arrest, prosecution, and punishment focused increasingly on the people who engaged in sex for money, in particular the sellers. Police departments vary, however, and some do give considerable attention to arresting customers and people who do not engage in prostitution directly, but who organize or profit from it.

Sentencing

The literature on sentencing has for some time drawn attention to the possibility that women are treated less severely than men by the courts because of chivalrous feelings of judges or because of their paternalism. Chivalry refers to ancient practices of being polite and caring toward women, and it is something of a stretch to assume that chivalry has been transported into courtrooms of the 20th and 21st centuries. Paternalism, which places men in control of meeting the needs of women assumed to be too childlike and unintelligent to manage their own lives, more accurately characterized women's treatment, and the result was not always leniency (Moulds, 1980). Paternalistic attitudes often resulted in long sentences for women. Prior to 1970, the law allowed differential sentencing for women (President's Commission on the Status of Women, 1963). The basis for differential sentencing was the belief that women were more responsive to rehabilitation and would benefit from indeterminate sentences that could be continued for many years (Temin, 1980). During the 1960s and 1970s, civil and women's rights activists, as well as federal task forces established to respond to the injustices that activists highlighted, exerted pressure to eliminate sex-based discrimination in sentencing (Feinman, 1985). The blatant practices of legislatively prescribed differential sentencing of women no longer continue in the United States.

Gender Bias in Correctional Programs

During the mid-20th century, when girls in the United States were institutionalized at a high rate for sexual activity, programming less adequately met their needs than did programming for boys, who typically were institutionalized for more serious lawbreaking. Despite the courts' concern with sexuality, programs did not offer sex or contraceptive education, and in fact some programs required that girls stop taking birth control medication (Chesney-Lind, 1973, p. 160). Girls also had fewer recreational options and poorer medical and dental care than did boys. When girls were provided with vocational programming, the emphasis was on traditional female occupations, such as cosmetology (Gibbons, 1970, p. 16). Girls spent most of their time watching television or in idleness, and their mail and their behavior were much more closely monitored than were the mail and behavior of the more seriously delinquent male offenders who were institutionalized (Chesney-Lind, 1973; Milton, Pierce, Lyons, & Hippenstead, 1997). Stereotypes of girls as passive, in need of tight controls, and restricted to traditionally female occupations permeated and were reproduced in the regimes of institutionalization.

There is much documentation that once women were committed to correctional programs, they also were groomed to fit into activities and jobs that were severely constrained by gender stereotypes. During the Progressive Era in the United States, prison reformers' recognition of environmental, social, and economic explanations of women's lawbreaking suggested correctional approaches that could meet women's needs and, of particular importance, led to the establishment of separate prisons for women (Freedman, 1981). Separate facilities for women provided them with each other's companionship and reduced exposure to sexual exploitation, but the separation also created a context in which it was simple to institute sex-stereotypic programs, such as housekeeping, and to treat women more like children than adults. Likewise in Great Britain, in the 1800s, women's prisons stood out from men's facilities in their different regimes—for instance, the much closer surveillance and control of female inmates that was accomplished by a network of refuges, asylums, reformatories, and shelters (R. P. Dobash, Dobash, & Gutteridge, 1986). Later, in the United States, when women were prepared for a greater variety of jobs in the workforce, the emphasis was on cosmetology, homemaking skills, and clerical work (Feinman, 1973; Glick & Neto, 1977). A court order issued in 1979 in the state of Michigan challenged and tried to correct the unequal access that women had to job training and other forms of education (*Glover v. Johnson*, 1979). The federal court's supervision of the Michigan Department of Corrections for this case ended in 2000, and there are concerns about reversion to less equitable availability of programs to women offenders; however, between 1979 and 2000, many programs, including preparation for work in the areas that are not traditionally associated with being a woman (e.g., the building trades) were made available. The case had an effect on other states, which tried to avoid lawsuits by providing more than the most stereotypical programming for women offenders. In most states, however, a majority of women are not exposed to work opportunities and training that challenges traditional stereotypes of women's work.

Advances in Theory

The overview of previously developed theory and its connection to responses to crime victims and offenders reveals how theoretical explanations have provided rationales for unjust practices. The flaws in prior theory and general improvements in social science explanations of social life have given impetus to the development of theories that represent a considerable advance over old knowledge.

Theory can be developed and improved in several different ways. One way is to discover new concepts that help to describe social reality and explain why people break the law, how people respond to crime and victimization, why laws are enacted or changed, and how laws are implemented. Another is to discover or confirm how concepts are connected to each other. Often, the reason that something occurs or a person embarks on a particular action or path is not easily predicted and is not linear in the sense that one condition always precedes and causes a particular outcome. Different circumstances and individual characteristics can have the same outcome, and the same circumstances and characteristics can have different outcomes. Some contemporary theories try to explain these alternative ways that social life unfolds. A third way that theory develops is through challenges to assumptions and the replacement of questionable assumptions with those that are tenable. Finally, explanations can be improved by integrating different theories and by developing more complex explanations that take into account different levels of influence and different contexts.

Concept development has been crucial to improving theory about gender, crime, and justice, because key aspects of life that are relevant to gender were not conceptualized at all in prior theories. It was not long ago, for example, that there was no name for sexual harassment:

> Women had to be experiencing and disliking work relationships before it was possible for sexual harassment to be invented. How frighteningly uncertain women must have been before they could know or say or "recognize," and therefore confidently *have* that experience. (Cain, 1989, p. 15)

Many of the oppressions and painful experiences felt by women and girls were not part of social science theory, and therefore they had to be discovered through observation, interviews, and self-reflection.

A theorist can make a contribution by drawing on knowledge that is outside the narrow confines of a particular discipline, in the case of the topics of this book, by *transgressing criminology* (Cain, 1990). For example, some theorists were able to understand how girls and women were controlled in the justice system only when they had a broader picture of how gender ideologies led to the control of women in the playground, in the family, and at work. (Cain, 1990, p. 7). Girls can be policed in everyday life by greater sanctioning in their families than is experienced by boys, by language that focuses on their sexuality, by an emphasis on marriage, and by precarious employment prospects (Cain, 1989). Taken together, the monitoring and pressuring of girls and women to behave in a certain way and fulfill certain roles limits their choices and opportunities. Similarly, before women are incarcerated, many have been imprisoned in more symbolic ways by social conditions in their communities, family circumstances, and abuse in their intimate relationships (Richie, 1996; Weston-Henriques & Jones-Brown, 2000, p. 272). Finally, just as girls and women are often judged and punished according to whether they fulfill expectations about whether they adequately conform to gender role expectations, so are gay, lesbian, and bisexual individuals sometimes judged and punished for this reason. Because oppression based on sexual orientation can result from gender stereotypes and ideologies, throughout this book, information on people who are not heterosexual is included to expand the scope of explanations. Awareness of forms of social control that are used outside the criminal justice system alerts us to look for the effects of similar gender ideologies in police, court, and correctional institutions (H. Allen, 1987; Eaton, 1986; Worrall, 1989), just as awareness of the applicability of explanations to diverse groups helps us to understand a greater span of human behavior.

Ways of Knowing About Gender, Crime, and Justice

Given so many examples of erroneous theories that have resulted in policy and program applications that perpetuate injustices, it is not unexpected that many scholars have asked what went wrong in the collection of empirical evidence intended to reflect and explain reality. *Epistemology* is the study of how knowledge can be obtained, what knowledge is, and the relationship between the knower and what can be known (Guba & Lincoln, 1994). A central question is whether researchers distort reality through their predispositions to think that certain things are important and their filtering of information through their senses. Research on gender, crime, and justice has been carried out using alternative epistemological approaches, and there is debate about whether different approaches can contribute to useful and valid knowledge.

Positivist approaches assume that there is a reality external to individual observers (including researchers) and that various methods are available to gather reasonably accurate information on this reality. The experiment, in which similar individuals are exposed to different treatments and then the results are compared, is one type of positivist research. Surveys, interviews, or observations also can be conducted to measure variables, and evidence that these variables are associated or occur in a particular sequence serves as supporting evidence for causal relationships. One direction that positivist theory development has taken is to test complex models that depict causal relationships between many different variables for which measurement is timed to reflect the time ordering of causes and effects.

Knowledge developed in the positivist tradition has been criticized for assuming that measured variables and the relationships between them accurately reflect social reality or complex causal processes. If a judge's race is related to her or his tendency to commit offenders to probation rather than to prison, what does this tell us? It would be more useful to understand how people's different life experiences lead them to reason about offenders, and how those life experiences are connected to racial inequities, and then to link certain types of reasoning to decision outcomes. When positivist research focuses on the relationships between variables that are not clearly linked back to a useful theoretical explanation, it is criticized as being *variable-driven research* or *empiricist*, which means there is measurement with no theoretical rationale or meaning.

The positivist approaches to building knowledge rely on deductive reasoning. Prior theory establishes the potentially causative variables that should be measured and the outcomes that are worth studying. A criticism of the positivist approach is that because so much of the early social science was developed by white, middle-class men to explain the lives of males, important dimensions of the lives and the social worlds of people differing in gender, race, and ethnicity might not even be considered in a theory, and thus will not be studied in research.

Many individuals who study gender have contributed to feminist theory, which focuses on the oppression and inequality of people because of their gender. One purpose of their theoretical work is to produce research results that are useful in reducing gender-related disadvantage. Scholars who work in the feminist traditions use many different epistemological stances and related methods of research, and many of them integrate across different theories and methods. Some of them do take a positivist approach that is referred to as **feminist empiricism** (Harding, 1990, Kruttschnitt, 1996). Feminist empiricism, and indeed all theory and research carried out within the positivist tradition, is most useful when it has been grounded in observation as well as in prior theory (Eichler, 1988). A grounding in observation ensures that the variables that are measured are salient in the lives of people and groups being studied. Many positivists, including feminists, assume that there is an objective reality. However, the researcher interprets that reality through political, cultural, economic, ethnic, and gender-related values, and therefore there are alternative interpretations of the same empirical reality (Guba & Lincoln, 1994).

Because of the shortcomings of positivist research, some social scientists work within alternative frameworks. *Constructionist* theorists highlight the process of human interaction that results in defining and labeling people, for example as believable victims, nonvictims claiming to have been victimized, sexually promiscuous girls, or offenders. At a more macro level, they look at the claims that groups and individuals make that result in the definition of certain patterns of behavior as social problems. Violence against women and hate crimes have been highlighted recently as social problems in the United States. The theory is that the various labels that are assigned to people in statistical reports, in the juvenile and criminal justice systems, and in the political arena are constructed; therefore, they are not necessarily an accurate reflection of social life. Some labels are the outcome of a process of thinking and interacting within a particular context. Official crime statistics are the outcome of record keeping and data manipulation. The constructionist theorists shifted attention toward how some people come to be labeled as delinquent or as criminal, and they have revealed how assumptions and ideologies pertaining to gender, race, and class affect labeling. Qualitative descriptions of the process of creating constructions of the self and of other people are seen as the most valid approach to developing knowledge. In the constructionist perspective, and in other epistemological approaches, measurement that is endemic to positivist research can also be viewed as producing constructions of reality rather than accurate reflections of it.

Research on Mexican American women in Detroit during the 1990s illustrates how data collection methods differ in the realities that they reveal.[5] Consistent with a positivist approach, women responded to several standard questions used in prior research. The questions asked women to report on the number of times that they and their husbands had been aggressive toward each other—for example, hit or slapped each other—during the last year. Questions were grouped into three areas: *expression of anger and rage* (for example, insults, doing things to spite a spouse, smashing things), *assault* (including behaviors like hitting, shoving, and kicking), and *attack* (beating, choking, forced sex, threatening with a knife or gun). A case example shows the erroneous picture created by the quantitative measure that is produced by adding up the number of times in the last year that the different incidents happened.

Equal fighting back and forth is suggested by the quantitative measure, though on each scale, the woman has a slightly higher score, indicating more aggression toward the husband than from him. For the last year, the woman reports more serious assault against the husband and none by him. In contrast, more descriptive information reveals that the primary issue for the couple is extreme control by the husband:

> [The most serious incident was] when he gave me a black eye and broke all of my furniture in the house, because a guy from work dropped me off from work. [He was trying to get me to] admit that I was cheating on him [because] just imagining me with another guy makes him act this way. [What makes things better?] Just being home with him so that he can get it out of his mind that I'm cheating on him.

In the example, the wife felt she had effectively limited the violence against herself by curtailing her own freedoms. Even though the quantitative measures suggest she is engaged in fighting back and forth with her husband on fairly equal grounds, she is in fact closely controlled by her husband, and her own acts are primarily responses to his extreme aggression toward and control of her. The qualitative descriptive information provides a very different picture than do the numbers.

Advocating for the use of detailed and rich qualitative description of behaviors and context, some social scientists argue that it is possible to avoid distorting the objects of study by starting with what is called a *grounded theory perspective* (Strauss & Corbin, 1990). A study of rape crisis programs used the grounded theory approach (R. Campbell & Ahrens, 1998). The research began with collaboration with personnel from innovative rape crisis programs. The researchers interviewed multiple types of service providers (e.g., police officers, nurses, rape victim advocates) who worked in innovative rape crisis programs across multiple communities throughout the United States. These community workers were asked to describe their programs in their own words, and the descriptive narratives were used to develop typologies of innovative programs, to describe each type of program in detail, and to guide the construction of an exploratory model articulating why these programs are beneficial to rape survivors (R. Campbell and Ahrens, 1998, p. 542). The study of rape services is somewhat unusual, because based on the grounded theory approach, the researcher developed a quantitative score reflecting the types of programs that were helpful to victims. Most people who use the grounded theory approach do not go on to use resulting findings as the input into quantitative research. However, they do develop concepts and explanations based on qualitative data.

Like constructionist theory and grounded theory approaches, *standpoint feminist theory* (Harding, 1990) questions whether positivistic science can contribute to valid social science knowledge and offers an alternative. According to standpoint feminism, the limitations of positivist research result because gender, race, class, and other status markers affect researchers' and subjects' perceptions of reality. If the researcher is in a different social location from the people being studied, she or he cannot accurately understand their reality. In the standpoint perspective, distortions in social science knowledge initially came about because white men conducted most of the research, and they did not have access to information about other groups. These groups would not open up their worlds to the dominant group, and the male researchers did not consider that their own standpoint might not afford them a full picture (Harstock, 1987; D. E. Smith, 1987). A solution is to carry out research that allows active participation of the people who are being studied, so they can shape theoretical explanations. Research from a standpoint perspective would not constrain subjects to answering preset questions with preset response possibilities. An objective of this sort of research is often described as *hearing women's (and others') own voices.* The researcher also would reflect on and write about steps taken to sift through and reflect multiple standpoints.

Standpoint theory is complicated by the recognition that each person's unique standpoint is affected not just by gender but also by race, age, ethnicity, and myriad other status markers. What is the accurate standpoint, and what is the researcher's role in developing knowledge that is fragmented by the many different standpoints of subjects and researcher(s)? Comack (1993) struggled with this question when she analyzed data from interviews on women's experience of abuse and their criminality. She described her resolution of the dilemma posed by multiple standpoints:

> It was when I was in the process of doing the research with the women in the prison that I realized how similar it was to quilt making. Each of the women I spoke with has been involved in constructing her own quilt piece. This work has involved the naming of her abuse and her own analysis of the ways in which abuse is situated within her biography. My role in this project was like that of a co-ordinator. By sewing the pieces together, patterns became visible in the ways in which the women have been rebuilding their lives over and around the abuse. Thus, while the heart of *Women in Trouble* is the voices of the women in the prison—their standpoint—the structure and design of the work represent my attempt to come to know and to make sense of the lives of all of the women who contributed their pieces to the quilt. (p. 300)

Comack's adaptation of the standpoint perspective recognized that study subjects' viewpoints are critical for obtaining insight into social life, but that the researcher must in the end look for patterns and exceptions in an effort to offer some explanation. Because the researcher's standpoint includes an awareness of social forces that individuals do not usually think about, she or he is in a unique position to incorporate the historical, community, organizational, and national context into a theoretical explanation (Cain, 1990; Gorlick, 1991).

Postmodern feminism is another epistemological stance. Many postmodernists, including those who focus on gender and crime, are highly critical of positivist, constructionist, and even standpoint methods for advancing knowledge. They emphasize that these methods oversimplify how and why things happen, because they impose incomplete models of causation that do not capture nonlinear ways in which certain things come about. Like constructionist and standpoint theorists, they caution that pregiven categories can be misleading, and they note that categories in which people are placed are constructions. The notion that the phenomena that social scientists study are in a constant state of being constructed and therefore being changed (Smart, 1995, p. 8) can lead to the conclusion that no patterns or causal relationships can really be known. Taken to the extreme, some feminist postmodernists see the world as endless stories or texts, many of which support current oppressive arrangements for gender, race, and other groups (Oleson, 1994). However, other feminist researchers have taken ideas from postmodernist theory into account but have not gone to the point of saying that there can be no knowledge of cause-and-effect relationships. Their empirical work focuses on understanding the language people use to construct their realities, and on examining how discourses influence social life.

This book presents advances in understanding that rely on research that uses a variety of epistemological orientations. Readers who do not consider some epistemological approaches to be valid may give less weight to theories that are supported by particular types of research. Postmodern identification of discourses and other previously neglected aspects of social life have opened up new themes for study, and their challenges to simple ways of understanding causality redirect attention to the importance of qualitative research. A look at research by postmodern theorists who study gender, crime, and justice suggests that within this perspective, there are analytical tools that connect empirical data to theory, and their work will be included in the book.

Ways of Thinking About Gender, Crime, and Justice

Much of the research presented in this book is informed by and adds to one or more general perspectives about inequities related to gender that are developed in social science and other fields of study. These general perspectives are called strains or branches of feminist theory (Daly & Chesney-Lind, 1988; Tong, 1998). No simple scheme can capture the variants within each strain of feminist theory or the full range of strains. However, there is some utility in being familiar with key perspectives and their implications for the sorts of social change that could increase justice.

Radical feminism stresses that the domination of women, the oldest and most widespread oppression in the world, is rooted in men's needs to control women's sexuality and their potential to reproduce.[6] Change would require overthrowing the existing social structure and obliterating gender differences. According to **liberal feminism**, gender differences in socialization result in oppression. If women are socialized differently and laws are equitable for females and are applied fairly, the oppression will be reduced or abated. The key is to give females and males equal access to education, opportunities, and resources. **Socialist feminism** highlights the ways that people are oppressed both because of gender and because of social class; thus, working-class and lower-class females are most disadvantaged. Change requires new gender arrangements and a move away from capitalism toward either socialism or communism. Different from the other feminist perspectives that focus on social structure (e.g., gender and class arrangements), **psychoanalytical and**

gender feminism highlights the unique psychological makeup of females that orients them to need to love and be loved in close relationships with other people. Critical of the other feminist perspectives, **multicultural feminism** and **global feminism** reject the idea that the idea of woman is invariant and stress that women who are privileged because of their race or class cannot speak for other groups. Multicultural feminism is centered on the idea of intersections; even in the same country, experiences of gender-related oppressions are altered by race, class, sexual orientation, age, and myriad other differences. Global feminism clarifies that gender oppression is heavily influenced by economic and political conditions that characterize First World, Third World, colonialist, and colonized countries. These and other variants of feminist perspectives (Tong, 1998) suggest which structural, social, and cultural changes will result in justice for females affected by crime, either by virtue of being involved in criminal activity or by being victimized. The perspectives can provoke thinking about the types of change that would be necessary to improve justice in relation to gender and crime.

In the next chapter of this book, "Gender and the Law," and in subsequent chapters, there is discussion of efforts to change laws and how they are implemented in order to improve justice. This approach to ensuring justice is preferred by people who adhere to the liberal feminist perspective; better laws and better implementation are seen as primary ways to reduce gender oppression. A question that readers of this book can ask about each topic covered is whether the legal approach brings justice, or whether more fundamental alterations in gender arrangements and in class, race, and other structures are needed.

Organization of the Chapters

The second chapter of this book focuses on gender and the law. The law provides an important framework both for understanding why certain people come into contact with the justice system as either victims or offenders and for understanding the responses of the system. Contemporary law is a result not just of tradition, but also of social movement activities and backlash against those activities, both of which are described later in the book. Also, communities, criminal justice organizations, and individual belief systems affect how laws are implemented. These influences also are considered in later chapters of the book.

Consistent with the problematic nature of categories emphasized by various epistemologies, a theme that cuts across chapters and promotes consideration of what it takes to produce justice is the artificiality in distinguishing between crime victim and crime offender. Some offenders also are victims, and gender has influenced both their illegal activities and their victimization. Both people who are labeled as victims and those who are labeled as offenders can be victimized by and in the criminal justice system, or alternatively, both can be accorded justice by that system and by other agencies.

For some group of girls and women, a proportion that is higher than for men, victimization precedes, and sometimes explains, their delinquent or criminal activity. By no means do all women follow this pathway, and not all gender-related victimization triggers illegal activity. However, there is some utility in starting with a look at victimization, then moving to a consideration of the responses of the justice system. Both victimization and justice system responses (or lack of responses) can be part of the explanation of why a subset of individuals breaks the law. For that group, the placement of the chapters on victimization and responses to it before the chapter on causes of offending mirrors the time ordering of events leading up to delinquent or criminal activity. Chapter 3 includes theories that describe and explain victimization that is concentrated on either girls, women, or people who are gay or lesbian. Chapter 4 presents theories that explain the influence of social movements on responses to victims, and Chapter 5 concentrates on the effects of community and organizational contexts, and of interactions and individual differences on responses to victims. Chapter 6 is focused on how gender is implicated in the etiology of illegal behavior, and Chapter 7 considers the effect of gender on responses to illegal behavior. Taken together, the chapters present the macrolevel, intermediate, and individual-level explanations of patterns of victimization and crime and responses to these phenomena. The concluding chapter, Chapter 8, provides an assessment of contemporary theory against the criteria set forth in this opening chapter, and it reflects on the state of knowledge and the needs for future research.

Throughout the book, the emphasis is on the experiences of the gender groups that have been most neglected by prior theory or that have experienced injustice because of their gender. Females, including those who are lesbian and bisexual, and gay men are therefore the victims who are discussed. Discussion of males' criminality against these groups is included in the chapter on victimization. In Chapter 6, when the focus shifts to offending behavior, theories are presented that postulate that gender is an influence on both males' and females' lawbreaking.

The theories presented in the book do not constitute an integrated, multilevel theory. They vary in the level of influence considered, in their attention to women's own voices, in their inclusion of the intersections concept, and in assumptions about agency. For each topic, passages are taken from research that exposes study subjects' own rendering of their situation and themselves. Also, to some extent the theories are consistent with each other. They provide some improvement over prior work reviewed in this first chapter, and they suggest bases for actions that would improve the situation of people who are disadvantaged by gender organization at the times and in the places where they are situated.

Key Terms

Agency	Feminist empiricism
Battered women's syndrome	Feminist theory
Criminal justice	Gender—individual level conceptualization
Discourse	
	Gender—macrolevel
Empowerment	conceptualization (including gender

organization, gender arrangements, the sex gender system, and gender stratification)

Gender definitions

Gender identity

Gender ideologies

Gender-role prescriptions

Gender-role stereotypes

Gender stereotypes

Global feminism

Globalization

Learned helplessness

Levels of explanation

Liberal feminism

Liberation thesis

Madonna/whore duality

Multicultural feminism

Patriarchy

Postmodern themes

Psychoanalytical and gender feminism

Radical feminism

Sex

Social location

Socialist feminism

Victim precipitation

Review and Discussion

1. Several early flawed theories are presented in this chapter. Using the criteria of contemporary empirical research, consideration of context and intersections, and recognition of people's agency, critique specific early theories that attempted to explain wife abuse, rape, incest, victim behavior, and girls' and women's criminality.

2. What levels of explanation were identified as causes of crime and victimization in specific early theories reviewed in this chapter?

3. What are the different ways that discourses are relevant to understanding crime and justice?

4. Given that historically unjust practices were supported by theories of the time, how could one guard against contemporary theories supporting unjust practices?

5. Explain the different perspectives on whether empirical research can validly reflect social reality. What is your own assessment of the validity of different approaches to connecting empirical research to theory?

6. What are the criticisms of different types of empirical data used to support theory, and what are some safeguards that can be used to ensure that empirical data reflect social reality with some accuracy?

CHAPTER 2

Gender and the Law

I n the United States, laws at the federal, state, and local (municipal and county) levels address victimization that is disproportionately concentrated on women and girls. Also, some laws are written or implemented in a way that disproportionately criminalizes women and girls. Types of victimization that are disproportionately concentrated on girls and women include incest, sexual assault, violence by an intimate partner, genital mutilation, harassment, and trafficking for sexual exploitation. People also are victimized by hate crimes when they are in racial, ethnic, or religious groups; because of their sexual orientation; because they are females; or because they have disabilities. Criminalization of abortion, prostitution, and certain forms of child abuse disproportionately affects females. In the case of child abuse, enforcement practices hold mothers more accountable than fathers for the safety and welfare of children. For prostitution, police more often arrest individuals engaged in prostitution (in the United States, usually females) than customers (usually men). Laws against pornography address the victimization of women that could occur if misogynist beliefs are reinforced by sexually explicit materials; at the same time, laws against pornography criminalize the behavior of women and men who make their living by working in the pornography industry. The first section of this chapter presents information on contemporary laws against gender-related victimization, and the second section describes contemporary laws that disproportionately criminalize the actions of women. Laws that pertain to prostitution and pornography are considered in separate sections. In the discussion of state and local laws, it is important to remember that states and localities differ considerably from each other, so although there may be some general trends across the nation, victims and offenders may confront quite different realities depending on where they live. The chapter ends with sections on international law, laws against consensual sex between same-sexed people, and limitations of the law in bringing about changes in behavior and social life.

Laws Against Gender-Related Victimization

In the United States, changes have been made in local, state, and federal **criminal law** and **civil law** to address violence that is disproportionately experienced by women. *Criminal law* pertains to conduct that is considered to be so harmful to society that it is prohibited and is prosecuted and punished by the state. *Civil law* deals with the rights of private citizens and conflicts between citizens; remedies include reparation, for example through economic relief from one party to another. Women's rights activists have influenced the development of a shared understanding about gender-related victimization that is experienced as traumatic, but that was not previously treated as illegal or highly damaging by the criminal justice system and the law as written or implemented. Over time, several new definitions of gender-related offenses were incorporated into law.

Sexual Assault

English common law, the basis for much law in the United States, defined rape as the "illicit carnal knowledge of a female by force and against her will" (Black, 1968, p. 1427). According to this law, only a female could be raped, and only a male could be charged with rape. At least minimal vaginal penetration was necessary. Married women could not be raped by their husbands, because sexual relations were considered expected. Finally, because an act is considered rape only if the woman does not consent,

> it is important for the victim to manifest her lack of interior consent by engaging in exterior acts of resistance (kicking, biting, screaming, protesting, pleading, crying) so that courts can determine whether it is the alleged victim who is telling the truth when she claims that she did not consent to sexual intercourse or whether it is instead her alleged rapist who is telling the truth when he claims that she did consent to sexual intercourse. (Tong, 1984, p. 96)

In 1974, the State of Michigan passed Public Act 266, the Criminal Sexual Conduct Act. In so doing, Michigan became a leader in the reform of legislation pertinent to rape cases. The laws in Michigan and in other states were reformed to correct several deficiencies. New laws and amendments identified victims as individuals who could be either males or females, reflected that rape could be committed by a spouse, abolished the requirements to prove victim resistance, dropped the requirement for corroboration of the victim's account, and specified degrees of sexual assault with corresponding minimum and maximum sentences. By specifying degrees of sexual assault, the law prohibited a larger range of behaviors than forced penetration. For example, unwanted touching and groping were illegal. In some states, reformed laws have replaced the requirement that victims resist assault with the requirement that defendants demonstrate that the victim consented to the act (Sanday, 1996, p. 277). **Rape shield laws**, which prohibited introduction of information on the victim's sexual history except under specified circumstances, were intended to shield victims from having to endure the degrading experience of reporting on their prior sexual activities, which was sometimes used as evidence that they deserved or encouraged the assaultive behavior (Matsoesian, 2001, p. 208). The new laws were intended to expand the scope of activities that are criminalized, to make it easier for victims to come forward, and to relax the requirements for conviction.

Despite reforms in the laws against sexual assault, it is not a simple matter for a prosecutor to make her or his case before a jury if there is little or no corroborative evidence or if, for some other reason, jurors do not believe the victim. The U.S. system of justice was set up to require evidence beyond a reasonable doubt before an alleged offender is found guilty. Although there are legal safeguards in each state, a person claiming sexual victimization can find that her or his sexual history is considered pertinent to the charge at hand, and thus is permitted as evidence. Thus, despite improvements in the laws, victims of sexual assault have no guarantee that juries will believe them or that their sexual history or other sensitive information will not be made public.

Intimate-Partner Violence

Intimate-partner violence includes violence directed against a person whom the aggressor is married to, living with, or dating. It also can include violence by a former marital partner or boyfriend/girlfriend or by a person who was previously cohabitating, including a person who has a child in common with the victim. Beginning in the 1970s, state-level case law established that intimate-partner violence was not a private matter but was criminal, and that it therefore could be punished by the state. More than a decade later, a backslide to treating intimate-partner violence as though it were a family problem rather than a crime was reversed in the findings from lawsuits, for example in New York City; Torrington, Connecticut; and Oakland, California.[7] In these lawsuits, police were held accountable for lenient treatment of men who assaulted their wives, because they thereby failed to protect the women. Over time, the laws as written and interpreted have also extended prohibitions against violence between spouses to other forms of intimate-partner violence. In some states, the reformed laws apply to violence between dates, people who were estranged or divorced, and people in same-sex relationships.

Depending on the state, new laws have made it either mandatory for police to arrest in intimate-partner violence situations or have allowed some police officer discretion but encouraged arrest. The first approach is called a **mandatory arrest policy**, the second a **presumptive arrest policy**. Liability when police fail to respond to intimate-partner violence or enforce protection orders is one reason that police have become more proactive in responding to domestic violence. Another reason is that social activists shaped existing laws and attitudes toward implementation. As with sexual assault laws, the resulting form and implementation of the law varies across the United States, but overall, the laws specify an increased range of behaviors that are considered to be illegal.

As a result of mandatory and presumptive arrest policies, arrest of a suspect in an intimate-partner violence case is increasingly common in the United States.
© Kim Kulish/CORBIS SABA

In spite of changes in the law, the outcomes of court cases continue to show that police in some jurisdictions or instances do not respond to victims of *domestic violence* and to domestic violence offenders with the same level of activity or force as they use when the case does not involve domestic violence (Blackwell & Vaughn, 2003). One example is a case in Los Angeles (*Navarro v. Block*, 1995).[8]

> Maria Navarro was celebrating her birthday at her home when she received a call from the brother of her estranged husband, Raymond, warning her that Raymond was on his way to her house to kill her and any others present. Maria immediately called 911 and told the operator about the warning. . . . Learning Raymond had not yet arrived, the operator replied, "OK, well, the only thing to do is just call us if he comes over there. . . ." Fifteen minutes later, Raymond arrived at Maria's house and shot and killed her and four others. (Blackwell & Vaughn, 2003, p. 140)

The court found in favor of Maria's relatives on the basis that the Los Angeles County Sheriff's Department policy assigned domestic violence 911 calls a lower priority than other calls. A similar example is the case *Hakken v. Washtenaw County* (1995).[9]

Jason Briggs, a sixteen-year-old, was dating twelve-year-old Greta Hakken. . . .
On February 13, 1993, while riding in the back seat of a car, Jason strangled
Greta into unconsciousness. The Washtenaw County Sheriff's Department
was dispatched to the scene where [mother] Kathleen asked the deputies to
intervene. Deputies responded that they could do nothing since Jason strangled Greta while in another county. . . . They made no arrest, even though
Jason admitted that he attempted to kill Greta. . . . On February 23, Jason
killed Greta while she slept in her bed; he then committed suicide. (Blackwell
& Vaughn, 2003, p. 138)

The court found the police department had failed to follow its own policies
regarding domestic violence and that it had a record of more lenient response to
aggressors against victims of domestic violence than to aggressors against other categories of victims. In these examples and in many other cases, after domestic violence laws were improved, individual officers and selected departments' policies
have been shown to continue to provide less protection to victims of domestic violence than to other victims.

Apart from changes in the criminal law, state and local laws have provided
women with the capacity to obtain what are called civil protection, personal protection, or restraining orders that prohibit contact between the offender and the victim.[10] If a person violates the order, he or she can be charged with civil or criminal
contempt, a misdemeanor for violating the order, or some combination. The viola-
tor also could be charged with a criminal act that occurred in addition to violating
the order, such as an assault. Although restraining orders hold promise for protecting victims, in fact violations are followed by arrest in half or even fewer, depending
on the jurisdiction, of the cases (Harrell & Smith, 1996; Mignon & Holmes, 1995).
When the victim was in an apparent high-risk situation, police in Boston made an
arrest regardless of whether there was a restraining order; for low-risk situations,
they were more likely to make an arrest if there was a restraining order, and an arrest
was made in just 44% of cases (Kane, 2000, p. 576). It appears that even when there
is a restraining order violation, officers consider additional factors, such as the presence of a weapon, before they make an arrest (Kane, 1999; Rigakos, 1997). Also, for
stalking victims, considered in the next section, in a Colorado police department
officers tended to charge offenders not with stalking but with the less serious offense
of violating existing restraining orders, which may limit the force of the law (Tjaden
& Thoennes, 2000b). Some victims do feel that restraining orders have been helpful
in protecting them (Ptacek, 1999), and many jurisdictions have increased the availability and the follow-up for this legal protection. However, these benefits are by no
means uniform across different jurisdictions or within a jurisdiction.

Stalking

Anti-stalking legislation is a recently developed area of law that is relevant
to intimate-partner violence. **Stalking** is "the act of deliberately and repeatedly
following or harassing another to create fear in the victim or to coerce him or her

to accede to the wishes of the stalker" (Buzawa & Buzawa, 2003, p. 14). It can include harassment through e-mail or phone calls. The initial attention to stalking was not related to gender but instead focused on Hollywood stars whom admirers had stalked (J. Best, 1999, p. 50). Once stalking had been defined and described, battered women's and victims' rights activists promoted anti-stalking legislation by linking stalking to domestic violence and by investing considerable resources in keeping stalking alive as a topic for public discourse and action (Lowney & Best, 1995). The ongoing activism coupled with several murders of stalking victims created an environment ripe for passage of new laws. Four women, all but one of whom had a restraining order against their killers, were murdered by former partners in Orange County, California, in a 6-week period in 1990. Soon after California enacted anti-stalking legislation, 47 additional states and the District of Columbia followed suit, and Maine began to charge stalkers under an anti-terrorizing statute (Lowney & Best, 1995). Although laws that prohibit and penalize stalking do not restrict the act to women stalked by men, most cases that come to the attention of the police involve males stalking females, and often the male is a former, present, or hopeful intimate of the female (Tjaden & Thoennes, 1998).

The Violence Against Women Act

By 1994, there was considerable public recognition of violence against women in the United States. The result was the introduction and passage of the federal-level **Violence Against Women Act** (VAWA). Initially, the VAWA focused on safe streets, safe homes, and civil rights for women. It was later extended to cover safe campuses and equal justice for women. The act defined gender-motivated crimes as hate crimes, and it included an amendment to federal civil rights laws, thereby giving victims access to civil as well as criminal courts. In the 2000 version of the federal Violence Against Women Act, substantial funds were committed to encourage the use of civil protection orders and other civil remedies as responses to domestic violence.

Much of the impact of the VAWA came about because of federal funding that encouraged state and local governments to alter criminal justice practices and to provide training for police officers, prosecutors, and judges. The act also funded women's shelters, a national domestic abuse hotline, and sexual assault education and prevention programs. It included relief measures for immigrants whose abusive spouses obstructed the victims' access to lawful status in the United States. Funding both for the VAWA and for efforts under the more general heading of the victims' rights movement has also supported the growth of victim assistance services, many of which are designed for victims of gender-related crime.

United States v. Morrison

The VAWA was created in response to extensive congressional testimony that supported the ideas that violence against women had negative economic effects on interstate commerce, and that inadequate responses of the states denied equal protection of the laws to victims. The specific economic impact was that domestic violence limited victims' ability to travel between states for employment and business, and as a result there was less productivity in the workplace and there was more unemployment and underemployment (Weissman, 2001, p. 1090). Documented bias and inadequacies of state and local court responses were the basis for creating a federal-level civil remedy for victims.

In 2000, the U.S. Supreme Court with a 5-to-4 vote struck down as unconstitutional the VAWA provision of a federal civil rights remedy for gender-based violence.[11] The justices discounted the connection of violence against women to commerce, and they expressed the opinion that the federal civil remedy did not correct deficiencies in state criminal remedies. They reasoned against the national, systemic character of violence against women, and reinforced the notion that instances of violence are situational and not part of a larger pattern.

Weissman (2001) has provided a critique of the outcome of the *United States v. Morrison* case. In her view, the Court did not adequately consider the extensive social science evidence of the impact of violence against women on the economy. The Court also did not consider that a common dynamic in an abusive relationship is the prevention of the victim's economic independence. The Court's decision reclassified violence against women from a pattern of behavior supported by cultural norms to individual illegal behaviors, such as sexual perversions and domestic disputes. The ultimate effects of *United States v. Morrison* are an important topic for future research, which must sort out whether other provisions and existing impetus of the VAWA have enough influence on the justice system to maintain progress in improving responses to violence against women, or whether there will be a backslide in the options and the assistance available to victims.

Female Genital Mutilation

As the United States experiences its most recent wave of immigration, and similarly for other countries to which sizable groups of Africans and South Asian people have immigrated, laws have been enacted to prevent female genital mutilation. **Female genital mutilation** (FGM) is the surgical removal of the clitoris and/or the labia minora or majora. It is sometimes accompanied by sewing together all but an opening necessary for urination and menstruation.[12] This latter practice means that for intercourse to occur, women must be cut open again. Often, nonmedical people in unsanitary situations perform the procedures involved with genital mutilation of girls, though some parents do arrange for FGM in medical settings. FGM is most common in Africa, but it also occurs in some Middle Eastern and Asian countries; and as people emigrate throughout the world, the practice has moved with them. According to the Centers for Disease Control and Prevention (CDC), an estimated 168,000 women and girls in the United States had either undergone FGM or were at risk for FGM in 1990 (W. K. Jones, Smith, Kieke, & Wilcox, 1997). Of these, 48,000 were girls younger than 18 years old. Although FGM that involves less severe cutting is viewed by some women as normal and as not interfering with sexual functioning, at least for women with the more extreme types of cutting, sexual pleasure is negatively affected, and serious, often life-threatening, medical and psychological results are common (Hopkins, 1999; Royal College of General Practitioners, 2003).

Countries that have criminalized FGM include Belgium, Canada, Denmark, France, Great Britain, Sweden, Switzerland, and the United States. The first law, passed in Sweden in 1982, outlawed the practice for both children and adults and prohibited adults' facilitating a person's leaving the country to undergo FGM. A 1985 British law similarly prohibited the practice not only within the country, but also as accomplished by taking a child outside the country, and it required social workers and teachers to report suspected cases (Messito, 1997–1998). A U.S. federal law that went into effect in 1997 criminalized FGM, but it provided no methods for enforcement and required no reporting.[13] It did, however, require that the Immigration and Naturalization Service provide immigrants from areas that practiced FGM with information about the harm from the practice and about the legal consequences of performing FGM in the United States or allowing a child under one's care to be subjected to FGM. The legislation also limited loans to other countries that had a cultural custom or known history of FGM and that had not taken steps to implement educational programs to prevent the practice.

Some people have argued that the law should not prohibit FGM because it is a religious and cultural practice. The **cultural relativity argument** that FGM is a religious choice has had a limited effect on blocking criminalization efforts. There is little information on the debates and discussions that led to passage of certain laws, but within countries and groups where FGM is practiced, long-standing activism against the practice (Winter, 1994) suggests that religious and cultural supports are by no means uniform. Also, the evidence of physical and psychological harm and of suffering is so blatant that it is difficult to make a case that religious freedom supersedes other fundamental human rights. In the United States, criminalization occurred at a moment when there were some dramatic publications of the practice and the resulting harm: a novel by a well-known author (*Possessing the Secret of Joy* by Alice Walker, 1992), a highly publicized situation of a young woman who fled her country and sought refuge in the United States to avoid FGM, and a television broadcast of a young Egyptian girl screaming in pain when she underwent FGM. Activists had laid the groundwork for the criminalization of FGM in the United states, and these events provided the immediate impetus for the federal legislation as well as legislation in a number of states.

Hate Crimes

Hate crimes involve the threat or use of violence that is motivated by hate of an entire group differentiated by race, color, religion, national origin, ethnicity, gender, disability, or sexual orientation. Before hate crimes were specified and criminalized in U.S. federal legislation, a variety of different coalitions pushed for legislation at the state level. As a result, several states have statutes that prescribe criminal penalties for hate-motivated crimes, and some states include crimes directed against people with a gay or lesbian sexual orientation and/or directed against women. Typical laws increase the penalty for previously designated crimes, for instance assault or homicide, if prejudice influenced the offender's conduct. The state-level statutes are broadly directed and most often cover prejudice based on race, religion, color, and national origins; less often, they specify prejudice based on ancestry, sexual orientation, gender, disability, creed, and ethnicity (Jenness & Broad, 1997, pp. 39, 42).

The first federal law concerning hate crimes was the Hate Crime Statistics Act of 1990.[14] It required that the Department of Justice collect data on crimes motivated by prejudice based on race, religion, or sexual orientation. Later, disability was added to the list. A particularly controversial law, the Violent Crime Control and Law Enforcement Act of 1994, went into effect September 13, 1994.[15] As was true for similar legislation in some states, opponents continue to argue that there should be no preferential treatment of offenders who commit hate crimes, and that pref- erential treatment disadvantages other victims and punishes offenders for their prejudicial thoughts rather than their illegal actions (Nearpass, 2003). Countering the criticisms of the 1994 act, proponents of the legislation were supported by the American Psychological Association's publication of research findings showing the greater harm caused by hate as opposed to other types of crimes (American Psychological Association, 1998; Herek, Gillis, & Cogan, 1999). The federal govern- ment gained further authority in investigation and prosecution with the Hate Crimes Prevention Act of 1999, which prohibited interfering with an individual's federal rights, such as voting, through violence motivated by the victim's race, color, religion, or national origin.[16] In 2004, the U.S. Senate passed the Local Law Enforcement Enhancement Act, which expanded federal hate crime protection to include disability, sexual orientation, and gender. Previously, the House of Representatives had refused to pass similar legislation, and lobbyists continued to argue that the law would result in unequal treatment of victims. The expansion of federal resources to enhance investigation and prosecution of hate crimes motivated by gender and sexual orientation continues to be hotly debated.

Some U.S. and state Supreme Court rulings have affirmed that gay, lesbian, and bisexual individuals can receive legal protection equal to that afforded to other peo- ple. In *Romer v. Evans*,[17] the U.S. Supreme Court upheld a Colorado constitutional amendment providing equivalent protection against discrimination based on sex- ual orientation and other characteristics (Feldblum, 2001). The Nebraska Supreme Court held that a county sheriff was accountable for failing to protect Brandon Teena, formerly named Teena Brandon, who had been raised as a girl. After two of his male acquaintances learned he was biologically a female, they raped him. He reported the case to the sheriff, whose only action was to tell the two attackers. The attackers then shot and killed Brandon Teena (Lambda Legal Defense and Education Fund, 2001; the story was portrayed in the 1999 film *Boys Don't Cry*, starring Hilary Swank). By its ruling, the Nebraska Supreme Court signaled that same-sex rape should be treated seriously by the criminal justice system, just as the U.S. Supreme Court had recognized that discrimination, including harassment, based on sexual orientation was illegal.

A memorial message after the 1998 killing of gay student Matthew Shepard by men who were motivated by hate of gay individuals.

© CORBIS

Summary of Trends in Laws Against Gender-Related Victimization

In recent decades, U.S. laws against sexual assault, stalking, intimate-partner violence, and hate crimes have brought a larger range of victimizations into the criminal justice system's realm of responsibility. In contradiction to the trends to increase legal interventions on behalf of crime victims, the federal civil rights remedy for domestic violence was removed through a Supreme Court ruling. Also, the U.S. law against FGM has been criticized for lacking any provision for enforcement and requirements for reporting suspected cases to authorities. Later chapters in this book will consider continuing efforts to reform laws and will review the empirical evidence on the uniformity with which laws against gender-related victimization have been implemented.

Laws Related to Reproduction and Child Protection

Historically in the United States, laws have prohibited the dispensing of birth control or access to abortion, have defined as a crime failure to protect a child from harm, and more recently have criminalized harming a fetus by taking illegal drugs while pregnant. Although these laws were developed and adopted at different times and for different purposes, they are tied together by a common theme, which is that they have disproportionate impact on women as childbearers and as mothers.

The United States is characterized by an extreme polarization on issues that are very important to politically involved religious conservatives, and these issues include abortion and sexuality (Evans, 2003, p. 87). This does not mean that there is polarization between people of different religions, but that, consistent with what is called *morality politics theory*, the religious polarization is limited to people who are active as Republicans and Democrats, political conservatives and liberals. Politically active groups have considerable influence on legislators, legislation, and ultimately public policy. Thus, laws pertaining to abortion and sexuality are the grist of much political activity and can reflect extreme viewpoints on the degree to which people are legally able to make decisions about reproduction. Some people have concluded that groups in the United States have been able to effectively use the "coercive power of the state to force their values on others arbitrarily" (Roh & Haider-Markel, 2003, p. 15). In particular, the claim is that a minority of politically active conservatives has had a strong influence on laws that limit access to abortion and constrain sexuality. As a result, laws may not reflect majority public opinion, but instead may reflect the preferences of a minority of the population.

Abortion

In 1973, the U.S. Supreme Court lifted several prohibitions against abortion in its decision in *Roe v. Wade*.[18] Unique from other countries that have increased women's access to abortion, a key rationale for the change in the United States was that women had a constitutionally protected right to privacy in making a decision in consultation with their medical providers. Since 1973, there have been continuous legal challenges, governmental policies and practices, and lawmaker actions intended to involve the state in deciding when, how, and whether women and girls can obtain an abortion. Activism both to increase access to abortion (the **pro-choice position**) and to restrict it (the **pro-life position**) has been pronounced, highly public, and widely publicized. It has included legal demonstrations and nonphysical harassment. It also has included illegal activities: civil disobedience and, especially for pro-life proponents, violence that includes attacks on people, bombing, acid attacks, stalking, and murder. The pro-life activism has had marked direct effects:

> [Some] physicians have stopped performing abortions, clinics have closed, and many women seeking abortions must now be escorted into treatment facilities. Protesters, too, have been injured at demonstrations while the violence attributed to the radical fringe appears to have eroded the foundation of the Pro-Life movement, reduced the numbers of people willing to protest, and diminished the financial resources available to these activists. (Kenny & Reuland, 2002, p. 356)

Despite setbacks on both sides, both pro-life and pro-choice activists have tried continuously to influence legislation. On April 25, 2004, hundreds of thousands (some estimates are more than 1 million) of pro-choice activists marched in Washington, D.C., to protest the U.S. president's policies that limited access to abortion. The pro-choice activists were met by large numbers of pro-life activists.[19] Unique to the United States, the antiabortion movement has had a strong influence on politics at both the state and federal levels (Lee, 2001), and it is not uncommon for people to base their votes on a candidate's stance on abortion.

Three years after the *Roe v. Wade* decision, U.S. Representative Henry Hyde introduced an amendment to a bill that has since been renewed repeatedly. The so-called Hyde Amendment eliminated Medicaid funding for abortions except in circumstances that included endangerment of a woman's life, rape, and incest.[20] Additional federal restrictions have prohibited medical insurance coverage for abortions for federal employees, women in federal prisons, low-income women in the District of Columbia, and teenagers who participate in the State Child Health Insurance Plan (Boonstra & Sonfield, 2000). Also, the Supreme Court has heard cases concerning the unavailability of public funding for abortions and has ruled that local, state, and federal governments are under no obligation to provide women with access to abortions, even if the woman's health is at risk.[21] Contradicting prior Supreme Court decisions, in 2003, the U.S. Congress passed and the president signed the Partial Birth Abortion Ban Act of 2003, which restricted abortion in cases when the fetus could be considered viable outside the uterus.[22] In 2004, the Unborn Victims of Violence Act was signed.[23] The purpose of that act is to allow a separate murder charge against a person who, by killing a woman, also kills a fetus she is carrying. The law therefore defines a fetus as a viable person, in contrast to *Roe v. Wade*. Proponents deny the contradiction on the basis that the Unborn Victims of Violence Act does not consider abortion to be homicide. Over time, the general trend in U.S. law has been increased emphasis on the rights and protection of the fetus, and decreased attention to the privacy and the rights of pregnant women who seek to consider and choose abortion.

State laws also have been adopted to restrict access to abortion. Typical approaches were to require the husband's consent, or in the case of minors, parental consent or notification, before an abortion is allowed (Ernst, Katzive, & Smock, 2004, p. 769). Limits are set on when during a pregnancy abortions are legal, and there are currently ongoing court battles about late-term abortions. Many state restrictions subsequently have been ruled unconstitutional in higher courts (Ernst et al., 2004, p. 770). However, some have not, so depending on the jurisdiction, women who choose to have an abortion can be required to delay for a 24-hour waiting period, minors can be required to obtain consent from a parent or guardian, and maintenance of medical records and reports on abortions can be required. Such requirements limit the amount of confidential interchange between patient and doctor as well as, in the case of minors, the choice to have an abortion. The restrictions on abortion have the greatest impact on girls and women with the least resources, whether they are young, low-level federal employees, or dependent on Medicaid for health care. People who are most affected by legal restrictions on abortion often cannot afford the cost of abortion and travel to another state or country, where they can obtain a legal abortion.

The United States, as the most powerful nation in the world, has reduced access to abortion in other countries, notably those that are in greatest need of foreign aid, which are also the countries with high concentrations of poor women and children. The U.S. Congress at one time denied funding to international organizations that advocated or supported abortion. After this restriction was dropped, it was reestablished in 2001, when President George W. Bush issued an executive order that stipulated that U.S. assistance would not be given to foreign family planning agencies if they used any source of funds to provide counseling or referrals for abortion, lobbied to make or keep abortion legal, or provided abortions. Political conservatives in countries dependent on U.S. foreign aid have used U.S. policies as a rationale for limiting women's access to abortion in their own countries (Ernst et al., 2004, p. 792). They have argued that they cannot liberalize access because they would jeopardize financial assistance from the United States.

Within the United States, the degree of legal restriction on abortion has varied depending on how abortion is characterized in the media and in political discussion and debate. For example, in New York, the pro-choice discourse redefined abortion from a criminal issue to a medical decision. The result was the repeal of the criminal law against abortion, and New York still is one of the more liberal states in regard to abortion (Nossiff, 1998, p. 251). Alternatively, in Pennsylvania, discourse concentrated on the definition of circumstances when abortion was and was not legal, and for two decades, Pennsylvania has had the most restrictive legislation in the United States. When abortion is seen as a medical issue, women whose physicians see a need for abortion are granted more choice. When abortion is viewed as a legal issue, legislators etch into the law specific circumstances that will limit women's choices.

Struggles over the criminalization of abortion are not limited to the United States. In France and the United Kingdom, women's rights activists in the 1960s initially sought to have birth control available through physicians. In more recent years, the effort has turned to making abortion available without medical regulation (Latham, 2001). In France, despite opposition, in 2000 it became legal for school nurses to prescribe emergency contraception (commonly referred to as *the morning after pill*) to minors without parental consent or a doctor's prescription. In the United Kingdom, emergency contraception can be obtained from a pharmacist by individuals aged 16 and above. Contradicting the approach in France and the United Kingdom, in May of 2004, against recommendations from a U.S. Federal Drug Administration (FDA) advisory panel and FDA staff, the agency ruled against selling the emergency contraception without a prescription. By June, the American Medical Association had issued a statement indicating that the decision was wrong and encouraging physicians to write advance prescriptions that women and teenagers could use as needed. A major reason for the AMA's position was that the medication could reduce the need for abortion and thus could limit complications from pregnancy and abortion. Cross-national themes in the discourse of activists

Abortion continues to be a hotly contested issue in the United States, as shown in images of pro-life and pro-choice supporters shown above and opposite.

© Leif Skoogfors/CORBIS

who want to increase women's access to contraception are that pregnancy limits girls' and women's control of their own bodies, and that neither the state nor the medical profession should make decisions for women.

U.S. religious groups are strong drivers of attitudes about abortion, and thus of particular lobbying efforts in both state and federal government. Religious beliefs also influence the personal stance taken by legislators, policy makers, and policy implementers. In parts of the United States where the Catholic Church is very organized, its representatives have successfully lobbied for restrictive legislation. Fundamentalist Protestants have also influenced public opinion (Deflem, 1998, p. 783). An unintended effect of pro-life efforts has been the strengthening of pro-choice groups and intensification of their activism to protect and extend access to abortion (O'Connor & Berkman, 1995; Staggenborg, 1991). By lobbying, campaigning, and taking other actions to make abortion more accessible, pro-choice groups responded vigorously to religion-based efforts to stop or limit abortions.

More fundamental than religion, basic beliefs regarding motherhood also shape a person's stand in the abortion debate. Regardless of religious affiliation, people

© Owen Franken/CORBIS

tend to take a pro-choice stance if they believe that women's ability to plan childbirth is "necessary to [their] fulfilling their potential as human beings" (Luker, 1984, p. xi). Alternatively, people who have tried to limit abortion believe that childbearing and childrearing are central to all women's lives, and they view abortion as a "symbolic marker between those who wish to maintain this [gender] division of labor and those who wish to challenge it" (Luker, 1984, p. 201).

In Canada, although higher courts have overturned the decisions, in some instances after decriminalization of abortion, lower courts prohibited abortions because of fetal and paternal rights, even though a fetus does not have legal rights and there was no actual filial bond between the unborn child and expectant father (Fegan, 1996). Judicial reasoning in the lower courts ignored the potential negative experiences of women who were being required to become mothers and highlighted the rights of fetuses and men who had impregnated the women to have their future rights protected. As is apparent from the Canadian example, the debate over motherhood and the resulting efforts to have the state intervene in decisions about abortion is only partly influenced by ethical concerns about whether a fetus is different from a baby. Activists on both sides are influenced by their views about ideal gender roles—and, most fundamentally, by their position on whether motherhood should sometimes be required.

Child Abuse Through Prenatal Exposure to Drugs

Existing child abuse laws have been used to criminalize women who use drugs during pregnancy. In an early case, the University of South Carolina Medical Center developed a policy of giving local police and prosecutors information about pregnant women who tested positive for illegal drugs (Jos, Perlmutter, & Marshall, 2003). If the women did not comply with mandatory prenatal care and substance abuse treatment, they were arrested and prosecuted. Thirty-nine black women and one white woman were arrested. Ten of the jailed women brought charges against the university, the police, and the prosecutor for, among other things, racial discrimination, unlawful search and seizure, and violations of confidentiality. A federal jury later dismissed all of the charges.[24] Subsequently, the South Carolina attorney general instituted a statewide policy that included the threat of arrest or removal of the child if women did not participate in treatment and that required health care professionals to test women and report evidence to authorities. In 2000, the U.S. Supreme Court declined to hear an appeal that obtaining evidence of drug use and exposure of a fetus to drugs during a medical procedure was a violation of the Fourth Amendment prohibition against unreasonable search and seizure.

No state has instituted laws that prohibit a pregnant woman from using drugs, but three types of existing laws have been used to bring charges against women. Women have been charged with child endangerment or abuse, with trafficking in drugs to a minor through the umbilical cord, and with fetal murder or manslaughter (Harris & Paltrow, 2003). Because child abuse statutes were developed to apply to living children, results of tests at the moment of birth have been used as evidence so that the mother can be charged with providing drugs through her body to a minor. By 2003, 35 states had criminally prosecuted women for the use of alcohol or other drugs during pregnancy, and additional states had used involuntary civil commitment to protect the fetus from drugs being used by a pregnant woman (Jos et al., 2003). It is usually poor women of color who are most affected by the laws, because they obtain their medical care from clinics, and they use the drugs that are considered harmful. Well-to-do women are able to see private physicians who see their drug use as a medical problem rather than as a child protection problem. Middle- and upper-class women's drugs of choice, particularly alcohol, often are overlooked as threats to the unborn child.

In every state but South Carolina, higher-level state courts have overturned cases that criminalize pregnant women who use drugs. Arguments against criminalization have been that a fetus is not equivalent to a child; that myriad different behaviors, such as working in a dangerous setting or smoking cigarettes, could be outlawed if failure to protect laws were extended to pregnant women who used drugs; and that there were negative effects of such applications of the law, including deterring women from seeking prenatal care or encouraging them to have abortions (Harris & Paltrow, 2003). For South Carolina, the United States Supreme Court recently did find that a diagnostic test to obtain evidence of a patient's criminal conduct for law enforcement purposes was an unreasonable search if the patient had not consented to the procedure (*Ferguson v. City of Charleston*).[25] Medical groups that have argued against criminalization include the American

Public Health Association, the American Medical Association, the American Nurses Association, and the American College of Obstetricians and Gynecologists. Overall, the use of the criminal law to address harm to a fetus by a pregnant woman who uses drugs appears to have been slowed if not halted, though it is used with some restrictions in South Carolina, and some states do have civil laws that allow physicians or others to take actions to protect the fetus (Harris & Paltrow, 2003).

Child Abuse Through Failure to Protect

In contrast to the criminalization of pregnant women who used drugs, which generally has not been supported by higher courts in the United States, the prosecution and conviction of abused women for failing to protect their children from witnessing abuse has been supported. Forty-nine states and the District of Columbia have child abuse statutes, and most of those include a provision that stipulates punishment when an adult fails to protect a child from abuse (Stone & Fialk, 1997, p. 206). There are many instances when failure-to-protect laws do benefit children from neglectful adults, and it is well established that even witnessing domestic violence can cause harm to a child. However, there have been several cases in which women who are themselves abused have been charged and found guilty of the failure to protect their children from witnessing this abuse. Some examples are

- the finding that mother and father neglected and abused a 3-month-old infant by exposing the child to the abusive relationship in which the father had beaten the mother for 7 years.
- termination of a mother's parental rights because she exposed her children to years of her own abuse and failed to leave her abusive partner.
- a finding that a mother was guilty of criminal neglect although she was unaware of the father's sexual abuse of the child.
- a finding that the mother had been neglectful and removal of the children even though when the mother had attempted to leave, the father threatened to kill the children. (Stone & Fialk, 1997, p. 206)

Consistent with the belief that mothers primarily are responsible for children's welfare, even when fathers abuse and threaten both children and their mothers, when failure-to-protect laws are used as the basis for action, the mother usually is the one charged (Roberts, 1993; Stark & Flitcraft, 1988; Stone & Fialk, 1997, p. 210). Action against the abusive fathers is rare. There also are many documented instances when, after a mother is convicted of failure to protect, custody is awarded to the abusive father (Baradaren-Robison, 2003, p. 236). A central part of legal reasoning when abused women are charged with failure to protect is that they have the power to stop the abuse or to remove the child from witnessing abuse, an assumption that is questionable when a woman herself is being victimized by abuse.

Courts often do not consider the reasons that mothers do not intervene and protect their children from witnessing abuse. These reasons include immediate or long-term threats to either the mother's or the child's safety should the mother attempt to remove the child. Legal scholars have argued against current practices on the basis that a mother should not be held responsible for situations she cannot control or affect (Enos, 1996, p. 230), or that law should criminalize the behavior of the abuser who exposes the child to domestic violence instead of criminalizing the behavior of the victim (Stone & Fialk, 1997, p. 210). A case in Minnesota in 1992 provides an example of circumstances that make the seemingly reasonable action to leave an abusive relationship untenable:

> Daniel beat and threatened Janice for over two years. Janice sought help from the Minnesota CPS [Child Protection Service] and the Minnesota police department, but they told her there was nothing they could do. Because these agencies do not keep records of the cases in which they fail to act, there was no documentation for Janice to present at trial. In the meantime, Daniel refused Janice's pleas for him to stay away from Janice and her children and Daniel repeatedly forced his way into Janice's apartment by smashing her windows. Janice previously had attempted to separate herself from her attacker, planned her escape, and was awaiting one more paycheck in order to fix her car and flee without Daniel's knowledge.

> Daniel's violence reached its crescendo when Daniel locked both Janice and her daughter in a bedroom and Daniel raped the daughter. Janice testified that she believed that if she had tried to escape, seek help, or intervene, Daniel would have killed her or her daughter. Thus, Janice told her daughter to comply with Daniel's demands. Similarly, when Janice's son came to the door to see what was wrong, Janice sent her son away, hoping he would notice something was wrong and call the police once he was out of Daniel's earshot. Despite the motivations behind Janice's actions, she was convicted for aiding and abetting in Daniel's rape of [her] daughter. (Enos, 1996, pp. 242–243)

Because dynamics of abuse include purposely isolating the victim from other people, making her economically dependent, and threatening retaliation if mother or child leave, it is not unexpected that abused women sometimes do not try to escape in the midst of violence, particularly when prior attempts to obtain help have failed. Laws are not written, and often are not applied, to take this common pattern into account.

Laws Against Prostitution

In the United States, federal law against prostitution concentrates on the prohibition of crossing state or international boundaries for the purpose of engaging in sex for pay or enabling someone to do so. State laws prohibit some of the acts of soliciting or arranging for or engaging in prostitution or profiting from it. In the United States, prostitution is in some way criminalized in every state except for selected counties in Nevada, where brothels are legal (Hausbeck & Brents, 2000). In some locations, municipal laws also have been adopted to stop prostitution, for example by prohibiting establishments like massage parlors, where prostitution is likely to occur.

Although there is relative consistency in the criminal laws against prostitution in the United States, internationally, laws relevant to prostitution are heavily influenced by the locale's history, the nature and amount of prostitution, and pressure by police, governmental units, community groups, health agencies, and occasionally collectives of prostitutes (J. West, 2000, p. 115). The result is much variation between places and periods in the form of criminal or regulatory law pertaining to prostitution. In some places, criminal law prohibits trading sex for money, profiting from prostitution, and/or buying sexual services. Sometimes manifestations of prostitution, such as soliciting, having control over prostitutes, and making agreement with clients, are illegal (Davidson, 1998, p. 21). Police intervention into the activities of people involved in prostitution can also take the form of charges for various public nuisance offenses, such as loitering.

The form of the law in a particular country is connected to the degree of collective organization by people who sell sex for money (J. West, 2000). In the United States, collectives of women engaged in prostitution have not had much influence, in part because of public and political concerns about disorder and abuse, and in part because of morality politics. The focus of U.S. law enforcement is primarily on arresting people who sell sex for money, though at some times and places there have been campaigns to arrest customers or to apprehend organized criminal groups. In some states in Australia, in New Zealand, and especially in the Netherlands, prostitutes' collectives have had more influence on the law. In the Netherlands, the conceptualization and discussion of what is called "sex work" as a reasonable, freely chosen occupation influenced legislation that was enacted in 1999. The legislation introduced very tough penalties for trafficking, coercion, and the involvement of minors but lifted the general ban on prostitution (J. West, 2000, p. 112). The change shifted criminalization away from people working as prostitutes and toward people who victimized or exploited them.

Canada provides an interesting example because its law does not criminalize prostitution. To address public distaste for prostitution on the streets, it instead criminalizes communication with the intent to arrange for prostitution. Based on the Fraser Report, the 1986 legislation prohibited communication for the purpose of arranging for the exchange of sex for money. Like the law it replaced, it also prohibited houses of prostitution. Local jurisdictions, however, could license places of prostitution. Legislators who supported the communications prohibition were concerned primarily with controlling street prostitution, which was seen as a serious problem, especially in Toronto and Vancouver. The law was to be enforced equally against people working as prostitutes and against customers, and the implementation did result in criminal charges against an increased number of would-be customers (Duchesne, 1997, p. 6; Fleischman, 1989, p. 41). Another effect of the law was the concentration of police apprehension and prosecution on street-level prostitution, coupled with tolerance of higher-priced, off-the-street prostitution (Lowman, in press). In the context created by this pattern of enforcement, less-advantaged prostitutes—for example, those who are homeless or addicted to drugs—and customers who have limited resources become involved in the justice system, but "the bourgeois styles of prostitution are accepted and flourish" (Duchesne, 1997, p. 13).

The pattern that was documented in Canada illustrates how contemporary enforcement of laws against activities related to prostitution can be selective and therefore discriminatory. Also, the threat of police intervention cuts off access to the police as a source for protection and help at the same time that it encourages women who prostitute to be in dangerously secretive settings and to make quick deals with potential customers. Enabled by the existence of laws that put prostitutes in jeopardy of arrest, in some countries, a high proportion of police become entangled in corrupt practices of demanding either money or sex for protection or for non-enforcement of laws (Bindman, 1997). Finally, when prostitution is defined as a crime rather than as a job, the normal protections that the state affords to workers are not available.

The negative results of criminalizing prostitution have been the basis for some countries to regulate instead. Regulation typically requires restrictions on where prostitution occurs, licensing of where it occurs, regular checks on the health of prostitutes, and prostitutes' registration with a central authority. When prostitution is regulated, there often are criminal laws that protect people who are engaged in prostitution from being exploited or forced to do sexual acts in exchange for money. In the Netherlands, for example, prostitution is considered a legal profession, and prostitutes have the right to hygienic working conditions and security in the workplace. They also must pay taxes. Prostitutes can have social insurance, be paid sick leave, and receive a pension if they work for a brothel or own a company. However, forced prostitution is illegal. Also, people working as prostitutes must work in state-regulated brothels or specified geographic areas (Leidholdt, 1991, p. 145; see European Parliament, n.d.). There are ongoing debates in many countries about whether people who sell sex should be viewed as victims who should be saved or as professionals working in an acceptable job. Positions in the debate are connected to alternative conceptualizations of a person who sells sex for money and related differences in opinions about appropriate laws.

Alternative Conceptualizations of Prostitution

Are people who become involved in prostitution victims of their circumstances and the individuals who trick and traffic them? Or are they freely choosing an occupation that has the most benefits for them under existing circumstances? Does criminalizing prostitution help people get out of a bad situation or deter them from getting into a bad situation? Or does criminalization punish people for making reasonable choices when trading sex for money is the only way, or the best way, they can survive? Alternative views of the culpability of people who sell sex versus the culpability of customers, entrepreneurs, and networks that support prostitution are enabled by conceptualizations of people who trade sex for money as **the prostitute,** the **prostitute as victim,** or the **prostitute as sex worker.**

The Prostitute

The term *the prostitute* is sometimes used to signify a **fixed identity** (Nencel, 2001, p. 31), which is a quality that sums up the totality of a person's life and personality and that does not change. The depiction of the fixed identity of women who prostitute differentiates them from other people and provides the rationale for whether prostitution should be criminalized and whether and how it should be regulated (Nencel, 2001, p. 31). For example, in Peru, regardless of whether they want to abolish (criminalize) or just regulate prostitution, people's discussions and writings have focused on women who engage in prostitution as the primary problem rather than on any supportive criminal enterprise or network of customers. Discourse about *the prostitute* concentrates on a distinct group of women who are poor, the object of lust, or dishonorable. Consistent with the idea that prostitutes differ from the rest of the population, the existing law and recommendations for its change call for criminalization or regulation that will support state intervention into the lives of people who prostitute.

The Prostitute as Victim

Some researchers and activists describe prostitutes as victims. They argue for criminalization of the behavior of customers, pimps, and others who benefit from a person's provision of sex for money, but for the decriminalization of the activities of people who prostitute. Their reasoning is that the majority of people who sell sex are severely constrained in their opportunities to earn a living. They take the vast social distance between most people who prostitute and their customers as evidence of the relative powerlessness of people who work as prostitutes. One U.S. activist compared the appearance of women who had been arrested for prostitution to the appearance of men customers who had been arrested:

> The prostitutes wait in the pens shivering—they are dressed in ragged clothing or underwear. They rarely have addresses: at most, I get the name of "a friend." Many are withdrawing from cocaine. They don't have telephones—I get the beeper number of "a friend." They have scars, cuts, and bruises on their faces, necks, arms, and legs. They are usually unemotional and compliant. They are largely African-American and Latin. They are either women or, occasionally, young men made up and dressed to look like women. . . .
>
> The johns, by contrast, are visibly upset—embarrassed and indignant. They wear business suits or work clothes. They have homes, telephones, and salaries. Their biggest concern is that I'll call their wives or they won't be able to get their cars back. They are all races. They are exclusively male. (Leidholdt, 1991, p. 135)

Activists and researchers point to the extensive research on the realities of many prostitutes' lives, which are marked by levels of victimization and poverty that make it difficult to believe that anyone would freely choose prostitution as a profession.

In several different countries, for both brothel and street prostitutes, there is a very high incidence of posttraumatic stress disorder, which can be both a result of making a living selling sex and a contributing influence that blocks access to alternative opportunities for getting money (Farley, Baral, Kiremire, & Sezgin, 1998, p. 419). Worldwide, when prostitution is regulated or legalized, there is usually little or no attention to physical and emotional harm connected to prostitution. When prostitution is legalized, the state's role is to make sure that people who sell sex are HIV- and STD-free, so that they do not jeopardize the health of customers, and to limit the location of prostitution activities so that they do not offend or disturb citizens. If prostitutes are viewed as victims, regulation does not make sense, and criminalization of customers and profiteers is the appropriate response.

The Sex Worker

There is no question that the lives of many people who sell sex for money are fraught with physical danger and exploitation and are negatively affected by police corruption. However, theory and related research has tried to broaden the view of people who trade sex for money to include those who work and live in a variety of different situations. In Spain, women working as prostitutes from their homes or other settings of their choice have described benefits of prostitution, for example better-than-average pay for a female worker and independence in structuring their work and their time (Ignasi, 1993). Similarly, some women in England and the United States maintain decent, stable, and even good incomes by engaging in prostitution with a select group of men (Davidson, 1998). People who consider this group or who are in it have argued that individuals should be allowed to make the decision to engage in prostitution, and thus these activities should be legal. Especially in Western countries, proponents of this position talk about the rights of prostitutes (and people portrayed in pornography or engaged in other types of sex work), recognize their work as a profession, and use the term *sex worker* instead of *the prostitute* (Nencel, 2001, p. 2).

At the same time that the term *sex worker* reminds us that some people freely chose to work in prostitution and accrue some benefits from selling sex for money, it obscures certain aspects of reality. Similar to the label *the prostitute*, *sex worker* limits attention to the person who sells sex, and it makes it possible to consider the person apart from any context (Barry, 1995). Around the world, the context of prostitution most typically includes backgrounds of childhood abuse, continuing exposure to violence, and individual and group benefit from the exploitation of people who have limited power and influence. The very act of selling sex, or having one's sexual availability and activity sold, is inconsistent with self-direction and free will. "[P]rostitution is better conceptualized as an institution which allows certain powers of command over one person's body to be exercised by another. The client parts with money and/or other material benefits in order to secure powers over the prostitute's person which he (or more rarely she) could not otherwise exercise" (Davidson, 1998, p. 9). Although some people self-define as sex workers, are not victimized, and are not coerced to prostitute, worldwide they are not the majority of people who sell sex.

The alternative conceptualizations of people who sell sex for money shift attention from one subgroup to another, and to alternative theories about the reasons a person engages in prostitution. Depending on the conceptualization, certain laws make more or less sense. If the focus is on immoral people who engage in prostitution, then it makes sense to criminalize the practice or allow for the application of laws regarding violations of public order to keep the prostitute out of view of people who do not want to be exposed. The view that prostitutes are victims suggests that the emphasis should be on criminalization of customers and of people and organized groups that profit from prostitution. Sex workers are treated as legitimate workers and thus have benefits, though they are typically regulated in order to protect the health of customers and to restrict the location of business. Subsequent chapters of this book provide insight into the evidence supporting different explanations of prostitution. The main point here is that acceptance of these theories and related perceptions of people who engage in prostitution lies behind alternative legal approaches.

Pornography and the Law

U.S. obscenity laws criminalize certain forms of sexually explicit, pornographic material. The basic logic is that written and visual materials depicting sexual acts or objects are not protected by the First Amendment guarantee of freedom of expression if the average person, applying contemporary local community standards, would find that the materials appeal to prurient (i.e., unhealthy) interest, are explicitly prohibited by state law, or lack serious literary, artistic, political, or scientific value. There has been considerable legal debate over whether pornographic materials harm people, and therefore whether constitutional guarantees of free speech should be curtailed.

Some activists have pushed for at least civil laws against pornography, because it adversely affects people involved in producing it and may stimulate sex crimes that are similar to acts portrayed in pornography. Neither the social science literature nor the courts provide undisputed evidence that pornography actually causes violence against women. There is some evidence, however, that suggests a connection between viewing pornography and sexually aggressive behaviors against women (Malamuth, Addison, & Koss, 2000). What is less clear is whether people prone to aggression seek out violent pornography, violent pornography increases a person's aggression, or causation occurs in both directions.

Even if they accept that pornography promotes attitudes that support violence, many people are uneasy about becoming allied with the religious right in pressing for limitations on free speech. One argument is that activism to criminalize pornography might divert resources from more direct legal action in response to violence against women or more fundamental attempts to bring about change through education. Or, if free speech is limited in the fight against pornography, activists' attention might be diverted to combating challenges to their own right to free speech. At the same time, women's rights activists will find themselves strengthening the religious right, which they have opposed because of disagreements about access to abortion and patriarchal family arrangements (Strossen, 1996). Overall, in the United States, the limits of illegal pornography continue to be set through case law decisions in the courts, and both activists who try to shape the law from a women's rights perspective and the courts have emphasized the protection of freedom of speech. However, there is continuing effort to apply laws that are violated in the course of producing pornography, particularly laws against the abuse and exploitation of children.

International Law

Human rights laws exist in each country's laws, and at the international level they are included in various treaties, covenants, and declarations. In the United States, foreign treaties that are ratified by the government become part of the law of the land, and thus state and federal courts are bound to enforce human rights principles contained in the treaties.[26] Also, state and federal law must be interpreted consistently with international obligations (Lillich, 1992). The International Covenant on Civil and Political Rights, which the United States ratified in 1992, guarantees fundamental human rights without distinction on the basis of sex.[27] International conferences and other forums that have recognized violence against women as a human rights violation have influenced the form of international law and have given nations the responsibility not just for abstaining from perpetrating violence, but also for eliminating violence against women.

Victims of acts that are criminalized by international law can seek to enforce their rights in their own country, at a regional level, or through the United Nations. For example, the United States is a signatory to many treaties that cover protection of human rights, and victims can turn to federal court by using the Alien Torts Claims Act (Women, Law and Development International, 1997, p. 110). An option at the regional level is the Inter-American Commission on Human Rights, which was created through the American Convention on Human Rights in 1969 (Shelton, 2000, p. 48). Upon receiving a complaint from a victim, the commission can submit a case to the Inter-American Court of Human Rights. Victims can also submit cases directly to the Inter-American Commission on Women, which was created in 1995 (Women, Law and Development International, 1997, p. 87). Finally, the United Nations offers several avenues of enforcement, including its Commission on the Status of Women and the Committee on the Elimination of Discrimination Against Women (Women, Law and Development International, 1997, pp. 36, 50). Typically, regional and national courts determine whether a nation's laws and practices provide adequate deterrence of violence against women and justice for victims.

The Hague Convention on the Civil Aspects of International Child Abduction, accepted by more than 70 countries including the United States, was drafted to address situations in which a father abducted a child and took that child to another country. However, most of the cases that have reached U.S. Courts of Appeals have involved women claiming that they have been abused and fled with their children to the United States (Weiner, 2003, p. 765). Worldwide, in 1999 there were 1,250 of this type of case, many of which involved more than one child (Weiner, 2003, p. 768). Additional cases went directly to national courts, involved countries that were not part of the Hague agreement, or were settled before going to court. Judges adjudicating Hague Convention cases considered whether the country where the father lived could provide adequate protection against future abuse, and negative findings were a cause for the child's not returning to the father. This type of sanction, particularly if repeated, can push countries to alter their programs and policies to improve the situation for victims of domestic violence and for their children (Weiner, 2003, p. 770).

International law has steadily increased protections for women and girls subjected to violence, but the United States has been inconsistent in its acceptance of international law. In Nairobi during 1985, a women's international conference of delegates from member states of the United Nations brought international attention to widespread human rights violations against women. They identified the elimination of domestic violence and other forms of violence against women as special priorities in the world community. What often had previously been defined as a private family matter was redefined as a state responsibility, and this redefinition subsequently has been reaffirmed in international meetings and agreements. Signaling increasing international attention to violence against women, during the 1992 creation of the Bosnian War Crimes Tribunal, the United Nations listed rape as a violation of international law and human rights for the first time (Scharf, 1997, p. 55). At the 1993 World Conference on Human Rights, 171 participating governments affirmed that human rights are the birthright of all people and that the first responsibility of governments is to protect human rights regardless of sex, race, color, language, national origin, age, class, or religious or political beliefs. The 1994 Declaration on the Elimination of Violence Against Women was adopted in a resolution by the General Assembly of the United Nations.[28] It sent a clear message that public international law condemns violence against women, including sexual assault and domestic violence, and expects states to help combat and end such violence. As a result of this declaration, the United Nations Human Rights Committee systematically evaluates the measures that states have taken to eradicate gender-related violence. An important 1995 women's international conference in Beijing brought renewed worldwide attention to violence against girls and women. The resulting treaty to end discrimination and violence against women has been ratified by 169 countries, which do not include the United States. Finally, at the beginning of the 21st century, the International Criminal Court was located in Rome as a separate entity from United Nations procedures for addressing human rights violations, and the Women's Caucus for Gender Justice in the International Criminal Court was established. The International Criminal Court Statute lists various types of sexual violence among the acts that constitute war crimes and crimes against humanity. These specifically include rape, sexual slavery, forced prostitution, forced pregnancy, and forced sterilization. The United States is not included in the 92 countries that have ratified this agreement, and no cases involving gender-related violence have yet been heard, but women's rights activists are hopeful that the International Criminal Court can be used to improve women's lives.

The U.S. position to not ratify or participate in key international law agreements is a result of a political process. In the U.S. Congress, there were many specific objections to ratifying the treaty to end discrimination and violence against women, and as a result there has not been an affirmative vote. The United States has not signed on to support the International Criminal Court Statute in part because the president and his advisers do not want U.S. military personnel to be charged and tried by an international court. People both inside and outside the United States have criticized U.S. actions to sanction human rights violations in other countries at the same time that it does not fully embrace international efforts to ensure the protection of women's and others' human rights.

Proponents of international law have pointed out that the laws have "transformed simple domestic rights claims into 'human rights' claims and 'international' claims" (Schneider, 2000, p. 55). However, critics point out that the United Nations must rely heavily on shaming other nations, which can be effective only if a country cares about the approval of United Nations members, or if those members impose other sanctions. Some people question the utility of international legal options, because these options are not used frequently (Shelton, 2000, p. 50). One drawback is that decisions of international tribunals are often difficult to enforce against unwilling governments (Women, Law and Development International, 1997, p. 20). Also, the United Nations has relatively limited resources for special issues affecting women; relies on monitoring but has no formal complaint mechanism; gives little emphasis to the violation of rights in the private sphere, where women are most often victimized; and sometimes accepts the cultural relativity arguments to justify violations of women's rights (Charlesworth, 1998, pp. 786–788). Respect for cultural differences can be the basis for noninterference with minority lifestyles, which are often supported by male leaders and are not necessarily acceptable to women and girls (Becket & Macey, 2001, p. 311). International law is best viewed as one tool that activist groups and individuals both inside and outside a country can use to create pressure for improvements in responses to gender-related violence and tendencies to criminalize homosexual sexual activity.

Despite criticisms of international law, women activists continue to explore international law as an option for enforcing their rights. International law can have effects beyond individual cases. International law enabled passage of the Violence Against Women Act (VAWA) in the United States. Specifically, the U.S. Senate Judiciary Committee reviewed internal law and conacuded that the VAWA was necessary because there had been state inaction to universally protect against domestic violence in the country, and because rape victims were unable to find either justice or protection in the justice system (Senate Committee on the Judiciary, 1993). The advances in international bodies of law can be helpful not only to victims who try to use them in the courts, but also as tools in diplomatic negotiations that pressure countries to improve protections for people subjected to gender-related violence (Koenig & Askin, 2000, p. 29).

Laws Prohibiting Consensual
Sexual Activity Between Same-Sex Adults

An opinion issued by the U.S. Supreme Court in *Lawrence v. Texas*[29] in 2003 provided a useful summary of the laws prohibiting consensual sexual activity between same-sex adults. The case involved police responding to a call about a weapons disturbance in a private residence. When the police entered the apartment, there was no weapons disturbance, but Mr. Lawrence was engaging in a consensual sexual act with another man. Both men were convicted of violating a Texas statute that forbid two persons of the same sex to engage in specified types of intimate sexual conduct. In ruling the arrest unconstitutional, the court reasoned that early American sodomy laws did not set a precedent for conviction, because they were not directed against homosexuals, but instead prohibited sexual activity that was not intended to result in procreation regardless of the sex of the parties involved. Also, the early laws were not enforced against adults acting in private. It was only at the end of the 20th century that American laws targeting same-sex couples were created, and just nine states singled out same-sex relations for criminal prosecution. Although the Supreme Court recognized that throughout history there had been powerful voices to condemn homosexual conduct as immoral, it defined its task as protecting liberty, not mandating a moral code. Thus, it decided that police intrusion into a private home and state power over very private sexual behavior were unacceptable. The Court further reasoned that there was no country or governmental interest that justified the compromise of liberty.

The U.S. Supreme Court decision was consistent with United Nations proclamations and agreements that people have the right to respect for private life and that discrimination based on sexual orientation is unacceptable. In fact, the Court's decision referred to several cases in international courts that had affirmed the right of consenting adults to engage in homosexual activities in private. For example, the European Court of Human Rights found that the following was inconsistent with the European Convention on Human Rights: An adult male who lived in Northern Ireland had been questioned, his home had been searched, and he feared prosecution because he had desired to be involved in homosexual behavior. The decision in *Lawrence v. Texas* pointed to this and other cases that had been in international courts as one of the justifications for its decision, and thereby illustrated how international law can influence national law.

Limits of the Law

Laws and legal processes can provide specific punishments or remedies on a case-by-case basis, and they can reflect either traditional or emerging norms about permissible behavior. However, the effect of laws can be relatively limited compared to the effects of other social forces. In research on domestic violence, Merry (1995, pp. 301–302) observed that the court of one Hawaiian town encouraged women to leave their violent parnters and to rely on the law and the legal system. This solution did not address problems that the women had with housing, support, child care, employment, or community acceptance. One woman said:

> I didn't ask him [the judge] for a no-contact TRO [temporary restraining order that prohibits contact], my dumb lawyer did. I'm angry at him. Now I can't ask for money for the bills. Now I got to go to the kids for money, and they ask him. (Merry, 1995, p. 301)

Similarly, in a Massachusetts court, judges who saw themselves as reformers and who believed and tried to understand the victims often fell short of providing help, because they did not recognize women's extreme economic distress and thus did not order child support or other types of financial aid (Ptacek, 1999). The law allows for an assertion of rights, but it "cannot do the job of providing safety and security. It cannot help a battered woman to change her life once the law has intervened" (Schneider, 2000, p. 53). More broadly, the law is not an instrument that can reduce or eliminate the root causes of violence against women. These limitations of the law have been referred to as an **unfulfilled promise of liberal legalism**.

Also illustrating the limits of legal reform, it is unclear whether reforms in sexual assault laws have translated directly into changes in the handling of sexual assault cases. Research before and after legal reforms showed that in Atlanta, Chicago, Houston, Philadelphia, and the District of Columbia, the conviction rates did not appear to change, but that in Detroit, three or four times as many individuals were indicted for sexual assault after institution of the reforms (Spohn & Horney, 1992). Also, a higher proportion of simple (as opposed to aggravated) reform cases were in the Detroit court (Spohn & Horney, 1996). The findings for Detroit suggests that in some areas, reforms may have encouraged more reporting, that prosecutors were charging in cases that they previously did not, or that public opinion unrelated to the reforms resulted in more charges. Victims who previously would not have had their cases heard before a court were now having their cases prosecuted. However, once cases were in court, the predictors of case outcomes were the same before and after reforms (Spohn & Horney, 1993). The reforms may have increased the flow of cases into court but not substantially changed decision making by jurors or judges. Also, the effects of reforms were not the same in the six cities that were studied.

There is some evidence of why a particular legal reform will have different effects depending on the local context. For the 48 continental states, several different factors influenced the effect of reforms in sexual assault laws on reporting and apprehension levels (Berger, Neuman, & Searles, 1994). In states where the new laws expanded illegal behavior to multiple forms of sexual assault and specified that victim and offender could be either female or male, reporting did increase. In states that shifted the definition of sexual assaults from acts that involve force to acts that fail to be done with consent, police apprehension increased. More generally, a context marked by liberalism and a strong feminist political thrust had an effect on apprehension rates separate from any effect of the new laws. Additional evidence of the effects of rape law reform was provided by an analysis of national statistics (Bachman & Paternoster, 1993). There was a slight (10%) increase in the proportion of sexual assaults that were reported after the reforms, and rape offenders were somewhat more likely to be sent to prison. Also, acquaintance rapes were treated as seriously as stranger rapes, not more leniently, as they had been before the reforms. After the reforms, police and prosecutors developed special units and procedures to improve the response to sexual assault. Because of either law reforms, changes in the justice system, or growing public intolerance of rape, sexual assault rates did decline after legal reforms occurred. Canadian experiences with reforms in rape laws has been similar to those in the United States: There were increases in reporting, but limited or no changes in how the criminal justice system responded (Roberts, 1992; Sanday, 1981). In assessing the reformed laws to address sexual assault, it is important to keep in mind that despite findings of limited impact on reporting, apprehension, and conviction, the reforms have resulted in more humane treatment of victims than characterized pre-reform interactions (Spohn & Horney, 1990). Additionally, there are indications that the new laws may have made the public less tolerant of the varieties of sexual assault.

Conclusion

U.S. laws and related policies pertaining to gender reflect ongoing political battles about women's rights and responsibilities, one result being that they are inconsistent with each other. More than 30 years ago, in *Roe v. Wade*, the U.S. Supreme Court recognized women's right to make medical decisions about abortion without state intervention, but federal and state legislatures have taken many steps to limit women's choices in this area, and the courts continue to hear cases to establish the continuation and the reality of this right. The basic tenet that a fetus does not have the rights of a person who has been born has been ignored in subsequent laws. Related to the issue of fetal rights, pregnant women have been charged with exposing their unborn children to damaging drugs. Consistent with the emphasis on protecting children, women also have been charged with exposing their children to violence by virtue of being victimized by abusive men. The theme running through much of the contest about the laws pertaining to women is that women and girls should be successful in protecting their children regardless of limitations that they face, and that they are responsible for the health of any fetus they carry, again regardless of personal or contextual limitations they may have. The limits on choice and high expectations for protecting fetuses and children fall most heavily on poor women who do not have resources to escape violence or locate private medical care.

Although with only the exception of some counties in Nevada, prostitution is consistently criminalized in the United States, this is not the case across the world. The U.S. laws emphasize the illegal nature of both the seller's and the buyer's engaging in prostitution and of supporting the act of selling sex for money through force, organized criminal activity, or some other means. Other countries have chosen to expend their criminal justice resources on public health concerns related to prostitution or on stopping exploitation or victimization of people who engage in prostitution. There is not a strong movement to challenge the emphasis on criminalization of prostitution in the United States.

A growing body of international law has developed to define women's and gay and lesbian individuals' human rights to include privacy, reproductive choices, and protection from discrimination and violence. The United States has played a complex and internally contradictory role in attempts to influence other nations. U.S. legislators were influenced by international law when they developed the Violence Against Women Act, and the U.S. Supreme Court, in *Lawrence v. Texas*, considered international law in making a decision about sexual activity between same-sex adults. In the United States, for both the Violence Against Women Act and sexual activity between consenting adults, international law led to increased protection of the rights of individuals. However, the United States has not ratified international treaties and agreements to reduce violence against women or to establish an international court. Also, inconsistent with its own Supreme Court ruling, it has taken steps to restrict access to abortion for women outside the United States. As for legal restrictions on the choices of women in the United States, restrictions on access to abortion outside the United States have had the most effect on the very poorest women from poverty-stricken countries.

The law and the criminalization that it accomplishes are just one type of influence on the specification of which acts are criminal and on responses to both victimization and crime. The remainder of this book considers theories that explain how macrolevel social conditions, community and organizational context, and individual beliefs affect patterns of crime and victimization and responses to both victims and offenders. These other influences have their effects within the constraints and the opportunities resulting from existing law. The law remains an important constraint because it criminalizes selected behaviors and limits responses to people who present themselves as victims and offenders within the justice system and the broader community. At the same time that the law is a constraint, as has been shown in the present chapter and will be shown in subsequent chapters, it can be challenged and changed.

Key Terms

Civil law	Presumptive arrest policy
Criminal law	Pro-choice position on abortion
Cultural relativity arguments	Pro-life position on abortion
Domestic violence	Prostitute as sex worker
Female genital mutilation	Prostitute as victim
Fixed identity	Rape shield laws
Hate crime	Stalking
Intimate-partner violence	Unfulfilled promise of liberal legalism
Mandatory arrest policy	Violence Against Women Act

Review and Discussion

1. Is it just that a U.S. woman's access to abortion depends on the policies and laws within the state where she lives, or should women have equal access to abortion regardless of the state where they reside? Explain your position.

2. What is the purpose of various laws against violence against women?

3. Compare and contrast U.S. law, international law, and law in particular countries mentioned in this chapter on (a) how they address violence against girls and women and (b) how they address prostitution.

4. What are the differences in the beliefs of people who promote alternative laws pertaining to access to abortion?

5. Is international law useful in promoting justice for women and girls and for people who are gay, lesbian, or bisexual? Justify your answer.

6. What are the pros and cons of criminalizing or regulating prostitution?

7. How could activists use international law to improve the handling of crimes against women or the criminalization of women in their home countries?

8. To what degree have injustices described in Chapter 1 been addressed by laws described in this chapter on gender and the law?

9. Is liberal feminism, as described in Chapter 1, a useful framework for understanding gender, crime, and justice? Explain your response.

Web Sites to Explore

The Web site for NARAL Pro-Choice America provides information about pro-choice issues and activities. NARAL stands for National Abortion and Reproductive Rights Action League. The NARAL changed its name to NARAL Pro-Choice in 2003. Separate sections of the Web site focus on contraception, equal access to abortion, science and women's health, sex education, the Supreme Court, and young women. http://www.naral.org/

At http://www.usccb.org/ the United States Conference of Catholic Bishops provides information about its pro-life activities. This is one of many religion-sponsored pro-life Web sites. Other religious groups maintain pro-choice Web sites.

CHAPTER 3

Gender-Related Victimization

Gender-related victimization is disproportionately concentrated on women and girls. Forms include sexual assault, intimate-partner violence, incest, genital mutilation, and trafficking for sexual exploitation. Some hate crimes are also directed at females. The concentration results because girls and women are victimized because of their gender. As Dorie Klein (1981) wrote, "in tracing the female experience through history and across cultures, one notices that women have often been injured *as women:* as child bearers, sexual objects for men, and nurturers" (p. 64). Sanctioning and abuse occur, for example, when a husband abuses his wife for not carrying out household chores in the way he thinks that women should. Gender-motivated victimizers who punish, harass, or in some other way aggress against people are motivated to enforce their own notions of gender-appropriate behavior or to express their hostility toward people who do not conform to those notions.

Because the process that leads to hate crime victimization of people who are gay, lesbian, or bisexual parallels the explanation for gender-related victimization, it is instructive to consider it along with the victimization of girls and women. Gay, lesbian, or bisexual individuals are victimized because they are not meeting other people's expectations about how females and males should act sexually or in other ways within intimate relationships. **Sexual orientation victimization** is an attack based on a person's sexual orientation.

Domestic violence, including sexual assault, does occur between same-sex individuals. An examination of the dynamics of same-sex relationship violence raises questions about the adequacy of theories that identify the patriarchal family structure and/or men's domination of women as the primary cause of violence against women. The rationale that the antagonists in same-sex relationship violence mimic traditional female and male gender roles, for example one woman or man being a more masculine "husband" and the other more like a wife, is a myth (Jablow, 2000).

Thus, violence between same-sex partners does not result from efforts to copy typical marital roles. The existence of same-sex domestic violence suggests that there can be alternative explanations for the violence between gay, lesbian, and straight partners. These explanations would not center on the importance of patriarchy and men's domination over women. They might apply primarily to same-sex couples but might still hold in some cases of violence against a different-sexed partner.

Theorists and activists have named and called attention to an increasing number of different forms of gender-related and sexual orientation–related crime and harassment. They have noted the overlap in oppressive and controlling behaviors that are not addressed in criminal or civil law but that are often part and parcel of constellations of behavior that include illegal acts. For example, eroding a partner's self-image is not illegal, but a pattern of criticism and belittling is often connected to physical abuse. Theorists also have linked gender to the *fear of crime*, which, although connected to the experience of victimization, is a separate influence on people's lives.

The next section of this chapter provides information on victimization patterns related to gender and sexual orientation. Theorists struggle, more or less successfully, to explain these patterns. The section is followed by information on improvements in conceptualizing and naming types of victimization, including exposure to what is called everyday violence. Literature that denies high levels of violence against women is presented and analyzed. This chapter also presents explanations that advance our knowledge of structural, cultural, and individual influences on victimization. The chapter ends with consideration of the effects of gender- and sexual orientation–related victimization.

Patterns of Victimization

Rates of Victimization

The National Crime Victimization Survey (NCVS) data have some unique advantages for highlighting broad patterns of victimization for males and females in selected racial groups within the United States. With support from the U.S. Bureau of Justice Statistics, annually the U.S. Census Bureau surveys a large and nationally representative sample of individuals age 12 and over, and it gathers information on the experience of personal crimes of sexual assault, other types of assault, and robbery. Although it is known that the survey results are affected by underreporting of victimization, especially highly personal experiences like intimate-partner violence and sexual assault, the NCVS does allow for comparisons of the victimization experiences of nationally representative samples of females and males in different racial groups. The survey does not, however, gather information on sexual orientation, so other sources of data need to be used to document crimes directed against people who are gay, lesbian, or bisexual. Similarly, it does not provide good information on sexual abuse of children. It also uses the categories of race (Asian, black, Native American, white), which obscure within-race differences and do not reveal ethnic differences, with the exception of Hispanics. Specifically,

Asians include many different ethnic groups, and Native American tribes can be very different from each other. Hispanics include people who differ in race. Finally, the NCVS results may be influenced by differences in the willingness of gender and racial groups to report to the interviewers whether or not they were victimized. Despite these drawbacks, the NCVS gives an overall picture of the profound differences in the patterns of victimization of groups that differ by both gender and race, and thus clarifies the importance of considering the intersections of gender and race in explaining these patterns. It also is the best available national victimization survey that has been done over time in the United States.

The relative rates of victimization for sex and racial groups depend on whether the focus is on crimes that happen in and around the home or in public places. These differences, which highlight gender and racial differences in people's experience of victimization, are shown in Table 3.1, which includes the results of an analysis of the NCVS data for 1993 to 1999.[30] The rates show the number of victimizations for every 1,000 people over the age of 12 in a 12-month period for each gender and racial subgroup.

Most personal victimization incidents are assaults or robberies, and a smaller proportion consists of sexual assaults. There are very large subgroup differences in the rates of personal victimization. For personal victimizations in and around the home, Native American females report the highest rate. There are nearly 30 victimizations for every thousand Native American females over the age of 12 in a 12-month period. The rate for Native American males is nearly as high, and the rate for black females is also high, at 20 incidents a year for every thousand females. In public places, Native American males experience the highest rate of personal victimization (76 incidents per thousand people), followed by black males (36 incidents per thousand people), and then by Native American females (35 incidents per

Table 3.1   Annual Rates of Victimization (per 1,000 people) at Home and in Public Places for Groups Differing in Sex and Race

	Place Where the Victimization Occurred	
	In or Around the Home	In a Public Place
Females		
Asian	4.9	12.0
White	12.6	16.6
Black	20.0	21.8
Native American	29.5	35.0
Males		
Asian	4.2	22.8
White	8.3	31.5
Black	12.2	36.2
Native American	25.2	76.2

SOURCE: Data are from the National Crime Victimization Survey, 1993–1999.

thousand). The largest gender differences in victimization involve offenses committed in public places, where males have the highest rates of personal victimizations. Native American females report higher rates of victimization in public places than do women of other races (35 incidents per thousand), just as they do for incidents in and around the home, but what is striking here is that their rate of victimization in public places is higher than the rates for males who are Asian (23 incidents per thousand) and white (32 incidents per thousand), and almost the same as for black males (36 incidents per thousand). Although males in general report higher levels of victimization away from the home, black females are also more often victimized away from their homes than are people in other subgroups. The home is a comparatively dangerous place for women of color, but black and Native American women are also quite vulnerable away from home. When white and Asian females do experience victimization, even if this is relatively rare, it typically is in or around the home.

Age also is related to differences in rates of victimization. An analysis of the 1994 NCVS data showed that boys (17 and under) were three times as likely as male adults to be aggravated assault victims, close to five times as likely as male adults to be simple assault victims who had sustained an injury, and almost four times as likely as male adults to be victims of simple assault without injury (Hashima & Finkelhor, 1999, p. 807). Girls were four times as likely as adult females to be sexual assault victims, and they were three times as likely as female adults to be victims of verbal threats of assault. Data sources apart from the NCVS have revealed very high rates of abuse of youth: One in five girls in Grades 9 through 12 reported physical and/or sexual abuse, and the proportion of sexually abused high school girls (12%) was more than twice than the proportion for boys (5%) (Harris and Associates, 1997). The high rates of sexual assault for young girls and the rates of other types of crime against boys and girls have very serious implications for health and emotional well-being.

Although there is no representative sample that allows for documentation of the pattern of victimization of gay and lesbian people, research does provide some information about the prevalence of victimization against people because of their sexual orientation. One study (D'Augelli & Grossman, 2001; also see Dean, Wu, & Martin, 1992; Garofalo, Wolf, Wissow, Woods, & Goodman, 1999; Herek, Gillis, Cogan, & Glunt, 1997; Otis & Skinner, 1996; Pilkington & D'Augelli, 1995) of a diverse group of gay, lesbian, and bisexual individuals aged 60 or older revealed that when the entire lifetime is considered, almost three quarters of them had experienced sexual-orientation victimization: 63% reported verbal abuse, 29% threats of violence, 16% physical attacks, 12% threats with weapons, 11% objects thrown at them, and 7% sexual assault. Also, 29% said they had been threatened with the disclosure of their sexual orientation. Men had experienced physical attacks nearly three times more often than the women. Only one third of all respondents reported no instances of sexual orientation victimization during their lives. People who were more open about their sexual orientation, and open at an earlier age, were most likely to have been victimized.

The NCVS does not provide information on sexual orientation of victims or offenders. Independent sources do suggest that within lesbian, gay, and bisexual relationships, there is at least the same level of physical violence as in heterosexual relationships (Cruz & Firestone, 1998; Turrell, 2000).

The Nature of Victimization

Most men and boys are victimized by other males; most girls and women are victimized by males, too. This finding is shown in Table 3.2 for NCVS data for 1993 to 1999.

Regardless of the victim's race, more than 90% of incidents perpetrated on males involved a male offender. Of the victimizations of Native American females, 65% involve a male offender, and for crimes against females in all other racial groups, this percentage is above 70%. Males are very rarely victimized by females, less than 10% for every racial group.

As shown in Table 3.3, females are much more likely than males to be victimized by someone they know. Women and girls interviewed for the 1993–1999 NCVS said that in 79% of their victimizations, they knew the offender; males reported that they knew the offender in 59% of their victimizations. When victim race and sex are both considered, the subgroup differences in whether the victimization is by a

Table 3.2   Estimated Percentages of People Victimized by Males and Females for Subgroups of People 12 Years of Age and Older, 1993–1999

	Sex and Race of Victim							
Offender Sex	Asian Female	Asian Male	White Female	White Male	Black Female	Black Male	Native American Female	Native American Male
Male	79.2	93.0	73.2	92.3	70.8	91.3	65.0	91.0
Female	20.8	7.0	26.8	7.7	29.2	8.7	35.0	9.0

SOURCE: Data are from the National Crime Victimization Survey, 1993–1999.

Table 3.3   Estimated Percentages of People Victimized by Someone Known or by a Stranger, for Subgroups of People 12 Years of Age and Older, 1993–1999

	Sex and Race of Victim							
Offender Known to Victim?	Asian Female	Asian Male	White Female	White Male	Black Female	Black Male	Native American Female	Native American Male
Knew/ had seen	65.8	40.7	78.9	58.9	79.9	62.1	86.1	60.5
Stranger	34.2	59.3	21.1	41.1	20.1	37.9	13.9	39.5

SOURCE: Data are from the National Crime Victimization Survey, 1993–1999.

stranger are very pronounced. At the low end, just 13.9% of Native American females' victimizations involved a stranger, and at the other extreme, 59.3% percent of male Asians' victimizations involved a stranger.

The concentration of nonlethal victimization of women and girls in their homes by people they know is mirrored in statistics on homicide. In 2000, in the United States, 65.2% of homicides involved a male offender and a male victim, 25.0% involved a male offender and a female victim, 7.2% involved a female offender and a male victim, and 2.6% involved a female offender and victim (Fox & Zawitz, 2003, p. 40). Between 1976 and 2000, female victims were more likely to be killed by an intimate or family member than male victims, whereas male victims were more likely to be killed by acquaintances or strangers (Fox & Zawitz, 2003, pp. 41–42). Similarly, in Canada between 1921 and 1988, the proportion of women killed by intimate partners stayed at about 50%, and women were most likely to be killed in their homes (Gartner & McCarthy, 1991, p. 309). As others have noted, "these features of femicide challenge the assumption that the home and family provide a refuge from victimization which is implicit in some perspectives on interpersonal violence" (Gartner & McCarthy, 1991, p. 309).

The striking differences between the nature and amount of violence against gender and sexual orientation groups is a starting place for theories about victimization and, as will be discussed in subsequent chapters, theories to explain why people break the law. The differences provide reason to expend considerable effort trying to understand why women and girls are at such high levels of danger in and around their homes, why males predominate as the offenders in the United States, and why females who are Native Americans, African Americans, and Hispanics are exposed to levels of violence not only higher than those for other females, but in some cases higher than for racial groups of males. The importance of explaining these long-standing patterns is reinforced by their replication in other countries.

Global Dimensions of Crimes Against Girls and Women

A consideration of developing countries and gender-related victimization is difficult because of spotty availability of data and omission of some forms of crime from official statistics, but there is evidence that various forms of gender-related victimization are higher than in the United States for some countries. In Papua New Guinea, 67% of women in rural areas and 56% in cities had been hit by their husbands (del Frate, 1995, p. 2). In South Africa, there is a virtual epidemic in rape of young women and girls (Meier, 2002). During the first month of the Bosnia war, an estimated 20,000 women were raped (del Frate, 1995, p. 8). These are but a few examples that reflect the magnitude of the numbers of women affected by gender-related violence at particular times and places.

Trafficking, which is the transport of people across local or national borders for the purpose of sexually exploiting them, is a crime that predominantly victimizes girls and women. Women, girls, and sometimes boys are tricked or forced into moving to another area of their country, often from rural to urban areas, or to other countries, where they are entrapped and forced to engage in prostitution. Some poor families sell female children to traffickers. Estimates are that 1 million people are

This girl, who was captured and forced to work as a prostitute in the Philippines, is freed by police, who are ready to retaliate if her captors attack.

© CORBIS

trafficked and sexually exploited worldwide each year (Hughes, 2000). Before the collapse of the Soviet Union, a criminal underground operated to circumvent and supplement the planned economies. After the collapse of the economic system, the context was ripe for expanded illegal opportunities, and the demand for women and the profits that could be made from them, along with limited risk compared to drug and arms trafficking, encouraged the growth of trafficking. Criminal groups have recruited and taken women and children from poor Asian countries (such as the Philippines and Thailand) and more recently from former Soviet republics such as Ukraine and Russia. Although the media have highlighted Europe, Asia, and Canada as the places where trafficked women are taken, the U.S. government has estimated that each year 50,000 women and children are trafficked to the United States, primarily from Latin America, Southeast Asia, and the republics that made up the Soviet Union (Raymond & Hughes, 2001, p. 7).

Fear and Everyday Violence

Survey results convey only a partial picture of people's actual experience of victimization, because they omit information on the context in which the victimization occurs, the feelings and thoughts of both the aggressor and target, and the aftermath of victimization. Increased understanding of the connection of gender to anticipation, fear, and terror of victimization has partly corrected the limitations of numbers in indicating victimization experiences. Efforts to name specific forms of gender-related victimization have drawn on descriptions of the context and consequences of victimization, and in so doing have extended understanding of the range in gender-related victimization.

Fear of crime results from a personal experience with crime or knowledge of other victims (Schlesinger, Dobash, Dobash, & Weaver, 1992), but it is a separate phenomenon with its own effects. Fear influences everyday routines, such as checking around the house upon first entering, and a variety of precautionary measures, such as carrying a weapon or not walking alone at night. Anticipation of victimization because of gender, sexual orientation, race, social class, or other combined differences in identity and physical characteristics—many of which are highly obvious—can put people in a state of discomfort ranging from periodic unease to high levels of terror. Stanko (1990) used the words "**everyday violence**" to describe fear-promoting experiences and circumstances that influence people to automatically take possible acts of violence into account. Everyday violence results in "measures to guarantee our safety—such as staying alert on the street, resisting arguments with our intimates because their bad tempers might lead to a beating, or avoiding certain public places that make us feel uneasy" (Stanko, 1990, p. 5). Consistent with the notion of everyday violence, fear of crime is most accurately indicated by the "wide range of emotional and practical responses to crime and disorder made by individuals and communities" or, more generally, "the impact of people's concerns about crime on everyday social life" (Pain, 2001, p. 901).

Depending on other correlates of social location—for example, poverty and race—girls and women, to varying degrees, have a sense that they need to alter their lives to manage violence that is disproportionately directed against females (Stanko, 1990). Gay, lesbian, and bisexual individuals also emotionally respond to and manage potential gender-related violence through routines and choices in everyday life. Fear of crime influences quality of life and reproduces social inequalities, creating and reinforcing exclusion from particular places and from some social interactions (Pain, 2001, p. 902) and restricting a person's actions. Individuals' beliefs that they need to adjust their lives to avoid gender-related victimization are a manifestation of their oppression.

Many people believe that girls and women are primarily at risk for sexual violence by an unknown male. This idea is communicated in persistent warnings to girls and to young women about avoiding walking in dark places, not talking to strangers, and not walking alone (Schlesinger et al., 1992, p. 167). Information about sexual violence and abuse by intimates or acquaintances or the risk of male-on-male violence is not similarly shared during social interactions. As a result of media and verbal warnings to women and girls, they are particularly fearful of sexual violence and harassment by male strangers. Also, harassment increases the fear of sexual violence (for a summary or supporting research, see Pain, 2001, p. 903). The harassment that exacerbates fear of crime is pervasive in the normal course of being in public places and/or in the workplace.

Women differing in race and ethnicity (white, African American, and Latina), age, and circumstances (for example, homeless African American teenagers in Manhattan and white upper-middle-class women in New Jersey suburbs) expressed similar worries about crime (Madriz, 1997, p. 344). They were very concerned about attacks from men in certain racial groups, especially men who were black or

Latino (Madriz, 1997, p. 345). They viewed criminals as "animalistic and savage, as monsters, and as lacking any human compassion" (Madriz, 1997, p. 345). Finally, they viewed new immigrants as potential criminals (Madriz, 1997, p. 347). The women pictured female victims as primarily white and middle class, submissive, innocent, and incapable of self-protection. Their imagery of victims sometimes incorporated descriptions of their own vulnerabilities: For example, undocumented Latinas talked about victims whom witnesses could not understand and who could not turn to the police for help. All of the groups of women focused on victimization through murder or rape, or, for a few, sexual harassment on the street. Women of color feared racial harassment (Day, 1999). The widespread imagery of victims and offenders reinforces stereotypes of men of color and of immigrants who are strangers as most dangerous, and it erroneously suggests that white women are most at risk for victimization and that rape by a stranger is the most typical type of victimization.

There is another way that race combines with gender to influence the perception and the experience, and therefore the fear, of criminal victimization. Some males believe and act on stereotypes that women of color are more available sexually or are rightfully theirs to become sexually involved with (Mama, 1989). The resulting greater harassment, confrontation, and other victimization of women of color accounts for their greater fear of rape (M. Gordon & Riger, 1989).

Sexual and other abuse by a current or former intimate partner and stalking by a nonstranger are unique forms of gender-related victimization because the perpetrator is known, is in close proximity to the victim on some regular basis, and has a history of aggression against the victim. The abstract concept "in or around the home," which describes the location of many girls' and women's victimizations, takes on a new dimension. When there is repeated victimization by an intimate *in and around the home*, there is persistent anticipation and fear of a high-probability attack. Some women experience continuous anxiety and terror knowing that a person who is often in close proximity is likely to strike out. They dramatically adjust their daily activities and their life plans, deciding where to live and work or whether or not to leave an abusive, life-threatening partner, based on whether their actions are likely to provoke violence against themselves and other people. For example, some women in abusive relationships feel they are constantly "walking on eggshells," always trying to anticipate and please the abuser to avoid any excuse or provocation for an attack.

Fear and boldness in relation to crime are not essentially male or female, homosexual or heterosexual qualities (Pain, 1997); they are influenced but not determined by gender and sexual orientation, and related experiences and social location. There are relatively bold women (lesbian, bisexual, and straight) and gay men of all racial and ethnic groups, as well as quite fearful heterosexual, majority men. Dominant culture makes fear unacceptable for males, so they report it less on surveys and take risks more often than do females (Goodey, 1997, p. 402). However, when interviews and open-ended questions instead of multiple-choice types of questions on written surveys are used to collect information on men's fear of crime, the types and effects of fear that are revealed can be just as great for at least some men as is the norm for women (Gilchrist, Bannister, Ditton, & Farrall, 1998; Stanko

& Hobdell, 1993). Despite variability within groups, however, on average women are more fearful of victimization than are men, and they more often compromise their activities in order to feel safe.

Naming Forms of Victimization

In addition to the expanded conceptualization of victimization to include fear and a related awareness of the potential for everyday violence, theorists, activists, legislators and policy makers have called attention to an increasing number of types of victimization experience. The words that identify the forms of gender and sexual orientation related victimization have fairly recently become important foci of criminological theory. They make it possible for people to talk about victimization that was frequently hidden, ignored, unspeakable, and difficult to communicate about. New terms to describe forms of violence concentrated on women include *domestic terrorism, marital rape, date rape, acquaintanceship rape, degrees of sexual assault, wife abuse, wife battering, intimate-partner violence, emotional abuse, stalking, sexual harassment*, and *gender harassment*. Threatening situations are not limited to crimes considered in national statistics, but extend to "obscene phone calls, being followed on the street, being felt up on public transport, and sexual harassment" (Stanko, 1995, p. 50). Recognition of the pervasiveness of such affronts helps to explain why women's fear of crime is high even in groups for which the statistically documented victimization is low relative to the statistics for men. Sexual harassment is so common that it has been referred to as **routine oppression** (Kelly, 1987, 1988). *Sexual orientation–motivated crime* and *hate crime* also are relatively new concepts. Hate crime can be motivated not only by dislike of gay and lesbian individuals but also by dislike of gender, racial, religious, or ethnic groups; it is unique from other crimes because the motive is hate of an entire group.[31] The extent to which conceptualization and naming have directed theoretical and practical attention to gender- and sexual orientation–related victimization is evident in several government publications that summarize statistics on violence against women and hate crimes (Rennison, 2003; Snyder, 2000; Strom, 2001; Violence Against Women Grants Office, 1998) and in federal and state policies and programs to prevent and control myriad sorts of violence. Highlighting each form of violence has called attention to a widened range of victimization.

Denial of Victimization

A small but persistently produced literature (e.g., D. G. Dutton, 1994; McNeely & Robinson-Simpson, 1987; Pearson, 1997; Steinmetz & Lucca, 1988; Straus, 1993) has insisted that women are *not* overrepresented as victims in any forms of aggression. This literature has challenged the validity of women's perceptions of their own lives and experiences, and by so doing it contradicts a major tenet of feminist theory: the need for theory and research to reveal and communicate women's realities. The NCVS finding that nearly one fourth of violent crimes against women but just

3% of violent crimes against men were perpetrated by an intimate partner (Rennison & Welchans, 2000, p. 1), though certainly an underestimate due to underreporting, is the basis for women's great concern with victimization by their partners. The overall lower rate of some groups of women's criminal victimization compared to rates for males does not diminish the prevalence of intimate-partner violence in women's lives.

There are problems of validity when researchers use self-reported instances of behavior, such as hitting or throwing objects, or counts of homicide from official records as the evidence that women and men equally victimize each other (R. P. Dobash, Dobash, Wilson, & Daly, 1992; Loseke, 1991). Specific acts of violence are disconnected and therefore decontextualized from any pattern of escalating violence, verbal intimidation, fear or terror, period and place. Acts are also divorced from resulting injuries, emotional distress, and what can be extreme measures that potential victims go to in efforts to prevent abuse. Dobash and her coauthors (R. P. Dobash, Dobash, Wilson, et al., 1992, p. 81) pointed out a number of differences in homicides that are committed by women and men. Men often kill their wives after a long sequence of violent acts, but this is rare for women to do. When a parent kills both the spouse and children, the perpetrator is most often the male head of household. When women kill a spouse, it is usually in self-defense, but this is not the case when men kill their wives. These patterns and differences are obscured when hits and killings are abstracted from the broader context. The data that ignore context and injury have been used to support the invalid conclusion that women and men are equally violent toward each other.

Explaining Victimization

Gender Organization

Klein (1981) broke a silence about the importance of social structure and culture in supporting patterns of violence against women and girls. She conceptualized gender organization, including divisions of labor and of resources, and other hierarchies of power, as being interconnected with economic arrangements. Gender organization explains why females are the "usual objects of child molestation, spouse abuse, rape, pornography, and sexual harassment" (Klein, 1981, p. 65). These sorts of physical force are a part of a larger system of gender organization characterized by male domination over women. In Klein's framework, an adolescent's pressure on his date to have intercourse, depictions of rape in pornography, and actual rape inside and outside marriage are elements in "the total systemic gender domination" (Klein, 1981, p. 77). Since she advanced this idea in 1981, theory and supporting research on specific aspects of social structure and on variation in culture have enriched the gender-organization explanation of violence against women and girls.

Consistent with Klein's (1981) theory, a study of 90 societies around the world demonstrated that the level of violence against women is connected to gender organization (Levinson, 1989). Women experienced less violence in societies where husband and wife shared decision making, wives controlled some of the family resources, there was not a premarital sex double standard, marriage was monogamous, and there was immediate social response to domestic violence. Economic and educational resources, along with culture, the two topics that are discussed next, have an important influence on domestic and other forms of intimate-partner violence.

Economic and Educational Resources

In the United States, poverty increasingly has been concentrated on women and children (Pearce, 1989). Census data for 1999 reveal that overall, 11.8% of people were living in poverty, but for women-headed households with no husband present, the poverty rate was 27.8% (Lott & Bullock, 2001). Additionally, 17% of the nation's children were poor by federal standards, even though most of them (77.6%) were in families with at least one working person. Compared with rates in 16 other developed countries, the child poverty rate in the United States was the highest (Annie E. Casey Foundation, 1999). Also, compared to both developed and transitional economies, the gender gap in poverty was highest in the United States, and the United States had the highest poverty rate for female-headed households (Pressman, 2002).[32] The poverty rate for women cannot be explained by their age or level of education. It can, however, be ameliorated by income transfer programs. In countries that, unlike the United States, have aggressive fiscal policies that transfer income to poor families, there are dramatically reduced poverty rates for female-headed households and for females in general. In the United States, for both children and adults, poverty rates are highest for nonwhite minorities. Thus, for themselves and their children, women's poverty restricts the rewards of participation in the legitimate economy and exposes family members to negative conditions of poverty. In the United States, the disadvantaged social location of women is high for Hispanics, who can be of any race, and for African Americans, and it is extremely high for Native Americans (Proctor & Dalaker, 2003).

As in the United States, in many developing and disrupted economies, girls and women are at a particular economic disadvantage. A study of 10 developing countries documented that poverty measures are higher for female-headed households and for females than for males with similar household types (Quisumbing, Haddad, & Peña, 2001). This inequity has profound implications for women's criminal victimization. People without money and the related access to housing, good neighborhoods, and reliable and safe transportation find it difficult if not impossible to live in safe environments (Baily, 1999). In the United States, racial discrimination in housing and in employment intensifies the residential segregation of black and Native American people. There is a multiplier effect for women of color, who are concentrated in environments where everyone is more likely to be victimized, but who are also the targets of female-directed, gender-motivated, and racially motivated offenses.

Comparative study of different countries has revealed a complicated connection of women's economic and other status markers to violence against them. Women typically are less likely than men to be murdered, but the difference between female and male rates of homicide varies considerably not only between countries but depending on the historical moment (Kruttschnitt, 1995). Women experience increased risk of homicide when they have nontraditional social roles, specifically when they marry at a later age, they divorce men at a higher rate, they are single parents, and they work outside the home.[33] However, the risk of increased violence for women in nontraditional roles is substantially counteracted and even reversed if they have economic, educational, and other resources (Gartner, Baker, & Pampel, 1990). In other words, women who take on nontraditional roles are more vulnerable to homicide *unless* they are well educated and well-off economically. If they are educated and economically well-off, they are less at risk for being murdered.

Cross-cultural and ethnographic studies explain how women's resources reduce their exposure to domestic violence (Kruttschnitt, 1995). Women who work and are well educated establish support networks in school or the workplace, and they can establish economic networks. The connections to other people, which are intermediate influences on victimization, serve as resources and result in less abuse and increased capacity to leave abusive relationships (Baumgartner, 1993; Levinson, 1989). Alternatively, wife beating is most frequent where husbands dominate all aspects of family life, including restricting women's access to divorce (Levinson, 1989). Women who attempt to escape traditional domestic and economic roles (but have not yet completed the transition) are at greatest risk of being beaten and killed by their spouses.

The effect of gender inequality on rape is similar to its effect on domestic violence. For 109 U.S. cities with populations over 50,000, from 1970 through 1990, increases in women's equality were associated with short-term increases in rape (Whaley, 2001). It is possible that men were resistant to women's greater status, and they responded with efforts to reestablish their dominance or in anger, which in some cases was expressed through rape. This explanation is called the **backlash hypothesis**. An alternative explanation is that when women become more equal to men, they are at greater risk for certain types of victimization because they are more often away from home. For the 109 cities, in the long run women's greater equality was related to lower levels of rape. It is possible that women and others influenced the investment of resources to prevent rape, or that over time men adjusted to women's greater status.

The relationship of sexual harassment to gender equality in the workplace is similar to the relationship of rape and abuse to inequality. When women begin to work in previously all-male settings, men degrade them and feel they are not qualified but were hired because of their gender (Beaton, Tougas, & Joly, 1997). Eventually, these negative views subside when "occupational segregation decreases, stereotypes about gender weaken, policies are written to solve new problems (e.g., sexual harassment, pay equity), [and] women gain decision-making power in relationships" (Beaton et al., 1996, pp. 533–534). The challenge and change to existing gender ideologies and arrangements appears to promote a variety of insults and injuries directed toward women, but greater equality eventually ameliorates the negative results.

The connection of women's limited power and influence to their victimization has been documented in the United States. In states where women are less equal to

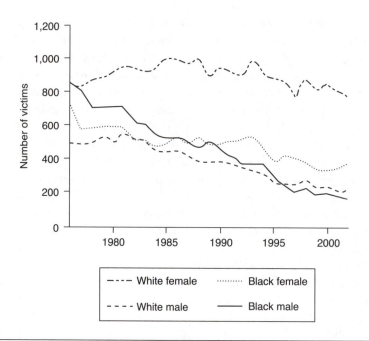

Figure 3.1   Homicides of intimates by gender and race of victim, 1976–2002

From http://www.ojp.usdoj.gov/bjs/homicide/intimates.htm#intgender. US Government Web site.

men in education, employment, occupation, and political participation and influence, rates of wife abuse (Yllo, 1983; Yllo & Straus, 1984) and rape (Baron & Straus, 1987) are higher. Perhaps women without power cannot influence legislation and the enforcement of legislation by agents in the criminal justice system in a way that affords some protection. Alternatively, women without resources may be unable to stay away from, leave, or influence potentially dangerous situations.

In the United States, the passage of the federal 1994 Violence Against Women Act (VAWA) resulted in increased resources to prevent and respond to violence against women. These resources included legislation that increased the power of the state to intervene, particularly in intimate-partner violence; programs to assist and empower victims; and policies and training programs to improve the implementation of laws intended to protect females. There is clear documentation of decreased violence against women after 1994. Specifically, women's rates of intimate-partner violence were lower in 1998 (7.7 per 1,000 women) than in 1993 (9.8 per 1,000) (Rennison & Welchans, 2000, p. 1). For males, the rates went from 1.6 to 1.5 per 1,000 men. For some demographic groups, there also has been a decline in homicide of intimates between 1976 and 2000 (Bureau of Justice Statistics, 2002; Rennison & Welchans, 2000). The group that has not experienced the decrease is white females. In comparison with white males and black females and males, white females have the highest intimate-partner homicide rate. However, rates of homicide by an intimate have dropped considerably for white males and for black females and males.

Changes in rates of intimate-partner violence may be due to growing intolerance for violence, various changes in the status of women vis-à-vis men, or other factors. In large U.S. cities, policies and programs that reduced women's exposure to their abusive partners were related to decreases in intimate-partner killings (Dugan, Rosenfeld, & Nagin, 2003). Increased welfare benefits were connected to lower rates of intimate-partner killings of African American men. This finding is consistent with knowledge that poverty is concentrated among African American women, who would not be able to leave abusive partners without welfare assistance. Aggressive arrest policies were connected to fewer deaths of unmarried intimates. Other policies that are related to lower homicide rates for at least some groups are availability of legal advocacy, mandatory arrest laws, and laws that allow arrest without a warrant. However, in cities where prosecutors were most willing to prosecute for violation of protection orders, some groups of women were more at risk for homicide; it may be that without adequate protection, increased prosecution places women at extreme danger of men's retaliation. Many of the programs and policies that are related to intimate partner homicide rates resulted from the VAWA. There are competing explanations of falling levels of intimate-partner violence. However, it is impossible to rule out, as an explanation for lower levels of intimate-partner violence, the possibility that the VAWA promoted gender rearrangements, giving more resources and influence to women and their advocates, and that this resulted in changes.

Internationally, females' economic marginalization in developing nations or nations with disrupted economies (for example, the nations that made up the former Soviet bloc) creates a context in which traffickers can recruit women and children. Although gender-related poverty is an element that makes trafficking possible, it is an influence only when it is coupled with two other things: motivated traffickers, usually operating in organized criminal groups, and countries or cities that are large sex industry centers where prostitution is tolerated or is legal. Although many areas of the world are poor and chaotic, it is only when traffickers are active that women and children are coerced or tricked into the sex industry (Hughes, 2001, p. 10). An example of a Ukrainian woman shows how lack of opportunity and criminal elements come together:

Irina, aged 18, responded to an advertisement in a Kyiv, Ukraine, newspaper for a training course in Berlin, Germany, in 1996. With a fake passport, she traveled to Berlin, where she was told that the school had closed. She was sent on to Brussels, Belgium, for a job. When she arrived, she was told she needed to repay a debt of US $10,000 and would have to earn the money in prostitution. Her passport was confiscated, and she was threatened, beaten, and raped. When she didn't earn enough money for the first pimp, she was sold to another pimp who operated in Brussels' red light district. When she escaped with police assistance, she was arrested because she had no legal documentation. A medical exam verified the abuse she had suffered, such as cigarette burns all over her body. (Hughes, 2001, pp. 10–11)

The recruiters (sometimes women allowed to escape their work as prostitutes), the pimps, and the traffickers, plus the international inequalities in chances for survival and a good future, are the essential influences on the movement of large numbers of women to settings where they are subjected to abuse and forced to prostitute themselves.

Toleration of prostitution in selected countries and the demand for it, coupled with women's depressed economic conditions, work together to maintain continuous recruitment of women. For example, in India moneylenders or their agents will visit areas that are affected by desperate poverty (Davidson, 1998). They promise jobs to girls and young women, and in some cases they make cash advances to the recruits' parents, and the young women must work until the debt is repaid. Moneylenders may own brothels, where they place the girls and women to work. In other cases, they may supply the women and girls to brothelkeepers for a fee, and then require them to work until the fee is paid off. The income for prostitution includes profit for the brothel owner, and just a small proportion is used to reduce the debt.

Once involved in prostitution, women are forced, in various ways, to continue. Asian-Indian women have reported to researchers that despite desires to stop, they continued prostitution because of illiteracy, beatings, starvation, rape by family members, and sexual exploitation in alternative jobs that paid less than prostitution, and that therefore created the reality that prostitution provided a higher rate of pay for sexual acts that they would have been forced into regardless of not working as a prostitute (Chattopadhyay, Bandyopadhyay, & Duttagupta, 1994).

Along with the economic marginalization of girls and women, race, class, and age increase the chances of exploitation through prostitution. In many national and international contexts, women's legitimate economic options are more or less constrained depending on their demographic characteristics. At the same time, stereotypes about which people are sexually attractive and desirable affect which groups are recruited. Preferences for sex with young girls and boys or with members of racial or other groups stereotyped as "exotic," "sexually desirable," or "passive" creates the "market" that entices some women and children to engage in prostitution and that encourages others to pressure or force them to do so.

The international scope of women's economic marginalization leads to their dislocation across the world, along with the resulting promotion of their involvement in the sex industry that crosses international boundaries. As a result of their greater economic disadvantage or because they are more expendable to their families and state policy makers, in some Asian countries, more women than men leave their countries looking for work, much of which is in low-paying and low-skilled jobs (Skolnik & Bootinand, 1999). They can then send money back home, creating an additional benefit for their country of origin. For instance, Indonesia's 5-year plans for both 1990 and 1994 included reducing unemployment by sending 500,000 women overseas (Skolnik & Bootinand, 1999). Along with the lure of opportunity to survive and even thrive by leaving one's homeland, for some women there is the push of governmental policy or families to leave home, both so they can send money to relatives and so they can seek their fortunes elsewhere.

Gender Inequality and Damage to Daughters

Around the world, a number of different practices result in physical and emotional harms to girls. In several countries, girl children are viewed as a drain on family resources, and having one or more sons and few or no daughters is valued. Thus, in China and India, girls are abandoned in public places or may be neglected as infants and therefore die; women in South Korea often abort a fetus that is known to be female (Das Gupta et al. 2003). Also, in several countries, including the United States, incest perpetrated by a father or stepfather against a daughter is relatively common, and in some groups, female genital mutilation is routine. All these practices reflect the lesser value of female children and the related dominance of males within the social group.

A pattern that cuts across the practices of elimination of female fetuses, abandonment of baby girls, incest, and female genital mutilation is that they are most common in families and cultural groups that "subscribe to highly stereotyped understandings of what it means to be a man and a woman" (Candib, 1999, p. 196):

> For instance, [incest] offenders think that the role of the woman in a family is to take care of the family, cook, clean, look after the children, be a sexual partner, help with money in a crisis, be loyal, keep the family together, stand by her man, be understanding, and maintain her physical attractiveness. . . . Men and women—and even therapists as well at times—subscribe to a belief in the man's "right" to get his sexual needs met within his family. . . . In fact, it is a common distortion among incestuously abusive fathers to believe "If my wife doesn't have sex with me, it's justifiable to have sex with my daughter" and "It's better to have sex with my daughter than have an extramarital affair." (Candib, 1999, pp. 196–197)

Fathers and potential husbands are viewed as having the right and the responsibility to rigidly control women's sexuality and girls' sexual desires through female genital mutilation, and girls are devalued because when there is gender inequality, they are likely to be economic burdens.

Limitation on the Birth of Females

Because most countries have banned or criminalized abortion and neglect for the purposes of having or keeping a male infant instead of a female, there are very limited statistics on the extent of these practices. Usually, an unbalanced sex ratio of boys to girls is used to indicate selective abortion of girls or neglect that results in their death. An unexpectedly low ratio of girls to boys is referred to as the problem of **missing girls**. Female-selective abortion is primarily but not exclusively practiced in China, Taiwan, South Korea, Pakistan, and India; it also is not uncommon for Asian immigrant populations, including those in the United States and Canada (B. D. Miller, 2001).

Abortion, life-threatening neglect, and abandonment to ensure that a daughter is not added to the family is related to cultural beliefs and to gender inequality. The influence of both culture and inequality is illustrated by findings from a survey in a very poor area of China (Li & Lavely, 2003). Women had a higher ratio of living male to female children than would be expected if there were no preferences for sons. Those with Confucian beliefs that only a son could perform important cere-monial duties for parents after the parents' death or carry on the family name, and those who anticipated ridicule from others because they had no sons, preferred sons. Also, women who were uneducated, had little or no financial resources of their own, and who expected their sons to care for them in old age preferred sons. In reality, in part because of their advantaged position in society, sons were more able than were daughters to economically support aging parents and carry out manual tasks, such as bringing water from long distances. Across countries, the greater the gender inequality, the greater the preference that people have for sons to be born into and survive in the family (Mason, 1987). Put another way, countries with the greatest number of missing girls are those having the most patriarchal gen-der arrangements, according to which males control property, have the only inher-itance rights, and have better employment options (B. D. Miller, 2001). In the study of rural China, female infants whose mothers preferred sons were twice as likely to die than others. Complementary cultural beliefs about sons support sex-related abortion in countries with resources to detect sex during pregnancy and for people who can pay for detection and abortions (F. Arnold, Kishor, & Roy, 2002; B. D. Miller, 2001), as well as neglect or abandonment of newborn girls in countries with less advanced economies and technologies.

Female Genital Mutilation

Girls who are born and who survive can be reminded of their inferior status through the practice of **female genital mutilation** (FGM). Specific beliefs and norms that promote the practice of FGM vary between countries, but in general the notion that women must be submissive to their husbands provides the rationale for continuing the practice. Women in regions of Africa where the practice is common believe that without the procedure, girls will "be wanton and will not remain a vir-gin before marriage or faithful afterward," and that FGM will protect them because they will not "seek sexual relations for pleasure, so their bodies belong totally to the men who marry them" (Candib, 1999, p. 190). Women support their male family members' requirement of FGM both out of concerns that their daughters will be married, which in some places is the only way that a female can survive economi-cally or socially, and also to avoid their own ostracism by being shamed, thrown out of the house, or divorced (Horowitz & Jackson, 1997).

Incest

In all societies, there is general recognition that incest, another way that daughters are damaged, is wrong and shameful. The high rates of incest in many different countries provide evidence that it cannot be explained by atypical, individual-level pathologies. There is considerable pornography, increasingly available through the Internet, that presents men having sex with girls, and though such information will not cause a man to become involved in incest, it provides material that he can draw on in his rationalizations about the acceptability of what he is doing and to demonstrate and justify the abuse to the child and to himself (Silbert & Pines, 1993; Trepper & Barrett, 1989). Also, men's beliefs that they have a right to control and supervise their daughters or to punish their wives by attacking the children sexually support their sexual abuse of their children (Candib, 1999, p. 196). The system of beliefs and relationships that characterize patriarchy include traditional definitions of daughters or stepdaughters as sexual property (Finkelhor, 1982), acceptance of inequality in male/female relationships, and veneration of youth (Bell, 1984). Consistent with available pornography and patriarchal ideals, incest perpetrators tend to view children as sexually attractive and motivated, and they endorse attitudes that support male privilege (Karl, Gizzarelli, & Scott, 1994).

Beliefs That Support Gender-Related Victimization

The idea that beliefs support gender-related victimization is important at different levels of explanation. Sometimes beliefs are associated with a culture that is shared by ethnic or national groups in an area where people live or originated. **Culture** includes not only beliefs, but also the values that members of a group share, the norms that they follow, and the objects and creations that they possess. Although culture is an important influence on behavior, it is not static or fully deterministic. In some situations, people alter beliefs, values, and norms. Alteration can occur when individuals are exposed to multiple cultures, or when adaptations are useful in managing within constraints imposed by economic hardships or other realities of day-to-day life. As examples of the malleability of culture, subgroups of European Americans incorporate into their thinking and traditions symbols and beliefs of Native Americans, there are so-called Western influences throughout the world, and there are examples of pan-culturalism, a melding of selected elements of many different systems of beliefs and traditions. People who move between different countries often adapt their cultural beliefs or incorporate elements of cultures to which they are newly exposed. However, even though there is some seeping of one culture into another, cultural distinctions relevant to gender-related victimization remain both between and within different countries. Also, the processes of cultural change can influence victimization.

Beliefs also can be shared, taught, and reinforced at the intermediate level of influence within smaller groups. Family and peer groups are important sources of beliefs that are consistent with sexual assault, with intimate-partner violence, and, as already discussed, with incest, preference for sons, and female genital mutilation. Beliefs consistent with rape and with sexual assault derive from both broad, though not necessarily uniform, cultural influences and from interactions with other people in peer networks.

Beliefs Consistent With Rape

In seeking an explanation of men's violence against women, it is helpful to recognize that the acts identified as violence are variants of men's power over women that many people do not consider to be unusual or unacceptable. Acceptance of men's pressuring and trying to force women into sexual activity are characteristic of many subgroups in and outside the United States. Of more than 3,000 women surveyed on 32 U.S. college campuses, 44% reported verbal pressure to have sex, and 12% reported that men had given them alcohol or drugs in order to have sex with them (Koss, 1989). In a study of 400 teenaged mothers, the most common explanation for having sexual intercourse was "inability to successfully resist pressure from the males" (Furstenberg, 1976, p. 150). U.S. college women (but not college men) who reported that they were pressured to have sexual intercourse also reported that they were greatly upset by the experience (S. J. Walker, 2001). The pressure toward intercourse and the constraints on resisting have been documented in many different countries (Wood, Maforah, & Jewkes, 1998), where popular imagery conveys that males should engage in sexual pursuit of women and that females should acquiesce to demonstrate their love.

Scholars have linked beliefs and norms that are common to at least some groups in the United States to rape. These beliefs are referred to as a **rape culture**. The term *culture* is used in a narrow sense to refer to specific beliefs. Rapists (and batterers) do sometimes express shame and remorse, but oftentimes they feel they are entitled to dominate women, and they try to justify their abusiveness and talk about their intentions to establish control (Lea, Auburn, & Kibblewhite, 1999; Ptacek, 1988). Also, men with a high proclivity to rape believe victims are responsible for the incident, have attitudes and beliefs about women and sex that support rape, and are insensitive to the negative effects of rape on the victim (Drieschner & Lange, 1999). Because they link sex with power, they do not feel sexual until after they have overpowered another person (Drieschner & Lange, 1999). Of course, not all individuals in the United States buy into the set of beliefs and behaviors that are consistent with a rape culture, but within the United States there are people who share and promote these beliefs.

Beliefs consistent with rape cannot be seen as individual abnormalities because they are often the result of peer interactions. In settings where women and men share the assumption that men are initiators of sex and women are either passive partners or active resisters, women seeking a long-term relationship are at risk for a brief *hookup*, an instance in which men use women as sex objects. In these environments, men often discourage each other from having long-term heterosexual relationships because such relationships threaten the solidarity among the men (Boswell & Spade, 1996). Males with peers who condone or encourage sexual aggression are more likely than others to pressure or force females to have sex (Kanin, 1985; Koss, Leonard, Beezley, & Oros, 1985; Krahe, 1998). Within a national or regional context, even if there is not uniform support for rape, it is possible to find support from selected peers and information sources.

National and smaller groups vary in their support of rape. Research on tribal groups in South Asia has illustrated how gender norms and related arrangements within different cultures vary (Sanday, 1986). In one group, males did not define their identities as opposite to those of women, and their separation from their mothers did not involve talk or behaviors that demeaned or established dominance over women. Even though boys matured to be independent men, they maintained bonds with their mothers and siblings throughout adulthood. The norms and values reflected by these practices resulted in little or no sexual abuse and aggression against women. In contrast to the culture that did not support sexual attack of females, in societies with limited resources—for instance, inadequate food and other types of severe deprivation—men and boys felt no control of their fate. Rape commonly was used to control women, display an image of masculinity, and induct younger men into masculine roles. The interactions of both women and men reflected and reproduced ideologies that supported rape (Box, 1983; Holmstrom & Burgess, 1983; Kirkpatrick & Kanin, 1957; Makepeace, 1981).

Beliefs Consistent With Intimate-Partner Violence

As with sexual assault, a strong predictor of which men will become abusive in courtship relationships is whether they have friends who explicitly and verbally tell them to abuse women under certain conditions, for example when women challenge men's authority or reject their sexual advances (DeKeseredy, 1988; DeKeseredy & Kelly, 1993). Men who are prone to abuse women form strong bonds of friendship with and spend a considerable time with other males who agree that there are circumstances in which abuse is acceptable. Their beliefs support domination and control of female partners—for example, the belief that a man has the right to decide whether or not his partner should work outside the home and the belief that he has the right to have sex with his partner regardless of whether she wants to (M. D. Smith, 1990).

When women are asked what their abusive husbands were trying to get them to do or say at the time of the abuse, their answers reflect the recurring theme of the men's belief in their right to dominate and control women. Three women answered the question, "What was he trying to get you to do or say?"

Just what is said should be done, because he said so, and right away.

That I should be an obedient, submissive person.

He doesn't want me to be me. He wants to be the head of the home. No 50–50, no 75–25.

Two women answered the question, "What makes him act this [abusive] way?"

He says I yell too much and I am not a good wife and mother.

I feel he is trying to fulfill a fantasy and that the person he is going out to drink with, also a friend, this person is a womanizer. . . . I have never drank or run around, and maybe in his mind, the drinking and sexual acts are attractive and he wants me to be as he sees other women in bars.[34]

The last woman quoted was forced by her husband to engage in sexual acts that she considered perverted. Often, men who abuse their wives are seeking tight control over them and are trying to enforce their ideas about how a good wife and mother should act. When men think that their partners are challenging culturally supported patterns of male dominance, violence is one way that they reinforce their domination (Gartner, Baker, et al., 1990).

For some immigrants, violence in families is influenced not only by norms and values reinforced in the United States, but also by the culture in the country of origin. Traditionally, people in South Asian countries have believed that men are entitled to control or discipline their wives (Dasgupta, 1998). This belief is a matter of dispute and social activism in South Asia. However, one way that immigrants and their offspring react to being in a foreign context is to hold rigidly to old traditions as a way of coping with the stress of a foreign language, lack of family and friends, and biases they may experience (Mazumdar, 1998).

To illustrate, in U.S. families of Mexican origin, changes in gender role expectations and performance, often an outgrowth of economic hardship, are a factor contributing to wife abuse (Morash, Bui, & Santiago, 2000). Women's dissatisfaction with men's performance of their gender roles and disagreements between men and women about appropriate gender roles led to violent episodes. One woman described why and how she changed:

> I'm working and not here at his beck and call. At first I was. Because of the economy, you cannot make it. Even though we don't live in [a wealthy community] . . . after two years of marriage and not having the things I wanted. He does not want me barefoot and pregnant, and eating beans and rice is not a life. Because times have changed, and people changed. He found living in America is not like living in Mexico. (Morash, Bui, & Santiago, 2000, p. 77)

Economic realities led to the wife's working outside the home, which changed family dynamics. Her husband reacted to changes with anger and abuse in an effort to reassert his dominance and control.

There is a similar pattern for Vietnamese immigrant families. Wife abuse is connected to arguments centered on disagreements about how traditional family life should be, whether women should work outside the home, who should do work around the house, changing norms and values, and education and discipline of children.[35] Violence against wives is related to disagreement and struggle over gender roles, what women should do, and what men could do.

The Dynamics of Same-Sex Relationship Violence

There is very limited research on the dynamics of violence between lesbians, bisexual individuals, or gay men. There is some evidence that women often experience same-sex abuse in the context of their first lesbian relationship (Ristock, 2003). In their first relationship, the abuser may be integrated into a friendship group, but victims often are unknown to the friends of the abuser, and they may have no status or support from lesbian friends. Victims' isolation, desire for a lesbian experience, and in some relationships their younger age may create vulnerability. The abusive partner, in contrast, may feel some immunity from criticism.

Also in lesbian abusive relationships, the direction of abuse from one person to the other often varies over the course of the relationship (Ristock, 2003). The abuse is not firmly connected to gender ideologies or to patriarchal family structure, so it is more variable. In some cases, the victim strikes back, and then establishes a pattern of abusing her partner. The issues do not typically involve women's performance in the roles of partner or mother, but rather center on such things as suspected attractions to men and related concerns that the victim is "not lesbian enough" (Giorgio, 2002). Some violence occurs around the complex issue of whether women are sexually involved with other lesbians or just are friends with them. Similar to the pattern with heterosexual relationship violence, abuse in lesbian relationships is signified not only by conflicts but also by control and coercion that are enforced by threats and violence.

Gender Identity

Masculinities and **femininities**, ideas about what it is to be male or female, are part of a person's identity and are shared and actualized through human interactions. **Accomplishing gender**—that is, acting feminine or masculine—involves behaving in a way that is consistent with one's gender identity. **Gender identity**, which is a person's sense of self as feminine or masculine, is connected to the forms and amounts of people's illegal behavior, and thus is relevant to understanding the undeniable patterns of men's violence against women and girls. It also is relevant to understanding violence against people who are gay or lesbian.

Although people do have the capacity to make choices about who they will be and how they will therefore act, the possibilities for accomplishing gender are limited by experience, knowledge, social location, and other conditions of life (Laidler & Hunt, 2001, p. 657). Because of both constraints and the agency people do have, there are many different forms of femininity and masculinity. **Hegemonic masculinity** is "the configuration of gender practice which embodies the currently accepted answer to the problem of legitimacy of patriarchy, which guarantees (or is taken to guarantee) the dominant position of men and the subordination of women" (Connell, 1995, p. 77). As part of a therapy session, one man who had battered his wife gave the following explanation of his hegemonic form of masculinity:

> What it means to be a man? Well, to me, [it] always meant to be in control over everything, not to be scared of nothing and never show your feelings or what we would call weak side because if we did we think it's a chump move or something so I always wanted to be in control and never let anyone control me and never showed my feelings. (Baird, 2000, p. 23)

Besides hegemonic masculinity, there are alternative, subordinate masculinities. **Subordinate masculinity** is related to subordinate statuses of race, class, and sexual orientation. **Oppositional masculinity** involves explicit resistance and challenges to hegemonic forms. For girls and women, **emphasized femininity** reflects stereotypical female qualities, such as passivity, dependence, and fragility, and is considered as complementary to the aggressive domination embodied in interactions that reflect hegemonic masculinity. The literature has not, unfortunately, explored alternative forms of femininity as thoroughly as it has considered alternative forms of masculinity.

Shifts in the global economy and related patterns of immigration affect the connection of social structure to some men's accomplishment of their gender identity through violence. There are many specific examples of this connection. The restructuring of the global economy has limited economic opportunity for entry-level working-class men in the United States, and conditions of poverty pushed Puerto Rican immigration to New York City. There, Puerto Rican boys grew up with fathers who asserted their power through violence against their spouses and partners, and who sometimes found themselves working for Puerto Rican women, who were more readily absorbed than men into the workforce (Bourgois, 1996). In this situation, some men in East Harlem, New York, in the late 1980s to the early 1990s actively viewed masculine dignity as the capacity to engage in interpersonal violence, sexual domination and economic parasitism (Bourgois, 1996). Similarly, for some British men who grew up marginalized by poverty, powerful masculine identity on the street involved drug use, drug dealing, and other crimes (Collison, 1996). Men with limited access to economic resources have limited possibilities for how they can act in accord with their images of masculinity. For many groups, in many places, the gendered division of labor, with men oriented to activities outside the home and women oriented to activities in the home, is central to development and management of gender identity (Connell, 1995). Unemployed and underemployed males may have particularly serious limitations on how they can actualize being the type of men they want to be. Many find nonviolent solutions, for example by developing a rebuttal culture in service industry workplaces (Newman, 1999). Others may define masculinity as domination of and violence against women.

Gender Identity and Violence Against Intimate Partners

Supporting the connection of men's inability to succeed in the workplace and their violence against women whom they date or marry, a particularly strong predictor of men's abuse of a partner is poverty (Moffitt & Caspi, 1999). Poor school performance, perhaps because of its connection to workplace success and other life achievements, also is a strong predictor of men's violence against women.

In the family, problems living up to masculine ideals may be especially acute for men whose partners are themselves working. In a 1993 survey of 8,461 Canadian women who had male partners, the women were at greater risk for abuse, particularly systematic, serious abuse, if they were employed and their partners were unemployed. Employed women with unemployed partners also were more likely to experience coercive patriarchal control; that is, they had jealous husbands who did not want them to talk to other men, their partners tried to limit their contact with family and friends, the partners insisted on knowing who the women were with and where they were at all times, and/or the partners prevented the women from knowing about or having access to family income (Macmillan & Gartner, 1999, p. 956).

Working Canadian women with employed husbands experienced less coercive control and less abuse than did other women. Unemployed men with employed female partners may feel that their dominance is threatened, and in an effort to maintain dominance in the relationship, exert controls that include physical abuse.

P. H. Collins (1990) also explained how a combination of the value placed on hegemonic masculinity and economic inequalities can increase violence against women. She theorized that black men have accepted "externally defined notions of both Black and white masculinity ... , and that these notions break with Afrocentrism and support battering" (p. 185). Something that is quite common— a violent reaction to suspicions of unfaithfulness—is an outgrowth of the image of black women as promiscuous whores. Such ideas and images are part of a larger context of domination of black women. They are echoed when black men internalize and act on "controlling images of the sex/gender hierarchy" that condone the rape of black women (P. H. Collins, 1990, p. 179).

The connection of ideas about masculinity with extreme economic disadvantage also can be used to explain violence against Native American women. Consistent with NCVS findings, small-sample studies of women from several specific tribes have documented high rates of their victimization by spouses (Hamby, 2000, p. 652). Because histories and current circumstances are not uniform, tribes differ in gender organization, culture, and economic marginalization. Yet, there are some commonalities that explain why on average there would be high rates of victimization of Native American women. Many tribes were separated from their land, and thus from their cultural traditions and economic resources. In the early part of the 20th century, large numbers of Native American children spent their school years in off-reservation boarding schools, which were plagued by physical and sexual child abuse. This history disrupted existing cultural practices that, for some tribes, historically had kept rates of violence low. With the loss of cultural traditions, the door was open for external negative influences.

Illustrating how a prevalent cultural orientation in the United States can stimulate wife abuse in minority racial and ethnic groups, one Navajo woman said: "A lot of women are having trouble with their husbands. The only model the men have is the *macho* white man. They try to copy him and Navajo women object" (Zion & Zion, 1996, p. 97).

Historical events and resulting realities have stimulated some men's development of identities consistent with the macho stereotype. Native American men have fared worse than women in their loss of traditional roles, and this structural disadvantage has led to alcohol abuse (Duran, Duran, Woodis, & Woodis, 1998; Hamby, 2000, p. 661) and to definitions of manhood that are divorced from Native American traditions. Further encouraging versions of masculinity that contradict egalitarian ideologies, in some places, U.S. government interventions into Native American life dismantled systems of public decision making in which women had a considerable say, and historical Western values were spread by providing girls with less education than boys (LaFramboise, Choney, James, & Running Wolf, 1995). The reduction of Native Americans' land and the resulting constriction of their ability to be self-sufficient, along with the forced education of children off the reservation, rarely led to the intended assimilation of youth into white society (Zion & Zion, 1996, p. 104). Instead, the youth returned to reservations where they felt alienated from the culture and lacked connection to their elders. After passage of the Indian Child Welfare Act of 1978,[36] children were returned to families that had no experience with child rearing. New parents who had grown up in off-reservation boarding schools and placements suddenly were faced with the challenges of raising their own children with no models. Many "unparented parents" had been raised in neglectful or abusive settings (Poupart, 2002, p. 152, also see Metcalf, 1976). The complex and multiple historical and economic influences on Native Americans suggest that it would be very misleading to attribute high rates of violence among Native Americans solely to some versions of masculinities or femininities. Violence is in part a product of the destruction of indigenous cultural values, which did not support men's complete dominance over women. It is also in part a product of the appropriation of selected values and practices of mainstream U.S. culture, and in part a result of economic disadvantage. Although the structural and cultural influences of violence remain, however, so-called macho identity can be viewed both as a reaction to these larger forces and as an influence on maintaining gender inequalities and related violence.

The links between economic dislocations of men and their use of violence against women to maintain patriarchal constructions of masculinity is not limited to any one part of the world. In sub-Saharan African nations, for many reasons, men have experienced extreme economic marginalization, and these extremes explain striking instances of violence against women. For example:

in the former South African Bantustan Qwaqua, [there was] a collective assault against working women by unemployed men. In the 1980s, women were attacked on the streets, stoned, and openly assaulted. The women targeted for the attack had recently joined the paid labor force as factory workers. The men who took part in this public beating rationalized the act saying that too many jobs were going to women. (Bank, 1994, p. 89)

Bank (1994) interpreted this incident as a struggle over whether women should control household income and whether men or women should perform household labor. Women's new roles and employment activities directly contradicted men's views of themselves as dominating heads of households.

Motivation for murder, the most extreme form of violence against an intimate partner, is directly connected to an exaggerated version of hegemonic masculinity, a version that embodies total ownership or control of a woman. Domestic homicides in Florida illustrate the point:

[T]he 102 Florida men [who killed an intimate partner] used violence against women for a long time before killing them. They did this either to establish control or to reassert control that they felt was ebbing away. (Websdale, 1999, p. 207)

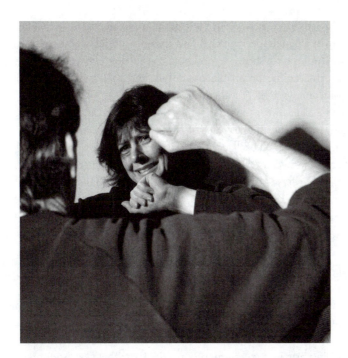

Men who kill an intimate partner typically are trying to establish or reassert control that they feel is slipping away. In contrast, women typically kill a partner when they feel trapped and that they or their loved ones are in danger.

© Getty Images

In contrast to the men, women who killed an intimate partner were fully trapped in their situation, and their actions suggested desperation, self-defense, and defense of children or other relatives.

Gender Identity and Sexual Assault

Some men believe that masculinity is characterized by dominance over women, extreme difference from and hostility toward females, and sexual aggression toward women. This constellation of beliefs has been described as **hypermasculinity** (Mosher & Sirkin, 1984). Men who are hypermasculine think that violence is manly and exciting and that callousness toward women is acceptable. A similar set of beliefs—that masculinity is signified by being dominating and in control, especially of women, and characterized by insecurity and distrust of women—is referred to as **hostile masculinity** (Malamuth, Scokloski, Koss, & Tanaka, 1991). The concepts of hypermasculinity and hostile masculinity are parts of psychological theories to provide individual-level explanations of behavior. The concept of hegemonic masculinity was developed in sociological theory that links identity to social structure, but that also explains individual behavior. However, hypermasculinity and hostile masculinity can be viewed as consistent with forms of hegemonic masculinity. A number of influences seem to contribute to men's development of hyper- or hostile masculinity. These include negative relationships with fathers

(Malamuth, Scokloski, et al., 1991) and frequent exposure to sexual language that is common in all-male peer groups and that objectifies women (Murnen, 2000). Numerous studies have shown a moderate connection between men's gender identity as hypermasculine or hostile masculine and their sexual aggression toward women (Murnen, Wright, & Kaluzny, 2002).

As noted earlier in this chapter, when women become more equal to men in a society, they experience higher rates of rape (Whaley, 2001). A microlevel explanation for this pattern is that some men's masculine identity is threatened by women's gains in equality, because their view of themselves as men requires that they be dominant. If they have no other way to exert their dominance, because of their own social location or personal limitations, they may use rape to reassert their positive sense of selves as men (Messerschmidt, 1986; Schwartz & DeKeseredy, 1997; Scully & Marolla, 1985).

Gender Identity and Victimization Based on Sexual Orientation

People who harass and attack others because they are gay, lesbian, or bisexual are "predominantly ordinary young men" (Comstock, 1991, p. 2).

> Gay-bashing provides young men in particular with a very useful resource for doing gender, especially for accomplishing hegemonic masculinity. . . . Gay-bashing . . . allows perpetrators to reaffirm their own masculinity, their own aggressive heterosexuality, in opposition to this nonconformist threat. (Perry, 2001, pp. 107–108)

The motivation to assert an aggressive, heterosexual masculinity through attacks on people who are gay is found not only in individuals, but also in groups. In order to attain and defend hegemonic masculinity, some individuals carry out hate crimes and form far-right groups that insist on a limited conceptualization of masculinity (Bufkin, 1996). The ideology and the actions of groups that engage in hate crimes are enabling resources that people draw on in an effort to assert and confirm hegemonic masculinity, which they feel that subordinated groups challenge through their lifestyles. Psychological measures of hypermasculinity are predictive of U.S. college students' antigay behavior (Whitley, 2001). One man in a nonstudent sample explained why a group that engaged in gay-bashing selected the blue baseball bat as a symbol:

> We chose the blue baseball bat because it's the color of the boy. The man is one gender. He is not female. There is no confusion. Blue is the color of men, and that's the color that men use to defeat the anti-male, which is the queer. (M. Collins, 1992, p. 193)

In a similar pattern, in the workplace, men sexually harass other men who do not fit the harassers' gender-role stereotype of heterosexual hypermasculinity (Stockdale, Visio, & Batra, 1999). Also, in a sample of college students, those who valued hypermasculinity were most likely to report their own physical violence or name-calling directed at people who they thought were gay or lesbian (Franklin, 1997). Perpetrators of sexual orientation–motivated bias crimes feel that people who are gay, lesbian, or bisexual are threatening and challenging to hegemonic masculinity, and that victimization can maintain the balance of power that favors their own ideas about what it is to be a man.

Immigration Through Marriage: The Confluence of Structural Inequality, Culture, and Beliefs About Gender

Women's global economic disadvantages and the limited opportunities that women have for attaining a good quality of life in many countries influence them and their families to actively seek opportunities for marriage to a person in another country (Banerjee, 1996). Men in countries that include the United States, Canada, and the Western European nations sponsor new wives as immigrants for many reasons. Some men who have immigrated want to marry a person with an ethnic and cultural background similar to their own. Some, including those who are and who are not themselves immigrants, seek out marriageable women from other countries because they hope that the women will fit stereotypes involving subservience and passivity, or that they will fulfill traditional roles as mother and wife more adequately than other available partners (Kojima, 2001). Numerous internet advertisements promise compliant women, for example this one:

> Asian Dating and Romance! Asian women and Thai ladies make the best wives, girlfriends, brides or mates. They are beautiful, exotic and wonderful thanks to their Asian culture. Thai women are especially great for a wife, girlfriend, bride or mate. They are beautiful and sexy while retaining a degree of modesty. Asian women and Thai ladies have skin as smooth and soft as silk, silky soft black hair, exotic Asian eyes, and personalities that are soft and sweet. They are respectful and supportive of their mates. (www.asiansweetheart.net/ Ladies/2201001_Nong/nong.htm, retrieved November 15, 2004)

Finally, men seek wives from other countries because they feel that, because of their own deficits in appearance or other attributes, they cannot successfully compete for desirable marriage partners.

Women who immigrate through marriage to a man whom they do not know or barely know are called **mail-order brides**. Mail-order brides are distinct from women whose marriages are arranged, a common practice in many countries. Traditional arranged marriages involve family members or trusted matchmakers who introduce potential marriage partners and their families to each other. Traditional practices of arranged marriage can protect women from abuse by providing family involvement and oversight of the relationship. However, sometimes the distinction between mail-order brides and arranged marriages is blurred, for instance when a matchmaker or acquaintance arranges a union between people with little knowledge of them or their families. Many women arrive as new brides in countries such as the United States, either as mail-order brides or in some cases through more traditional arranged marriages, with no friends or family, limited language ability, and no resources of their own. They usually are sponsored with the U.S. Immigration and Naturalization Service by their new mates, and therefore feel dependent on them for the opportunity to remain in their new country.

Women's economic (and often educational) disadvantage and men's expectations that women will live up to stereotypes about traditional wives, be passive and subservient because they are from a particular culture, or will willingly engage in particular sexual activities can place women at great risk for abuse. A case analysis of South Asian immigrant women revealed that men were able to control abused women in large part because immigration law gave them the power to determine whether a wife whom a husband sponsored could remain in the United States, and therefore whether she would be separated from her children (Dasgupta, 1998).[37] Men even purposely failed to file the appropriate paperwork with the U.S. Immigration and Naturalization Service, leaving their wives "undocumented" and therefore at great risk for deportation if the abusive husband revealed her status to authorities. In many countries, marriage defines one's social status and worth as a person, divorce is unacceptable, the highest value is placed on keeping a family intact, there is emphasis on women's tolerance of and compassion toward the husband (even if he is abusive), and there is an acceptance that an unhappy marriage is a deserved fate. Cultural ideologies from countries of origin result in women feeling pressures to marry and, if the man turns out to be abusive, to stay in the relationship.

Victimized Offenders

Substantial numbers of women and men are simultaneously victims and perpetrators of crime. Although all children and youth do not respond in the same way, the experience and witnessing of violence teaches some that attacking and hurting other people is a reasonable route to self-protection or to get one's way. Alternative influences can counteract and mitigate the connection, but for some people victimization leads to their own future violence (Widom, 1996).

The popular image that people who do violence are irrational monsters (Madriz, 1997) may extend to violent offenders, suggesting no hope for change in the offender and justifying a primarily punitive response. But a person's dual status as victim and offender raises difficult questions about justice. Some teenagers "partly as a result of their abuse, may well present themselves as uncooperative and unattractive, and as perpetrators as well as victims, reflecting and perpetuating the social and emotional handicaps that come with abuse, and hence deflecting and derailing the very help they need" (Simpson, 2001, p. 67). If parents and social and educational institutions fail to provide models for alternatives to violence, and if they do not protect youth from victimization or even are the victimizer, is it just to ignore an aggressor's own victimization in the rush toward punishment?

There are numerous examples in many countries of the ways in which people are at the same time victims and offenders. Ninety-two percent of the girls who were interviewed for a 1998 survey of youth in the California juvenile justice system reported a prior history of physical, sexual, and/or emotional abuse, often on multiple occasions (Acoca, 1998, p. 565). A 1995 study of women in California, Florida, and Connecticut state prisons also revealed that 92% of the women had histories of abuse (Acoca & Austin, 1996). The dual status of victim and offender is repeated throughout the world.

There is a strong connection between childhood abuse and prostitution. Across different nations, a high proportion of women and girls involved in prostitution have been victimized as children (Farley, Baral, et al., 1998, p. 408). In the United States, boys and men involved in prostitution have backgrounds that are not dissimilar to those of females who sell sex for money or trade it for drugs. Many left home before age 16 and had been physically or sexually abused, the majority lacked a high school education, and many used multiple drugs (Morse, Simon, & Burchfiel, 1999, p. 87). In Nigeria, half of 150 Nigerian teenaged prostitutes had been sexually abused as children (Adedoyin & Adegoke, 1995). In the United States, girls and women involved in prostitution also reported high rates of various types of prior abuse during childhood. In one study, 90% of women in prostitution said they had been battered as children, 74% reported sexual abuse by family members, and 50% reported sexual abuse by nonfamily (Giobbe, 1991; Giobbe, Harrigan, Ryan, & Gamache, 1990).

In the United States, economic, community, and family characteristics both explain the childhood abuses and running away that put girls at risk for involvement in prostitution and leave them with few opportunities to escape the violence in other ways. Professionals who have worked with abused girls and women in clinical settings have described them as severely traumatized and having self-destructive thoughts and behaviors, contempt for themselves, feelings of shame and worthlessness, substance abuse and eating disorders, and sexual aversions and compulsions (Herman, 1992). People who suffer in these ways can have lifestyles and coping strategies that place them at risk for further sexual and physical trauma (Browne & Finkelhor, 1976; Terr, 1991).

In addition to prior sexual abuse, many people who engage in prostitution are victims of exploitation by illegal business operations and customers of these businesses. Preferences for sex with young girls and boys or with members of racial or other groups stereotyped as "exotic," "sexually desirable," or "passive" create the markets that entice some people to engage in prostitution and give organized criminal groups and individuals incentive to pressure or force them to do so. Conditions hospitable to **sex tourism**, which is travel for the purpose of purchasing sex, include pronounced economic disparities between countries, extreme poverty within countries, and demand by both indigenous and visiting people, most often men, who have means to pay for sex. In Sri Lanka, in a common pattern of trafficking in children and women, local pimps trick or force primarily boys, but also some girls from rural areas, to go to tourist destinations, and the traffickers keep them in rented houses that are frequented by European pedophiles (Ratnapala, 1999, p. 216).

In the Dominican Republic, which is extremely poor, both girls and boys engage in prostitution beginning at ages 11 or 12, and in the 1980s, more than half of their clients were tourists (Moya & Garcia, 1999). Fears about HIV have resulted in less tourist demand and increased violence as children took more risks to earn money from fewer clients. In India and Bangladesh, where there are large numbers of boys who trade sex for money, sex work is a survival strategy for people who are homeless, hungry, poor, and powerless (Kahn, 1999, p. 195). They sell their bodies in exchange for money, food, shelter, or clothing. Whether the providers of sex are adult women, girls, or boys, they are disadvantaged by either age, poverty, or gender. Ironically, many customers consider them sexually desirable because of the demographic characteristics that place them at a disadvantage.

Prostitutes in countries with very different cultures and contexts (South Africa, Thailand, Turkey, the United States, Zambia) report extremely high rates of brutal victimization in their histories and while they work as prostitutes (Farley, Baral, et al., 1998). In a sample of 475 people from these five countries, predominantly girls and women but including males, since entering prostitution, 73% had been physically assaulted, 62% reported having been raped, and at the time of the interview, 67% met criteria for a diagnosis of **posttraumatic stress disorder** (PTSD). (PTSD is a constellation of difficulties: rethinking the experience of the trauma, avoiding stimuli that are similar to the trauma and a general numbing of responsiveness, and anxiety.) Similar victimization of prostitutes has been documented in areas as different as Norway (Hoigard & Finstad, 1992), Glasgow in the United Kingdom (McKeganey & Barnard, 1996), and Canada (Baldwin, 1992). In San Jose, Costa Rica, boys who submit to homosexual relationships are treated violently and cruelly (Schifter & Aggleton, 1999). One 34-year-old woman who had been involved in prostitution in Toronto for 10 years described the level of day-to-day violence:

> There have been fights with knives over crack, over 20 pieces in a crack house. I was almost raped because I did not want to give this guy a blowjob after he gave me a toke . . . I had my jaw broken (by my boyfriend) when I was partying with this girl. [Why?] Because I smoked without him. (Erickson, Butters, McGillicuddy, & Hallgren, 2000, p. 777)

Some of the violence is mutual, fueled by drugs, self-defense, and women's own aggressive inclinations (Erickson et al., 2000). More often, women are the sole victims in the incident. One crack-addicted woman who was involved in prostitution explained why prostitutes are often beaten up:

> [C]ause we open our mouths and we say stupid shit and they don't take, dope men don't take no disrespect from nobody. . . . And you say something they don't like, they'll smack you in the mouth in a heartbeat. Because they, they feel like they can get away with it. You know because we're gonna come back o them and we're gonna forgive 'em. Because after they hit us, they're like, "oh baby I'm sorry" and everything like that, you know "I just had a bad day." And you know, and they give you dope because they know it's gonna get you more

hooked, you know to come back and you're gonna spend more money with them and they're gonna keep abusin' you, and they know they can get away with it. (J. Miller, 1995, pp. 443–444)

Pimps or other people who attempt to control and profit from prostitution victimize those who exchange sex for money; and people involved in prostitution are vulnerable to the abuses of men who seek to purchase access to their bodies.

Often, it is an oversimplification to label a person as a victim or an offender. The misleading quality of one or the other label is exemplified by women trafficked into the United States and other countries. Interviews revealed some common scenarios:

> Organized businesses and crime networks, such as escort services, bars, brothels, clubs, "biker gangs" and the mafia, were instrumental in recruiting the international (60%) and U.S. women (40%). U.S. servicemen have also been involved in recruiting Asian women, especially from Korea, Vietnam and Japan into the sex industry in the United States. Often the servicemen marry prostituted women around military bases abroad, bring them to the United States and pressure them into prostitution. A large number of foreign military wives become victims of domestic violence, displaced or homeless, and end up in prostitution around U.S. military bases. (Raymond & Hughes, 2001, p. 9).

Domestic violence in some situations has resulted in foreign women's leaving their husbands and continuing or beginning prostitution to support themselves. Women are also threatened and battered by pimps, some of whom are husbands, if they do not engage in prostitution (Raymond & Hughes, 2001, p. 10).

Not only do victims of gender-related offenses become involved in the justice system as offenders, but offenders also are at risk for gender-related victimization while they are incarcerated. For juveniles, there is evidence that girls in California institutions view it as routine to be strip-searched and to have their private parts visually examined in an open space with male staff casually observing (Acoca, 1998, p. 579). The tremendous increases over the last two decades in the number of women and men who are in U.S. jails and prisons means that more people experience the vulnerabilities that come with being institutionalized, often in places that are overcrowded and not adequately staffed. Drug addiction and the very limited resources of many incarcerated people create an environment where sex in return for drugs or other favors is not uncommon. The power imbalance between prisoners and correctional staff increases the potential for staff to sexually exploit offenders (Morash & Schram, 2002). Twenty-one percent of incarcerated men in seven Midwestern prison facilities reported on an anonymous survey that they had experienced at least one episode of pressured or forced sex while in prison (Struckman-Johnson & Struckman-Johnson, 2000). Depending on the facility, in the same Midwestern region, between 7% and 27% of incarcerated women reported sexual abuse or rape while they were incarcerated. Although there are exceptions, the typical pattern is for women offenders to be victimized by male correctional staff, whereas other inmates more often victimize male prisoners.

The placement of people into categories of victim *or* offender is misleading. It obscures the possibility that the structural and cultural supports for victimization also can result in the victim's illegal behavior. It also denies that victimization can have effects on people that result in illegal behavior. In practice, many correctional programs do address the harm done to offenders through prior or current victimization. Some, however, do not—or, more damaging, some correctional facilities are the settings for continued victimization of offenders.

Effects of Gender- and Sexual-Orientation–Related Victimization

Gender-related and sexual orientation–related victimization can be particularly traumatic because potential victims are at risk by virtue of gender, which for women and girls is readily apparent, and because it can be motivated by misogyny, dislike of gay and lesbian individuals, and other forms of hate directed at the very identity of a person. For women and girls, because victimization is so often within the family or circle of acquaintances, there is the additional disquietude introduced by violation of trust and the potential for continued contact with the victimizer.

Research has demonstrated severe and complex effects of gender-related victimization. In addition to physical injury and in some cases disability, battering can result in depression, anxiety, and PTSD. A report sponsored by the World Bank concluded that throughout the world, wife abuse is a serious threat to health and quality of life, results in injury or death, and has negative spillover effects on children, the workplace, and the broader community:

> The most endemic form of violence against women is wife abuse . . . 35 studies from a wide variety of countries . . . show that in many countries one-quarter to more than half of women report having been physically abused by a present or former partner. An even larger percentage have been subjected to ongoing emotional and psychological abuse, a form of violence that many battered women consider worse than physical abuse. (Heise, Pitanguy, & Germain, 1994, p. 5)

Domestic violence has particularly pronounced effects on disability and death among women of reproductive age in both the industrial and developing world (Heise et al., 1994, p. 17). For the individual women, the result can be both injury and permanent disability and disfigurement, as well as psychological effects that include "fear, anxiety, fatigue, and post-traumatic stress disorder" (Heise et al., 1994, p. 18).

Some victims of incest and other forms of child sexual abuse, wife battering, and stalking are traumatized over a lengthy period. Compared to women who are infrequently stalked, those who are relentlessly stalked over a period of time not only are at greater risk for physical, sexual, and emotional abuse but also suffered more depression and PTSD (Mechanic, Uhlmansiek, Weaver, & Resick, 2000). Repeated victimization can produce long-term changes in how survivors regulate their emotions, self-perceptions, and relationships with other people, and the meanings they attach to actions and events (Herman, 1992). One woman who was traumatized during her involvement in prostitution described her feelings:

> It's a process. The first year was like a big party, but eventually progressed downward to the emptiest void of hopelessness. I ended up desensitized, completely deadened, not able to have good feelings because I was on "void" all the time. (Farley et al., 1998, p. 409)

The term **complex posttraumatic syndrome** refers to these sorts of long-term changes.

Compared to other crime victims, gay and lesbian survivors of hate crimes are more depressed, angry, anxious, and stressed; they also have more crime-related fears and more often describe personal setbacks that resulted from attacks (Herek, Gillis, & Cogan, 1999). Victimized gay and lesbian youths from both rural and urban areas reported high rates of suicide attempts (Waldo, Hesson-McInnis, & D'Augelli, 1998). Many victims of sexual orientation–motivated hate crimes are afraid to report their victimization, and some turn their feelings inward and feel shame or guilt about their identities (D'Augelli & Grossman, 2001; Waldo et al., 1998).

A survey of prisoners who were sexually abused by other incarcerated people (typically incarcerated males abusing other males) or by correctional staff (typically male staff abusing incarcerated females) in Nebraska revealed that emotional harm is a likely outcome (Struckman-Johnson, Struckman-Johnson, Rucker, Bumby, & Donaldson, 1996, pp. 67–68). This harm includes rape trauma syndrome and a resulting loss of self-esteem and decreased ability to trust others. At the very least, correctional settings where there is sexual abuse would reinforce the negative results of prior experiences with being exploited and would undermine programming designed to empower people who are incarcerated to take control of their lives.

The economic effects of gender-related victimization could be profound. Many people who are battered in intimate relationships, stalked, raped, and exploited by people who benefit financially from their prostitution are economically marginalized by their victimization. If they are physically or psychologically traumatized, they may be unable to work in legitimate settings. Aging prostitutes who work in groups controlled by "the man" are marginalized even within their world "of last resort":

> Traded as chattel, often stripped entirely of property in the process of exchanging "men," and finally disowned when competition from other more naïve, more attractive, and more obedient women becomes too strong, street women find themselves doubly jeopardized by capitalistic-patriarchal structures that are pervasive in "straight" society and profound upon the street. (Romenesko & Miller, 1989, p. 109)

Whether or not individuals simultaneously hold the statuses of victim and offender, the economic impact of gender-related victimization can result in immediate loss of financial resources and long-term declines in quality of life if it is necessary to live in less desirable neighborhoods.

Despite the strong and sometimes long-lasting effects of gender-related victimization, many individuals who are affected and their advocates prefer to talk about themselves as *survivors*. The term *survivors* denotes that even if there are long-term effects, people who have lived through their victimization are capable of independence and self-direction. They are not so overcome by their experiences that they cannot or should not exercise agency in the various facets of their lives.

Conclusion

For women and girls, the experience of violent victimization often involves attack by an intimate partner, relative, or acquaintance, and it is likely to occur in or around the home. The reality of victimization in one's home and the widespread (though misleading) fear of victimization by a stereotypical black or Latino male stranger make everyday violence a part of many females' day-to-day lives. An international perspective reveals that the victimization of females extends beyond personal attack to trafficking in women and children, abortion of female fetuses, abandonment of girl infants, and female genital mutilation. In some cases, women who have been victimized through trafficking are labeled as offenders, and women and girls who have committed crimes have past and current experience with gender-related victimization (DeKeseredy, Alvi, Schwartz, & Perry, 1999, Jargowsky, 1997; Krivo, Peterson, Rizzo, & Reynolds, 1998; Wilson, 1996). All of these practices signify that females have low value, and that they are subject to male domination, control, and violence.

One advance that has been made in understanding gender-related victimization is the documentation of how gender inequality and the concentration of poverty on women, particularly women who are black, Hispanic, and/or Native American, has exposed them to victimization. This is a major step away from early theory, which focused on the psychology of the victim, sometimes the psychology of the offender, and the family system as the source of violence against girls and women. Worldwide, women's poverty places them at risk for being lured or forced or enticed into situations where they are trafficked within and outside their countries for sexual exploitation. In regions or countries where women are most disadvantaged because of their gender, they are most at risk for sexual assault and for domestic violence. They also turn to prostitution as a way to make money, and thus are exposed to victimization by pimps or customers. When gender inequality decreases, women may experience a backlash of violence by males who resist the change. However, over time, decreased gender inequality typically translates into decreased violence against women.

Although women's and girls' disadvantage places them at risk, it is important to recognize that violence against women is not directed only at those who are poor, but that there are beliefs and norms that can be found in many social classes or groups to support men's violence. Some male peer groups, families, and media messages convey that men's dominance over women is acceptable and preferable to more equitable arrangements. In some cases, men who are economically marginalized use violence against women because they see no alternative ways to assert power, which they feel is essential to express their masculinity. However, men who are well-to-do also may choose to assert their dominance over women through violence.

A result of globalization is that images and beliefs that support gender-related victimization are readily available to people in widely diversified settings. Another aspect of globalization is the movement of large groups of people from their countries of origin. While international mobility opens up opportunities for many individuals and provides human resources to support legitimate economies, it also results in trafficking, a criminal activity that primarily affects women and children. Also, women who immigrate to the United States or to other countries through marriage sometimes find themselves with very limited resources and are subject to wife abuse or turn to prostitution to escape abusive relationships. Husbands may use abuse to enforce traditional gender role expectations that their wives no longer agree with due to influences in the new country. Globalization has several negative results connected to gender and crime.

This chapter has emphasized the structural and cultural explanations, and compatible intermediate- and individual-level explanations that focus on beliefs about masculinity, because those theories are empirically supported and they explain the quite-well-documented concentrations of particular forms of victimization among girls and women, and gay and lesbian people. Gender arrangements, gender inequality, changes in gender inequality, and culture and its adaptations explain persistent patterns of violence. Complementary theory along with supporting evidence shows how certain individuals accomplish their gender-identity through violence against girls, women, and people who are gay or lesbian.

Key Terms

Accomplishing gender	Hypermasculinity
Backlash hypothesis	Mail-order brides
Complex posttraumatic syndrome	Masculinities
Culture	Missing girls
Emphasized femininity	Oppositional masculinity
Everyday violence	Posttraumatic stress disorder
Female genital mutilation	Rape culture
Femininities	Routine oppression
Gender identity	Sex tourism
Gender-related victimization	Sexual orientation victimization
Hegemonic masculinity	Subordinate masculinity
Hostile masculinity	Trafficking

Review and Discussion

1. Examine the tables presented at the beginning of this chapter (Tables 3.1–3.3) and list gender and race differences in victimization. What theoretical explanations explain these patterns? Which patterns are not well explained?

2. What is the connection of women's poverty, both in the United States and in other countries, to their vulnerability to particular forms of victimization?

3. Given that culture changes and is adapted, how can it be used as a concept that explains gender-related victimization?

4. Compare and contrast macro- and microlevels of explanation for gender-related victimization. Are they consistent with each other?

5. How are different levels of influence on gender-related victimization connected to each other? Specifically, how is culture related to economic opportunity? How is gender identity related to economic opportunity?

Web Sites to Explore

The U.S. federal government supports the Office on Violence Against Women in the U.S. Department of Justice. Its Web site includes information on current activities, interventions to stop violence against women, and research results and promising practices related to domestic violence, stalking, batterer intervention, child custody and protection, sexual assault, and welfare reform. www.ojp.usdoj .gov/vawo/

In December, 1999, the General Assembly of the United Nations designated November 25 as the International Day for the Elimination of Violence against Women, and it invited governments, international organizations, and nongovernmental organizations to organize activities designated to raise public awareness of the problem on that day. Women's activists have marked November 25 as a day against violence since 1981. This Web site describes activities to address violence against women around the world. www.un.org/depts/dhl/violence/

CHAPTER 4

Social Movements and the Response to Victims of Gender-Related Crime

C rime victims can be believed or doubted, they can be recast as nonvictims or even as offenders, they can be provided with criminal justice system and other types of help, or this help can be withheld. This chapter considers macrolevel influences on the responses to individuals who have experienced gender-related victimization. Issue-oriented activists have worked to shape the responses of other people to victims of crime at the same time that traditional practices in the justice system and backlash have worked against these changes.

Activists with a focus on women or people who are gay, lesbian, or bisexual have joined social movements or worked independently in a struggle to define, spread understanding about, and prevent gender-related victimization. They also have tried to improve official responses to victims of gender-related crime. The results of social activists' work are new legal, theoretical, and popular definitions of certain crimes. New legislation, policies, and programs also have resulted. Theory and research have provided insights into how activists achieve their results. Activists have made a reciprocal contribution to theory by expanding and making specific the different types of gender-related victimization and by emphasizing patriarchal gender arrangements and related beliefs as root causes of damaging and unhelpful responses to crime victims.

More than for other types of offenses, when a person alleges to be a victim of rape, other forms of sexual assault, intimate-partner violence, or sexual harassment, responders question the veracity of the account, discount any recent or potential harm to the victim, or blame the victim for instigating the offense (Best, Dansky, & Kilpatrick, 1992; Jordan, 2001; P. Y. Martin & Powell, 1994; Sloan, 1995). It is not unusual for children and adults reporting sexual assault to be asked and persuaded by police or prosecutors to take a polygraph test as evidence that they are

Victims who are asked to take a polygraph test may feel they are being revictimized by the justice system.

© Karen Kasmauski/Getty Images

telling the truth (P. Y. Martin & Powell, 1994; Sloan, 1995). Following the same pattern, school officials sometimes blame adolescents who are subjected to anti-gay harassment for their own abuse (Filax, 2003). Also, laws may be interpreted or implemented so that they do not keep victims safe or restore their losses. These damaging practices, which are called **secondary victimization** (R. Campbell & Raja, 1999; R. Campbell, Sefl, et al., 1999), are also sometimes referred to as the **second assault** (P. Y. Martin & Powell, 1994), or in cases of sexual assault, the **second rape** (Madigan & Gamble, 1991).

Secondary victimization can have a number of negative effects, undermining victims' confidence that the justice system will or can protect them, creating additional trauma, and making it unlikely that victims will request assistance in the future. Although one study found that victims' experiences in the medical and justice systems were unrelated to mental and physical distress (Martin & Powell, 1995), other research has documented that the prosecution of rape cases actually decreases victims' emotional well-being (Matsoesian, 1993; Sloan, 1995). Also, even when rape victims held positive attitudes about police officers who investigated their cases, they were frustrated by the overall criminal justice system response (Frazier & Haney, 1996). A statewide sample of licensed mental health professionals with experience treating rape survivors also reported that secondary victimization was widespread, particularly if their client base included women of color (R. Campbell & Raja, 1999). Similarly, in a sample of rape victims in Chicago, half of the women experienced contact with the legal system as hurtful, and one third experienced contact with the medical system as hurtful. In contrast, the vast majority found their contact with mental health professionals, rape crisis centers, or religious communities to be healing (R. Campbell, Wasco, Ahrens, Sefl, & Barnes, 2001,

p. 1250). Since the emergence of concern with secondary victimization, numerous programs have been developed either to change responses or to support victims as they encounter police, emergency room staff, prosecutors, judges, and juries. Although there have been changes, secondary victimization continues to be a concern of activists and of service providers who work to ameliorate the negative outcomes. Current evidence of secondary victimization is described in the next chapter, which includes sections on how communities, organizations, and individuals respond to victims of gender-related crime.

This chapter opens with a brief description of the Feminist Movement, in which much of the work to challenge and change responses to gender-related victimization has occurred. It then describes how activists have brought attention to a full range of the types of gender-related victimization, have focused attention on the root causes of these problems, and have addressed the unique difficulties of victims of varying ethnic, racial, gender, and immigrant statuses. As appropriate, information on the related problem of sexual orientation victimization is presented to show parallels with gender-related victimization and to raise questions about the adequacy of existing theory in explaining how social movements address responses to violence.

The Feminist Movement

Women in many countries have mobilized in efforts to establish gender equality and to address problems that are common to girls and women. The **Feminist Movement**, which is also referred to as the Women's Movement, has struggled over the appropriate roles of women and men in both developing and postindustrial societies and over gender inequality in access to resources and power.

In what is called the **first wave of the Feminist Movement**, between 1848 and 1919 in the United States, there was a strong focus on women's right to vote and on other aspects of their participation in society. Not only well-to-do European American women participated in the movement. Similar to women's clubs formed by European Americans (Gere & Robbins, 1996), African American women's clubs campaigned for woman suffrage. They also worked to improve conditions for and to reduce discrimination against both male and female African Americans (McKinley-Floyd, 1998; Meis Knupfer, 1996). Many of the employed immigrant and other women in the working class marched in suffrage parades and encouraged male coworkers and relatives to vote to give women the right to vote (Schrom Dye, 1980). Although diverse groups of women did come together on certain issues, activists in the different race and class groups also concentrated on issues of particular concern to their own groups.

During the **second wave of the Feminist Movement**, which began in the 1960s, in a revised and renewed effort to create social change, activists concentrated on equality in the workplace, the value of women's work in the home, women's right to control their own bodies, and myriad other issues (Caputi, 1992; Davies, 1994; Schneider, 1992). For example, black women who worked as data terminal operators in hospitals drew on their kin- and family-based networks to organize the workplace, opposed management's view of their work as unskilled, and provided informal leadership in efforts to obtain better working conditions (Sacks, 1988). Similar groups with varying racial composition, called labor feminists, sought to eliminate sex-based disadvantages in their places of work by working within the labor movement (Cobble, 2004). In fact, the Coalition of Labor Union Women is still an active force. Women who were, and some who were not, involved in the various types of activism also historically worked and currently work on the issues of abortion, reproductive rights, and inadequate prevention and justice system response to violence against women.

A number of writers (e.g., Denfield, 1996; Heywood & Drake, 1997; Walter, 1999) have called the Feminist Movement from 1980 through the present the **third wave of the Feminist Movement**. Third wave feminism is characterized by heightened awareness that gender oppression varies or is accompanied by other sorts of oppressions depending on age, race, ethnicity, and numerous other differentiations.

In the period of third wave feminism, people who are experiencing and/or concerned about gender and other oppressions grapple with negative images and opinions about "feminism" and "feminist." Some do not want to be associated with feminism because they feel it is rigidly defined, and that the definition does not make sense in relation to their own experiences (R. Walker, 1995). For instance, some women of color and lower-class women feel that feminism is a middle-class white ideology that has not recognized critical problems of racism. Also, in the period of third wave feminism, at least for some racial, ethnic, and class groups, some of the benefits of earlier feminist activists have been realized. In the United States, abortion is legal, there is greater gender equity in education, and affirmative action programs have been instituted. However, many poor women, who are disproportionately women of color, do not benefit from affirmative action in the workplace because they lack education to be eligible for hiring or promotion. Also, because of the concentration of poverty among and the lack of medical insurance for women of color, activism to obtain health care is a primary focus of black third wave feminists (Taylor, 1998). Third wave feminist activists directly acknowledge the great variety in the lives and experiences of girls and women with different backgrounds and social locations.

Despite the emphasis on multiple social locations and multiple standpoints, there are some commonalities among third wave feminists. Both majority and minority contemporary feminist activists in the United States recognize the distortions embedded in media portrayals of women and girls. In fact, a common movement tactic has been to publish low-cost newsletters, often distributed through e-mail, to counteract distorted media images. Also, third wave feminists are connected into networks, though unlike first and second wave feminists, these connections are often through Internet technologies that can be used to pull divergent groups together around current issues or to share common experiences such as incest, sexual assault, and discrimination (Findlen, 1995; Garrison, 2000; Schilt, 2003).

Although the contradictions and differences in the Feminist Movement are most apparent in recent years, in the United States and internationally, the Feminist Movement has always been characterized by more or less interconnected networks of people rather than by a single unified group (Ferree & Hess, 1995). These networks consist of decentralized coalitions of groups, organizations, and individuals, including scholars and politicians. In the United States, the second wave of the Feminist Movement recruited membership into networks from two strands: older women who were working in bureaucracies, often as professionals, and younger women who were politically active at the grassroots level. The two strands have been described as **bureaucratic activists** and **collectivist activists**. The existence of the two strands is a source of strength for the movement because it allows different women to find a place in the social movement (Ferree & Hess, 1995, p. 73).

The initial group of educated urban female activists recruited new participants into the movement from within their own networks. As a result, "few working-class women—old or young, black or white—were available for mobilization via these interpersonal influences" (Ferree & Hess, 1995, p. 93). The activists did include African American and Hispanic professional and educated women, however. There continues to be considerable diversity in terms of social class, but often racial and ethnic group minority women have developed their own activities to address special concerns in minority populations (Ferree & Hess, 1995).

Although some networks focus on a geographic area, many are organized around a particular issue, notably health and mental health, education and politics, cultural and entrepreneurial alternative institutions, or the topic of this chapter, one or more forms of gender-related victimization (Ferree & Hess, 1995, pp. 102–115). Activists are often part of more than one network. Many states have coalitions against sexual *and* domestic assault. Gay and lesbian people and their advocates work within and in cooperation with coalitions that address violence against women. Increasingly, there are global connections as activists share information and strategies through international meetings and the Internet (Arizpe, 1999; Ferree & Hess, 1995, p. ix; Hawthorne & Klein, 1999; Spender, 1995).

The choice of issues for the focus of activism is often related to social class concerns characterizing the network of people involved in a particular branch of feminist activities (Ferree & Hess, 1995). Because racial and ethnic groups are differently distributed across social classes, activities also concentrate on addressing problems that are particularly common in certain ethnic or racial groups. An example of the influence of social class on the choice of issues is found in movement efforts to address concerns about reproductive rights. In the 1970s, more than one feminist organization focused on abortion and, more generally, reproductive rights. Dr. Helen Rodriguez-Trias, a medical doctor, was a founding member of one of these organizations, The Committee for Abortion Rights and Against Sterilization Abuses. As a physician with working knowledge of both Puerto Rico and New York City, she was aware that women of color and with physical disabilities were more often sterilized, often without being informed of the consequences, than were white, middle-class women. Thus, her work addressed not only the right to an abortion but also the right to refuse sterilization. Also beginning in the 1970s, another group, the National Abortion Rights Action League chapter in Boston, which was supported heavily by middle-class feminists, singled out legal abortion as its primary issue, but its members ignored the problem of forced sterilization. Historically, alternative focuses of interest and membership, often related to social class, characterized different networks of activists. Some organizations, however, have worked to include multiple agendas relevant to the lives of girls and women in their priorities.

Expanding the Focus to a Full Range of Gender-Related Victimizations

Feminist activists have formulated definitions of victimization that emphasize oppression by dominant, heterosexual, white males. **Dominant** refers to the privileged status of people who are a majority and/or who—because they have uniquely ready access to resources, opportunities, and power—can exert some control over other people. When the focus is on victimization by the dominant gender group, numerous phenomena fit under the umbrella heading "gender-related victimization." These include sexual assault by a stranger, sexual assault by a spouse or boyfriend, obscene phone calls, gay-bashing, harassment through unwelcome sexual advances or requests for sexual favors (**sexual harassment**), and harassment that is directed against a gender group and that creates a hostile environment or interferes with performance (**gender harassment**).

Sometimes legal definitions restrict the range of victimizations included. Sexual harassment is a violation of *criminal law*, which defines violations against the state, only when it includes some other criminal activity, such as forced sex or stalking. People may feel sexually harassed when unwelcome sexual advances or implications that there will be some reward if there is compliance with sexual requests are directed at them, but these are violations of civil law (which defines violations of the rights of private citizens) only when these behaviors occur in limited contexts defined by law, for example, the workplace or academic settings. There are common underlying ideologies, structures, and gender arrangements that influence responses to a greater range of gender-related victimizations than is covered by the law (Bush, 1992; Rose, 1977). Each type of gender-related victimization involves hurtful acts by a person with greater power against a victim with lesser power.

Without the documentation of the many types of verbal and physical assaults experienced by previously ignored groups of victims, it would not have been possible to establish legal, prevention, education, crisis intervention, and victim assistance programs that are far reaching and that address a multitude of victim concerns (Jenness & Broad, 1997, p. 70). For some types of victimization, grassroots activists began to speak out about "the unspeakable," that is, crimes that were stigmatizing, unsettling, and embarrassing to victims. For others, new terms were developed to describe victimization in all of its varieties.

Incest was one of the early concerns of activists. The widespread psychoanalytic approach to incest that predominated in the 1950s and 1960s denied women's reports that it had occurred. Women's reports were considered to be fantasies that women had about their relationships with their fathers. As part of the Feminist Movement, both scholars and practitioners emphasized the very real experiences of incest that had affected many women during their childhood (Herman &

Hirschman, 1981; Rush, 1990), and women who had experienced incest talked openly about the experience.

Social interaction and the political actions that were part of the U.S. Feminist Movement extended the definition of rape beyond vaginal or anal penetration by a non-intimate. The new term **sexual assault**, referring to the range of sexually aggressive behaviors that people experience as traumatic and assaulting, captured the behaviors that people experience as traumatic and assaulting (e.g., touching), and it recognized that marital and dating partners can commit sexual assault.

Early grassroots organizing as well as more recent collaborative efforts between victim advocates, service providers, and theorist/researchers were the means through which definitions of violence against women were established. Sanday (1996) cited one woman's description of how in the 1960s discussion among women activists led to a reframing and renaming of shared experiences:

> I must say, at first I didn't see it [rape] as an issue for us. . . . I thought prostitution was much stronger. But then one of our women was raped, hitchhiking home from a college weekend. . . . Then we organized a "Speak-Out on Rape," and different women stood up and told how they'd been raped. One woman described how a medical student took her "to see the residents' quarters," and raped her. Afterward, he said, "I'm sorry that happened. I suppose we should go out and eat." And what enraged her in retrospect, she said, was that *she went.* You see, what we all realized was that women accepted the fact that men are conditioned to be rapists, but they *don't* accept the fact that they are conditioned to be *victims.* (p. 171)

By the 1970s, the anti-rape movement was incorporated into other change-oriented feminist activities. Talk and action turned to the trauma of rape and extended to the identification of rapists who were acquaintances and family members: "friends, schoolmates, a gynecologist, a psychiatrist, a therapist, husbands and dates" (Sanday, 1996, p. 172). The term *sexual assault* recognized that rape is but an extreme of other assaults that involved forced sexual intimacy, including touching and fondling. **Date rape** and **rape within marriage** reflected the reality that forced sex does occur within intimate relationships. **Wife battering** refers to repeated physical force within a marital relationship; **wife abuse** reflects women's experience of a range of emotional and physical attacks, including emotional abuse, from their husbands and from other partners; and **intimate-partner violence** opened the door to thinking about violence that occurs not only in marital relationships but also in a wide range of intimate relationships. Even more generally, **relationship violence** extends beyond heterosexual relationships to include relationships between people with the same sex. In similar patterns, advocates, activists, and victims have described and given names to *stalking* and *hate crimes.* These and other terms are now commonly used in the media, in law, and in professional and popular discourse to sum up the experiences of victimization. They are also key concepts in theoretical explanations of crime causation, explanations of responses to victimization, and explanations of how laws develop and are implemented.

Advocates, activists, and victims have described and given names to illegal behaviors such as stalking.

© Anna Clopet/CORBIS

Addressing Secondary Victimization

Activists not only have increased their focus to include a wider range of oppressive behaviors but have also moved beyond a sole concern with *primary* victimization. They have worked to document and reduce secondary victimization. The emphasis on secondary victimization grew out of the social movements against rape and battering. An activist explained:

> The stories we heard of women who, after being raped, were hounded by the police in a kind of inquisition as if the woman had provoked the rape, created a terrible pain in us. We moved to act there, to stop the bleeding there. After numerous speak-outs were held, in which women stood up and told of having been raped, and then abused by the police and the judicial system, after giving ourselves the so desperately needed time to speak about a long hidden injury, we worked to change these more outrageous injustices inflicted on us by the very system which claimed to protect us. (Susan Griffin, cited in Sanday, 1996, p. 170)

The effort to address secondary victimization encompassed situations involving sexual assault, intimate partner violence, incest, and sexual harassment.

Issues, Locations, and Strategies of Activism to Address Gender-Related Victimization

In the United States, the types of gender-related victimization that currently occupy most of the attention of activists are sexual assault, intimate-partner violence, stalking, and sexual and gender harassment. The grassroots and the governmental (local, state, and federal) attention to each of these issues vary. In recent years, federal resources to reduce violence against women have been concentrated on domestic violence (Burt et al., 2000), with the result that attention to incest and to sexual assault is limited in many localities.

Incest continues to be a concern of survivors and the professionals who provide them with therapeutic help, but absent is the highly visible grassroots organizing and the heightened government attention that has been given to other sorts of violence against women. This may be because of the dominance of child welfare and mental health professionals among responders to incest and because of the inclusion of incest, which was viewed as rooted in patriarchy, as but one category of childhood sexual abuse. Child welfare and mental health professionals have tended to emphasize personal recovery rather than the patriarchal sources of child sexual abuse (Naples, 2003). Consistent with the de-emphasis on power imbalance related to gender and the emphasis on individuals who are to blame for incest, in a sample of staff in 87 sexual abuse prevention programs, more than 80% placed responsibility for avoiding the abuse on the usually female victims (Plummer, 2001). Also consistent, most home visitation programs designed to prevent child maltreatment have focused on mother and child and have ignored fathers (Guterman, 2001). Programs that take alternative approaches—for example, a Vermont social marketing campaign that encourages sex offenders to seek treatment—are quite rare (Paradise, 2001). Critical scholars have argued for research and related practice and activism that recognize the reality that most childhood sexual abuse is perpetrated by males against females, and that mothers in some cases are additional victims of abusive perpetrators; the mothers therefore risk their own and their children's safety by trying to intervene in the abuse (Risley-Curtiss & Heffernan, 2003). Critics of the child abuse professionals' approach to incest have argued that it is important to expand attention beyond individual recovery to include political action intended to "contest limited medical and psychiatric analyses of survivors, individualist theories of incest and childhood sexual abuse, and disempowering healing strategies" (Naples, 2003, p. 1177). However, there is no widespread movement to do this.

Worldwide, rape crisis centers, where women can obtain counseling, support, and advocacy, have been key places where feminist activists initially worked to change perceptions and responses to sexual assault victimization. Similarly, the opening of the first shelter for battered women in 1971 in Great Britain is often viewed as the start of the movement against domestic violence (R. E. Dobash & Dobash, 1979). Staff and volunteers in domestic violence shelters continue to provide services and advocate for improved response to intimate-partner violence. Shelter staff have given safe haven for victims and their children, described and publicized the problem of abuse, formulated and lobbied for new legislation, and stimulated the development of government policy and government-supported programs in a number of different countries.

Just as some people who provide services to incest victims focus on individual need to the exclusion of broader social change, in some places, professionals who deliver services to wife abuse victims take positions that contradict advocacy for social changes. This pattern is illustrated in very distant and different settings, for

U.S. battered women and, in India, for **dowry burning**, which involves a husband setting his wife on fire as an expression of dissatisfaction with the dowry provided by the wife's family to the husband's family. For both forms of violence against wives, the result can be death or disfigurement. Movements against both forms of violence succeeded in getting violence against women recognized as a troubling and serious social problem. However, in both nations, there was inconsistency between activists' view that the root cause of the violence was a patriarchal family structure that left women without power and influence and the social work, mental health, and governmental stance that the problem was with a limited number of anomalous dysfunctional families and individuals (Bush, 1992, p. 600). Government and professional approaches that seek to treat anomalous dysfunction are inconsistent with social movements that try to alter culture and gender organization. When nonfeminist professionals and activists (whether or not they are professionals) try to work together, there can be considerable tension (Morash & Robinson, 2002b; Radford & Stanko, 1996).

The collectivist and bureaucratic activists who do work for structural and cultural change are not always clearly distinguished from each other. There is not a direct evolution from activist, social change–oriented organizations to bureaucratic, service-oriented agencies. Instead, there are a variety of existing programs and groups, each with its own peculiar mix of strategies and practices. Many people in state and local agencies are former grassroots advocates or have been heavily influenced by them, with the result that advocates for battered women and sexual assault victims work with state agency personnel to improve the community and justice system response to violence against women (Ferree & Hess, 1995, p. 105; Reinelt, 1994). Some grassroots organizations and service providers continue to use change-oriented strategies but have obtained government support and/or are housed inside governmental agencies.

Often, different strategies to promote change are carried out within the same organization, group, or network, without any apparent disagreement or conflict. The rape crisis centers that are most often involved in public demonstrations and prevention programming tend to be those that are older, are not part of other agencies, use collective decision making that includes clients and all levels of staff, and value social change (R. Campbell, Baker, & Mazurek, 1998). A newer genre of rape crisis center is organized more hierarchically and is affiliated with a larger agency. Although the newer form is not as active in public demonstration and prevention programming as older forms, it is involved in political lobbying. Consistent with the interpretation of Ferree and Hess (1995, p. 73), the existence of both collectivist activists and bureaucratic activists can strengthen the movement by involving a range of people who carry out different tasks.

In the United States, the balance between grassroots organizations that are outside the official system and programs that are part of the criminal justice or health delivery systems has shifted toward the latter (Schmitt & Martin, 1999). For example, in Lansing, Michigan, responding to referrals from the police, Project CARE volunteers who are trained in victim advocacy visit all potential victims of intimate-partner violence, regardless of whether an arrest is made. The program and its budget are in the city police department, but activities include victim services throughout the county and advocacy aimed at improving police, prosecutor, and judicial response. Similarly, the Southern California Rape Crisis Center (SCRCC), which is housed in a not-for-profit hospital, shifted from demonstrating to negotiating, a strategy that is called **unobtrusive mobilization** (Schmitt & Martin, 1999, p. 368). The SCRCC does not "stand outside [the system] and allocate blame, as many early rape crisis activists did. Instead, they used an 'occupy and indoctrinate' strategy to persuade outsiders to adopt their version of laws, police officer training, rape exams, and school health education messages" (Schmitt & Martin, 1999, p. 379). The shift to incorporation of victim advocacy programs within the justice system has occurred in part because the early activists were successful in getting resources to establish local, state, and federal programs within mainstream organizations.

Efforts to improve the responses to victims of gender-related crime flourish and have their greatest impact when they grow out of a preexisting organizational base, specifically preexisting feminist groups and organizations that have connections to the social work, mental health, and legal professions (Tierney, 1982, p. 211). A preexisting base and connections to the professions provide activists with a viable network. The relevance of the connection to the professions is consistent with the idea that strength results from the combined efforts of collectivist and bureaucratic activists. Additionally, groups most successful in bringing about change are those with a flexible organization in which activists can adapt in their degree of centralization and can vary in membership, goals, and strategies depending on the situation at a particular moment. Successful local movement groups receive the resources, input, and actions of national groups, but at the same time they can flexibly adapt to local conditions (Tierney, 1982, p. 212). In sum, the arrangement of multiple networks that can come together in a flexible way, and that can draw in members from several different types of places, has made it possible for the Feminist Movement to produce major changes in how people understand and respond to victims of gender-related crime.

When countries are compared, feminist activists have been most successful in addressing violence against women if their efforts have been complemented by strong women's policy groups within government (Weldon, 2002). Depending on the country, these groups take different forms, including women's commissions, women's bureaus, and offices on women's status. However, they share the capacity to place feminist bureaucrats inside the government, where they can give outside activists access to decision makers and resources for research and organizing. A comparison of development of policy directed at violence against women in multiple countries showed that government response to the full range of violence against women issues was greatest when the inside bureaucrats worked with outside activists to shape the government agenda. Weldon, who conducted the comparative research, concluded that for the most responsive governments, those of Canada and Australia, "the women's movement was responsible for articulating the issue of violence against women, but the presence of a women's policy machinery made it possible for femocrats inside government to push for the inclusion of violence against women on the decision agenda" (Weldon, 2002, pp. 154–155). Again, the joint activities of collectivist and bureaucratic feminists seem to promote the greatest change.

Movement Activities Aimed at Diverse Populations

Although social movements to address violence against women have historically included activists with a focus on diverse groups, there is some recent resurgence of particular attention to this diversity. In the past several decades, the United States has shifted from an almost exclusively white, European-origin population with a black minority to one that is more racially and ethnically diverse and that includes an increased proportion of immigrants. Statistics on race, ethnicity, country of origin, and foreign language use reflect the diversity. As of 2000, just 75.1% of the population was white, and almost 5 in every 100 households were considered to be linguistically isolated, which is defined as having no person in the household over the age of 13 who speaks English "very well" (see the data at the U.S. Census Bureau Web page at http://factfinder.census.gov). In California, Florida, New York State, Hawaii, and New Jersey, between 16.7% and 26.2% of people were foreign born, and in Texas, Colorado, Nevada, Washington State, and Illinois, between 10% and 16% of residents were foreign born (U.S. Census Bureau, 2004). Immigration in the last decades has had important influences on the demographic makeup of the population in several other countries, for example Australia, Canada, England, Hong Kong, Denmark, and Germany.

Culture and national origin affect which responses will be most helpful and accessible to victims of intimate-partner violence, sexual assault, and incest (K. A. Baker & Dwairy, 2003). In some places, community and health services programs, as well as special criminal justice programs, have developed models for service delivery to address sexual assault in diverse populations. However, the literature provides a much more thorough understanding of efforts to address the needs of racial, ethnic, and immigrant women affected by wife abuse than of efforts to provide culturally sensitive responses to sexual assault or incest. Culture and the related factor of national origin heavily influence attitudes toward a husband's physically or emotionally attacking his wife, and cultures and countries differ in the degree to which they are characterized by beliefs that act as barriers to women's obtaining justice system and other interventions that might assist them in stopping or recovering from victimization. The literature also provides some information on activism to improve responses to people victimized because they are gay, lesbian, or bisexual.

Racial, Ethnic, and Immigrant Groups

Population diversity creates special problems for delivery of victim assistance services and for access to the criminal justice system (Bauer, Rodriguez, Quiroga, & Flores-Ortiz, 2000; Kanuha, 1996, p. 35; Preisser, 1999, p. 684). Access to the justice system or to victim assistance programs will be very limited if translators or employees who are bilingual are unavailable for immigrants from non–English speaking countries. Bui (2004) provided a translated excerpt from an interview in which a Vietnamese American battered woman described the language barrier:

One time, I called 911 when my husband hit me, and he tried unsuccessfully to flee before the police arrived because I kept his car key. When the police arrived, he told the police that we had arguments because I was jealous and kept his car key to prevent him from going with his friend. When the police learned that he was the car owner, they ordered me to return him the key. I tried but couldn't make the police understand that he had hit me and wanted to escape. . . . They even told me that they would arrest me if I refused to give the key back to my husband. . . . The last time I had contacts with the police was two months ago. On that day, his friend called and asked him to go gambling. . . . This guy usually called my husband to go gambling and I hated him. The next day, I called this guy and swore at him on the phone. . . . This guy retaliated and caused me troubles by calling the police and lying that my husband needed to go to the emergency room. When the police arrived, they were angry and accused me of lying to the police. I tried to explain the situation, but I was so nervous that I couldn't know what to say. . . . It seemed to me that the police didn't want to protect me. I felt like people who couldn't speak English did not deserve police protection. (p. 58)

When an abuser has greater command of English than the victim, it is possible for him to use this advantage to further disadvantage the victim. The language barrier is found throughout justice system processing, sometimes even in victim assistance programs, and it can leave victims misunderstanding why decisions are made, unable to give their own accounts, and vulnerable to being accused of being the aggressors.

In South Asian and Hispanic communities, which include two substantial immigrant groups in the United States, and particularly for people who are least acculturated to life in the United States, the norm is to rely on an informal support network if there is a problem with violence in the family (Balgopal, 1988; Kohn & Wilson, 1995; Santiago & Morash, 1994). Many South Asian women come to the United States and other Western countries for an arranged marriage; they are dissuaded from revealing problems with wife abuse by their belief that disclosure would bring dishonor on the two families that were joined by the marriage, on themselves, and on their ethnic group in their new country (Krishnan, Baig-Amin, Gilbert, El-Bassel, & Waters, 1998; Yoshioka, Gilbert, & El-Bassel, 2003). One study reported that less than half of abused Hispanic women in Detroit turned to social service agencies for help, and only half of them felt the help they received was useful (Santiago & Morash, 1994). A lack of culturally and financially accessible services is a likely explanation for why Hispanic women receive limited help (Pinn & Chunko, 1997). Another explanation is that Hispanic women are especially bound by a norm of loyal motherhood: "They tend to be married younger, have larger families, and stay in relationships longer" (Gondolf & Fisher, 1988, p. 48). Battered Hispanic women who are least acculturated are least likely to seek help (Caetano, Schafer, Clark, Cunradi, & Raspberry, 2000; C. M. West, Kantor, & Jasinski, 1998). There are special barriers to using the justice or other systems to help with battering for Hispanic, South Asian, and other women from collectivist cultures that emphasize the group, including the family, much more than the individual.

Some African American women who are victims of intimate-partner violence hesitate to report the crime because they feel that the U.S. courts treat African American offenders with undue harshness.

© Bertram Henry/Getty Images

For women who are of African heritage but are not immigrants to the United States, the problem of limited accessibility may result from the erosion of community services in many low-income neighborhoods (Gondolf, Fisher, & McFerron, 1988; Pinn & Chunko, 1997). African Americans are disproportionately overrepresented in poor neighborhoods. There also is research that demonstrates that African American women often feel that the justice system will mistreat African American men, and therefore, to preserve their communities, they should avoid seeking help from the justice system and from other service providers (Gondolf, Fisher, et al., 1988). Thus, for many different groups, there are unique prevention and service needs related to accessing the justice system when a person is victimized.

Currently, both scholars and activists in and outside the United States struggle to extend to diverse groups an understanding of gender-related victimization and the utility of alternative reactions to it. The importance of considering the diversity among national and cultural groups is illustrated by consideration of Native Americans in the United States. Because of differences between Native American tribes in the United States, there is no standard way to effectively reduce victimization. Hamby (2000, p. 666) described several differences between Native American tribes that are relevant to solutions to problems of domestic violence. For example, the Blackfoot value autonomy very highly, and thus would be receptive to community-based domestic violence interventions. Interventions among the Apache would need to consider the central importance of endurance and respect in the culture. Also, in many American Indian cultures, there is not a pattern of gender disparagement, and this can be used to bring about positive resolutions to domestic violence. Effective means for rearranging patriarchal relations in one population are not always transferable to other groups inside or outside a country.

Some victim assistance providers and advocates have taken steps to address the unique needs of ethnic and immigrant women. For example, the organization Manavi[38] was established in 1985 as a battered women's program with a focus on South Asian women in the United States. Manavi has a goal of providing culturally and linguistically relevant empowerment strategies for South Asian women by designing training for victim service providers and developing effective intervention models.[39] As another example, the Domestic Violence Counseling Program serving the Vietnamese Community of Orange County, California, provided programming for men who batter and who ranged from having little education to a college education, and who also ranged considerably in years in the United States and type of occupation. Service providers and activists target assistance and social change efforts on a variety of culturally distinct groups at the same time that they work to make the criminal justice system more responsive to these groups.

Gay and Lesbian Anti-Crime Movements

There is limited research information on access to services for gay, lesbian, and bisexual people who are crime victims. Since the early 1990s, numerous social movement organizations have sprung up to work to stop violence motivated by hate of gay and lesbian people and to offer supportive services to victims. Some of these initiatives developed in response to a particular incident, but many others grew out of more general concerns of gay and lesbian organizations and broader attention to victimization in the United States (Jenness & Broad, 1997, p. 54).[40] Civil rights, religious, peace, gay and lesbian, and ethnic groups worked as a coalition against hate crimes and influenced the passage of the U.S. Hate Crimes Statistics Act, which, beginning in 1993, required the federal Attorney General's office to maintain statistics on hate crimes (Jenness & Broad, 1997, p. 37). Because local law enforcement agencies were required to produce the statistics, they were sensitized to the extent and nature of hate crimes in their jurisdictions, and this may have translated into more prevention and detection efforts. To date, the primary activity of groups working against the victimization of gay and lesbian people has been to document the extent and nature of crime. Some effort also has been made to broaden awareness of hate incidents, violence within the gay and lesbian community, and "'invisible' incidents of gay/lesbian victimization such as same-sex incest, child abuse/neglect, unwarranted HIV testing, and domestic abuse/violence" (Jenness & Broad, 1997, p. 64).

International Priorities

The amount of social movement emphasis given to one or another form of gender-related victimization varies across nations. In countries where girls and women are most disadvantaged, activists struggle with HIV/AIDS infection spread by

These Ugandan children are the product of two brothers and several wives. One of the brothers has the AIDS virus and probably has passed the disease on to his wives and possibly some of the children seen here. When basic health and human rights issues exist in a country, activists are spread thin in their efforts to address the multiple problems that confront women and their children.

© Jeff Cadge/Getty Images

husbands who refuse to use protective measures or through widespread rape, beliefs by some men that sex with a virginal girl will cure AIDS, lack of adequate and nutritious food for women and their children, lack of decent shelter, the use of trickery and force to get large numbers of girls and women trapped in brothels, and female genital mutilation. Wife abuse often includes forced sex or refusal to use protection during sex, with the result that it exacerbates the problem of HIV and AIDS infection for women (World Health Organization, 2000). Sexual assault and childhood sexual abuse also may leave girls and women with limited skills to protect themselves in the future, less confidence in their own worth and their personal limits, and an inclination to accept victimization as part of being female (Heise et al., 1994). In sub-Saharan Africa, young girls who become involved with older men to get money to go to school or for basic necessities, or in exchange for gifts, are at very high risk for both violence and unprotected sex (Luke, 2003). The enormity and life-threatening nature of extreme deprivation and rampant abuse consume the time and resources of activists who work for basic human rights on a massive scale.

Similar to the developed countries, in developing nations shelters for battered women are a key site for activism to reform the response to violence against women (del Frate, 1995). Beginning in the 1980s, governments in countries as diverse as Thailand, Trinidad and Tobago, Malaysia, Egypt, Zimbabwe, and India began to provide financial support for what had been voluntary organizations. However, the levels of funding in relationship to the problems of violence against women typically are very small in comparison to funding levels in the United States and Europe.

Backlash

Social movements typically are resisted by countermovements against change (Zald & Useem, 1987). The antifeminist **backlash** is part of a broad-based political effort called the New Right. The New Right is characterized by a philosophy that emphasizes "traditional conceptions of masculinity, including displays of male strength, control over others, hierarchical power relations (from God to husbands and fathers to women and children), and competitive success" (Ferree & Hess, 1995, p. 148). New Right themes characterize resistance to efforts to address gender-related victimization.

Reflecting the backlash, newspapers, magazines, and public discussion include reference to the naturalness of male aggression, conceived of as a powerful force that cannot be regulated, and they claim unwarranted rape hysteria (Sanday, 1996, p. 245). The media have extensively criticized research showing college women's experience of rape, often by a date, for creating a "phantom epidemic of sexual assault" (Schwartz & DeKeseredy, 1997, p. 25; also see Schwartz & DeKeseredy, 1997, p. 26). It was a short stretch from this criticism to suspicions about women's motivations for pressing for the state's increased involvement and response to sexual assault; women were accused of making false accusations against men, not being in touch with reality, and being vindictive and hysterical. In the 1990s, a tabloid called the *Inquirer* referred to the "shark infested waters of modern dating," meaning that women claiming rape are akin to sharks aggressing on men by falsely accusing them of sexual assault (Sanday, 1996, p. 238); and a *New York Times Magazine* article claimed that date rape was a myth, and that women claiming rape had invited or imagined the experience (Roiphe, 1993, p. 26). After initial attention to child sexual abuse, including incest, as a problem in the 1980s, the media message shifted and began to emphasize that "false allegations are frequent, that many innocent people are being unfairly stigmatized, and that professionals are being overly zealous in reporting possible cases of sexual abuse" (L. Jones & Finkelhor, 2001, p. 7; see also Beckett, 1966; J. B. Myers, 1994). These examples of backlash are not unusual, and television, radio, and newspapers continue to put forth the messages of the New Right.

As with larger-scope efforts to more fully involve societal entities in supporting victims of gender-related crimes, attempts to enact and implement laws against hate crimes have met with resistance. One backlash response is denial that there is any such thing as hate crime. For example, James Jacobs and Kimberley Potter (1998) argued that hate crimes should not be differentiated from other illegal aggressive acts. They reasoned that crimes such as the following dramatic example can and should be handled by usual laws against murder and assault:

> Shepard [a gay man], a university freshman at the time of his death, succumbed to massive head injuries in October 1998, five days after police say he

was lured from a bar near the university campus and robbed and beaten while being driven to the outskirts of Laramie. He was then tied to a wooden fence, beaten again with a .357 magnum pistol and left to die. (Kenworthy 1999, p. 3)

They further argued that the differentiation creates animosity between groups, specifically between people who are homosexual and heterosexual in their sexual orientation.

The backlash argument essentially denies that there are special, gender-related or anti-gay types of victimization at particular historical moments. Part of the denied reality is that groups that are persecuted by other people want and feel helped by legal specification of what is happening to them and how victimization is related to their place in society and the relative power they have (or do not have). Another denied reality is that special health and mental health problems, along with self-imposed restrictions in order to feel and be safe, are harms that are unique to groups affected by hate crimes. Refusal to acknowledge hate crimes suggests that the law should not address such problems except when they are similar to other types of criminal victimization. This reasoning narrows the scope of the law and the state response allowed by it by eliminating from consideration the special motivations, victim experiences, and patterns of gender-related criminal victimization.

Both historically rooted attitudes about gender and backlash against the Feminist Movement and the gay rights movement can result in an ambivalent or inconsistent reaction to people who come to police and the courts as victims of gender-related and anti-gay crimes. Depending on the context, the processes of interrogation by police, interaction with prosecutors, and going to court can be riddled with elements of the backlash or can reflect reforms that have improved responses to victims in the last two decades. Regardless of reforms, in some settings the legitimacy and validity of victimizations and victims therefore continue to be questioned both blatantly and subtly, and as a result, secondary victimization persists.

Conclusion

Theory has provided description of the social movements to improve responses to victims of gender-related crimes. Activists, including scholars, in many different countries have been highly successful in expanding the scope of actions considered as gender-related violence. In some cases, not just popular but also legal definitions and theoretical concepts have been broadened. The expansion of concepts and definitions has been the basis for transgressing criminology, that is, going beyond what are narrowly conceived as the types of victimization that should be considered as within the subject matter of academic work on criminal justice and criminology. By expanding the scope of both practical and academic concern to a broad range of ways in which dominant groups negatively affect other groups, the door is opened for a study of structural inequalities and cultural orientations that support and are reproduced in the actions of individuals.

In many parts of the world, activists and government entities have been heavily focused on a multitude of immediate threats to girls' and women's physical viability, including not only violence perpetrated through abuse, sexual assault, or incest, but also HIV/AIDS, genital mutilation, and abject poverty. Violence against women and girls is part of a conundrum of these problems, because sexual violence and oppression of wives feeds into exposure to HIV/AIDS and other health problems, and all of these contribute to women's extreme poverty. Health problems and poverty then put females at greater risk of violence.

Theory has clarified how social movements develop, gain force, and have their effects in shaping responses to violence against girls and women and to hate crimes. Networks with flexible structure and with both collectivist and bureaucratic activists seem to create the most social change. Countermovements respond to social change efforts, and they create a backlash by using tactics of denial of the existence of some forms of victimization or minimization of its prevalence. In the United States, there has been tremendous pressure for change in responses to violence against women, in part because of federal funding and new laws. Yet, traditional approaches and backlash create the situation that a particular response to a victim will very much depend on time and setting.

The Feminist Movement in the United States includes networks that concentrate on particular social classes, indigenous populations, and racial and ethnic groups. The influx of immigrants into many different countries throughout the world has provided additional challenges to activists who are trying to improve responses to gender-related victimization. Particularly in the case of wife abuse, special advocacy services exist for groups differentiated by ethnicity and immigration status. Circumstances of women's immigration—for example, immigration through marriage or to escape extreme poverty—can create special needs within the group or special risks for battering. For both those who are and those who are not immigrants to a particular country, differences in culture can result in differential effects of the same responses to victimization.

Key Terms

Backlash	Gender harassment
Bureaucratic activists	Intimate-partner violence
Collectivist activists	Rape within marriage
Date rape	Relationship violence
Dominant	Second assault
Dowry burning	Second rape
Emotional abuse	Second wave of the Feminist Movement
Feminist Movement	Secondary victimization
First wave of the Feminist Movement	Sexual assault

Sexual harassment

Third wave of the Feminist
Movement

Unobtrusive mobilization

Wife abuse

Wife battering

Review and Discussion

1. Note the characteristics of the Feminist Movement that have led to successful efforts to address responses to gender-related victimization. If you were part of the Feminist Movement to change responses to gender-related victimization, what strategy would you use?

2. Differentiate between professionals in social work and mental health who focus on individual dysfunction as the cause of gender-related violence, collective activists, and bureaucratic activists. How do their goals and their strategies for addressing gender-related violence differ?

3. Compare the quality and the type of evidence that is used to support the position of people in the Feminist Movement and in backlash movements who address responses to gender-related violence. Information from Chapter 3, "Gender-Related Victimization," may be useful in making this comparison.

4. How has the Feminist Movement changed in its orientation to making changes that will affect victimized women in different social classes and different racial, ethnic, and immigrant groups?

5. What are the ways in which macrolevel influences, particularly social movements, can influence the organizational, community, and individual responses to gender-related victimization?

Web Sites to Explore

The National Organization for Women Web site provides information on U.S. feminist movement issues and a list of current alerts. www.now.org/

The Doctors Without Borders Web site documents violence against women and numerous issues of poverty and illness that are concentrated on women throughout various parts of the world. Search for the terms "girls," "women," and "violence against women" in the site. www.doctorswithoutborders.org/

The Web site www.un.org/womenwatch/ is supported by the United Nations. It includes a review and appraisal of the Beijing Declaration and Platform for Action, news and highlights relevant to violence against girls and women and other results of gender inequity, and search capability for materials on girls and women throughout the world.

CHAPTER 5

The Influence of Context and Individual Differences on Responses to Gender-Related Victimization

B road social forces set the stage for how victims will be treated, but community and organizational contexts and individual differences have intermediate-level and individual-level influences on responses to victims. This chapter will first consider community, then organizational contexts that influence responses to victims of gender-related crimes. It will end with material on how individuals make decisions about and respond to victims within communities and organizations. Although context does influence people to respond to victims in particular ways, individuals within a particular context have some degree of autonomy, and thus they vary in their responses.

Community Characteristics and Response to Victims

Some community contexts support both a pattern of gender-related victimization and negative responses to victims, with the devastating result that tolerance of victimization encourages more of it. Many college campuses are relatively closed communities that include aggressors, victims, police agencies, and counseling and medical services. Sanday (1990) opened her book on gang rape with a striking description of one campus environment that was characterized by centrally located fraternities with housing quality far greater than available to women, and with residents who openly harassed passing women and held parties at which the common goal was to have sex with women who attended. By tolerating the environment, the university symbolically sanctioned the dominance and sexual pursuit of women. Women recognized the tacit support of existing gender arrangements and exploitations, and they believed that the administration did not take rape seriously. The setting was complicated by the presence of feminist women and men on campus who did speak out against violence and the institutional practices that allowed sexual aggression (Sanday, 1990, p. 61). Despite efforts to change existing gender arrangements, many members of the university community, including official representatives of the administration, denied the documented incidence of rape, and in so doing they made irrelevant and invisible the feelings and experiences of victims. The overall outcome was that high rates of victimization persisted in this setting.

In sharp contrast to community contexts that support both primary and secondary victimization, in communities with a very high level of resources, rape victims received many types of help across the criminal justice, mental health, and health systems (R. Campbell, 1998). Often, they received help without any advocacy to locate or access assistance. In large part due to the Feminist Movement and the resulting resources from the federal government, large numbers of U.S. communities, including university settings, have worked to increase resources for victims of gender-related crime. They have developed innovative, **coordinated community responses**, which bring together all key stakeholders to coordinate a consistent response to the offender and in the assistance of victims and are intended to communicate that victimization is not tolerated and to enhance the assistance that is provided to victims.

Although coordinated community responses are developed for different kinds of victimization, the approach is most often used to address domestic violence (Burt et al., 2000, p. xiii). Through inclusion of educational, social service, business, governmental, and religious organizations (Clark, Burt, Schulte, & Maguire, 1996), coordinated responses reach beyond the legal and criminal justice systems and tie together an array of stakeholders, so that batterers are made accountable for their acts and victims remain safe (Pence & Shepard, 1999). The first coordinated community response, referred to as the *Duluth model*, was developed in Duluth, Minnesota, in 1980. Subsequently, in 1991 the Minnesota legislature mandated the establishment of an intervention project by a battered women's advocacy group in each of the 38 legislative assignment districts in the state. The Duluth model created a freestanding organization with responsibilities for promoting cooperation and institutional change. Coordination was achieved through interagency agreements, routinization of communication (for example, through regularly scheduled meetings), and the development and application of guiding principles (Pence & McMahon, 1997). The local shelter movement, criminal justice agencies, and human service programs agreed to the same principles that identified the ideal response to domestic violence. In Duluth, the various stakeholders have continued to change and adapt the community response to domestic violence, but the central idea that the response should be coordinated remains.

Two additional models are commonly used to coordinate responses to crime victims within a community. One gives responsibility for managing interaction, communication, and coordination to a new program in an existing organization, for example in the prosecutor's office or in a domestic violence shelter (Gramache & Asmus, 1999; Hart, 1995). The other sets up a domestic violence coordinating council that includes members from the various entities to be coordinated. As in the Duluth model, the aim is to bring together representatives from police departments, prosecutors, courts, victim advocates, and service providers who can contribute to an effective and just response to both victims and offenders.

There is evidence that coordinated responses alter the behaviors of people in the agencies that interact with victims and offenders, but little is known about the actual results for women. For instance, in San Francisco the coordinating council approach increased interactions between agencies, promoted broad changes in institutions, and made service systems more responsive to battered women (Clark et al., 1996). Also, the staff in several councils in one state perceived positive changes that resulted from the coordinated effort in their communities (N. E. Allen, 2001). A national survey of recipients of federal grants to improve response to violence against women also found that practitioners felt that working with other agencies in their community had increased the number of victims asking for assistance, and the research team concluded from site visits over 4 years to 16 states and more than 80 programs that women were most helped when there was a coordinated community response (Burt et al., 2000, p. x). Although it would be useful to have victims' assessments of the outcomes of attempted coordination, a case can be made that advocates in a community have a unique and reliable viewpoint on the quality of services and justice system responses that victims and offenders receive. Thus, it does appear that coordinated responses have desired effects.

Domestic violence courts are an example of a program within an existing agency. They stimulate coordination and collaboration with substance abuse services, other therapeutic programs for offenders, victim services, police, and correctional agencies. They may or may not exist in a community that uses other approaches to develop a coordinated community response. Evaluations of specialized domestic violence courts, estimated to number more than 300 across the United States, have shown some promising results (Gover, MacDonald, & Alpert, 2003; Karan, Keilitz, & Denaro,1999). There also are studies that show that the degree of penetration into the justice system and the type of sanction either does (Murphy, Musser, & Maton, 1998; Seyers & Edleson, 1992) or does not (Steinman, 1990) affect recidivism. However, the recidivism studies do not reveal whether arrest was followed by prosecution, conviction, and a particular sanction, so they shed little light on how coordinated the response is or on what the particular intervention is. Further research is needed on how the different forms of coordinated response translate into effects on the number of victims served, the progression of victims through the justice system, the variety and intensity of services received, and the eventual outcomes for the victims.

A particularly innovative and encompassing study of the nature of coordinated community-based programs developed to assist rape victims identified different coordination models that are used (R. Campbell & Ahrens, 1998). One model is to

Clothesline projects are used to represent the number of people who support a stance on an issue or the number of victims of violence against women. In either case, they create a sense of community that supports crime victims.

© Catherine Wessel/CORBIS

establish a site for integrated services, for example the Sexual Assault Response Team (SART), which brings police, prosecutors, medical professionals, social workers, and advocates to a central place, often the hospital, rather than requiring that the victim schedule multiple appointments at different times and places. An advocate from a SART described the result:

> The program relieves women of some of the burden of chasing all over town trying to get information and referrals from six or seven different agencies. Many women give up long before they get all the information they wanted— and who could blame them? Here, the community takes a more active role in helping survivors than the traditionally passive, and frankly, revictimizing role, it's worked under for decades. (R. Campbell & Ahrens, 1998, p. 553)

Because not all sexual assault victims go to the same place for help, integration also involved spreading information, professional help, and training to many different places, including substance abuse programs and domestic violence programs, where victims might reveal information about their own sexual assault. The most highly coordinated communities also had reform groups that focused on community education about sexual assault and the need to change policies and procedures. One rape survivor described the clothesline project, for which T-shirts that had the stories of rape victims on them were hung for public display:

> It was amazing to see—men and women openly crying after reading these T-shirts . . . to know, I mean really know, that I wasn't alone anymore . . . to

know that other people in my town really cared about this, cared enough to bring this demonstration to our park. It was like this big public declaration that our own town understood and wasn't gonna put up with rape and domestic violence anymore. (R. Campbell & Ahrens, 1998, p. 565)

A critical feature of the reform efforts was the creation of a culture of acceptance for the rape victim and public disapproval for the offenders, which in combination with integrated services provided considerable support for victims. Like coordinated responses to domestic violence victims, the coordinated responses to sexual assault victims helped them to obtain needed services to a greater degree than would be possible in more traditional communities (R. Campbell, 1998), and thus it reduced secondary victimization.

Organizational Context and Response to Victims

Given the highly decentralized nature of criminal justice in the United States, departments and agencies vary tremendously. These variations influence traditional practices and organizational reactions to legal and other reforms. After legal reforms were put into place, increased reporting and apprehension rates for violence against women were most characteristic of the more professionalized and the larger police departments (Berger et al., 1994, p. 17). Size, professionalization, organizational culture, and leadership influence responses to crime victims in criminal justice, medical, and victim services agencies. Organizational culture had its influence among more seasoned officers (Stalins & Finn, 1995), who learn to be pragmatic in their decisions about how to handle domestic violence; experienced officers most often considered the potential for the offender to be dangerous, the likelihood that the evidence was strong enough to support the charges, and the probability that the victim would pursue prosecution.

In addition to explicit goals related to their primary missions, organizations have implicit goals that meet internal needs. Prosecutors' offices provide a prime example of how organizational goals influence the decisions of employees. Whether prosecutors, who are elected officials, win or lose cases is a highly public result, and thus there is tremendous incentive to avoid going to court with a weak case and thereby appearing to be an ineffective prosecutor. Prosecutors have considerable discretion in whether they will take a case to court, and the organizational goal of winning can mitigate against taking a case to court.

Prosecutors consider what are called **blame and believability factors** when they reason about whether the jury will believe the victim, and therefore about whether a case can be won. In Detroit during 1989, six blame and believability factors were the only predictors of whether prosecutors filed charges in rape cases (Spears & Spohn 1996; also see Spohn, Beichner, & Davis-Frenzel, 2001, p. 206). Prosecutors were least likely to file charges if the victim knew the suspect, the victim did not scream or physically resist, the victim waited more than an hour to report the crime to the police, and the police file included information about the victim's prior sexual activity, alcohol or drug use, prior criminal record, or work as a prostitute, as an exotic dancer, or in a massage parlor. Prosecutors also were less likely to proceed with cases if the victim had engaged in some sort of risky behavior, like walking alone late at night. The legal considerations, specifically the severity of the crime (e.g., weapon present) and the quality of the evidence, did not have as much influence as did the extra-legal considerations. The organizational goal of keeping difficult-to-win cases out of court explains the reliance on believability factors in decision making about prosecution.

Primary objectives of police and prosecutors are "building cases, arresting suspects, collecting and verifying evidence, discrediting victims' accounts, bargaining with others in the network, and complying with statutory and case law procedures" (P. Y. Martin & Powell, 1994, p. 878). For emergency room medical staff, the primary objective is to save lives. Traditionally, neither criminal justice nor medical organizations have placed priority on victim services (P. Y. Martin & Powell, 1994, p. 879), although in recent years they have been challenged to do this, and some organizations have met this challenge. Responses that are helpful to victims include offering comfort, expressing regret, validating the victim's feelings, and confirming her or his experiences (Koss, 1993). These responses can be inconsistent with and can undermine organizational objectives of determining whether the victim is or will appear to be truthful and preparing her for a tough round of questioning by other people. Thus, the addition of new objectives often is not a simple solution to the complex problem of meeting victims' needs.

Just as there are documented examples of community changes to better support victims of gender-related crime, there are examples of organizational change (P. Y. Martin & Powell, 1994). Police officers have been trained to provide greater support to victims. Prosecution units have specialized in sexual assault or intimate-partner violence. Results are increased prosecutions and, for intimate-partner violence, referrals to diversion programs that provide some check on violence. One approach to meeting victim needs in criminal justice and medical settings is to sensitize staff through training and to reward them for providing assistance to victims. Another is to place specialized personnel within the organization, for example, victim advocates in prosecutors' offices, or teams of domestic violence advocates and police officers jointly responding to potential intimate-partner violence (Whetstone, 2001). As long as the advocates are not co-opted into meeting organizational needs, the inclusion of victim advocates within criminal justice and medical settings allows for *unobtrusive mobilization*—that is, criticism and change from within.

Restorative Justice and Peacemaking Models

The **restorative justice model** and **peacemaking model of justice**, which have been suggested for domestic violence cases, provide an alternative to both traditional and reformed organizational responses to victims. These models eschew the formal court processes and instead focus on repairing harms done to the victim and restoring the offender to the community as a positively contributing member. Typically, the perpetrator of harm is engaged in a process that would enhance his or her understanding of the extent of harm done and responsibility for that harm.

The traditional justice system serves as a backup should the perpetrator continue to harm the victim or refuse to participate in the alternative process.

Community conferences, a form of restorative justice, would include people who are close to the offender and who would shame the offender and encourage reintegration. Victims would not have to worry about the interaction disintegrating into "court talk" that disempowers them, and they would have a forum in which the offender's violence would be revealed to other people. At conferences, people can confront men's misogynist values and actions and can model antiviolent masculinities (Braithwaite & Daly, 1994). Conferences could be used in a step between detection of the offense and formal response. The availability of existing formal responses would be a necessary complement to increase the chances of effectiveness.

Some cultural groups may find that community conferences are congruent with historical and contemporary practices. Among the Navajo, for example, mediation is commonly used to solve interpersonal disputes and disagreements (Zion & Zion, 1996). Consistent with Navajo tradition, the person who presides over the mediation would actively correct any power imbalance between the attacker and the victim. One scholar described the mediator: "[T]he Navajo *naat'aanii* is not neutral. He or she can be related to the parties, and most often that person will have a definite conviction about domestic violence as evil" (Zion & Zion, 1996, p. 106).

There is some evidence of positive effects for victims when community mediation was used in the Navajo nation (Coker, 1999). The offender's family members could be confronted, and if they had been supporting the abuse, they might become part of the solution to stopping it. Also, traditional practices for involving the offender's family in making reparations, along with referrals to community social services, can empower women. Punitive, nonconciliatory U.S. law, with its emphasis on punishment and removal, often makes little sense to groups that seek to right wrongs and prevent further harm, but that at the same time do not want to expel people from the group (Yazzie, 1994).

Despite potential benefits, peacemaking and other restorative justice models could be subject to some of the same difficulties as traditional legal systems. Victims might be pressured to participate, and people presiding over the process may have personal beliefs about the acceptability of ending a marriage even if that resolution is best for the woman (Coker, 1999). Restorative justice models and more traditional criminal justice settings have both overt goals related to delivering justice and internal goals that involve maintaining harmony in the work group and satisfying external stakeholders in the community. Also, individual beliefs and other differences can counteract and undermine organizational and group goals. For instance, many traditional cultures stress respect for elders, so alternative approaches to justice must guard against overlooking or excusing violence by an elder (Zellerer, 1999). Thus, it is important to assess the likelihood of unintended effects of new peacemaking and community models against the potential for positive outcomes of victims in a particular contest. Perhaps emphasizing physical safety of the victim, prohibiting any blame of the victim, screening out offenders who are unlikely to change, presenting the victim with alternatives to the process, and including the fallback of the coercive legal system would reduce unintended effects (Presser & Gaarder, 2000).

There is considerable controversy among feminists and others about the use of restorative justice to address problems with intimate-partner violence (Strang & Braithwaite, 2002). Some proponents see it as the culturally appropriate way to handle violence for some groups, and point to the failure of other approaches in groups such as specific Native American tribes. Others feel that with proper precautions, the approach would be useful with all groups. Individuals who are in favor of restorative justice often feel that these processes give more choices to the victim and allow her to voice her thoughts and opinions most openly. Alternatively, individuals who disapprove of restorative justice point to the need for legal processes to make it clear that intimate-partner violence is a serious crime, and they do not feel that precautions will adequately protect victims. There is very limited evidence of the outcomes of restorative justice for victims of intimate-partner violence, and the stakes for the victim, in terms of the potential for physical and emotional harm, are very high. In light of these realities, there has been limited experimentation with the approach.

Individual-Level Influences on Responses to Victims

At the level of the individual, beliefs and assumptions about gender influence the decisions and actions of police officers, prosecutors, judges, and others who come into contact with victims. The discourse, the "talk," of people during police-citizen encounters and at the courthouse contains evidence of these beliefs, and at the same time it reinforces the beliefs by exposing other people to them.

Particularly in locations touched by organizational and legal reform, there are positive interactions and communications with victims. A study of the district courts in Dorchester and Quincy, Massachusetts, examined judicial responses to women seeking restraining orders, which prohibit a threatening person from contacts with the victim (Ptacek, 1999). Several judges saw themselves as reformers, and they "used their authority to make women feel welcome in court, to express concern for their suffering and to mobilize resources on their behalf" (Ptacek, 1999, p. 99). Similarly, the widely implemented innovation of community-oriented policing has potential for involving police officers with staff from shelters and crisis centers to jointly address gender-related crimes and to improve responses to victims (Morash & Robinson, 2002b). Community policing emphasizes partnerships within the community to improve quality of life. In large part because of federal funding to stop violence against women, many police, prosecutor, judicial, and medical personnel have received special training to learn about the needs of crime victims and to develop strategies within their organizations for meeting these needs.

When victims appeared before a judge to obtain a restraining order in one Wisconsin jurisdiction, advocates and court personnel had three distinct styles of relating to women seeking the order (Wan, 2000). Some exhibited a good-natured demeanor and offered support, physical protection, and advice to the women. A second group was more bureaucratic. Bureaucratic judges limited their comments to the law, and bureaucratic advocates, perhaps to deal with the stresses of heavy caseloads, provided routine advice but did not spend extra time explaining proceedings or listening to the victims. A third group of court personnel, primarily judges, demeaned the women, minimized the threat and past abuse, joked about women's circumstances, and even sided with the targets of the restraining orders. This third group exhibited patriarchal beliefs about men's rights in their own homes and the insignificance of women's complaints about abuse. These individual styles are no doubt connected to personal ideologies and beliefs about gender and, more specifically, about domestic violence.

Despite reforms and increased training and education about the needs of crime victims, there is recent evidence that some criminal justice officials, medical personnel, and members of the general public doubt and disempower victims of gender-related crime. The theory that has provided the most insight into individual responses to victims has highlighted the effects of people's beliefs about gender, race, and crime on how they respond to victims. These beliefs include stereotypes of typical crimes and typical victims. When victims do not fit the stereotypes, they can be reclassified as not being *real victims*. In a parallel process, reclassification occurs because of assumptions and beliefs about people who are gay, lesbian, or bisexual. Ideologies also establish appropriate gender role behaviors that are differentiated for racial and ethnic groups, and when victims act outside the defined gender roles, they also may be reclassified as not being real victims.

Stereotypes of Typical Crimes

Many people believe that strangers commit most crimes. In fact, the **violent stranger myth** is sometimes perpetuated by government advice that stresses that women should prevent victimization by adopting various individual precautions to reduce their encounters with male strangers (Stanko, 1995).

Because of the violent stranger myth, rape victims are taken more seriously and are seen as more convincing if a stranger has attacked them. For a sample of rape victims in Chicago, "[a]ssaults that fit a more 'classic rape' profile (e.g., stranger rape, physical injury, and weapon use) were . . . more likely to be prosecuted: 80% of the prosecuted cases involved stranger rapes, and 20% were nonstranger rapes" (R. Campbell, Wasco, et al., 2001, p. 1247). Even in resource-rich communities, where services to rape victims were readily available, it was the women who were the stereotypical victims, women assaulted by a stranger with a weapon, who were most favored in the allocation of resources (R. Campbell, 1998). The violent stranger myth explains why victims of stranger rape are more likely to receive information about HIV risk and testing options than are victims of rape by an acquaintance or an intimate (R. Campbell, Wasco, et al., 2001, p. 1247). The stereotypical victim may be seen as being more innocent, and thus as being more in need of information that might protect her health, than a person who is viewed as suspect and tarnished. Finally, medical students also saw rape victims in a more positive light if a stranger rather than an acquaintance had attacked them (C. L. Best et al., 1992, p. 179). Women who have been raped by an acquaintance or someone well known to them and who have not had a weapon brandished at them are most disadvantaged when they seek help from the justice system and various helping agencies.

Victim Behavior That Falls
Short of Others' Expectations

Just as there are ideas about typical crimes, there are expectations about how real victims will act. Many of these ideas are quite specific to gender-related crimes against women. When victims' behavior falls short of what other people think would be usual or appropriate, the response may be disbelief that the crime occurred or a moral judgment that the victim does not deserve the support of social, medical, or justice services, because she is responsible for the offense (Fischer, 1986).

In their interactions with the police, sexual assault victims struggle and negotiate, and succeed or fail, to be seen as legitimate victims. Whether they fought back against the assailant and the timing of their report of the crime to the police can be critical considerations for police, who sometimes do not believe that the offense even took place (Du Mont & Myhr, 2000, p. 1110). In Sussex, England, in the mid-1990s, after the reform of practices and procedures for responding to allegations of rape, officers continued to doubt that reported rapes were valid. One officer said:

> You get a feel for something and how genuine it is or isn't by the demeanor of the victim, by the time it has taken her to report it, whether she does or doesn't know the offender, whether there is a history between her and the offender previously. . . . I think one of the first points that causes concern is when she is making an allegation five days later. And then she knows the assailant and is thinking it through. (quoted in Temkin, 1997, p. 516)

The cited officer's many doubts, including his doubt that an actual victim would wait so long to report the assault, and his knowledge that the accused was not a stranger led to his skepticism about a 15-year-old girl who reported rape. He never considered whether the girl did not report the crime because she was "ashamed, embarrassed, or afraid" (Temkin, 1997, p. 516). In fact, a national survey that was conducted in the United States revealed that delayed disclosure of childhood rape is very common, and long delays are typical, particularly for young children and for those assaulted by someone known to them (D. W. Smith, Letourneau, et al., 2000). The officer responded based on presuppositions rather than available knowledge about how real victims act.

Besides timing of reporting, victims also may be less believable because they are not emotional and seem to be in control of their feelings when they report to authorities. Medical students who participated in a study saw a videotape of a young woman who did not appear distressed after she had been sexually attacked by a person she had met once before in a bar. They viewed her as less innocent than a woman attacked by a stranger in a parking lot, and they felt the first woman did not adequately resist the attack (C. L. Best et al., 1992, p. 179). British police officers who were generally empathetic toward rape victims were not much influenced by the victim's style of presentation (Baldry, 1996). However, like the medical students, less empathetic officers found the victim to be more believable if she was emotional when she described the rape. It seems that there is a combined effect, on an individual's response to a victim, of the predisposition of that individual who is responding to a person who has been victimized with the nature of the crime and the characteristics of the victim.

Secondary victimization of battered women that results from assumptions about why they did not leave abusive relationships is illustrated by a study of medical staff. Ironically, the staff were implementing protocol to increase their discovery of battering and promote their helpful responses to women in a hospital setting (Kurz, 1987). One medical staff member criticized battered women for not coming immediately to the hospital:

> Why do anything for people who do not take responsibility for themselves? What good does it do when they won't come in and do something for themselves? Last night we had a battered woman. It took five hours for her to be convinced to come in by neighbors. (quoted in Kurz, 1987, p. 75)

Another expressed the opinion that most battered women provoke their abuser: "A lot of women do things to provoke a man. Probably most of them do. I know there are some real crazy women around here" (quoted in Kurz, 1987, p. 76).

These quotations are taken from a study done prior to the enactment of the Violence Against Women Act and the resulting training in medical settings and dissemination of information about domestic violence from public media and forums. Even if such responses would be less characteristic in contemporary hospital settings, they illustrate how some victims are seen as undeserving of services because they do not live up to expectations about suitable victim behavior. This finding may explain why battered women report that they do not seek health care assistance—because providers seem to be uninterested, uncaring, or uncomfortable about domestic violence (J. Campbell, Rose, Kub, & Nedd, 1994; Gerbert et al., 1996).

Stalking victims are particularly vulnerable to doubts about whether they are truly victims, because they often maintain some contact and communication with the stalker in an effort to keep his emotions and behavior in check and to avoid causing trouble for other people (Dunn, 2002). One woman (referred to as *K* in the quotation presented below) who had been stalked described how the police officer (*I*) implied and made her feel her complicity in continuing a relationship with the man who stalked her. She had been told that the man who stalked her was in the reception area where she worked, and she later defended her decisions to see him after police insinuated that she willingly remained in contact with him:

> K: When he showed up at my office, I didn't have to go down to reception. You know, I could have said, "Send him away." But I didn't want to create problems, so I would go down, and see him.
>
> I: Were you thinking that if you talked to him. . . .
>
> K: That he would leave me alone. . . . Other times it would be, he'd want to get into a discussion about, "Let's get back together, I love you, I miss you, I'm sorry," you know. . . . I was still speaking to him, where I, I shouldn't have done that at all. (quoted in Dunn, 2002, p. 89)

Stalking victims often recognize the double bind that they are in when they interact with the offender in an effort to minimize disruption to their and others' lives and to reduce the potential of danger to themselves. Many women try to maintain a civil relationship so that they do not incite the abuser to become more intrusive into their lives. By being civil, they raise doubts in the minds of criminal justice system employees, medical staff, and family and friends about how frightened they really are and whether their claims of victimization are made in earnest. In playing out their prescribed roles, defense attorneys help to solidify the impression of the false claims of victimization by using the courtroom as a place to cast stalking victims as disturbed, hopelessly in love, and giving mixed signals—all of which are assumed to be indicated by the victim's maintenance of some relationship with the stalker.

Some criminal justice or social services employees have many doubts and misunderstandings about women who have been exposed to repeated intimate-partner abuse, but have not left the abuser. They are not aware of a number of logical reasons that a victim would try to hold the relationship together. They do not recognize the realistic fear that women have that if they leave, the result will be a lethal attack (J. Campbell, 1992; Mahoney, 1991). They may not understand the degree to which women fear for their own social standing and respectability, both of which can depend on their marriage, within a cultural or national group. The result is that many responders see victims of repeated domestic violence as insincere, inconsistent, and wavering.

In general, victims of gender-related crimes are expected to resist and to report offenses to authorities quickly, and in the case of domestic violence or stalking, to terminate the relationship with the abuser. These expectations extend to incest and to sexual harassment. For instance, although it is known from research that girls sometimes do not resist incest as a way to avoid other physical abuse, school professionals, including psychologists, teachers, and counselors, blame children for the sexual involvement if they did not resist (Ford, Schindler, & Medway, 2001). Also, victims who did not report sexual harassment immediately were seen by a sample of undergraduate college students as more to blame than those who did report quickly (Balough, Kite, Pickel, Canel, & Schroeder, 2003). The common theme is that victims are expected to have the knowledge, capacity, and sense of security to report gender-related offenses immediately. This expectation can be challenged on the grounds that some girls and women are from cultural groups where reporting is heavily discouraged if not prohibited, and also because some women have had prior negative experiences when they did report offenses. Fear of not being believed is an important consideration for women who hesitate to turn to the criminal justice system, employers, academic officials, or other official sources of help. Whether there are negative responses to victims because they did not report on time, act to avoid the perpetrator over time, or live up to some other expectation for appropriate victim behavior, or there are no responses because the victim stays silent and does not report, the result is the same. Groups targeted by gender-related crimes remain vulnerable to either no response or a negative response from both the justice system and other agencies that could be helpful to them.

Victims Who Violate Traditional Gender Role Expectations

Females who do not conform to common ideas about appropriate and moral behavior and appearance for girls and women are sometimes not taken seriously as victims or are blamed for their own victimization (LaFree, 1989; Schulhofer, 1998; White & Humphrey, 1991). One study presented scenarios to college students and asked them to report their assessments of victims and offenders. In the eyes of white undergraduate students, drinking disqualified black female domestic violence victims from the law's protection (Pierce & Harris, 1993). Another study of college students found that women who were harassed were seen as less trustworthy and less feminine if they reported the incident to authorities and labeled it sexual harassment than if they did not apply this label (Marin & Guadagno, 1999). Research showed that adolescents also more often blamed rape victims for the offense if they had worn suggestive clothing (Cassidy & Hurell, 1995). When the victim engages in behavior that is considered inappropriate for girls and women, even if this behavior is motivated by a desire to protect herself, she is more likely to be blamed, and the offender is more likely to be exonerated for the incident.

Victim-blaming attitudes are not uniform within the population. People who adhere to traditional beliefs about appropriate gender roles are more likely to blame victims for both sexual assault and intimate-partner violence (Brems & Wagner, 1994; Caron & Carter, 1997; Simonson & Subich, 1999). Among employed women, those who held the most sexist beliefs felt that respectable females should be able to resist unwelcome sexual behaviors, and thus women who were harassed were not respectable (Jensen & Gutek, 1982). In contrast, for both employees and students, a more egalitarian gender ideology translated into less blaming of harassment victims (De Judicibus & McCabe, 2001).

Individuals who have traditional gender role expectations often also have what are referred to as **benevolent sexist beliefs**. At the same time that they stereotype females, they have a positive and affectionate view of them, seeing them as weak and in need of protection. Benevolent sexism leads people to categorize females as either good or bad, as either having the appreciated attributes of a female or lacking these positive attributes. Male college students who were high in benevolent sexism were more likely than other men to blame victims for acquaintance rape (D. Abrams, Viki, Masser, & Bohner, 2003). Women and men with high scores on benevolent sexism placed more blame on acquaintance rape victims who were unfaithful to their spouses than on those who were not (Viki & Abrams, 2002). People who have attitudes of benevolent sexism are more likely than others to expect women to conform to restrictive gender roles. They also are more hostile toward women, including those who have been victimized, who do not conform.

The several studies that have been done of college student or general public attitudes toward victims do not necessarily generalize to people who work in criminal justice or other organizations that regularly come into contact with victims. However, there are some consistent findings from research on the justice system. Police officers with less liberal attitudes about women are more likely than others to blame date rape victims for their own victimization (R. Campbell & Johnson,

Even though it might help women to escape victimization, fighting back is sometimes seen as an indicator that victimization did not occur, because the woman does not fit the stereotype of a victim.

© CORBIS

1997). Also, women are more likely to be classified as nonvictims when they act with a level of aggression that is inconsistent with female gender stereotypes. For example, one stalking victim acted in a way that could not possibly be construed as compliance with the stalker's interest in continuing the relationship (Dunn, 2002, pp. 95–97). She admitted that she had on occasions hit her alleged stalker with a lock, hit him with a baseball bat, and grabbed him and pulled his shirt so the buttons came off, and that she kept a knife with her to protect herself. In court, she boldly threatened to the accused man that she would protect herself. She explained that her aggressive stance was necessary, because in the past the police had not responded to her calls for help. The defense lawyer argued that this woman could not be a victim of stalking, because she apparently was not living in fear. Her behavior was inconsistent with the view that real female stalking victims are passive and unable to defend themselves.

Although most of what is known about secondary victimization pertains to heterosexual women, male sexual assault victims also are negatively viewed because of ideas about behavior that fits with gender role expectations (Washington, 1999). In examples from opposite ends of the world, police in Queensland, Australia (Stewart & Maddren, 1997) and in Georgia in the United States (Finn & Stalans, 1997) more often blamed men than women victims for their own victimization through sexual assault, because they felt that men had more control of the situation by virtue of being stronger and more powerful. Similarly, police are less sympathetic to men than to women victimized by domestic violence, even when the men have been seriously injured (Buzawa & Austin, 1993). Police often erroneously consider same-sex domestic violence to be mutual combat and do not try to determine whether one party is the primary aggressor (Letellier, 1994), because they assume that men are equally powerful and controlling. Rape or domestic violence directed against boys and men contradicts expectations about males having the power to ensure that other people do not physically overcome them.

Usually, female survivors of same-sex violence do not report to the police or use hotlines, support groups, or legal advocacy (Girshick, 2002a; Renzetti, 1992; Ristock, 1991). If they do seek help, it is from friends or therapists. The pattern of seeking help is understandable. Except in some large cities with special programs for lesbian, gay, and bisexual individuals, services to assist victims of same-sex violence are not mentioned in announcements or written materials (Girshick, 2002a). In some states, victims may fear being charged under laws that make it illegal to have sex with another women (or for two men to have sex). Also, because many people assume that all women are nonviolent, victims of attack by another woman often think they will not be believed. When police do get involved, they may jump to the conclusion that the woman who appears to them to be more masculine is the aggressor, and thus arrest that person, who in fact could be the victim (Giorgio, 2002, p. 1243). Some people stereotype African American women as more masculine than women of other races, with the result that police are especially likely to arrest a female African American victim who has been assaulted by a female white offender (Giorgio, 2002, p. 1243). Here is a case example.

> Angel is a twentyish, African American woman whose older, White, female abuser convinced the police that she put Angel in handcuffs to subdue her from the drugs she was on. Despite the fact that Angel was not on drugs and that she was covered in bruises from Dawn's beating, the police arrested Angel. (Giorgio, 2002, p. 1243)

Lesbian batterers, including those who sexually assault their partners, may convince both police and victim assistance services that they are indeed the victims of abuse, because the people responding to the abuse cannot use their usual gender cues or explanations based on patriarchy to identify the primary aggressor. These many reasons explain the very low reporting rate for same-sex violence between lesbians. (Girshick, 2002a, p. 1516).

There is useful documentation of continued negative effects of gender ideologies and stereotypes and of assumptions about same-sex violence on responses to victims, but there is not longitudinal research to demonstrate whether, in general, there have been overall changes in the thinking of people who respond to crime victims. Given the very active second wave Feminist Movement, as well as the training and advocacy instituted to assist victims, one would certainly expect some change. In the general public, successive generations in the United States have become less traditional in gender attitudes (Amato & Booth, 1997; Thornton, 1989; Twenge, 1997). Research that documents continuing problems is important for the stimulation of improvements in response to victims, and it can reveal the ways that race, ethnicity, and immigration status interact with gender. However, it is important to keep in perspective that continuing problems are not necessarily at the same frequency, but in at least some settings may have been reduced substantially over time.

Recasting Victims as Offenders

A remarkable recasting occurs when a victim is reframed as an offender. Whether this is a common problem in intimate-partner violence cases has been the focus of some debate. There is concern that battered women who defend themselves are reclassified both in criminological theory and in criminal justice practice as participants in mutual combat, and therefore are seen as being as equally culpable of violence as their assailant (Ferraro, 1993). The tendency for women to strike their partners primarily in self-defense rather than as part of mutual combat is supported by research showing the predominance of the self-defense pattern. A study of 52 battered women revealed that the most frequent reason for their use of violence or what the women often called "fighting back" was self-defense (Saunders, 1986). A more recent study of a nationwide representative sample of nearly 2,000 Canadian college students found that although women committed a large number of violent acts in dating relationships, very few injuries resulted, and again, a substantial proportion of these acts were committed in self-defense (DeKeseredy, Saunders, Schwartz, & Alvi, 1997). Although mutual combat situations do exist, evidence of greater injury to female victims of domestic violence and the self-defense motivations for fighting suggest that mutual combat is not the norm.

When a **dual arrest** is made in a domestic violence incident, both parties are arrested. An increase in dual arrests has fueled the debate about whether these arrests are justified by actual instances of mutual combat between two equally aggressive people (Chesney-Lind, 2002). In some cases, it is clear that the dual arrest occurs because each person has aggressively attacked the other, and neither has acted solely in self-defense. Both parties are victims and offenders. However, evidence of harm to both parties and of who is the primary aggressor is not the only influence on whether a dual arrest is made (M. E. Martin, 1997). In Connecticut, for 69 police departments that were studied, there was tremendous intradepartmental variation, from 0% to 45%, in the proportion of dual arrests. Some departments emphasized the need to avoid being sued for not making an arrest when it was warranted, while others emphasized the need for officers to use their discretion in identifying the primary aggressor. Replication of a similar pattern of departmental variation in another part of the United States (S. L. Miller, 2001) confirmed the importance of organizational policies and context as influences on individuals' decisions.

For the same Connecticut study, another finding raised the possibility that women are more often arrested than men when they are acting in self-defense. Forty-one percent of the men in dual arrest situations had a prior history of arrest for family violence, but the corresponding figure for women in dual arrests was just under half that, at 19%. Also, for none of the men, but for 40% of the women, the police had written down on the forms they filled out that there had been a prior victimization. Consistent with evidence that mutual combat is not the norm in intimate-partner violence, these findings suggest that when there is a dual arrest, women previously have been victimized but have not previously been the aggressors.

There can be quite serious results for victim caught up in a dual arrest situation. Women who have been arrested along with their partners are understandably less likely than others to take steps to promote prosecution, and they are placed in an adversarial position rather than the position of someone in need of help and protection (Bui, 2001). Distrust and avoidance of the justice system promoted by dual arrest can increase vulnerability to interpersonal violence and can be a barrier to seeking help.

Like some victims of intimate-partner violence, some sexual assault victims are discounted because their behavior or appearance suggests that they are actually offenders (Frohmann, 1997, p. 532). When women from a high-crime, black ghetto area reported being sexual assaulted, the prosecutors did not initially believe them because they associated prostitutes, women who lie, and "garbage" (i.e., immoral and criminal activity) with the neighborhood. The prosecutors suspected the women were not assaulted by a sexual predator, but were trading sex for drugs, and then claimed rape. After questioning the women, the prosecutors changed their minds and did believe them, but they assumed the women would have no credibility with jury members, who also would think they were untrustworthy prostitutes. The prosecutors' assumptions about the probable thoughts of jury members reduced the likelihood that women victimized in lower-class, ghetto areas would have their cases prosecuted. There was too much risk that the jurors would consider the rape victims to be offenders whose allegations of being victimized could not be believed. The dichotomous thinking, that a person is either a victim or an offender, is particularly problematic because indeed, many victims of sexual assault are prostitutes who are therefore unlikely to receive the full range of help available from the justice system. As with domestic violence cases, organizational policies and practices have considerable influence on individual decision makers, and thus on outcomes for victims.

Transforming the Victim Through Court Talk

Mirroring the backlash against legislation to criminalize and penalize gender-related victimization, criminal laws pertaining to gender-related crime can be transformed and undermined at the level of courtroom drama. The U.S. system requires that elements of a crime as identified in the criminal statute be present before the accused can be proven guilty. This requirement is met in an adversarial courtroom process in which the defendant's lawyer tries to show the client's innocence and the prosecutor tries to prove guilt. In the adversarial system, when a case is tried there is **court talk**, which is accomplished by the defense lawyer, the prosecutor, and the judge. Court talk is about the law, the merits and the realities of the case, and what should be done by the state to and for both the alleged victim and the alleged offender. Through the dynamics of court talk, the judge and the jury are convinced that a person is or is not guilty of a crime. As part of this convincing, some gender-related crime victims are reconstructed as unbelievable, not real crime victims.

Despite the intent of individuals who supported and fashioned the rape shield laws, the pattern and content of discourse that occurs in rape trials can cast doubts on victims (Matsoesian, 2001). The trial of William Kennedy Smith received much media attention because he was a relative of former U.S. president John F. Kennedy. William Kennedy Smith was charged with the rape of Patricia Bowman, a single mother who had accepted an invitation to see Smith's home after meeting him at a party. The reconstruction of her as other than a victim involved questioning that depicted her as illogical and as wearing sexually suggestive clothing. This last bit of framing of Bowman as a nonvictim was accomplished by referring to her underwear as "panties."

DA: When you got to your house [after the alleged rape] you stayed there for . . . *several hours* without removing those panties.

V: I—I'm not quite sure how long I was at my house but I—but I—the underwear was still on me.

DA: It was at *least* a couple of *hours* wasn't it.

V: I—I'm not sure.

DA: And when you went to your mother's house, when you left your house and went to your mother's house you kept those same panties on didn't you?

V: Yes.

DA: And when you uh went from your mother's house to go to pick up Johnny Butler you still wore the same panties.

V: I was pretty terrorized I—I—I'd—never I just It's like you're—you're just functioning and—and Mr. Abbot told me tuh-tuh be at the sheriff's office? . . .

DA: Even though you—you felt *dirty*, you felt *awful* and what have you, you kept those same panties on. . . . (Matsoesian, 2001, p. 43)

Through questioning that required the victim to repeat certain information again and again, rhetoric that left an impression that the victim exhibited illogical behavior repeatedly, and emphases and pauses (some of which are omitted from the above quotation), the legal defense constructed a complex image of the victim as illogical, therefore untrustworthy, and somehow inviting her own rape by being sexually inviting. In the end, the existence of the rape shield law provided little protection, though unquestionably in some courts for some women, the law has the intended effect.

Court talk also is used to transform people accused of acts of domestic violence. The domestic violence cases that end up in court tend to involve repeated and escalating acts by men against women rather than arguments between equally powerful and aggressive men and women. However, attorneys' accounts of the circumstances of fighting emphasize the mutual combat portrayal of intimates fighting (Erez & King, 2000). The mutual combat depiction is accomplished by spotlighting the testimony of male batterers, a testimony in which they set forth their own views that they were engaged with an equal in a fight rather than abusing and terrorizing a person they dominated. In fact, defense and prosecutorial attorneys for cases of intimate-partner violence feel that the most effective defense is that "the woman initiated the incident and the man was using just enough force to protect himself from her aggressive behavior" (Erez & King, 2000, p. 213). By recasting the incident as mutual combat, attorneys' questions and comments minimize the criminal responsibility of the defendant and at the same time characterize the complainant as responsible for bringing the abuse on herself.

Additional defense tactics that are commonly used in domestic violence cases exploit or manipulate documented dynamics of abuse and myths about domestic violence (Hartley, 2001, pp. 534–542). Arguments of self-defense, of diminished capacity of the offender because of alcohol or mental health problems, of minimal harm done, and that the offender did not attack the victim all are mirrored in the reasoning of men who are repeatedly abusive (Healey, Smith, & O'Sullivan, 1998). In some cases, defense rests on the lack of corroborating evidence of the abuse. This tactic is not surprising, because many abusive men cut their partners off from family and friends and are very careful to not have witnesses (Kirkwood, 1993). Similarly, the defense that women could not have been particularly fearful because they did not fight back flies in the face of the reasonable possibility that fighting back might result in heightened levels of abuse. In some cases, expert witnesses bring the dynamics of abuse to the attention of jurors and judges. However, there still is the potential that limitations on testimony along with myths and lack of understanding about domestic violence will combine with defense tactics to result in a not guilty verdict when in fact an offense has occurred.

Court talk is limited by various rules and procedures. This can leave the victim quite dissatisfied because she cannot describe the situation in her own words. One Scottish woman who had been battered by her husband described what happened in court:

> He pleaded guilty so I didn't need to say anything. I just sat with the other people who were waiting to go up. He never even let me stand up there in the courtroom and give evidence because he always pleads guilty. (Lewis, Dobash, Dobash, & Cavanagh, 2000, p. 195)

Just because the legal procedures and rules of the courts are followed does not ensure that victims who appear before the court feel that justice has been done.

The Media

The media are one of the influences on how people picture and respond to victimization. A study of nearly 2,000 newspaper reports on violent incidents in Great Britain during 1992 showed that the stories emphasized female victims and offenders who were strangers to the victim (Naylor, 2001). Another assessment of newspaper stories about four highly-publicized sex crimes in the United States during the 1980s revealed that sexually suggestive language was used to describe crime victims, and there was more attention to crimes against white women than to crimes against women of color (Benedict, 1992). The stereotypes that are sometimes reinforced through community- and organization-level interactions are also reinforced by media coverage.

A specific example of coverage of an abusive husband's shooting of his wife and two of her friends during divorce proceedings illustrates how the media can present a story to emphasize a victim's responsibility or deservingness for being murdered (Consalvo, 1998). The story was about Tim Blackwell, who had seen his future wife's photograph in a catalog, *Asian Encounters*. After they had corresponded for a year, he had traveled to the Philippines and married her. Subsequently, he had been extremely abusive toward her, until the point at which she was in court to obtain a divorce. In describing the murder of Susan and two friends who were with her at the court, the *Seattle Times* emphasized Tim's and his lawyer's accusations that his wife, Susan Blackwell, whom he described as being involved in a mail-order-bride fraud, had duped him. The *Seattle Times* also inconsistently described Tim as in control of what he was doing and "snapping" because of his anger at his wife. In the Blackwell story and in an analysis of other coverage of domestic violence incidents, the press commonly presents violence against women as a response to the victims' provocation (Meyers, 1997). Specific to the Blackwell story, the *Seattle Times* emphasized that Susan was a foreigner from a very poor background, and this created the impression that she was marrying just in order to come to the United States. Coverage of Susan Blackwell's murder also focused on lax courtroom security, whereas alternative presses included separate stories on domestic abuse and pointed to Susan's ties to friends and family. News coverage sometimes portrays victims of domestic violence as precipitating acts against themselves and, in the case of Susan Blackwell, as taking advantage of their attackers.

Decisions About Victims of Gender-Related Crime

Although people in and outside the criminal justice system subject victims of gender-related crime to unique responses and think about gender as they interact with the victims and formulate their opinions and decisions about them, there is not always a clear translation into decisions about a case. In a classic study that showed this lack of connection, LaFree (1981) found that the "most important determinants of arrest, charge seriousness and felony screening were legal. Suspects experienced more serious outcomes when: (1) the victim was able to identify a suspect, (2) the victim was willing to testify, (3) the incident included sexual pene-tration, (4) charges were more serious, and (5) the incident included a weapon" (p. 582). Similarly, in 1992, spousal assaults and assaults by acquaintances and strangers in Victoria, Australia, were treated almost the same at the charging, plea, and sentencing stages (Laster & Douglas, 2000). The few differences were that, for the cases involving intimates, the charge and resulting conviction were more likely to be for *intentionally causing injury* rather than a less serious crime. However, when police and prosecutor case files were compared, there was more loss of infor-mation about the seriousness of harm done to the victim when an intimate was the offender. Also, charges were more often dropped for intimates who were offenders. Although there were few outcome differences for cases that came to court, the process was affected by an earlier bias toward less severe treatment of intimate part-ners who assaulted women. It may be that certain decisions are not affected by the stereotypes and ideologies of the decision maker, or that the effects of these beliefs occurred earlier in the criminal justice system process.

Research that shows no differences in the ultimate outcome of cases does not negate victims' experience of secondary victimization through interactions and reactions that are affected by gender ideologies, stereotypes, and assumptions. In one state, police who responded to questions about vignettes did not differ much from each other in whether they said they would make an arrest in response to domestic violence, but they did report a greater potential for responding to victims with hostility (Stith, 1990). Officers who were violent toward their own wives had much more negative views of abused woman victims; those who were experiencing marital stress and who did not buy into sex role egalitarianism also were more neg-ative. Some police apparently have a mind-set of anger toward women that results in negative response to female domestic abuse victims. They may make an arrest as required by law, but secondary victimization is still accomplished through their reactions.

Victims Exercising Agency

Because everyday violence, intimate-partner violence, sexual assault, and hate crime historically had been ignored and denied both in the legal system and more widely in society, it was important to clarify the extent of harm and to profile the worst case scenarios. Media coverage emphasizes cases of femicide and tends to ignore women who have successfully resisted abuse (Caringella-MacDonald & Humphries, 1998; Ptacek, 1999). The most common media conception is that the vast majority of crime victims are permanently disabled by their victim status. Also, fear of crime can be stimulated by constant media attention to violence.

Despite the theme of everyday violence that runs through women's lives, fear waxes and wanes, it is not universal, and women exercise their agency to set their envi-ronments up to reduce, if not eliminate, fear. For instance, women establish routines in how they use space within their neighborhoods or larger towns and cities, and in so doing they actively reclaim it from people who are threatening or annoying.

By their presence in urban space, women produce space that is more available not only for themselves but also for other women. Women's spatial confidence can be interpreted as a manifestation of power. Hence, at the level of the whole society, women's safety in public arguably is improved more by women going out than by them staying inside (Pain, 2001, p. 904).

Like "Take Back the Night" initiatives, for which people demonstrate by marching through areas after dark to reclaim them as safe from rape, individual initiatives to reclaim safe space depend on the level of gender equity and the related amount of power that potential victims have. However, there are many instances in which women and girls, and gay and lesbian and bisexual people, have, by their very presence, made safe places for themselves.

Turning to the aftermath of victimization, the psychiatric label of posttraumatic stress disorder (PTSD) has been the basis for some people thinking and acting as though all people victimized by violence cannot ever fully function. Even though the effects of trauma through victimization are serious and may be long lasting, most crime victims are neither fully nor permanently disabled, either physically or psychologically. The majority of childhood sexual abuse victims do not show severe symptomatology over the long term (Finkelhor, 1990; O'Dell, 1997). Similarly, although almost all victims of rape have PTSD in the weeks after the victimization, for most, there are no symptoms 2 years later (Rothbaum, Foa, Riggs, Murdock, & Walsh, 1992). A negative result of thinking that victims are incapable of constructive self-direction is the assumption that victims who *are* in control of their lives and emotions are not "convincing victims" (Lamb, 1999, p. 110). Another negative result is the belief that victims cannot reasonably be expected to act with agency, and thus decisions must be made for them.

Policies and interventions can increase crime victims' agency. The mere existence of a law and a process that are designed to stop domestic violence, even if that law and the process operate imperfectly, can be empowering. One Caribbean woman's effort to obtain a protection order "was deeply influenced by her ability to retain agency over the long process of negotiating with disparate actors and legal processes, including contending with the police, filing charges, sustaining adjournments, and telling her story to clerks and magistrates" (Lazarus-Black, 2000, p. 401). In the end, the court personnel made a mistake and failed to summon her husband to court for one crucial hearing, and her case was dismissed because her employer would not let her take additional time off from work. Another researcher, who studied a small Hawaiian town during the years when activists developed a woman-centered approach to domestic violence, also found that when cases came before the court, victims were reaffirmed in their right to protection, and offenders found themselves in a place that did not support their sense of male authority (Merry, 1995). The court appearance in itself was helpful to victims and addressed the power imbalance in the family. Finally, a study in New Haven, Connecticut, discovered that battered women felt empowered by virtue of judges and prosecutors listening to them when they sought restraining orders (Chaudhuri & Daly, 1992). Even when outcomes are not considered ideal, the existence of laws and legal procedures makes it possible for victims to take some steps to stop abuse, and if there is not secondary victimization, they can feel empowered because their desires are known and the illegality of abuse is publicly recognized.

Apart from legal interventions, for women abused by intimate partners, advocacy intervention by paraprofessionals (trained university undergraduate students) increases access to resources outside the justice system (C. M. Sullivan, Tan, Basta, Rumptz, & Davidson, 1992). Primary concerns of women who were leaving a battered women's shelter were material goods or services, for example, furniture or the assistance of a plumber, social support, education, transportation, financial help, legal assistance, health care, employment, and child care. Although they continued to have similar problems with abuse after 10 weeks, women who were assisted by advocates were able to access more community services than were others, and they felt better about their own actions to achieve their goals. After 2 years, women who had worked with advocates had a higher quality of life and social support, and they more easily obtained community resources (C. M. Sullivan & Bybee, 1999). Empowerment was promoted by altering their access to concrete services in the community.

When interventions take power and related decision control away from victims, the result is by definition disempowerment. For example, a key in recovery from victimization from incest is that women can choose when and how they use treatment and other types of assistance (Herman, 1992). It is important to recognize that crime victims are in some cases overwhelmed, much in need of advocacy, and physically and emotionally injured. However, it is just as important to understand and recognize that many are capable of being and want to be actively engaged in making their own decisions.

The Self-Directed Crime Victim

Theorists have brought into the spotlight information on how crime victims see themselves and their experience with crime, how they view and feel about justice system staff and other responders to them, and how they try to, and sometimes do, shape what happens after the crime. For victims of ongoing and oftentimes escalating domestic violence, there is quite a bit of practitioner and scholarly emphasis on why women remain in the relationship. Sometimes there are very obvious reasons, such as restricted access to divorce within religious or national groups (Gartner, Baker, & Pampel, 1990). U.S.-based organizations that assist abused women have highlighted the importance of "cultural factors that differentiate the family structure of immigrant families, the problem of tactics of control used by the abuser within the immigrant context such as the 'green card' factor, language barrier, and lack of information or access to support services" (Abraham, 1995, pp. 458–459).[41] Other influential and restricting reasons that women stay in abusive relationships include the desire to protect the future of children or to live in decent housing. Yet, even within the constraints, in a variety of ways, women do act to escape and prevent violence.

People who are victimized repeatedly by a spouse or other intimate partner typically are active decision makers. They quite accurately size up the seriousness and danger in relationships marked by violence, and they realize that they are most at risk for life-threatening abuse when they threaten to or actually try to leave their partners (Hamby, 1997, p. 347; Ptacek, 1999). Thus, they may stay in relationships or places that expose them to escalating abusive behavior against themselves or their children, pets, or other relatives because they know that if they try to leave, they and others will be in greater danger.

Victims of domestic violence think through whether or not they should call the police (Coulter, Kuehnle, Byers, & Alfonso, 1999, pp. 1290–1291). Fear of retaliation, prior unhelpful experiences with the police, and, as might be expected, prior experience with dual arrest all mitigate against calling the police in a particular situation. In light of the increasing risk of dual arrest and other negative outcomes of police intervention, women who do not call the police are not necessarily lacking agency (Bui, 2001; Haviland, Frye, Rajah, Thukral, & Trinity, 2001; M. E. Martin, 1997; S. L. Miller, 2001). Women in public housing face an additional problem, because a call to the police might alert public housing authorities to the violence, and no-tolerance policies for violence or drug involvement of any household members could be used to evict them (Vrettos, 2002). For a number of reasons, victims of domestic violence might anticipate or have experienced negative outcomes of police involvement, and therefore purposefully avoid police contact.

Despite the many reasons that domestic violence victims have for not calling the police, many do take this step, and the numbers are increasing over time (Rennison, 2001, p. 7). The proportion of female victims of intimate-partner violence who did report the crime to the police increased from 48% in 1993 to 58% in 1998. Men and women reported at similar levels in 1993, but women more often reported in 1998. Aside from calling the police, abused women seek help in other ways, especially if the abuse is escalating or repeated (Gondolf & Fisher, 1988, pp. 37–38). Most leave their partners, and many of them then seek restraining orders to prevent their abusers from coming after them (Ptacek, 1999). Not psychological strength, but material empowerment in the form of legal help, a job, education, money, child care, social support, and transportation are most important in women's decision to try to find help (M. A. Dutton, 1996, p. 112; C. M. Sullivan, 1991, p. 1). When women do seek help from the legal system, their purpose is primarily to obtain immediate and lasting protection (Lewis et al., 2000). Sometimes they feel that the experience of arrest and court proceedings, and occasionally programs mandated by the court, will reform their abusers' behavior. When women act to involve the justice system, they engage in a lengthy decision-making process, during which they weigh the potential for the benefits of safety and less abuse against the costs of seeking help.

Ethnic and racial minority groups within a country face some complex dilemmas as they figure out what to do about their own abuse and the abuse of family members (Haj Yahia, 2002). They may feel an allegiance with their abuser on the basis of race or ethnicity, or because they recognize potential bias against him by the justice system. Also, in many cultures, marriage has a very different meaning than in the European-origin U.S. culture. In Arabic and Asian countries, a marriage is an arrangement that ties together two families, and divorce or discord brings shame on the entire extended family. A woman has no significant social standing unless she is married, and children will not have a bright future if the family

Despite the many difficulties that women face when they leave an abusive relationship, an increasing number of women take this step. Here, a mother and her two sons who have suffered domestic violence leave their home carrying their belongings.

© Viviane Moos/CORBIS

is broken (Morash & Bui, 2002, p. 15). Women who separate from the abuser can lose their financial support, experience increased welfare department surveillance of and intervention in their families, and end up separated from family members, including the offender, who have in the past provided some help in a foreign environment (D. I. Martin & Mosher, 1995). The actual calculus that leads to an abused woman's decision must be understood so that one avoids the mistaken assumption that she is not acting with agency because she either stays in the relationship or does not contact the legal and criminal justice systems as sources of help.

When abuse occurs within a same-sex relationship, the same influences on staying together, such as financial dependence, can be operative. Another consideration is the further stigmatization that gay, lesbian, and bisexual people would feel, in addition to that already directed against them because of their sexual orientation, if they were to come forward publicly with the problem of abuse (J. D. Smith & Mancoske, 1999). Same-sex partners often share friends within a homosexual community, and if one partner reports abuse by the other, the friends may no longer support the victim (Giorgio, 2002). This can leave the victim without a community and with antagonism from community members who previously have been essential parts of a friendship network that addressed negative reactions and stigmatization directed against people who are gay, lesbian, or bisexual.

Many female victims of rape also are not so overcome by their experience that they cannot take many different steps to increase the chances of a positive outcome of their trials. Some figure out the dress and demeanor that will allow them to be seen as true victims, and they present themselves accordingly (Konradi, 1996). They may prepare themselves by doing library research.

> I was on the rampage of having this information, you know. . . . So I got a lot of information just from reading. I went to the library and found out about laws, um, the laws and what the defense attorneys could do, I mean, I read it in the [California Penal Code]. (quoted in Konradi, 1996, p. 421)

Rape victims rehearse their testimony, try to produce feelings and emotional displays that they feel will be appropriate in the courtroom, organize supportive people to be present at various stages of the trial, and locate and bring to court information to support their cases (Konradi, 1996). The activity and self-direction of women who have been raped contradicts notions of a total victim status that implies an inability to act on one's own behalf. Ironically, some people who have been victimized by rape recognize that to be seen as true victims, they must convince a jury and judge of their limited agency, and they act to fill the role of powerless victim. Others purposely speak and act in ways that contradict common stereotypes of women as "not real" rape victims.

Like victims of intimate-partner violence, victims of sexual assault exercise their agency by deciding not to report to the police. Overall, the reporting rates for sexual assault are very low, but there are some differences between cases that are and are not reported. Women most often report cases that involve serious injury (Felson, Messner, & Hoskin, 1999). For adults, juveniles, and children, reporting of sexual assaults is least likely when the victim knows the offender (Finkelhor & Ormrod, 1999; Hanson, Resnick, Saunders, Kilpatrick, & Best, 1999; Ruback, Menard, Outlaw, & Shaffer, 1999).[42] When the offender was a current or former husband or boyfriend, three quarters of victimizations were not reported to the police (Rennison, 2002, p. 3). For strangers, 54% of completed rapes, 44% of attempted rapes, and 34% of other types of sexual assaults were reported. Although the reporting rates were higher when assailants were not as well known or were strangers, the vast majority of cases still were not reported to the police.

There are many different reasons that individuals do not report sexual assaults. Female college students who had been sexually assaulted did not report incidents to the police when they thought that their actions, such as drinking before the assault, would be judged negatively by other people (Finkelson & Oswalt, 1995). Because alcohol consumption is involved in a large proportion of campus sexual assaults, many women therefore have doubts about being believed and even blame themselves for the assault (Koss, Gidycz, & Wisniewski, 1987). Moreover, assailants encourage self-blame as a way of getting away with rape (Pitts & Schwartz, 1993). When female victims know their assailants, they sometimes do not report because they fear retaliation by the offenders (Bachman, 1998; Greenfeld et al., 1998; Tjaden & Thoennes, 2000a). Also, some sexual assault victims feel embarrassed about being victimized or do not believe that reporting the assault would lead to an arrest (Bachman, 1998; Finkelson & Oswalt, 1995). Finally, victims consider the potential for secondary victimization in the justice system should they report sexual assault to the police (Coleman & Moynihan, 1996).

Victims also may not report because they do not define a sexual attack as a crime (Koss, 1988; Pitts & Schwartz, 1993), or they think that others will not believe that a crime occurred if it does not fit the **classic rape profile**. The typical rape has been erroneously depicted as being perpetrated by a male stranger against a female in an unfamiliar or deserted place, and as resulting in obvious physical injury to the victim (Weis & Borges, 1973). There is considerable evidence that when rapes do fit the classic profile, victims more often report them (Bachman, 1998; Finkelhor & Ormrod, 1999; Fisher, Daigle, Cullen, & Turner, 2003; Gartner & Macmillan, 1995; Pino & Meier, 1999). The two markers of classic rape that seem to be the most important are that force was used and that serious injury resulted (Du Mont, Miller, & Myhr, 2003). Female victims may themselves think that attacks that deviate from the classic rape scenario are not technically rape or illegal assault, or they may recognize that other people will not regard them as real. Both of these lines of reasoning can reduce reporting.

Men who are raped either by heterosexual males or within intimate relationships are least likely to report (Pino & Meier, 1999). There is limited research on their decision-making process, but the stigma of a male's being raped and being unable to fend off attackers, expectations of not being believed, and shame and embarrassment no doubt affect men's decisions.

Similar to victims of other gender-related crimes, stalking victims also consider expectations about appropriate behavior for females before engaging in interaction with criminal justice system professionals. Women who have experienced stalking are keenly aware of how people in the criminal justice system may see their responses to stalking as out of form for what women should do. They alter their actions to achieve their objectives for successful prosecution of the case (Dunn, 2002, p. 1).

By trying to act like a stereotypic real victim in order to obtain a positive outcome from the justice system, crime victims can present themselves in a way that reinforces stereotypes. Alternatively, some victims try to overcome the negative effects of stereotypes and erroneous assumptions about real victims and real crimes. For example, victims who think that criminal justice officials will not believe them because they delayed reporting a rape can provide the prosecutor with evidence that results in a conviction, despite the dissonance of late reporting with ideas about true victims (Konradi, 1996). One successful court outcome might influence prosecutors to take on future doubtful cases, which in the past they hesitated to do because of their assessment that there was little chance of a guilty verdict. Thus, patterns of interactions between criminal justice officials and victims can either reinforce stereotypes or challenge or change them.

Constraints on Agency

Even though people have agency at some times and in some places, there are limitations. Assuming consistently high levels of agency is as misleading as ignoring it. In many of the cases of exercise of agency that have been described, the forces limiting a person's actions are as apparent as the actor's capacity to act with intention.

A teenaged girl described what she considered to be consensual sexual involvement with an adult male:

> If you go out with an older guy, like, let's say it's not a good relationship and you know, you feel that you have to like, put on an act for, not an act, but you have to make them happy. Like you forget the fact that you are in a relationship, a two-way relationship, which means they have to make you happy also. And all you think about is, well, I have to make sure he's happy. I have to make sure I talk to him the right way. I have to make sure I'm living up to his standards. And then you start to lose sight of what a relationship is. (quoted in Phillips, 1999, p. 102)

Even though the girl has freely involved herself in a relationship, within that relationship she sees little choice about how to act and whether she can express her true feelings. The girl's choices are severely constrained by age and gender differences, which translate into power differences within the relationship.

Much of the talk about why people do not remove themselves from relationships in which they are repeatedly abused focuses on the need for people to move to independence. Of course, the possibility of being independent rests heavily on being able to obtain a job at a decent wage. In the United States, women of color with dependent children join Native American and poor black men as the groups with the least economic opportunity (Pollack, 2000, p. 73). Welfare legislation has been reformed to allow battered women to request a waiver from work requirements and the lifetime benefits limits on the basis that compliance would prevent women from leaving abusive relationships and endanger them. However, the reform left in place incentives from the federal government for the state to deny benefits in order to keep costs low, in most states there were not comprehensive screening procedures to establish eligibility for waivers, and women were not aware of their eligibility (S.A.D. Moore, 2003, p. 483). Recent welfare policy developments stand as an additional barrier to women's leaving abusive relationships.

Culture and class can limit conceivable reactions to victimization, particularly for gender-related victimizations, rape, and various forms of family violence. In South Korea, for example, being raped brings such shame on oneself and one's family that reporting is rare. There is a special crime with a Korean name that roughly translates to "family breaking." Perpetrators break into the home and steal valuables while a woman is there alone. Knowing that the shame of being raped will stop most women and their families from reporting to the police, they also rape the woman. Gender-related attitudes about being tarnished and spoiled by rape have a powerful influence on whether women will report or their families will encourage or support their doing this.

Ideas about appropriate masculine behavior can influence men not to report or talk about victimizations. Men in Great Britain reported being hesitant to report their own victimization and ask for help because such action would be inconsistent with "being men" (Stanko & Hobdell, 1993). One man said:

> Looking back on it, I wasn't really able to actually look at it in a way that would have been helpful . . . because the male bit in me said, "You ought to be able to

cope, you ought to be able to be strong enough to face aggression when necessary." . . . it's irrational. (quoted in Stanko & Hobdell, 1993, p. 404)

Gender identity mitigates against some actions and makes others more reasonable choices.

Too Much Criminal Justice System Involvement?

Between 1980 and 1996, a period during which most U.S. federal and state domestic violence legislation was passed and implemented, the U.S. arrest rate for aggravated assault increased substantially. The change is likely due to mandatory and presumptive arrest policies (Blumstein & Beck, 1999, p. 32). There are several rationales behind the increases in arrest. Criminal violations are crimes against the state, and the state should treat offenses uniformly. Victims might be intimidated by the offender to drop charges and not cooperate, and pro-arrest and pro-prosecution policies would taken the onus off the victim. In some cases, women who do not fully support arrest and prosecution later find that the outcome of being involved in the system is favorable for them. Finally, early research on policies that increased arrests for domestic violence, which have since been largely discredited (L. W. Sherman, Schmidt, et al., 1992), initially suggested that arrest had a deterrent effect.

Aggressive police intervention has been helpful to many women (Belknap & Hartman, 2000, p. 163; Stephens & Sinden, 2000). Also, widespread domestic violence training has made police rethink the assumptions that previously mitigated against arrest when the parties were involved in a homosexual relationship (Younglove, Kerr, & Vitello, 2002). Even though arrest has become the usual response to domestic violence in the United States, victims are not always satisfied. Prior to the institution of pro-arrest policies, women who were domestic violence victims were most satisfied when police honored their preferences regarding making an arrest, no matter what those preferences were, and even if there was a serious injury but they preferred no arrest (Buzawa & Austin, 1993). After the change in policies, women continued to favor being allowed to drop charges to improve their situations (Erez & Belknap, 1998, p. 260). At the same time that mandatory arrest and **no drop policies** make some women feel that they have lost control of what is to be done with the offender, victims cannot truly be empowered because of the current social welfare context, which is characterized by increasing scarcity of concrete help such as child care and welfare assistance (Landau, 2000, p. 155). When policy changes highlight women's extreme needs for protection, there is always the danger that domestic violence victims will be seen as needing protection for their own good, and gender inequities will be reproduced (Bush, 1992; C. M. Sullivan, 1991). There is no easy answer to the dilemma posed by the mixture of negative and positive benefits from increased arrest and prosecution as responses to domestic violence, because new policies have met the needs and desires of some victims at the same time that they have left others feeling more victimized.

Conclusion

Although social movements invested considerable energy into and altered responses to gender-related crime victims, community, organizational, and individual responses to victims perpetuate some level of secondary victimization. Specific responses to victims in the United States, which has a very decentralized and locally controlled justice system, are likely to depend heavily on the community and organizational context and on how fully local, state, and national activist groups have affected a locality.

The mid-level influences of community and organizational context on response to gender-related victimization are undertheorized and underresearched. More is known about macrolevel social movements and about individual-level beliefs and ideologies. What is not known is the degree to which individual-level beliefs and ideologies are reduced or overcome by community coordination and organizational and legal reforms. There is need for better understanding of how organizational and community change can alter or reproduce patterns in response to victims.

The ideologies and attitudes about gender and victimization that activists have tried to address still persist to some extent. However, research has not provided complete information on the amount of change (or continuity) in the beliefs held by medical, justice system, and other personnel. It is increasingly clear that beliefs about race, ethnicity, immigration, and sexual orientation interplay with beliefs about gender to influence how crime victims are treated. Efforts by the movement, the community, and organizations; backlash; and continued individual variation in thinking about gender and crime create a fluid dynamic in which the response to particular victims is quite unpredictable across times and locations.

Sometimes there are incongruities in the objectives of people working at different levels of influence. For example, feminist activists initially supported policies that encouraged or required arrest in domestic violence cases, because these policies affirmed the seriousness of harm and the victim's need of and right to legal intervention. However, at the level of individual interactions, for some victims the policies contradict their immediate desires, and victims feel they are disempowered by limited influence on police or prosecutor actions. This sort of tension gives rise to continuous critique and reassessment of the best policies to ensure justice where there is gender inequity in access to resources and freedom to act according to one's wishes.

Also, some organizational and individual influences lessen the effects of context. R. Campbell's (1998) research on responses to rape victims showed that not only the level of resources characteristic of the community context, but also individual-level characteristics of the victim and of the offense, contributed to how multiple systems responded. Women whose cases did not move far into the justice system were more often drinking alcohol just before the rape. Women who received help from the medical but not the justice system were more likely to have been raped by someone they knew and by someone without a weapon. Women who had been raped by an intimate, an acquaintance, or a person who was not using a weapon frequently received no help from any system. The no-service group also included women of color who had been raped by white men. Even in communities with resources explicitly dedicated to gender-related victimization, the judicial, medical, and mental health systems sort rape victims into those who are and are not deserving of or eligible for certain types of help. The justice system is most selective of the different types of agencies. Despite the important role that both activists and victim advocates have had in determining the nature of responses to gender-related victimization, theory points to persistent and newly discovered forces and patterns of interaction that maintain gender inequities.

Key Terms

Benevolent sexist beliefs

Blame and believability factors

Classic rape profile

Coordinated community responses

Court talk

Dual arrest

Green card factor

No drop policies

Peacemaking model of justice

Restorative justice model

Violent stranger myth

Review and Discussion

1. What types of organizational or community change strategies might be undertaken to counteract the persistent negative influence of some individual beliefs, common ideologies, and stereotypes on responses to victims of gender-related crime?

2. What are the different ways that communities try to deliver a coordinated response to crime victims?

3. What are the pros and cons of expanding coordinated responses to gender-related victimization before additional evidence of the effectiveness of different models is available?

4. What rationales do people use to justify their conclusions that people claiming victimization are not, indeed, real victims?

5. Is the distinction between victims and offenders helpful in understanding the behavior of individual people who break the law or who are victimized? Does it promote justice?

6. Discuss the degree to which victims of gender-related crime have agency, and the potential for increasing that agency through empowerment.

Web Sites to Explore

Most states have coalitions that work to stop sexual assault and domestic violence. In some states—for example, Michigan—a coalition that addresses both types of violence has posted information on how to develop and improve a coordinated community response to domestic violence. www.mcadsv.org/mrcdsv/CCR.html

The Tribal Court Clearinghouse maintains a Web site on domestic violence among Native Americans. www.tribal-institute.org/lists/domestic.htm

CHAPTER 6

Explanations
of Illegal Behavior

C hapter 3, "Gender-Related Victimization," presented statistics on a well-established pattern of males' disproportionate involvement in violence. Those statistics were based on the reports of a national sample of people over the age of 12 who reported on their victimization. Other studies that gather information on self-reported involvement in illegal behavior and on individuals who are involved in the justice system have also shown that girls and women break the law less often than boys and men, and when they do break the law, they are generally less violent (Dell & Boe, 1998; Duffy, 1996; Elliott, Huizinga, & Menard, 1989; Maguire & Pastore, 1997; Osgood, Johnston, O'Malley, & Bachman, 1988; Snyder & Sickmund, 1999; U.S. Department of Health and Human Services, 2001; Wolfgang, Thornberry, & Figlio, 1987). In the United States, even though there is some narrowing of the gap in rates of crime by females and males (Heimer, 2000; U.S. Department of Health and Human Services, 2001), women and girls still exhibit markedly lower levels of serious crime and violence than do men and boys. Females and males are most similar in offenses that do not involve violence, such as theft and the use of alcohol and drugs.

Despite considerable research showing that girls are less violent than are boys, some people have concluded that, in fact, girls are equally aggressive. The reasoning to support the conclusion is that girls show their aggression differently than do boys, and that the alternative forms of aggression are increasing. A book titled *Odd Girl Out: The Hidden Culture of Aggression in Girls* (Simmons, 2002) sets forth the argument that girls are just as aggressive as are boys. Working as a journalist, Simmons visited 10 schools across the United States and talked to girls of different ethnic and class backgrounds. White girls in particular told her about rampant competition and jealousy that led girls to be emotionally and even physically abusive against each other. Research has shown the damaging effects of girls' negative looks and gestures that are intended to hurt and exclude other girls (Underwood,

2004). The conclusions of *Odd Girl Out* have been confirmed by social scientists, who have written that girls are just as aggressive as boys if nonphysical aggression is considered (Crick & Grotpeter, 1995).

Should there be sanctions against nonphysical aggression? Clearly, nasty faces are not illegal, so any sanctions would be outside the purview of the formal justice system. There are other reasons for being cautions about imposing either formal or informal sanctions against girls' covert aggressive behavior. Many girls are socialized to be conciliatory and to avoid conflict so that they are not excluded from relationships and are not disliked by other people (Brown & Gilligan, 1993; Underwood, 2003; Zahn-Waxler, 2000). Indirect acts are sometimes the only way that girls can express their anger. As one psychologist put it, "There is reason to question any approach that potentially serves to discourage females from expressing anger and aggression and reminds them of their subordinate positions in society" (Zahn-Waxler, 1993, p. 81). Also, although some studies find that girls exhibit more relational aggression than do boys, other studies reveal no gender differences (Crick & Collins, 2002; Crick & Grotpeter, 1995; Rys & Bear, 1997). Some studies show greater relational aggression by boys, partly because they sexually harass girls and because they are aggressive in dating relationships (Hennington, Hughes, Cavell, & Thompson, 1998; McMaster, Connolly, Pepler, & Craig, 2002). There may be justification for encouraging and teaching both females and males to express their feelings assertively but not aggressively, but there is not clear justification for zeroing in on girls' social interactions as highly aggressive.

For adult women, except for murder, the gender gap in illegal behavior did shrink between 1960 and 1997 (Heimer, 2000), but it still persists:[43]

- Larceny declined for both genders, but the female rates dropped off gradually and the male rates dropped off more sharply.
- For forgery, female rates increased but male rates declined somewhat.
- For embezzlement, arrests of females increased, but arrests for males declined between the late 1980s and 1995.

For the serious property crimes of burglary, motor vehicle theft, receiving stolen property, and arson, there has been a very slight or no decline in women's arrest rates, but a modest decline in men's rates of arrests.

The extensive and consistent research findings about the differences in the patterns of females' and males' illegal activity are the basis for asking several questions about gender and the causes of crime. Why are boys and men more likely (than are girls and women) to be violent and to commit serious offenses? Why are the types of offenses that females commit different from the types that males commit? Why is there a narrowing of the gap between males' higher rates of property crimes and women's lower rates? Why do some girls and women break from the norm and carry out violent illegal acts or other serious types of illegal behavior? The theories that are included in this chapter consider gender as a key concept that can be used to answer these questions.

Gender conceptualized at multiple levels of influence explains patterns of illegal activity. At the macro level, gender has its effect through differences in beliefs about how females and males should act, work opportunities, and access to influence and resources. Intermediate-level explanations concentrate on community context, family, peers, specific life events, and other influences that combine to promote certain patterns of lawbreaking over the course of a person's life. At the level of the individual, a person's gender identity is relevant to crime and delinquency. People generally act consistently with how they see and define themselves. At the same time that they have agency, they also are constrained and conditioned by their history and by their social location. Finally, there is evidence of biological influences on illegal activity. Advances in theory linking gender to crime causation are discussed in this chapter under subheadings that reflect the different levels of influence: the macro level, especially *economic marginalization;* intermediate influences over the *life course*, including community, family, and peer groups; and the individual-level influence of *gender identity*. Community and family contexts and opportunities for both legal and illegal action can affect gender identity, and regardless of context, people do make independent choices. Recent biological explanations for illegal behavior are considered in a separate section.

At the macro level, the bulk of criminological literature has neglected the force of economic marginalization in stimulating women's and girls' lawbreaking, though feminist theorists have worked to correct this neglect. Life course theorists have concentrated on the development of delinquency and crime through experiences that people have at different life stages and in different contexts. With but a few exceptions, they have concentrated on males. However, there is a small but compatible body of research that describes not girls' and women's life courses, but the similar idea of pathways through which girls and women move toward engaging in (or desisting from) illegal behavior. Theorists who focus on identity have most directly addressed the influence of gender on delinquency and crime, though the preponderance of what we know is about how males with certain definitions of masculinity use particular types of crime to live up to ideas about being "real men." Less is known about the connection of women's and girls' gender identity to their illegal behavior. Advances in understanding biological influences on human behavior are just recently being integrated into explanations of crime and delinquency. The sections below present data-grounded and innovative explanations of the connection of gender, conceptualized at multiple levels, and of biology to the patterns and the nature of illegal behavior.

Economic Marginalization

A dominant explanation of males' criminality and delinquency is that when there are not legitimate means to obtain money, boys and men seek the financial rewards of illegal activity. At the individual level, many theories about males' breaking the law have emphasized the stresses and strains associated with difficulties achieving economic success. For example, drug trafficking, especially given the ease of entry into the crack cocaine market, provides financial rewards for people without other ways to earn a living (Block & Block, 1993). Male gang members work in illegal enterprises when they cannot feasibly enter legitimate markets (Hagedorn, 1988; Padilla, 1992). As a final example, a study of boys in the three New York City neighborhoods showed how illegal and legitimate opportunities, race, and ethnicity came into play as influences on boys' delinquency (M. L. Sullivan, 1989). African American boys from housing projects, who were most restricted in legitimate access to money, solved their economic problems by robbery, often away from the neighborhood because project residents could identify them. Latino immigrant boys who lived in a desolate neighborhood dotted with factories and warehouses turned to joy riding in stolen cars, and eventually to professional car theft to supply parts to local auto-repair shops. White working-class boys started out with delinquent behavior similar to that of the other groups, but as they grew older, they relied on relatives and neighbors to obtain legal part-time jobs. Some of them eventually began stealing from the workplace. The local communities provided a cultural milieu that was consistent with particular options for "getting paid," and individual differences affected the choices that particular boys made, including abstinence from illegal activity. However, because groups of boys in each community did have a similar pattern of delinquency, they reinforced and reproduced the culture of the community. For males, many different theorists have explained illegal behavior as the result of economic opportunities and motivations, both of which vary depending on racial, ethnic, and immigrant group status.

Fewer theorists have emphasized economic realities, illegal opportunities, or cultural adaptations to economic conditions that influence women and girls to size up and choose illegal options when they want or need resources (Naffine, 1987). The idea that economic struggle and motivation explain women's lawbreaking opened the door for a critique of gender-related economic inequities and for recommending policies and reforms to address these inequities. The attention to race and ethnicity in neighborhood contexts reinforced the importance of intersections of gender with other differentiating characteristics as influences on women's lives.

An example from Jamaica illustrates the international dimension of economic motivations to break the law and women's criminality (Sudbury, 2002). African Caribbean women are held in jails and prisons for drug smuggling in the United States, Great Britain, and other countries. One Jamaican woman explained:

> They do it mainly for the kids, to support the kids. You have a mother who has four or five kids, two is very sickly, every time she visit the hospital or the doctor, you have to pay to register, you have to pay for medicine, you have to pay for an X-ray. Everything costs money. So anything comes up they're going to jump at it, the easiest way to make money. (Sudbury, 2002, p. 67)

Of course, some of the women who smuggle drugs have different motivations— for example, a desire to assist a man who is supplying the drugs—and some are even unaware that goods they transport include illegal drugs. However, in many countries, women have been burdened disproportionately by financial strains because they are the sole source of support for their children and sick or elderly relatives. In the United States, several policy changes in the 1980s reduced women's access to legitimate decent-paying jobs. These policy changes include "cutbacks on public sector employment, the scaling back of local government services, health and education, increases in the cost of public utilities . . . , and a dramatic decline in real wages" (Sudbury, 2002, p. 69).

Economic motivation to exchange sex for money has been linked to national settings in which women are expected to assume full responsibility for children should the children's fathers not provide support and where the labor market is segmented so that women have only the lowest-paying jobs available to them. In Sri Lanka, women had few legal rights and had heavy responsibilities for children, with the result that many of them turned to prostitution as a way to earn money (J. Miller, 2002). An additional problem in Sri Lanka is that women who have been married are not seen as "pure," so remarriage is unlikely, as is marriage for girls and women who are not virgins. Without the benefits of marriage, prostitution becomes an economic solution to problems of basic survival.

Before reviewing additional evidence of economic explanations of women's criminality, this chapter will add information on women's economic inequality to what was provided in Chapter 3.

A resident of Chile, 23-year-old Pamela has four children. First pregnant at the age of 14, she wants to raise her youngest children herself while another family member looks after her two eldest children. She currently lives with the father of the two youngest children, and he is unaware of her work as a prostitute. Her mother is a former prostitute, and she baby-sits the children while her daughter goes out to work.

© Elisa Haberer/CORBIS

Public Policy and Women's Poverty

In the United States, the trend has been and continues to be to reduce welfare assistance. Welfare policies have undergone a nationwide overhaul, beginning with the 1996 federal welfare reform legislation, the Personal Responsibility and Work Opportunity Reconciliation Act, which replaced Aid to Families with Dependent Children with a state block grant system, the Temporary Assistance to Needy Families. The new legislation eliminated any entitlement to federal cash assistance, set time limits for financial aid, and allowed states the discretion to emphasize work rather than cash transfers for families in need. The results are that more of the poor are working, and there is less flexibility to obtain education and training during the period when welfare benefits are available. Thus, fewer people can move from welfare to a job that will lift them out of poverty. Because women with children are major beneficiaries of welfare assistance, the move from welfare to employment has concentrated women in traditionally female jobs with limited stability of employment and few or no medical or other benefits (Peterson, Zong, & Jones-DeWeever, 2002). Women who are single heads of households and their sons and daughters are most adversely affected. Requirements that mothers who receive public assistance leave welfare for work have destabilized their housing arrangements, increased homelessness, and resulted in hunger for them and their children (Burnham, 2001). Women and children have been constrained in neighborhoods characterized by having few legitimate opportunities to earn money, increased illegitimate opportunities, and limited and strained public health, mental health, and educational services.

Women who obtain public benefits and those who are counted among the working poor struggle to cover basic expenses for food and housing. Even if they are

A Seattle, Washington, neighborhood with few legitimate opportunities to earn money and limited social and educational services.

© Paul Edmondson/Getty Images

receiving welfare, most work very hard to meet rent, food, clothing, and transportation costs. Many spend considerable time seeking out charitable support, doing odd jobs, and using other time-consuming strategies to make ends meet. Women working in low-paying jobs may actually fare worse than those on welfare, because they lose Medicaid for their children after a year of not receiving welfare, they have work-related expenses, and their time to seek help from charitable organizations is limited (Edin & Lein, 1997). One woman described why she sold crack to supplement the income she received making 10 dollars an hour as a sporadically employed nursing assistant:

> Even though I have a good job when I work and stuff like that, it's hard raising two kids by yourself. . . . [Y]ou get used to having money every day and you don't have to worry about the electric being off or the rent being paid . . . I'm not going to McDonald's. McDonald's is not going to pay my rent. That's what they want you to do. I have two kids to support. Where am I going to live with them? In a shelter, making five dollars an hour. I'm not going to subject my kids to something like that. I'd rather just do my prison time if I have to do it and get rid of all of this. (Ferraro & Moe, 2003, p. 20)

The woman who preferred to go to prison rather than work for a low wage that could only support her living in a shelter did not see welfare support as an option. Prior to welfare reform, many women opted to receive welfare instead of being part of the working poor, because they could not obtain medical care for themselves or their children if they did work.

Welfare support has decreased because of the reforms. Before welfare reform, women surveyed in Boston, Chicago, Charleston, and San Antonio uniformly reported that welfare benefits needed to be supplemented by other sources of income to meet basic expenses (Edin & Lein, 1997). Many women violated welfare agency policies by working at jobs without approval, thereby committing welfare fraud. Smaller proportions of women (between 2% and 19%, depending on the city) supplemented their incomes with illegal activities, such as dealing drugs or prostitution. The source of supplementary income depended heavily on the availability of legitimate jobs. One unmarried, 25-year-old former drug offender relied on public assistance and temporary agency work as her only sources of income. She described her struggle to regain custody of her three children, obtain work, and find suitable housing:

> The worst part is now I have lots of [criminal] charges, so no one wants to hire me. When I get my kids back, no one will want to rent to us. No one will believe I am going straight and it will be hard to find a suitable place. I cannot pay for the deposits, application fees, rent and utilities and still support everyone by making $6 an hour . . . so I might have to do some stealing and [selling] drugs again. (Holtfreter & Morash, 2001)

Welfare reform, coupled with a faltering economy during a downturn or for an extended period, create the conditions in which some women turn to illegal opportunities to make money.

The reality of poverty that is concentrated on women and juveniles, and its link to criminality, highlights the importance of theories that connect women's criminality to economic realities. Current public policies, which if fully implemented will require every mother who is not disabled to work after receiving welfare for 2 years, make it all the more important to understand this connection.

Economic Marginalization and Women's Criminality

Women's worsening economic situation, reflected by increased divorce rates, formation of female-headed households, fathers' failure to support their children, and the segregation of women in low-paying, traditionally female occupations—a constellation of situations referred to as the **feminization of poverty**—is tied to their increased involvement in consumer-based crimes, such as shoplifting and welfare fraud (Steffensmeier & Streifel, 1992). The most economically disadvantaged cities in the United States have the highest rates of homicide, aggravated assault, burglary, and larceny by both women and men (Steffensmeier & Haynie, 2000). The connection of economic disadvantage to crime is stronger for men, particularly for homicide involving strangers. Being a woman does not, however, negate the connection of economic marginalization to breaking the law. It is therefore critical to keep economic marginalization in the picture for explaining women's criminality, but to additionally consider other theories (for example, theories about pathways into crime and theories about identity) as useful explanations of the connection of gender to crime. We need to understand why women are similarly affected, but not as much affected, by the economic conditions that influence men's illegal actions.

Women's increasing representation among poor people in the United States suggests that over time, the ratio of the rate of females' offending to the rate of males' offending will become smaller; that is, that the gender gap in crime would narrow. The narrowing of the gender gap results from an increased prevalence of female-headed households, a persisting gender gap between the wages of high school–educated workers, increases in the unemployment of female heads of households, and the erosion of welfare (Heimer, 2000). In other words, there is a direct tie between the feminization of poverty and the decreasing gap between women's and men's rates of nonviolent economic crimes.

Neighborhood Context

One way that economic disadvantage affects criminality is through neighborhood context. In particular, the context of poor, socially disorganized neighborhoods with inadequate education, inadequate job training, and lack of sustainable community-level employment can promote involvement in an alcohol- or drug-related lifestyle (Wilson, 1996). African American women and their children are disproportionately residentially segregated in poor areas, particularly for female-headed households. At the same time that African American women bear the brunt of gender-related victimization, they disproportionately experience limited choices for supporting themselves and their children and for keeping their families safe in crime-ridden communities.

In the neighborhood contexts of the truly disadvantaged, substance abuse, prostitution, and other crime can perpetuate each other. Women become involved **in the lifestyle** (Mancuso & Miller, 2000). Economically motivated prostitution promotes drug use as a way to handle stress and stigmatization, and the cost of drug use requires the financial rewards of prostitution. In turn, drug dependency creates the motivation for illegal activity that involves women in the underworld and criminal subcultures, which then increases exposure to deviant networks that provide support and opportunity for more illegal activity. Women in the drug economy, especially crack cocaine dealers, commit some violent acts to survive on the streets when they are attacked by robbers or competitors for business (Kruttschnitt, 2001). The physical threat from other dealers, customers, and suppliers stimulates the adaptive use of violence for protection of self and property (Baskin & Sommers, 1998). Individual differences along with local variations, like the unavailability of deviant networks, can lessen the relationship between economic marginalization and crime, but overall there is a connection.

There is some debate about whether the ease of manufacturing and selling crack opened unprecedented opportunities for women to sell drugs in some settings (Baskin & Sommers, 1998), or whether gender, race, and ethnicity limit girls' and women's entry into the drug economy (Maher, 1997). On one hand, during the crack cocaine epidemic in New York City, a group of African American teenage girls and young women from a disadvantaged area sold drugs and committed violent crimes (Baskin & Sommers, 1998). One woman described her economic motivation to sell cocaine:

> I had lots of little jobs, but selling cocaine was always how I really made my living. My last job was, I was 18, I was a receptionist at a showroom. I was there maybe 1 year. It was okay. But I was already into selling cocaine. I started that much earlier when my father went to jail. I knew my father was selling coke. . . . And I felt that as my duty as taking care of my family I started selling coke. Now, I'd be selling for about 7 years. I went up and down. I could make $500. I could make $3000 a week. . . . I never stood on the corner and sold bags or anything like that . . . I was selling ounces with some Colombians. They became like my suppliers and stuff. I started like with myself; when my father came out I started like working with him. Then I stopped working in offices altogether. (Baskin & Sommers, 1998, p. 89)

The economic motivation to sell drugs placed women in situations where it was necessary to commit violent acts in response to robbery or aggressive competitors for business (Baskin & Sommers, 1998; Kruttschnitt, 2001). On the other hand, observation of a very active drug market in Brooklyn, New York City, confirmed that in that setting, men nearly totally dominated the managerial and supervisory activities in the network that distributed drugs (Maher, 1997, p. 87). Even when women were involved, their opportunities for higher-level involvement in the drug market depended on support from a male partner (Koester & Schwartz, 1993). One woman explained:

I moved up to Harlem, and um, I hooked up with this guy that was selling heroin. We used to get the quarter bag, and we used to cut it, and the shit used to be good. So I used to tap the bags, the quarter bags. . . . I didn't know I had a chippy (mild habit) till like about three years later, when he finally found out that I was messing with it—and all that time he trusted me. And I was handling the money and everything; everything was right there with me. But as soon as he found out that I was messing with it, it was like I was cut off. (Maher, 1997, p. 88)

In the New York City drug market, when women worked selling drugs, they were usually temporarily allowed involvement because "men were arrested or refused to work or . . . it was 'hot' because of police presence" (Maher, 1997, p. 88). The ease of entry was limited by gender-related differences in power and influence in the particular neighborhood context, and one result was that women were not as violent as were men.

Also in Brooklyn, the intersections of gender, race, and ethnicity shaped the opportunities that women had to earn money illegally and affected their support networks (Maher, 1997, pp. 177–189). The neighborhood was predominantly Latino, and Dominican men controlled drug distribution. Latinas from the neighborhood were involved in prostitution. Because they lived in the neighborhood, most started out by informally arranging with acquaintances to provide sex for money. Even when they worked on the streets, they often had connections to kin and friends in the area. African American and European American women had a history of working as prostitutes, were not from the area, and had previously worked and currently worked with a pimp. The European Americans could command higher prices for prostitution because of the prejudices and preferences of potential customers. Both African and European American women blamed local Latinas who were addicted to crack for the low market prices for sex, and thus they resented them. Aside from gender-related lack of opportunity, cultural prohibitions and stigmatization restricted Latinas involvement in selling drugs (also see G. Moore, 1992). European American women were restricted because they looked "out of place" in the neighborhood context, so they were considered to be too vulnerable to police detection to sell drugs. Although each racial and ethnic group of women that Maher studied faced illegal work opportunities that were limited by gender, the particular reasons for the limitations and results were different depending on whether they were European American, African American, or Latina. As might be expected, cross-group social support was most common for African and European American women. The two groups from outside the area were unified by their blame of Latinas for lowering the price of sex work. Race and ethnicity would be expected to have different effects on opportunities for illegal work depending on the local context, but in many settings they change the effects of gender. It is critical to consider women in the neighborhood context where they work or live. Otherwise, it is impossible to see the patterns of inclusion and exclusion.

White-Collar Crimes at the Workplace

Many women who on the surface may not seem to be economically marginalized do commit white-collar crimes at work because of financial strains. Many men but few women who were before several federal courts in the 1980s for white-collar crimes (bank embezzlement, income tax fraud, postal fraud, credit fraud, false claims and statements, bribery, and all antitrust and securities fraud) fit the profile of highly placed, powerful, financially well-off employees (Daly, 1989a). The majority of women white-collar criminals were clerical workers, and compared to their male counterparts, they were more often nonwhite, without a college education, and with few economic assets. Financial problems provided motivation to break the law.

There are additional gender differences in white-collar criminals and their behaviors (J. M. Collins & Collins, 1999). Among federal prisons, women tended to be other- rather than self-motivated. Unlike the men, women typically committed their offenses because loved ones (husbands, parents, or children) were in financial trouble or had health care–related financial needs. Their capacity for empathy was similar to that for non-offending women in similar managerial positions. In fact, their empathy with loved ones in need of financial help often motivated their offending behavior. Women's greater orientation toward caring for others (Gilligan, 1982) sets them apart from men who commit similar white-collar crimes.

The gendered dimension of the white-collar crime phenomenon is clear only when the label is unpacked to show the relative disadvantage that women in the category have relative to similarly categorized men. Compared with men, the women tend to experience gender disadvantages in the workplace and often are motivated to meet the needs of others through their illegal behavior.

Public Policy and Involvement in Crime

The connection between crime rates and the size of the disadvantaged population is weaker in metropolitan areas with high levels of welfare assistance (Hannon & Defronzo, 1998). Consistent with this research finding, for women offenders in two U.S. cities, poverty was the most significant predictor of recidivism (Holtfreter, Reisig, & Morash, 2002). Women who lived in poverty were almost 5 times as likely to be rearrested, and they were 12 times as likely as other women to be probation or parole violators. After 12 months, obtaining public assistance was by far the strongest predictor of desistance from criminal activity (Morash, Holtfreter, & Reisig, 2002). The research on criminality and poverty raises serious questions about the potential effectiveness of policies that maintain welfare assistance below subsistence levels and force increased numbers of women into low-paying jobs.

Consistent with findings about the connection of obtaining public assistance to desistance from criminal activity, when the Supplemental Security Income program was terminated for individuals who were addicted to drugs or alcohol, individuals' criminality increased (Swartz, Martinovich, & Goldstein, 2003). Previously, Supplemental Security Income and treatment were available because addiction was considered a type of disability. For those who were disqualified and who did not have another qualifying disability, there were moderate increases in crime, especially for drug and property offenses. The increased drug use was highest 6 months after loss of benefits, and the other illegal activity was highest at the 2-year point after loss of benefits. The policy change produced a crime-prone population of drug users with limited access to treatment.

Parallel to policy trends in the United States, in Great Britain, girls' economic choices have been severely restricted by policy changes in the last few decades. Youth aged 16 and 17 can no longer claim social security benefits, and the rate for benefits has been reduced for people under 25 years old. There also have been cutbacks in training programs, people 18 and under are excluded from the minimum wage protection, and housing costs have risen. The result has been increased youth involvement in such illegal activities as shoplifting, begging, drugs, and—for young women especially—prostitution (Phoenix, 2002, p. 71). In and outside the United States, reductions in public benefits have created conditions conducive to crime for women and girls. Public policy is an important variable that explains illegal behavior.

Questions Answered by Macrolevel Explanations

Poverty-based explanations of illegal behavior address the question of why some women break the law for economic gain. Public policies, such as cuts in welfare benefits, also appear to explain some increases in girls' and women's breaking the law for economic gain. More than for men, women's white-collar crime can be explained by their economic needs. Their motivation, more often than for male white-collar offenders, is meeting the needs of loved ones. Just as women are marginalized from the legitimate economy, they are marginalized within the illegal economies that operate within some impoverished neighborhoods. This second marginalization explains why females commit different sorts of offenses than do males. Thus, macrolevel explanations shed light on why males and females break the law in different ways. The macrolevel explanations do not, however, explain the lower rate of serious offending among girls and women. We must look to contextual and individual-level explanations to address those questions.

The Life Course and Pathways Perspectives

Life course theories have challenged and corrected explanations for delinquency and crime that do not attend to the timing and sequencing of potential influences on an individual's illegal behavior. In a **life course theory**, a combination of events, context, and characteristics—including age and the related concept of stage in development—ultimately influences whether or not a person breaks the law, continues breaking it, or stops. Key events at particular points in time can start or interrupt a trajectory in a pattern of delinquency or adult offending. Life course theory identifies those key events, circumstances, and conditions that influence people to differ in whether or not they engage in illegal behaviors over time and in the nature of any lawbreaking.

Life course theorists who focus on delinquency work primarily from a psychological or social psychological child development perspective. Although they sometimes concentrate on behavior that is officially considered to be delinquent, they generally subsume delinquency under broader concepts, including aggression and what is called **conduct disorders** (also referred to as *antisocial behavior*).

Conduct disorders are indicated by some of a set of aggressive behaviors, including aggression to people and animals (such as bullying or intimidating others and stealing from victims while confronting them), destruction of property, deceitfulness along with lying or stealing, and serious violations of rules set by the family or school.

Girls may follow a unique gender-related *delayed-onset pathway* to delinquency and, unlike boys, rarely exhibit what is called *childhood onset conduct disorder* (Silverthorn & Frick, 1999).[44] Some boys' delinquency is the end result of a *childhood onset* pathway, in which conditions present in childhood spark a pattern of antisocial behavior while the youth are young. These conditions include cognitive and neuropsychological deficits, dysfunctional family environments, and the child's callous and unemotional interpersonal style. Girls with the same negative family conditions or individual characteristics as the boys who are labeled as having conduct disorder in childhood do not typically act in an antisocial way before adolescence. However, they are *more* likely than boys with a similar background to be antisocial during adolescence (Silverthorn & Frick, 1999).

The distinction between *childhood* and *adolescent onset* antisocial behavior may have important practical implications for girls. Even if girls have problems and backgrounds that are related to antisocial behavior in boys, some research has shown that almost no girls are antisocial during their childhoods (Silverthorn & Frick, 1999). Almost all of the girls who had behavior that was categorized as antisocial in adolescence had negative outcomes, including arrest, when they were adults (Silverthorn & Frick, 1999). Because girls with predispositions and family experiences that are predictive of continuing and increasingly serious criminality after adolescence rarely have preadolescent behavior problems, it is likely that high-risk girls do not receive special educational and family-oriented programming or interventions available to similarly predisposed and situated boys.

With but a few exceptions, life course theorists have emphasized the structural, family, and neighborhood contexts that shape boys' delinquency. In contrast, **pathways theory** and research has paid attention to the effect of sexual and other victimization and of relationships with other people who support crime, especially relationships to men who are intimate partners and/or sexual exploiters, on girl's and women's criminality. This emphasis in the pathways research is justified by the higher incidence of abuse among girls and women than among males, as well as the later onset of females' illegal behavior, which often begins in adolescence or early adulthood.

Girls' and Women's Pathways Into Delinquency and Crime

Observations, case studies, and intensive interviews that expose pathways into illegal activity provide the most detailed, direct, and humanistic picture of contexts, events, and choices over the life course that result in some girls and women breaking the law. Available data in court and other agency records also can be pieced together to provide detailed pictures of women's lives.

Daly (1992) analyzed presentence investigations for a federal court to develop a framework for differentiating the ways that women's lives lead up to an incident or a pattern of illegal activity.

- *Streetwomen* had been severely abused in childhood, lived on the streets, and were in court for crimes related to supporting their drug habit, for instance selling drugs, prostitution, and stealing.
- Like streetwomen, *harmed and harming women* were abused as children, but they responded with anger and acting out; for some, the use of alcohol or drugs contributed to their violence.
- *Battered women* typically had little or no criminal record, and they had harmed or killed men who had violently attacked them or threatened to do so.
- *Drug-connected women* used or sold drugs as a result of relationships with a male intimate, children, or their mothers, and also had a limited criminal record.
- *Economically motivated women* committed crimes to cope with poverty or out of greed.

Daly's typology pinpointed key gender-related influences on crime. These include childhood abuse, victimization by intimate partners, and the central role of relationships with men.

Childhood Abuse

Chesney-Lind (1989; Chesney-Lind & Rodriguez, 1983) drew attention to the effect of childhood victimization, particularly sexual abuse, as the starting point for girls' eventual involvement as offenders in the juvenile and later the adult justice systems. Many abused girls and young women who have run away from home, often after the courts failed to stop the abuse, become involved in prostitution or petty property crimes in order to survive (Chesney-Lind & Rodriguez, 1983). Although the outcome for abused girls is not always running away and living on the streets, when it is, some of those with no marketable skills continue to support themselves with illegal activities in adulthood. Criminality can be the outcome of what are sometimes lengthy histories of abuse and the failure of the juvenile courts to help girls, and the girls' continuing attempts to escape abuse and survive away from home (R. Arnold, 1990; Chesney-Lind, 1997).

Qualitative data from one recent study clearly illustrated the role of past victimization in girls' delinquency and subsequently in adult women's criminality. For a 20-year old woman, who was currently drug-free and participating in a women's support group for former prostitutes, the pathway into illegal activity began with sexual abuse by a relative. After her repeated unsuccessful attempts to stop the abuse ("no one believed me"), she ran away and sought protection, food, and a place to stay by joining a prostitution ring. The pimp who provided housing was physically abusive and encouraged her to begin using crack cocaine. She reported that after she became addicted at the age of 14, she would do anything for her pimp to get his drugs, she didn't know what else to do, and she could not go home (Holtfreter & Morash, 2001).

Some girls run away from home to escape abuse. Later, they become involved in illegal activity in order to survive on the streets, and some use drugs and alcohol to deal with their distress.

© Kevin Horan/Getty Images

The causal connection of sexual abuse and chronic traumatization to running away, followed by illegal activity, is strongly supported by additional research on women engaged in prostitution. In several parts of the world, between 60% and 90% of prostituting women have been sexually assaulted as children (Farley & Kelly, 2000). One woman provided a poignant, from-the-streets assessment:

> We've all [the prostitutes] been molested. Over and over, and raped. We were all molested and sexually abused as children, don't you know that? We ran to get away. They didn't want us in the house anymore. We were thrown out, thrown away. We've been on the street since we were 12, 13, 14. (Boyer, Chapman, & Marshall, 1993, p. 16)

Some women and girls react to their own criminal victimization by escaping from abuse into a lifestyle marked by illegal behavior and continued abuse by others.

Victimization of children also is connected to their involvement in illegal behavior through the use of multiple types of drugs. One 15-year-old explained the connection of prior sexual abuse to drug use:

It [the abuse] hasn't had an effect. I hurt when he did that, not physically but in my head. So I do a lot of "fat rail" [drugs]. Then I don't feel it. You think about—the stupidest shit. Sometimes I just cry all day. (Acoca, 1998, p. 571)

Although the girl claimed that abuse did not have an effect, it clearly did result in emotional problems. The use of illegal drugs to block out confusion, distress, and pain resulting from abuse or other sources is referred to as **self-medication**.

Another outcome of abuse is summarized in Daly's (1992) typology under the category *harmed and harming women*. One of the few studies of women who have killed children revealed the serious psychological harm that can result from childhood abuse of girls (Crimmins, Langley, Brownstein, & Spunt, 1997). The women had all been neglected or abused during childhood, but not all had followed the pathway of running away, prostitution, substance abuse, or other criminality. Their childhoods were uniquely marked by extreme unavailability of predictable adults to meet their needs and keep them safe, coupled with the lack of other supports. Homicide is a rare outcome of abuse, but because girls are more often and more frequently sexually abused than boys, the study provides important insights on the connection of girls' abuse to later criminality.

Taken together, knowledge about life course events and involvement in illegal behavior and about girls' and women's pathways into crime suggests that in similar neighborhood environments and families, girls and boys will have different experiences, and these experiences can have different meaning and therefore different effects. Both male and female offenders have experienced childhood sexual abuse at higher levels than are found in the general population, but for girls the abuse starts earlier and lasts longer (Chesney-Lind, 2001, p. 141). For girls, the result is often running away and substance abuse; for boys, it is more often aggression.

Women Who Kill Abusive Intimate Partners

Research on incarcerated women shows how they came to kill an abusive partner. The women had adjusted to living conditions and attacks on themselves, and sometimes their children, which were increasingly severe, and when they felt there was an "unprecedented threat," that "he had never done *that* before," they took lethal action against their abusers (Browne, 1987, p. 130). An unresponsive justice system is one of the influences on women's perception that they had no alternative but to kill or be killed. Women's rates of committing homicide are related to two measures of potential help: the amount of domestic violence legislation and the availability of shelters and other services (Browne & Williams, 1989). Regardless of other strong predictors of women's homicide rates, both legislation and resources are important additional predictors of homicide by women. When women live in parts of the United States where laws and resources do not help them, abuse by male partners more often escalates to the point that the women strike back at their abusers as a last resort.

The Centrality of Relationships to Other People

Alternative theoretical explanations of girls' and women's illegal actions have recognized that women's investment in relationships with family members or other intimates affects their criminality. As noted above, women white-collar offenders frequently committed their offenses to help other family members in need of cash. Also, battered wives have endured escalating violence in an effort to understand the batterer and keep the family together, but when the violence becomes life-threatening, some respond by killing the abuser.

Based on in-depth interviews, Richie (1996) showed how the nature of women's relationships with abusive men explained how they came to break the law. A complex interplay of socialization and immediate circumstances entrapped New York City jail inmates in relationships that led to various criminal outcomes through several different sequences of events. When the abusive relationship resulted in the death of a child, some women were charged as accessories or perpetrators.[45] Constant beatings by one man resulted in one woman's murdering another man who seemed to be threatening her with a similar beating. Some men forced women into prostitution and beat them if they would not bring in adequate income, and some would beat women unless they brought home illegal income, for example from stealing from their employers. Black women in particular, who tended not to use social services to get help, killed their abusers in retaliation. Battered women also took drugs in an attempt to share an activity and intimacy with their abusers, or to numb the pain caused by abuse. Resulting drug dependency fueled criminal activities. All these scenarios revealed that gender ideologies and gender-related power inequities entrapped women in relationships that led to their criminal behavior. **Gender entrapment** involves women being lured into a compromising act, and it can result in some women being forced or coerced into crime because of their gender role expectations, violence in intimate relations, and their social location, which limits access to resources (Richie, 1996, p. 133). African American women in particular were entrapped by circumstances.

Alternative Pathways Into and Out of Illegal Behavior

The book *Street Woman* (E. M. Miller, 1986) detailed the lives of Milwaukee women offenders who were recruited to the study through halfway houses, correctional institutions, and the suggestions of women from these places of other women to interview. The women, who were interviewed in 1979, were disproportionately minority in relation to the city's population, had children, were in their twenties, and had limited education and little legitimate work experience. Although data were collected in 1979, *Street Woman* still stands as one of the best explanations of how individual choice, life's circumstances, immediate social context, and particular events come together to influence women's pathways into delinquency and crime. Even though childhood sexual victimization, intimate-partner violence, or some other critical experience can explain many women's involvement in crime, quite different events and circumstances can lead to the same end, and similar events and circumstances can result in different outcomes.

For the women described in *Street Woman*, diverse life circumstances, ranging from extreme poverty to economic stability, typified women who broke the law. Women's involvement in crime was affected by context, specifically neighborhood conditions, and family relations. Deviant street networks, often overlapping with family networks, were essential to recruiting, maintaining, and supporting women active in prostitution, selling drugs, stealing, and other "street hustles." Miller documented that strict or abusive families or families that generated income through illegal means could promote women's offending. Girls often ran away from strict or abusive families, and this move exposed them to pressures and opportunities to break the law. Even if their family networks did not overlap with deviant groups, runaway girls could locate themselves in deviant networks on their own. Additionally, girls' and women's own agency, reflected in desire for excitement or money, had an impact on their lawbreaking. For both males and females, individual decision making, often related to identity, can counteract circumstances and situations in the family and community that support crime and delinquency.

Many of Miller's (1986) findings have been confirmed in more recent research. A study conducted in the 1990s in New York City (Maher, 1997, p. 93) verified the importance of preexisting social and kinship networks for providing women access to participation in the drug economy that Miller had identified decades before. In New York, female-centered deviant street networks provided information and support that enable lawbreaking (A. Campbell, 1990; Maher, 1997, p. 35; J. Moore, 1991). Also, there has been some interesting, data-driven revision to prior theorizing that girls are not typically involved in gang-related delinquency, and if they are involved in a gang at all, it is as a girlfriend and member of an "adjunct" group to the boys' gangs (Chesney-Lind & Hagedorn, 1999).

A good example of an advance in research on girls and gangs is a study in Milwaukee. The study had two features that produced especially valid information (Hagedorn & Devitt, 1999). First, the sample size was relatively large, at 72 women who had been members of gangs when the groups took their names, and 176 additional women who were identified as being members of the eight gangs that the original group belonged to. Second, female gang members worked collaboratively with the researcher to develop the questions and carry out the interviews. The research could therefore shed more light on the standpoint of girl gang members than could previous studies that tried to understand girls by asking questions of the male members or by having a male researcher observe the gang. The study findings challenged several assumptions about the connection of girls to delinquent gangs and the nature of the girls' delinquency.

Although Milwaukee boy gang members in an earlier interview had described girls as not really in the gang, as allowed into the gang only with agreement by the male members, or as under the control of male gang members (Hagedorn, 1988), both African American women and Latinas felt they had started their gangs without male involvement, often based on early childhood friendship groups (Hagedorn & Devitt, 1999, p. 266). Some Latinas said that the gang was led by a man, but none of the African Americans said this. The Latinas who were least acculturated to the United States held traditional views of gender differences, most often said that a male had "called the shots" in their gang, and most often felt that their experiences in gangs were primarily negative (Hagedorn & Devitt, 1999, p. 268). Less-traditional Latinas described more self-directed and positive involvement with gangs. There was disagreement between gang members about who the other members were and, for girl gangs or parts of gangs, about the importance of males in allowing membership and providing leadership. A person's ethnicity and gender affected how experience in the same gang was constructed. Additionally, members of the different gangs provided evidence that girl gangs varied greatly from each other in how they were formed, whether they were involved in drug selling, and how and whether they were related to groups of males who self-identified as gang members. Miller's finding of the great diversity in females' responses to similar circumstances is repeated by the more recent findings about girls in gangs. Depending on ethnicity and gender, gang members differed in their perceptions of girls in gangs, and the girls differed markedly from each other in their experiences in gangs that stimulate delinquency.

Research also has confirmed the variation in how adults end up in the same patterns of illegal behavior through different routes. In a study conducted at the end of the 1990s (Erickson et al., 2000), 30 women gave diverse accounts of how they ended up working as prostitutes and addicted to crack. Explanations for initially using crack included multiple life crises, such as being raped or losing a child, wanting to escape feelings of depression, or progression from other drugs. Some of the women engaged in prostitution after they began using crack in order to support their lifestyle and buy the drug. Others were already making money through prostitution before they used crack. One woman explained how she self-medicated by using drugs to deal with multiple people touching her in the course of working in prostitution:

> I've been doing it (prostitution) since I was 15 years old, that's like what I know best. I started prostitution to support my habit for alcohol and marijuana . . . when you have so many people touching your body, I did the drugs first. I got addicted (to crack) when I was 18 and I've never stopped since that. (Erickson et al., 2000, p. 775)

For the women addicted to crack cocaine, a common thread in their lives was that at some point, the desire for drugs that made them feel good sustained their involvement in prostitution.

Many women are influenced to begin, to resume, or to stop using illegal drugs by their concerns and experiences with maintaining custody of children. In-depth interviews with women in the Pima County, Arizona, Adult Detention Facility provided examples of women desisting from drug use in efforts to obtain custody of their children; however, because they could not accomplish the logistics of establishing a living quarters, meeting sometimes intensive probation supervision requirements, or in some other way, they ultimately permanently lost custody (Ferraro & Moe, 2003). Two women explained their relapse into patterns of drug use. One woman said:

They told me again that they were going to take my kids away, so I started doin' drugs again. And then, prostitution came in. (Ferraro & Moe, 2003, p. 30)

The other said:

They said I had a drug problem, and I don't even know where they got that. I wasn't even doing drugs. I did start drugs after I lost her. About two to three months later, I did it. It was like, "Hell, they said I did it." I didn't have nothing to lose then. I had already lost her, so that's when I started doing drugs. (Ferraro & Moe, 2003, p. 30)

Other women explained how they stopped using illegal drugs and alcohol and were able to regain custody of their children. For both groups, the motivation to use or not use drugs was custody of children.

Regaining custody of children, obtaining a decently paying job, finding a place to live, or establishing a relationship with a non-abusive and supportive partner are the sorts of events that have been referred to as **hooks for change** (Giordano, Cernkovich, & Rudolph, 2002). They are life events that, in combination with immediate context and a person's inclinations and motivations, influence desistance from patterns of criminal activity. As Miller and others have previously demonstrated, women come to the same point through different series of events, decisions, and circumstances. The pathway leading to and leading away from repeated illegal behavior is certainly affected by gender, race, and ethnicity, but there are no standard routes for females, just as there are no standard routes for males (Laub & Sampson, 2003).

So far, discussion of context has centered on how family, networks, and relationships explain how some girls and women become involved in breaking the law and why they continue doing so. Both familial and other networks open up some, but not other, possibilities for lawbreaking. Context also limits the type and the amount of illegal activity that girls and women do. The limitation results in part from the effects of context on gender identity. Thus, the connection of gender identity will be discussed next, and it will be followed by material on the way that context influences identity.

Gender Identity and Crime

At the individual level, the concepts of *hegemonic masculinity* and emphasized femininity help to explain gender differences in amount and type of lawbreaking (Heimer, Unal, & DeCoster, 2000). **Hegemonic masculinity** implies a high degree of power and influence over other people. These other people include women and men who have subordinated masculinities and who are working class, homosexual, or ethnic minorities. **Emphasized femininity** implies behaviors that support hegemonic masculinity. Both masculinity and femininity result from societal beliefs, norms, and attitudes that promote particular *gender definitions*. Family members encourage behavior consistent with particular gender definitions, and gender segregated play groups tend to reinforce these definitions in childhood and during adolescence (Heimer, Unal, et al., 2000). When they play, boys encourage each other to be tough, competitive, and aggressive. In contrast, girls typically play in small and intimate groups. They encourage each other to be concerned with relationships in the group, and they focus on appearances, emotional skills, and nurturing each other.

School curricula, extracurricular activities, interactions with teachers, and the media may contain mixed messages about appropriate behaviors and attributes of girls and boys, but ideas consistent with hegemonic masculinity and emphasized femininity are readily available in the media in the United States and elsewhere, and in many families and social groups. On the whole, definitions of masculinity are more consistent with breaking the law than are definitions of femininity.

There is a fairly large literature on how males' different forms of self-identification as boys or men contribute to some of them being criminal and committing particular types of illegal acts. Perhaps there is the emphasis on masculinities and crime because so many more males than females break the law. In theoretical explanations of females' behavior, the focus has been on how traditional emphasized femininity limits the forms of girls' and women's illegal behavior. This literature has addressed the question of why males are so much more seriously delinquent and criminal than are females. Identity that incorporates emphasized femininity stresses passivity, subservience, caring for others, and the activities of wife and mother, and all of these are incongruent with aggressive lawbreaking. Theory has paid relatively little attention to what forms of gender identity support females' involvement in illegal behavior, though the limited work in this area is quite interesting. In contrast, theory about males' gender identity has described criminal activity as a handy resource for accomplishing quite a variety of different forms of masculinity. Overall, the various theories that have been developed to explain crime and delinquency posit that feminine gender identity limits women's and girls' possibilities for illegal activity. For males, theories attend to the intersections of masculinity with race and class inequalities as important influences on the amount and type of crime a person commits. This is clearly an unbalanced view: Females are most fully understood by examining limitations resulting from gender, and males, while limited by class and race inequalities, are depicted as active and resourceful in using available resources, including crime, to construct a masculine identity.

Boys and Men Breaking the Law

Alternative masculine identities, which are more or less possible depending on social class and related contexts of daily life, support alternative types of criminal activity (Messerschmidt, 1986). At the same time, one or another type of criminal activity makes it possible to live up to an image of a successful man, and therefore to accomplish a particular form of masculinity. Within a capitalistic society like the United States, in particular social contexts, different groups of men—for example, chronically unemployed men in urban ghettos or managers in U.S. corporations— interact with their peers, and through this interaction they construct and negotiate what it is to be masculine. Capitalism stimulates an interest in the acquisition of material goods, so that even a wealthy individual will seek more fortune, perhaps by breaking the law, as a mark of being a successful male. Different notions of manliness are linked to different ways of doing gender, and some men accomplish gender through particular sorts of crime.

As an example, shop-floor men steal goods in the workplace in groups to "beat the system" and impress each other, but managers commit corporate crimes when profits shrink and they feel their identity as successful businesspeople is challenged (Messerschmidt, 1987). Following are descriptions of other types of masculinities that support various sorts of crime and violence:

> Men's rape and assault of women reflects a masculinity of domination, control and humiliation, and degradation of women. Other types of harmful conduct involve a shameless masculinity or a masculinity of unconnectedness and unconcern for others. When called to account for exploitative conduct, men's responses may be rage rather than guilt, or an amplification of non-caring identities such as "badass." (Braithwaite & Daly, 1994, p. 222)

The main idea is that alternative masculinities support various types of both lawbreaking and law-abiding behaviors.

In some families, physical violence is routinely used as a means to solve problems, and therefore violence provides boys with a plausible and meaningful way to construct masculinity and become attached to an admired adult male, for example one's father (Messerschmidt, 2000). Based on his research on a small number of boys who were either physically violent or who engaged in sex with younger children, Messerschmidt (2000) concluded that the key influence on these behaviors was the family conception of what it means to be a real man. Boys saw sexual aggression and physical fighting back as a resource for accomplishing masculinity, of being what they defined as real men acting with power and control in the context of family and school, where other resources were not available. Another life history study of a teenager who pressured and rewarded a much younger cousin to engage in sex over a period of several years also illustrated how a boy who could not act according to his image of a man used sexual coercion to "be masculine" (Messerschmidt, 1999). The boy had been repeatedly teased and rejected by classmates who saw him as "fat," "a wimp," and an outcast. He failed at his attempt to demonstrate his manliness by losing weight and playing football. He explained how his sexual coercion of his younger female cousin helped him feel successful as a male:

> It made me feel real good. I just felt like finally I was in control over somebody. I forgot about being fat and ugly. She was someone looking up to me, you know. If I needed sexual contact, then I had it. I wasn't a virgin anymore. . . . [With my peers] I could now talk about sex with them if I had to. I knew what it looked like and how it felt now, kind of thing. So I felt I fit in more. (Messerschmidt, 1999, p. 205)

Case information like that presented above provides support for general conclusions about the connection of masculinity and criminality. When a boy or man feels his masculinity, however he defines it, has been called into question, or when sex categorization is ambivalent and masculinity is "on the line"—if there are not legal ways for a person to accomplish his idealized version of masculinity, criminal behavior can provide a solution. Alternative masculinities are developed in part from childhood experiences with family or guardians, and in part in reaction to the realities of available ways to fill one's image of a "real man" in light of personal physical characteristics and the cultural and economic resources that are available.

There is another take on the degree to which masculinities come into play in the production of violence. Alder and Polk (1996) used Australian coroner files to develop descriptions of men who killed a person under 18 years old. The murdered children varied from infants who died at the hands of stepfathers or birth fathers to teenagers killed by young men not much older than they were. For confrontations between young men and for spousal fighting that resulted in the death of a child, either inadvertently or on purpose, the criminal acts appeared to affirm a particular version of masculinity, and indeed seemed to be provoked by a direct threat to hegemonic masculinity. Polk (1994) provided an example involving an adult victim:

Mick F. [age 36, unemployed] started his drinking at the house of a friend late in the afternoon, and then the two of them moved off to their local, the Victoria Hotel. They continued drinking "shout for shout" for some time (Mick's blood alcohol was later found to be 0.147).

In the middle of the evening, the group was approached by Jimmy S. (age 53), another of the pub regulars. Jimmy, also feeling the effects of alcohol (some hours later, his blood alcohol was still found to be 0.197), upbraided Mick for some insulting comments he had made towards his "missus" (observers commented that a trivial exchange had occurred between the two earlier in the day, or at least in their view the comments were trivial). There were mutual insults and challenges, and finally Mick hauled back and struck Jimmy, a short fight ensued, with Jimmy being rather badly beaten. Hurt as well as drunk, Jimmy needed help from bystanders to make his way out of the pub.

After Mick and his group settled back to their drinking, they were interrupted by Jimmy's *de facto* wife, who proceeded to abuse Mick for his beating of Jimmy. Then, Jimmy himself re-entered the bar. Without a word he walked up to Mick, pulled out a knife, and stabbed him once in the chest. As before, Jimmy was set upon, this time by the friends of Mick. Jimmy was assisted out of the pub by his *de facto* spouse. Help was summoned for Mick, but the knife had penetrated his heart and he died before he could reach the hospital. (p. 178)

Key features of this and similar examples are the public nature of the accomplishment of masculinity, a contest of honor between males, and the offender's lower-class status, which limited alternative means for publicly establishing the men's version of masculinity.

It is important to keep in mind that the vast majority of men in poor neighborhoods or in financial straits do not identify as hustlers or aggressors in order to feel that they are successful men (Newman, 1999). The so-called working poor, who include large proportions of African Americans and Latinos, have a strong work ethic and work at jobs that most other people would not accept. They maintain their dignity and, as the title of Newman's book states, they feel there is "no shame in my game." One recent immigrant from Jamaica who lived in a tough section of Harlem explained how he maintained his pride in the face of peers who taunted him for making a living "flipping burgers":

> What I did was make Sam [the general manager] save my money for me. Then I got the best of clothes and the best of sneakers with my own money. Then I added two chains. Then [my friends] were like, "Where you selling drugs at?" and I'm like, "The same place you said making fun of me, flipping burgers. That's where I'm getting my money from. Now, where are you getting yours from?" They couldn't answer. (Newman, 1999, p. 100)

People are inventive, and they can cope with limited opportunities in a variety of ways, one of which is to take pride in scratching out a living in the service economy and avoiding criminal activity.

In low-opportunity neighborhoods, the working poor outnumber residents who break the law. They see themselves as having a strong work ethic and being on the right side of the law.

© Patrick Bennett/Getty Images

Girls and Women Breaking the Law

Correcting the relative inattention to gender identity and girls' illegal activity, there is theory and research on girls and gangs that considers this topic. The lasting quality of traditional gender ideologies (that is, *emphasized femininity*) has been used to explain the typical roles that girls play in gang activities. Sometimes, female groups are primarily an annex to male gangs, and the girls support boyfriends and others in the group but are largely controlled by them and involved in gang activities in minor ways (A. Campbell, 1991). In contrast, other girls describe themselves as full-fledged members of gangs that include males, and the male members agree with the girls' account. Interviews with 24 Latinos and 9 Latinas who were former gang members in Phoenix, Arizona, revealed that in order to escape patriarchal family practices that emphasized girls' roles taking care of the household or siblings and that afforded them little personal freedom or independence, girls were with the gang for part of each day, sometimes for very extended periods (Portillo, 1999). Those who grew up in the neighborhood with the male members and those who were "jumped in" (beaten) by other members as part of initiation were routinely accepted as members, and many of them expressed in dress, speech, and behavior a type of **oppositional femininity** that included characteristics of loyalty, bravery, willingness to fight, and fighting ability. Some Milwaukee girls who were members of gangs, including all-girl gangs, were similarly proud of their fighting ability (Hagedorn & Devitt, 1999). One Milwaukee female gang member responded to questions:

Q: When you were active in the gang, how did you personally feel about fighting?

A: I loved it.

Q: Why?

A: 'Cause I used to kick ass! (Hagedorn & Devitt, 1999, p. 257)

Milwaukee girls who fought just because they liked to, which was the predominant motivation for African American girls, had less of a male-centered outlook than did girls who fought primarily to show their solidarity with other gang members. The African American fighting girls were less likely to be in a relationship with a man and did not see a male partner as essential to ensuring a good future. Overall, girls' fighting was "mainly tied to adolescent rebellion from home, school, and traditional gender roles" (Hagedorn & Devitt, 1999, p. 275). It also was tempered by some limits on rebellion, including not using firearms or violence to the extent that males used them because of lack of access or knowledge, or an inhibiting sense of self. Fighting girls at times adapted when they were with family or were expected to be more traditionally feminine in some other way by a boyfriend or other peers, and motherhood or moving out of the area eventually interfered with some girls' ability to be part of a gang. Yet, there are instances when girls defy emphasized femininity for extended periods and they act in ways that produce different forms of femininity.

Young women who hang out together on the same corner in their Brooklyn, New York, neighborhood drink malt beverage and practice their technique for hiding a razor blade in their mouths, for use as a weapon.

© Marc Asnin/CORBIS SABA

Like the researchers in Milwaukee, Laidler and Hunt (2001, p. 657) questioned the assumptions in prior work that either (a) girls in gangs are stereotypical girls in their roles as sexual chattel, personal property, or maladjusted tomboys; or (b) they are seizing the streets, gaining independence from, and almost competing with, their male counterparts. Their research was unique in its inclusion of Vietnamese, African American, Samoan, and Latina heritage girls and young women in the San Francisco Bay area. They first considered the different ways that femininity was constructed within the girl gang members' families, and then how girls renegotiated and managed the paradoxes of femininity at home and on the streets.

That the young women held traditional notions about femininity was evident in their ideas about respect (Laidler & Hunt, 2001):

> Respect has a lot to do with the way she [a girl] presents herself. The way she acts around guys and girls at all times. She isn't a ho [whore], she's not all desperate with the drugs. She acts like a woman. Some girls kick back and don't have respect from the guys. Some homegirls [gang girls] see each other, and they start cussing [at each other and at the guys]. . . . It starts getting ugly, and he'll hit her. Better calm down. They [those homegirls] got no respect for themselves. (p. 664)

This view of respect differs from the emphasis on power and control that is tied to notions of masculinity. It limits sexual behavior and overt expression of aggression. Other statements by the girls revealed their concerns with being good mothers. However, the context of street life made it unrealistic to completely refrain from seemingly unfeminine aggressive behavior, even when broadly defined. Respectability also meant being able to stand up for oneself (Laidler & Hunt, 2001). The girls aggressively postured and engaged in violence with each other in an attempt to "look bad" and to protect themselves in a hostile street environment (Laidler & Hunt, 2001; also see Maher, 1997). Given the constraints of their social location both on the streets, which were dominated by powerful men, and as lower-class girls of color within the larger society, fighting brought status and honor and therefore made it possible for girls to confirm they were "decent" and "nobody's fool" (Laidler & Hunt, 2001, p. 675). The girls were negatively affected by their social locations, and their buy-in to some aspects of emphasized femininity constrained them, but they also improved their position through their seemingly unfeminine actions. They modified the stereotypical feminine identity accordingly.

The history of the Black Sisters United (BSU) girl gang also reveals forms of femininity that supports and reproduces noncompliance and resistance to hegemonic masculinity (Venkatesh, 1998). The group, which was a collection of "sets" or other groups, was the largest coordinated all female gang in Chicago. Members initially formed an alliance to help each other respond to problems such as harassment and abuse by males and to provide numerous social activities. The group operated fairly formally, with a coordinating board that drew representatives from groups scattered across the city.

In response to the urban economy's polarization into a high-wage corporate sector and a low-wage service sector, younger members increasingly wanted to cooperate economically, not just socially, with an all-male gang that was engaged in drug trafficking. As research in Brooklyn, New York, has shown (Maher, 1997), the amount and nature of women's participation was affected by gender differences in power and influence: "the [drug] economy was fundamentally gendered vis-à-vis historic control of supply lines, street distribution sites, and regulatory systems by men who at the street level retained an affiliation" (Venkatesh, 1998, p. 106). As a result, BSU's "participation never reached equity status, and the roles available to them were almost always subordinate to the roles of male gang members. Generally, BSU rank-and-file members received a small allowance in exchange for monitoring police activity or holding drugs and cash for male gang members" (Venkatesh, 1998, p. 106). With dominance in the drug economy, males used harassment and abuse to limit BSU members' attempts to increase their profits from drug-related activities.

Although realities of power differentials for women and men in Chicago constrained the activities of women and limited the outcomes of their efforts, BSU members did act in their own economic and social interests. BSU members did not just internalize, but they also modified and reproduced feminine gender identities. The group initially formed to address problems of male dominance and abuse, and even as some of the members were drawn to cooperate with males and be subordinated in drug dealing markets dominated by males, others consciously chose not to. In fact, they purposely took steps to disband the BSU when they thought it was becoming a support system for men's operations. The typologies of types of masculinity and types of femininity do not fully reflect the way that people develop their own gender identities to depart from pure types or how they change their identities over time. In some forms at some times, a criminal activity can support a person's notion of femininity, just as criminal activity can support different notions of masculinity. More broadly, context has an impact on a person's gender identity and influences the amount and the type of a person's illegal behavior.

Gender Identity in Context

Gender Differences in the Amount of Delinquency

Identity develops in the context of family, peers, community, and larger structures of inequality that characterize many families, neighborhoods, illegal markets, and peer groups. Some promising new theories to explain how girls' and boys' differing experiences during adolescence result in boys' greater violence and other serious lawbreaking have taken context and gender identity into account. According to **everyday practices theory**, gender differences in everyday patterns of action and practices, especially in the family and among peers, account for the gender difference in delinquency by making some illegal activities unavailable as resources for accomplishing gender (Bottcher, 2001). In **gender definitions theory**, a combination of gender definitions and ideas that are more or less favorable to breaking the law (Heimer & DeCoster, 1999) explain why boys break the law more than do girls, and traditional views of gender are among these definitions. A third explanation, **power control theory**, is that gender differences in delinquency result from the degree to which families are patriarchal rather than egalitarian, that is, characterized by shared power and decision making by mother and father (Hagan, Gillis, & Simpson, 1985; Hagan, with Simpson & Gillis, 1988). The idea is that different forms of gender identity are supported by families that are patriarchal than are supported by those that are more egalitarian. Each of the three theories considers gender-related restrictions on girls, and each reveals the supports (and limits) for gender identities that can and cannot be accomplished by breaking the law.

Everyday Practices

An examination of what high-risk adolescents in California actually do on a day-to-day basis showed how several key practices that were different for girls and boys explained why sisters of highly delinquent boys less often broke the law than their brothers, even though they were exposed to the same communities and families (Bottcher, 2001). In the practices of making friends and having fun, partly as a result of parental concerns about girls' becoming pregnant and partly because of peers' view of different activities being appropriate for boys and girls, males more often belonged to large peer groups and gangs, spent time with unsupervised peers, "received social support to be delinquent, had access to privacy and to time and space away from home, and enforced gender-defined friendship group boundaries" (Bottcher, 2001, p. 910). Different from the boys, the girls became sexually involved with single partners at a young age, were independent from their families earlier, and when they had children, assumed responsibility for their care (Bottcher, 2001,

p. 917). The context of neighborhoods with few economic opportunities provided boys with incentives that, because of practices of having fun with friends and delayed assumption of parental responsibilities, influenced them to stay away from home and break the law for enjoyment or profit. Girls were often excluded from the crime-supportive contexts by parents and peers, or by their own sense of responsibility for caring for their offspring.

To explain the California sisters' and brothers' different levels of delinquency, Bottcher conceptualized gender differently than Messerschmidt and others who adopted his emphasis on masculinities. For Messerschmidt, gender involves structure and action. Social patterns, for example the division of labor between females and males, define what it means to be feminine and what it means to be masculine. For example, when males and females conform to stereotypical divisions of labor in the family, with the women and girls cooking and the men and boys doing the yard work, they are in effect affirming the division of labor and re-creating existing structures. Bottcher instead saw gender as a set of social practices in a particular context. Social practices that work against girls' involvement with delinquency include girls' greater restriction to their homes and their tendency to seek and assume child care responsibilities at an early age. Despite these differences, both theoretical approaches connect gender to the level of resources and opportunities available in a person's immediate social context. Because she considered both girls and boys in her theory and research, Bottcher (2001, p. 926) was able to reveal how power relations, shown for example when boys restricted girls from some illegal activities, helped to determine who "needs" the delinquent options and, among the "needy," who gets them. This understanding helps us to make sense of the emphasis that characterizes criminological theory—that crime is a resource for accomplishing masculinity, but in girls' day-to-day practices, the resource of crime often is not available and may be less needed to accomplish femininity.

Gender Definitions

It has long been recognized that people who see or define things in a way that supports lawbreaking more often commit crime and delinquency, and that definitions are learned and supported during interactions with other people (Sutherland, 1924). Girls are less likely than boys to learn definitions favorable to breaking the law (Heimer & DeCoster, 1999). The bond that daughters have with their parents and the time they spend together reduce girls' learning of definitions that are consistent with crime and violence. Also, girls' violence is reduced because they learn traditional definitions of gender that portray females as nonviolent. Poverty and the related experience of living in high-crime neighborhoods foster delinquency through associations with other people who promote a way of looking at the world that is conducive to crime, but this happens more for boys than for girls.

Power Control Theory

Both *everyday practices* and *gender definitions* explanations emphasize the consistency with which girls are less delinquent than are boys. In contrast, in power control theory, whether girls and boys differ in their levels and types of delinquency depends on the nature of the family. In egalitarian families, mothers and fathers have equal power; but in patriarchal families, fathers dominate in decision making and control. Patriarchal families are characterized by greater differentiation of roles considered ideal and acceptable for males and females. Therefore, girls and boys are treated quite differently, and they are expected to act very differently. Research to test power control theory has had mixed results (Morash & Chesney-Lind, 1991), but there are continued refinements and retests, in part because the explanation attends to variation within gender groups, not just differences between girls and boys.

Tests of power control theory at first produced findings that because of stronger paternal controls, in patriarchal families girls are less likely to be risk takers, and therefore may engage in less delinquency than girls in more egalitarian families (Grasmick, Hagan, Blackwell, & Arneclev, 1996, p. 193). The implication for egalitarian families is negative, because they seem to support girls' delinquency. Given documented low levels of girls' involvement in serious delinquency, a more important finding is that the active role of mothers in the egalitarian family, along with the tendency to provide boys with similar supervision and treatment to what is provided to girls, appears to put a damper on boys' delinquency. In the more egalitarian family, boys do not tend to be high risk takers, they are less likely to believe they can act with impunity, and they are less likely to be delinquent than are boys in patriarchal families (McCarthy, Hagan, & Woodward, 1999). Also in the more egalitarian family, boys more than girls feel they will be more embarrassed if the people whose opinions they value know that they have been involved in various delinquent acts (Blackwell, 2000). That boys in egalitarian families experience more involvement and control by their fathers than do those in patriarchial families may explain their greater embarrassment, because youth often most identify with the same-sexed parent. Overall, research has shown that boys in the egalitarian families less often exhibit characteristics that are associated with the versions of masculinity that support delinquent behavior in the more patriarchal families. Although the egalitarian family may offer girls some leeway to break the law, at the same time it suppresses the greater problem of boys' delinquency (Blackwell & Reed, 2003).

The Salience of Gender Identity in the Causation of Crime and Delinquency

Theories that emphasize masculinity and femininity as explanations of lawbreaking assume some congruence of a person's gender identity with his or her behavior. It is not necessarily the case, however, that violent and other illegal behaviors are a response to threats to one's gender identity or difficulties in living up to definitions of femininity or masculinity. Some crime and delinquency may have nothing to do with gender identity. In a group of primarily lower-class men who had murdered a child, the variation in their views and expression of masculinity were not connected to their social class status (Alder & Polk, 1996). Adding further complexity, individual men seemed to have contradictory aspects to their masculinity. For example, they simultaneously valued nurturing behavior toward children and the use of aggressive behavior to control them. Because there are incongruous and multiple influences on people, it is important to consider self-definitions of identity in context.

Consistent with the idea that people are not necessarily motivated to break the law in order to fulfill their gender identities, Maher (1997) concluded that for women involved in sex work in a severely disadvantaged neighborhood, there were no instances in her study where "crimes by women could be interpreted as a way of separating from all that is masculine" (p. 119) in the way that males break the law to separate from notions of femininity, and in so doing to reaffirm their masculinity. One woman gave an example of the thinking behind women's emphasis on sex work and other hustles that were different from methods that males used for making money:

[Could girls get a hold of like guns and go in and rob stores or people—do they do that?] They could do it but it's not done, right? It's not Hollywood. This is the real deal out there. . . . See what I'm sayin'? So they (girls) work their con—go for their own kind of bullshit. (Maher, 1997, p. 119)

As a result of the distribution of power, the threat that men would react violently to women who intruded on their money-making schemes, and the resulting divisions of labor within the neighborhood, only some forms of illegal activity were available to women. The women committed crimes not to enhance their femininity, but to get money in settings characterized by gender divisions in work.

For people involved in prostitution, specific sexual acts are not usually a way to accomplish some form of gender identity. If they are forced by other people or by a desperate need for money, both children and adults who work as prostitutes may see their actions as contradicting their identity. Boys who trade sex for money do not typically use this experience as a resource for establishing themselves as masculine (Schifter & Aggleton, 1999). Individuals manage their gender identity more or less successfully within the constraints of broader societal and market forces, but by no means is all behavior a way of accomplishing that identity. In some cases, they can accomplish their identity as a girl or woman, or a boy or man, by breaking the law, but in many cases they accomplish this identity in spite of breaking the law.

Biological Explanations for Females' and Males' Illegal Behavior

A key tenet of modern biological theories to explain human behavior is that biological tendencies may or may not result in specific behaviors, depending on the environment and on social learning that occurs in that environment, including the family, school, and peer groups (Fishbein, 2001).[46] Typically, males have higher levels of testosterone than do females, but there is variation in both groups, and thus some females may have higher concentrations than do some males. There is increasing evidence that testosterone concentrations correlate with violent behavior in both female and male populations (Banks & Dabbs, 1996; Dabbs & Hargrove, 1997). The direction of causation, or whether there is cause and effect in both directions between aggression and testosterone, is unclear; aggressive behavior can result in increases in testosterone (Mazur & Booth, 1998). Thus, heightened levels of testosterone might result from aggression or might cause aggression, or the causation could be in both directions. For females, there is some evidence that prenatal and early postnatal exposures and events that interfere with sex hormones are characteristic of those who exhibit higher levels of aggression than do other women (Banks & Dabbs, 1996; Berenbaum & Resnick, 1997; Dabbs & Hargrove, 1997; Dabbs, Ruback, Frady, Hopper, & Sgoutas, 1988). The biological explanation has provided some understanding of why some males are more violent than other males, and why some females are more violent than are other females. However, it is not clear how important hormones are relative to other influences, including gender as conceptualized at different levels, in influencing violence.

Some research has suggested that males more often have predisposing traits that lead them to be involved in antisocial behavior as young children (Moffitt, Caspi, Rutter, & Silva, 2001). For example, boys more often exhibit negative emotions, such as worrying and being nervous, as children (Moffitt et al., 2001). This can limit their capacity to build personal resources by relating positively to other people (Harker & Keltner, 2001). Boys also are lower than girls in constraint, which is characterized by traits such as being disciplined and responsible. Boys also are more at risk than are girls for attention deficit-hyperactivity disorder, which makes it difficult for them to concentrate on and understand written and verbal communication. All these tendencies are related to antisocial behaviors in children, and childhood antisocial behavior is connected to illegal activity during adolescence and adulthood.

The interpretation of the effects of inborn tendencies must be done very carefully. It is widely recognized that the family and the larger social context can modify various tendencies, and that individuals also have some control over their own development and formation of identity. Females with the same biological and personality traits that predict boys' antisocial and illegal behavior are less often delinquent than are males with the same risk factors. The different experiences of girls' growing up, many of which have been reviewed in this chapter, likely have a powerful effect in moderating the influences of biology. These experiences are malleable and depend on the family, community, and broader social support context. Although the emerging research on the biological bases of antisocial and illegal behavior provides some information on why boys might be more delinquent than girls, predispositions are only a small part of the explanation.

Offenders Exercising Agency in Choosing to Break the Law

For some types of illegal activity, it is quite clear that although there may be constraints, people do make their own choices to break the law. This is most obvious when a person commits an economically motivated offense. For some sorts of illegal activity, it is less clear whether people are exercising agency. In particular, scholars, social critics, and people who make money by "selling sex" debate about whether individuals who work as prostitutes can be viewed as exercising agency.

There is no question that people who are forced or tricked into prostitution are not exercising agency. Moreover, a case could be made that if prostitution is the only means for financial survival, or if drug addiction is promoting an uncontrollable need for money or the drugs themselves, people involved in prostitution have little agency. A multicountry survey of prostitutes provided evidence that the job was not an acceptable, let alone an attractive, career choice for many people. Most of the people who were interviewed wanted to leave prostitution (92%), but they lacked asylum (73%), job training (70%), and health care (59%) that would make leaving possible (Farley, Baral, et al., 1998, p. 420). Consistent with the picture of prostitution work as dangerous and unpleasant, and not very profitable, Maher (1997, p. 159) described the effects of crack cocaine on sex work. In a neighborhood where many addicted women would sell sex for very little money, the result was cheaper "rougher" dates. Women had little power to select or negotiate with customers, and violence against the women was common, either when customers were dissatisfied or other people in the area stole from them. Prostitution may not be a true choice for a person who is addicted or in a place where alternatives for meeting basic needs are very limited.

Rejecting the no-choice perspective on prostitution, some people who earn money by prostituting call themselves sex workers and say that prostitution is a job like any other (Zatz, 1997). They feel they have considerable agency, and they protest against criminalization and regulation that limit their choices. Most contemporary social scientists have come to the conclusion that despite constraints of the historical moment, social structure, personal limitations, and culture, there are some individuals who break the law and who chart their own course in life. Their actions are influenced by how they see things, their own drive, and the resources they use. Some prostituting people who select their customers and their sexual activities and who control the environment where they work have more choice in what they do than many people who work in the legitimate economy (Kahn, 1999, p. 196). People who have alternatives but still engage in prostitution are best described by the term *sex worker* because they are often in a position to leave their job. Lorraine's interview with Magda, who supported herself through prostitution, revealed that, within constraints, some people do opt for making money through prostitution, and they exercise some control in interactions with customers:

Magda: Sometimes they [customers] become vulgar, but I throw them out with their clothes and tell them they can call the police if they want to but nobody is going to force me to be with you. Not only that, I have already taken my pants off, and they are paying to look at me.

Lorraine: Do you only work on this street or are there others?

Magda: I used to work on another street, but we had to leave the area because some of the women working there were crooks. The police raided the street looking for them. Since they all hid, the police took us in instead. That is why we left and came here. It is a lot closer to where we bring the men. (Nencel, 2001, p. 101)

However, for all but the most well-placed people engaged in prostitution, at the same time that they take steps to control their fate in their day-to-day interactions and activities, there are restrictions on their mobility, their space for maneuvering, and negotiating. The women who engaged in prostitution in a disadvantaged neighborhood in New York City in the 1990s could sometimes resist or avoid requests for disturbing sexual activity, and thus they could maintain their dignity and self-respect (Maher, 1997, p. 139). However, their appearance as physically sick and "strung out on drugs," the domination by men over the more profitable ways of making money in the area, and their sense that there was no place else to go limited their choices (Maher, 1997, p. 139). The strong connection between poverty and work as a prostitute that exists for most people translates into threats of death, sickness, and danger on almost a daily basis at the same time that they struggled to survive within a changeable and insecure economic situation (Nencel, 2001, p. 215).

In the United States and in other countries, about half of women involved in prostitution have tried to leave work involving sex for money, some repeatedly (Raymond & Hughes, 2001, p. 12). However, these efforts often are unsuccessful. Responding to a survey, 27% of international women and 52% of women in the United States indicated that they could not leave prostitution because "economic necessity, drug dependencies and pimps who beat, kidnapped, and/or threatened them or their children prevented them from leaving" (Raymond & Hughes, 2001, p. 12). In studies of multiple countries, the majority of people who sold sex for money did not feel that prostitution should be legalized, and they would not recommend it to other women as a way to earn money. They usually saw prostitution as the final option. The majority of people involved in prostitution do not see themselves as having much, if any, choice, but instead their comments reflect the tremendous imbalances of their personal power and efficacy in relation to that of customers and controllers.

Individuals can become empowered to take group actions when they realize that their own emotional turmoil and suffering are not springing solely from within themselves, but that there are external influences that elicit the same responses from similarly situated people. People involved in prostitution, who often hold the statuses of victim and offender simultaneously, are often relieved when their emotional distress is labeled as PTSD (Farley, Baral, et al., 1998, p. 408). The diagnosis affirmed that the women were experiencing stress from material conditions rather than because of any personal deficits. At the least, this recognition provided the basis for some expectation of medical and psychological care and protection from violence, and at most, some change in the negative context. The recognition of the person-context-structure connection serves as a springboard for political and other social change–oriented strategies.

This chapter has recognized that individual who break the law do have varying degrees of agency. It also has emphasized the countervailing forces that limit this control. There are people who work in prostitution and other sex trade occupations (e.g., phone sex, pornography) who see themselves as having considerable choice. Some participate in efforts to educate the public and politicians about the sex trades and themselves. Educational efforts and organized activities by sex workers also have concentrated on decriminalizing their work. The next chapter includes a section on how sex workers have exercised their agency in efforts to bring about social change by shaping the law and related reactions to people who do this sort of work.

Conclusion

Contemporary theory and related research have spotlighted the previously neglected influence of the feminization of poverty on the illegal activity of both women and their children. The influence results when women and children increasingly live in low-resource, crime-ridden neighborhoods, where there are limited opportunities for education and for legitimate jobs. At the same time that women are isolated in poor neighborhoods where some of them turn to crime to earn money, other women move between countries to better their economic situations. For example, women become involved in smuggling or move to internationally recognized centers for prostitution, like Amsterdam. Poverty both keeps women and children entrapped in settings where illegal activity is a means to survive and get by and also motivates women to move to settings where they can or must earn money illegally.

Careful examination of women's own viewpoints and their activities reveals both the power of gender to shape their lives and women's capacity to fashion altered versions of femininity to fit their circumstances. Women do sometimes take major roles in drug markets, but research has revealed that at least some moments of women's doing their own "business" were responses to men's dominance, and in some cases were stopped by men's reassertion of their greater control of drug dealing as a way to make money. Apart from instances of women's being in control of some part of a drug market, generally girls and women have survived on the street by filling their own niches in illegal markets, and their activities were more risky and less profitable than those available to males. Reinforcing the importance of intersections, women in minority racial and ethnic groups had the most limited and risky illegal work opportunities available to them.

Recent theory has corrected prior inattention to key events and circumstances in girls' and women's lives that account for some of them becoming involved in illegal activity. Childhood abuse (including sexual abuse), victimization by an intimate partner, and the centrality of relationships with others are important influences on females' illegal activity. Similar to the recent exploration of men's pathways into and out of crime (Laub & Sampson, 2003), however, overall the pathways research on women shows tremendous diversity in how women and girls respond to adverse circumstances. The pathways research also shows the importance of family structures and racial and ethnic group–based networks as causes of illegal activity.

Although they have been useful "ideal types" for promoting thinking about how identity is connected to resources and opportunities in a particular context, concepts like emphasized femininity and hegemonic masculinity are best considered to be heuristics. They help us to think about how people actualize gender identity in a particular context, with its constraints and its opportunities. They do not fully describe actual personal identities, but they lead to theory and research on how women and men think of themselves, and on what their identities have to do with whether they break the law. The literature has emphasized how males use several different kinds of criminal activity to be more masculine, and it has emphasized how females have a harder time using illegal activity to boost a positive sense of self as feminine. Among other things, parents and peers restrict girls from illegal involvement, and girls' and women's sense of responsibility for caring for their offspring often counteracts inclinations to break the law. Theory reproduces social reality to some extent, in that even crime is less of a resource, or is a more problematic resource, for women and girls than it is for men and boys. The solution is, of course, not to open up the opportunities for crime, but to reduce the need for turning to crime for money or a positive identity.

The structural, intermediate, and identity theories fit together to some degree. Gender inequality is relevant to explaining girls' and women's experiences at the macro level of influence, families and peer groups act in accord with gender ideologies that influence the amount and the nature of illegal behavior at the intermediate level, and gender identity has an influence at the individual level. Gender inequality also is relevant to boys growing up in communities where many families are supported only by women, and gendered family and peer group experiences affect the illegal behavior of males. Versions of masculinity have been identified as central influences on boys' delinquency and men's crime. Although gender is not always a salient influence on crime and delinquency, it can explain a considerable amount about why people do or do not break the law. Even though there is evidence of several levels of influence on illegal behavior, it is increasingly recognized that individuals do make choices, and that particular events at particular times can result in an individual's illegal behavior.

Key Terms

Conduct disorders	Hooks for change
Emphasized femininity	In the lifestyle
Everyday practices theory	Life course theory
Gender definitions theory	Oppositional femininity
Gender entrapment	Pathways theory
Feminization of poverty	Power control theory
Hegemonic masculinity	Self-medication

Review and Discussion

1. In light of life course and pathways theories that emphasize the many different routes that people take into a pattern of crime, what types of programs would a community need to prevent illegal behavior? Would the programs be different for females and males? How?

2. What are the assumptions about why people are not in the workforce that underlie current tendencies to limit welfare support? Are these assumptions consistent with, inconsistent with, or unrelated to research evidence about people who break the law?

3. Do you think that female offenders should be considered as victims too? Use research results in this chapter and from other sources to support your position.

4. How well has theory done in explaining why girls are less seriously delinquent than are boys, and why women are less often offenders than are men?

5. What are the different ways that gender influences girls and women who break the law?

Web Site to Explore

International Sex Worker Foundation for Art, Culture and Education is a site developed by sex workers. The site includes a special section for students who are writing papers on prostitution. www.iswface.org/

CHAPTER 7

Gender and Response to Lawbreakers

Avery Gordon: I'd like to begin by asking you to describe what is meant by the "prison industrial complex."

Angela Davis: Almost two million people are currently locked up in the immense network of US prisons and jails. More than 70 per cent of the imprisoned population are people of colour. Approximately five million people—including those on probation and parole—are directly under the surveillance of the criminal justice system. Three decades ago, the imprisoned population was approximately one-eighth its current size. While women still constitute a relatively small percentage of people behind bars, today the number of incarcerated women in the state of California, where we live, alone is almost twice the entire state and federal women's population of 1970. In fact, the fastest growing group of prisoners are Black women. . . .

Penal infrastructures must be created to accommodate this rapidly swelling population of caged people. Goods and people must be provided to keep imprisoned populations alive. Sometimes these populations must be kept busy and at other times . . . they must be deprived of virtually all meaningful activity. . . . All this work, which used to be the primary province of government, is now also performed by private corporations, whose links to government in the field of what is euphemistically called "corrections" reveal dangerous resonances within the military industrial complex. (A. F. Gordon, 1999, pp. 145–146)

S ince Avery Gordon interviewed Angela Davis and had the exchange cited above, the number of people in U.S. prisons has gone beyond two million. A contemporary examination of gender and the U.S. response to people who come to be labeled and processed as offenders must start with recognition of the growth of the **prison industrial complex**, an emphasis on punitive incarceration as a response to crime, and the related shrinking of the proportion of federal, state, and local budgets that are available to deliver financial help, social services, mental health care, crime prevention, and rehabilitation programs. The extreme growth of incarceration of women and of men is unique to the United States.

In the last several decades, detached from any increase in violent crime rates (Currie, 1998), the United States has become the nation with the highest incarceration rate in the world. Contenders are China and Russia, and there are indications that Russia is in a period of decarceration. England may be following the United States by dramatically reducing welfare and mental health programs, but along with other European countries, it does not seem to be moving to the extreme increases in incarceration that United States legislators and policy makers have promulgated (Downes, 1999). In the United States, several legislative trends and political movements have brought more people into the justice system and moved them into incarcerative settings. These influences include determinate and mandatory sentencing laws that attach specific lengths of sentence to specific offenses, truth in sentencing laws that require people to serve their full sentence, extra charges and penalties for people who have broken the law repeatedly (e.g., three strikes and you are out laws, habitual offender laws), the criminal justice system's war against drugs, pressures from private corporations that want to continue to supply incarceration services, and beliefs that crime is increasing throughout the nation and that getting tough on crime will improve safety and quality of life.

Gender, in interaction with race and other status markers, comes into play in the **mass incarceration society** that the United States has become. Because women's illegal activities disproportionately involve nonviolent drug and other offenses, the sweep of drug offenders into penal institutions has disproportionately increased the number of females in jails and prisons. In fact, compared to other types of offenses,

> [d]rug offenders account for a far greater share of the total growth in the [prison population] among females (43 percent) than among males (28 percent). The differential is even larger between white and minority inmates: drug offenses account for 17 percent of the increase among whites compared with 36 percent among blacks and 32 percent among Hispanics. (Blumstein & Beck, 1999, p. 26)

Because of stringent drug legislation, more women are arrested, and of those who are arrested, more are sentenced to prison for extended periods (Blumstein & Beck, 1999, pp. 54–55).

For women sentenced for drug-related offenses, welfare reform has provided continuing punishment beyond the penalties imposed by the courts. The 1996 U.S. welfare reform act stipulated that individuals who were convicted of a state or federal felony offense that involved the use or sales of drugs would be subject to a lifetime ban on receiving cash assistance or food stamps.[47] Many states eliminated or modified the ban, but as of early in 2004, an estimated 92,000 women were still affected (The Sentencing Project, 2005). These women included more than 44,000 who were white, nearly 35,000 who were African American, and just under 10,000 who were Latinas. Seventeen states denied benefits entirely, 10 denied benefits partially, and 12 made benefits dependent on participation in drug treatment programs. The remaining 11 states and the District of Columbia did not participate in the ban. By providing additional punishment beyond what the courts stipulated, the lifetime ban on receiving welfare assistance and its modifications restricted opportunities for legitimate sources of support, particularly for minority women, and placed children in a situation where their mothers could not support them.

The transfer of ideas across national boundaries, an important aspect of globalization, has stimulated increased use of incarceration in several countries and for foreign nationals entering selected countries (Sudbury, 2002). In the 1980s, the U.S. government used its economic clout to influence the most industrialized nations (Britain, Canada, France, Germany, Italy, and Japan) to comply with U.S.-promoted criminalization of drug use and to address drug use and distribution with incarceration. This influence spread to other United Nations members, with the result that women (and men) have been incarcerated as part of a U.S.-initiated multi-country war on drugs.

There is anecdotal evidence that judges sometimes single out foreign national women as examples to their ethnic or racial group members, and punish them more severely in order to send a signal to other people. For example, one foreign woman incarcerated in England explained:

> The judge when he sentenced me said he's going to use me as an example. Because he knows I've been set up, but he has to give a message to the world: "Don't bring drugs." He used me as an example because he knew I was pregnant. I was set up by a friend of mine, if you call him that. And they knew that. But still he said that's why they're using women to bring drugs to the country because they think that the system is not going to be as hard on women as on male prisoners. He said that's not the case. (Sudbury, 2002, pp. 66–67)

The multicountry spread of women's incarceration as part of a war on drugs is intricately linked to the feminization of poverty on a global scale. Women's poverty increases their incentives to carry drugs across national borders, or to in other ways break the law inside and outside their countries of citizenship. In many countries, similar rhetoric and political pressures have defined subsisting on state support and being in the presence of drug dealings and dealers as signs of flawed character that have been used to justify limited availability of welfare support and increased use of incarceration.

In the United States, race is a powerful influence on a high rate of incarceration for both women and men. In some court jurisdictions, seriousness of offense and past criminal record being equal, unemployed, minority men are more likely than other males to be sentenced to a term in prison (Spohn & Holleran, 2000). The result is highly disproportionate imprisonment of certain groups (Garland, 1999, p. 6). The effects of race extend beyond the huge number of black men who are incarcerated, to women they are attached to and any children they have. An increased number of households headed by black women are exposed to poverty, relegation to high-crime neighborhoods, criminal victimization, and limited opportunities for jobs or education.

Macrolevel Influences on Responses to Lawbreakers

Guided by a variety of theoretical explanations of incarceration rates, Greenberg and West (2001) obtained empirical evidence to explain why some states have very high incarceration rates, and why in some states rates of incarceration grew especially quickly between 1971 and 1991.[48] As expected, for the combined group of women and men, state imprisonment rates were partly explained by violent crime rates. Less expected, states with more financial resources and increasing resources imprison more people. Beyond these influences, a large black population and low investment in welfare are connected to high rates of imprisonment. Greenberg and West interpreted their findings: In many places, a concentration of black people leads to racial stereotyping of them as a threat to be contained by a punitive criminal justice system (Greenberg & West, 2001, p. 640).

When women and men were considered separately, again violent crime rates explained state imprisonment rates for each gender group (Bridges & Beretta, 1994). Also, for both women and men, higher rates of hospitalization for mental illness and use of parole were connected to lower incarceration rates. As known from other research, the higher the concentration of blacks, the greater the incarceration rate for both black women and black men.[49] The incarceration rates of women and men are affected by similar influences, and sex differences in incarceration rates can be explained as resulting from sex-specific rates of labor force participation and hospitalization for mental illness. At a macro level, public policies of low investment in mental health and welfare flourish where there is high investment in incarceration, and this dynamic has affected both women and men.

Alternatively, the more that states invest in welfare support for the poor, the lower the rates of incarceration (Greenberg & West, 2001). Because conservative politicians, who have been the majority in many states for more than a decade, favor both cuts in welfare and punishment-oriented crime control policies, in recent years, the relationship of incarceration to welfare cuts has become stronger (Beckett & Western, 2001; Greenberg & West, 2001). With the feminization of poverty, women would be expected to be most affected by whether a state favors the use of welfare and avoids harsh treatment of the poor, who are the majority of criminal court defendants. The dynamics of limiting welfare and increasing incarceration, and the concentration of the result on women, explain the quicker increase in women's versus men's incarceration rates in the last few decades. Fueling the increase in prison populations, these broad policies have operated along with sentencing legislation to create the dramatic boom in the women's prison population.

England provides an example of how public policies have resulted in increased confinement of girls who work as prostitutes (Phoenix, 2002, p. 71). Increased numbers of girls have become involved in prostitution since minimum wages for youth were decreased and welfare benefits have been cut. The recognition that girls have previously been victimized justified more aggressive policing and more use of confinement "for their own good." Ironically, the emphasis on the harms of prostitution grew as the recognition of public policy–induced youth poverty decreased, so that there was little public attention to the root cause of girls working as prostitutes. In England, child welfare policies also had their influence by stressing the need to confine girls, who were typically in their late teens, and shifting attention away from their economic stresses.

The huge number of people in U.S. prisons and jails, along with even larger numbers on probation and parole, occurs at a time when many prison and probation departments in many states have shifted from an emphasis on rehabilitation to a focus on processing and monitoring masses of people. Specifically, in some settings, most notably large surveillance-oriented prisons, rehabilitation has been replaced with assessment of the risk that offenders pose and related practices to manage and warehouse them. Ironically, certain justice system methods, such as boot camps and supermax prisons,[50] seem to stimulate and reproduce the most undesirable aspects of stereotypical masculinity in both the keepers and the kept— a lack of emotionality related to isolation from positive human interaction and capitulation to authority-driven and to hypermilitary-like regimes (Morash & Rucker, 1990). These are the very characteristics that theories have identified as consistent with a masculinity that supports some types of illegal activity.

Epitomizing the shift toward punishment, women in Maricopa County, Arizona, participate in a chain gang that does public work such as picking up trash and burying "unclaimed bodies" in the county cemetery.

© CORBIS

The shift away from rehabilitation is less clear for juvenile offenders than it is for adults. The juvenile courts were established to provide care and helpful interventions for children who have broken the law. Changes in police responses to domestic violence have resulted in more arrests for girls who strike a family member (American Bar Association and National Bar Association, 2001). In recent years, there have been increases in the number of juvenile girl offenders who are being arrested for assaults and confined in detention and residential facilities (Belknap & Holsinger, 1998; Chesney-Lind & Okamoto, 2001; Schaffner, 1999). At the early stages of contact with the justice system, the influx of girls is most apparent for minorities. To some extent, the "get tough on crime" approach has resulted in more girls being confined in detention or residential facilities. For judges who favor alternatives to confinement, but see a need for youth to receive mental health and other specialized services, the lack of community-based programs suitable for girls results in their being released to troubled home situations or sent deeper into the justice system. In their initial contacts with the juvenile court, girls may be handled more leniently than are male offenders (MacDonald & Chesney-Lind, 2001). However, research on Hawaii has shown that if they are convicted, especially if they are girls of color, they are handled more harshly than are males (MacDonald & Chesney-Lind, 2001). The patterns of increased arrests of girls and harsher treatment at sentencing account for disproportionate representation of minority girls in the most confining juvenile justice programs.

For adults, pockets of rehabilitation and even empowerment in gender, ethnic, and racial group–specific programming exist in some location-limited programs in prisons, therapeutic courts, restorative justice processes, and community corrections settings. Also, in response to growing concerns that large numbers of offenders are beginning to be released from prisons without preparation or resources to manage, the federal government and some states are emphasizing increased use of parole and preparation for reentry. The result is a mixture of the rehabilitative and the people-management approaches, sometimes in the same institution or program, and often across a state system.

Countermovements Against Incarceration

There has been a steady stream of criticisms of the U.S. mass incarceration society on humanitarian grounds and based on findings from social science research (Mauer & Chesney-Lind, 2002). Additionally, political pressures and economic shortfalls in state budgets have forced reconsideration of mass incarceration as a preferred public policy, and in some places there is a stemming of the tide and even reversal of the number of people in prison. However, even if police and judicial actions change to limit incarceration, decades of long sentences have populated prisons with people who face many years of incarceration. For those whose release is imminent or who can be released through relaxed parole policies, prisons and jails usually have not provided help with managing mental health problems, including drug abuse, and with integration into contemporary job markets. There is no quick fix for the damage done by the high levels of incarceration with limited programming.

Families Against Mandatory Minimums (FAMM) is a grassroots, collective activist organization started by the families of lawbreakers who often had no criminal history, but who because of changes in sentencing legislation were incarcerated for a lengthy period. FAMM has advocated against mandatory sentences and has supported sentencing guidelines that promote guided judicial discretion. FAMM uses television, e-mail, and written publications to humanize the people who are incarcerated. Prisoners are reframed as mothers, productive young adults with drug addiction problems or momentary lapses of good judgment, and members of families that wanted and cared for them. FAMM has been active in lobbying, supporting legal appeals, and garnering public support. For instance, largely because of FAMM activities, in Michigan, which had some of the harshest penalties of any of the states, in 1998 the law requiring life in prison without parole for anyone convicted of intent to deliver 650 grams of more of heroin or cocaine was repealed. In 2003, state legislation changed Michigan mandatory minimum sentencing for nonviolent drug offenders by allowing earlier parole and discharge from lifetime probation. In 2004, FAMM supported the reform of what are called the Rockefeller drug laws in New York State. State legislation ended the 15 years to life sentences for the highest-level offenders and reduced the time to 8 to 20 years. It also doubled the weight of drugs an offender must possess or intend to sell in order to trigger a mandatory prison sentence. In 2004, FAMM chapters existed in 27 states, and other similar groups operated in states without a FAMM chapter. The groups lobby for the return of discretion to judges so that punishments can fit both the crime and the offender. They highlight the damage of the soaring incarceration levels to offenders and their families.

Families to Amend California's Three-Strikes Law demonstrate at the California Institute for Women. The third-strike law imposed long sentences on third-time crime offenders. The families are victims of the law in that their mothers, daughters, and loved ones are imprisoned for a minimum of 25 years for nonviolent and petty offenses.

© Ted Soqui/CORBIS

Activism has concentrated on limiting the numbers of both women and men in prison, but only for women has there been talk of gender-specific or gender-responsive programming. Gender-responsive programming would be tailored to the special needs and circumstances of women. In Canada, many women's sentences are 6 months or less, or even 14 days or less (Shaw, 1999, p. 195). The short sentences suggest that incarceration may not be necessary or helpful in many cases. There is concern that a focus on gender-specific programming may have diverted attention away from efforts to reduce the use of imprisonment and toward the nature of programs for women.

In the United States, even when there are pockets of programs considered to be empowering within an institution or community, most programs do not challenge gender stereotypes or give women substantial access to resources. For programs that are empowering, a major task for staff is to struggle along with each woman offender to address increasing problems connected to lack of affordable housing, cuts in welfare benefits, new foster care policies that quickly terminate relationships between mother and child, and other diminishing resources for the people who are incarcerated.[51] Very different from the social movement to improve justice for victims of gender-related offenses, there are relatively limited efforts that raise questions about whether incarceration is an appropriate use of public funds. Efforts to alter the nature of programming for female offenders have received more attention, primarily from activists and victim assistance groups that have reached out to women offenders who have experienced incest, intimate-partner violence, or sexual assault.

Organizational Context and Responses to People Who Break the Law

The next sections of this chapter concentrate on organizational sites where people think about and respond to people accused of breaking the law and on how gender affects what is done for, with, and to offenders. Consistent with the structure of other chapters in this book, broad social arrangements that resulted in the mass incarceration, particularly of minorities, were considered first. The larger context provides the setting within which organizational members talk, interact, and act.

Within organizations, gender norms are maintained when they are reflected and reinforced by common practices. Patterns of police, prosecutorial, and judicial decisions and related courtroom dialogue are influenced by ideas about which people are deserving of leniency even if they have broken the law, and which are not (Arnot & Usborne, 1999, p. 6). By and large, these decisions and dialogues reinforce existing norms, though challenges and debates can create exceptions. Existing norms provide information about acceptable and unacceptable behavior for people of a certain gender. Offenders who do not conform to ideas about appropriate gender behavior are treated most harshly.

Although there are predictive statistics to show race and gender inequities, there is limited evidence of how decision makers actually think about gender, race, and other status markers when they choose a response. The ways that people talk, their discourses about offenders, provide some insight into their choices. Discourses are used to authorize and justify painful and penal practices, and in some cases discourses are painful to the subjects of discussion (Cain, 1990, p. 7).[52] Discourses include writing and talk of experts and written and verbal communication among people within organizational settings. The following sections report on predictors of decisions about offenders and on the discourses that surround these decisions, and they therefore give insight into the influences on decisions.

Police in the United States

There is limited research on the influence of gender on police behavior that is directed at suspects. One study published at the beginning of the 1980s documented that police tend to treat women and men who did not fit gender stereotypes more sternly than those who did fit them. Specifically, females who were not submissive or were nonwhite were more likely to be interrogated and arrested when they were suspected of a crime (Visher, 1983). Also, women but not men offenders' rearrest was predicted by their drug use and their prior record, two indicators that they had broken with expectations about acceptable females (Uggen & Kruttschnitt, 1998). Because legal violations committed by women are seen as particularly at odds with their prescribed gender roles, women were subjected to more police control, regardless of current levels of offending and drug use.[53]

Juvenile Court

Compared to the convincing documentation of the juvenile court's role in criminalizing girls in an effort to control their sexuality (Chesney-Lind & Shelden, 1997), contemporary processing of girls through the juvenile justice system is relatively less understood. We have statistics, but limited revealing research, on how people who assess and respond to girls make their decisions. One exception is an analysis of how the justice system responded to girls before the Philadelphia Juvenile Court (Simkins & Katz, 2002). For some girls, the judge had no information on prior history of abuse, and it was not uncommon for a girl to be released into the custody of an abusive family member or to be punished by confinement for striking out at that person. For cases that did have extensive information on file, the most common mental health diagnosis was "oppositional defiant disorder." It is possible that oppositional behaviors are symptoms of posttraumatic stress disorder, a common response to abuse in the family (Beyer, 2000; Cauffman, Feldman, Waterman, & Steiner, 1998). For example, when a parent or a law enforcement official is overly controlling, a common reaction of a person with PTSD would be to think back to instances of controlling abuse, and a common response would be to strike back. Despite this possibility and the very high rates of abuse for girls before the court, the diagnostic information that the court considered typically focused on the girls' most recent behaviors rather than their histories of abuse. Even when a judge had detailed information on the reason for a girl's behavior and saw the need for mental health treatment, often professional help was not available because of limited programs and limited resources (Simkins & Katz, 2002).

For girls, there is a serious problem of secondary victimization in detention facilities, training schools, and other residential settings. The use of physical constraints and force can constitute secondary victimization. The use of physical constraints increases when facilities are overcrowded (F. T. Sherman, 2001). Because there are not adequate programs for girls, girls' programs often are overcrowded. Also a serious problem, staff in juvenile facilities sometimes play on girls' vulnerabilities and either entice or force them into sexual involvement. These control strategies and sexual abuses within juvenile justice settings can trigger flashbacks of prior assaults and revictimize the girls.

Another exception to the limited research on juvenile court responses to girls is a 1993 book that described how in Australia, girls living in publicly supported housing and Aboriginal communities were most likely to be moved through the juvenile justice system when they were seen as sexually promiscuous or defiant against their parents (Carrington, 1993, p. 112). The girls who went deepest into the system and were placed in residential settings tended to be homeless, in the custody of the state, or living in incestuous or otherwise intolerable families. At the root of girls' penetration into the justice system were the prior failures of welfare and other social services supports for them and their families. This is a different explanation from the one that sees the courts as enforcing sexual purity standards as the reason why girls are drawn deep into the justice system. Instead, it was the failure of earlier interventions that results in some girls' institutionalization. Also, girls were not uniformly drawn into the system; it was primarily minority girls who were in the most restrictive correctional settings.

There is also scant research on how court staff think about minority youth, especially minority girls. One study did find that individuals who prepared juvenile court records attributed different causes of offending to minority as opposed to majority male adolescents. The different attributions explained why minority youth were punished more severely than others (Bridges & Steen, 1998). Similar patterns of discrimination may exist against minority girls, at least in some jurisdictions. For African American girls, there is a tendency to bootstrap status offenders into institutions for delinquents by treating family arguments as criminal assaults (Bartollas, 1993; Robinson, 1990). Apart from this limited evidence, recent studies of the effect of race and sex on juvenile justice processing is scarce, and the topic is largely untheorized in the sense that the thinking behind such decisions is not documented.

Finally, there is some research that suggests that the juvenile courts have categorized girls' behaviors that formerly would have been considered as status offenses or as matters to be handled informally to violent delinquency. Once girls have been categorized as delinquent, especially if they are in a racial or ethnic minority group, they are more often detained, their cases are forwarded to court, and they are committed to institutions (Chesney-Lind, 2002). For more than 2,000 girls who were referred to Maryland's juvenile justice system for "person-to-person" offenses, nearly half of their cases involved physical fighting between parent and child

(Mayer, 1994). A review of the cases of almost 1,000 girls in California revealed that most of the charges for delinquency were for "non-serious, mutual combat, situations with parents" (Acoca, 1999, pp. 7–8). In Honolulu, Hawaii, between 1991 and 1997, there was a shift in policy of treating schoolyard thefts by younger boys and by girls more formally (Chesney-Lind & Paramore, 2002). Girls and young boys are increasingly being arrested for offenses that in the past would have been handled by adults informally, if at all. The findings that less serious offenses of adolescents are more often official police and court cases than in the past are consistent with self-reported decreases in violence by girls and a slight decrease in the already low rate of homicides committed by girls (Chesney-Lind, 2002, p. 85). The increased punishment of girls at the same time that there is evidence of decreased serious delinquency suggests increases in negative labeling of girls and, in the case of schoolyard robberies, younger boys.

Women and Men Before the Court

Much of what we know about gender and court processing comes from research on adult offender attributes and jurisdiction characteristics that are predictive of particular outcomes at the points of plea bargaining, preparation of a presentence report to make sentencing recommendation to the judge, and the judge's choice between sentencing alternatives. Offender's race and the racial makeup of the population in the jurisdiction compete or combine with offender's gender as potentially biasing influences on who is most punished.

Legal Representation

Women accused of crime may be at a disadvantage because of their legal representation. Offenders often enter a plea of guilty for the promise of a sentence that is not as harsh as it could have been if the case went to trial and the jury decided on guilt. A study conducted in the early 1980s showed that offenders were more likely to plea bargain when their charges were serious, but because women have less serious charges, they bargained less often (Figueira-McDonough, 1985). Even when they did plea bargain, they were not rewarded with the lighter sentences that the men who plead to a lesser charge received. This one somewhat dated study stands alone in shedding some light on gender as an influence on legal defense.

Presentence Report

Once a person is found guilty, judges often order preparation of a presentence investigation by a probation officer, who provides a rationale and makes a recommendation for case disposition. Australian probation officers wrote presentence reports that presented women who committed violent or drug offenses as more pathological than similarly charged men, and as more readily rehabilitated; as a result, judges sentenced the women more leniently (Wilkie, 1993). Presentence reports in New Zealand similarly described women's criminality as primarily a result of psychological disturbance, though the evidence of psychological dysfunction was weak or questionable (Heather, 2000; also see Gelsthorpe, 1992). Consistent with international research, after sentencing reforms in Pennsylvania, one of the reasons that judges departed from the guidelines more often for women than for men was mental health considerations (Kramer & Ulmer, 1996; Steffensmeier, Kramer, & Streifel, 1993; Steffensmeier, Ulmer, & Kramer, 1998). In some settings, framing offending women as mentally unstable or ill may have the negative effect of stigmatizing them, but the positive effect of justifying lenient sentences. Alternatively, men before the courts may be less stigmatized by the mental illness label, but treated more harshly.

Gender, Familial Paternalism, and Sentencing

In several U.S. courts where sentencing practices were reformed to reduce discretion based on factors other than the seriousness of the offense, at the point of court sentencing, there is evidence of more lenient responses to women. After sentencing reforms in Chicago, Miami, and Kansas City, women still received more lenient sentences than did men charged with similar crimes and with similar criminal histories (Spohn & Beichner, 2000). For drug offenders in federal courts, postguidelines sentencing disparity was associated not only with offense-related differences (e.g., type of offense, use of weapon) but also with legally irrelevant factors such as race, ethnicity, gender, and noncitizenship (Albonetti, 1997). Again, women fared better than did men. Pennsylvania judges departed from sentencing guidelines to treat women more leniently because of a nonviolent prior record, physical health problem, parental responsibilities, a minor role in the current offense, and a demonstration of remorse (Kramer & Ulmer, 1996; Steffensmeier, Kramer, et al., 1993; Steffensmeier, Ulmer, et al., 1998). Generally, the judges felt that female defendants were less dangerous and less culpable than their male codefendants, and that the women had more responsibilities and ties to the communities because they cared for dependents (Steffensmeier, Kramer, et al., 1993, p. 433). Finally, several years after the implementation of sentencing guidelines in Minnesota, gender was still a significant predictor of more lenient sentences for women (Koons-Witt, 2000). Despite the institution of many state-specific schemes to link the severity of the sentence only to legal considerations, such as crime seriousness or injury to victims, in general women do seem to be sentenced more leniently than are men.

There was a tremendous advance in theory development when, breaking from most prior and subsequent research that emphasized statistical model testing to show the predictors of judges' decisions, Daly (1987b) interviewed court officials (prosecutors, defense attorneys, probation officers, and judges) in an effort to understand their thinking about both women and men at the point of sentencing.[54] She discovered, and with expanded samples validated, that neither simple gender stereotypes nor paternalistic concern about women explained their treatment by the courts. Instead, **familial paternalism**, a concern with the welfare of the family members who were dependent on the defendant, influenced case outcomes.

Familial paternalism is characterized by a concern about the impact of removing parents from their children, with particular emphasis on the negative result if a mother could not meet the psychological needs of her offspring. Some men were given more lenient sentences because of possible negative effects on their children, but judges described men's contribution to children's welfare as mainly economic, and thus other types of involvement with children were not sufficient reason to avoid a jail or prison sentence. Also, some judges felt that economic support could be replaced by state support, whereas maternal care could not. Most mothers were seen as so important to their children's psychological development that they were irreplaceable. Although gender did not by itself explain differences in sanctioning, it was an important part of the explanation.

At the same time that Daly wrote about familial paternalism in U.S. courts, Eaton (1994) wrote about police and solicitors' presentations of women to judges in Great Britain. She also used evidence of the actual reasoning of people involved in making decisions about defendants to show how gender-related ideologies were enacted and reproduced in criminal justice settings. Often, bail was allowed because of interest in keeping women at home to take care of children. Also, bail was sometimes allowed because a husband was available to exert social control over his wife. The assumption underpinning the reasoning is that women should and could be let out on bail when they fulfilled their roles taking care of children and when a male head of household was available to, in effect, police them. Women without children and without husbands were at a disadvantage.

Gender, Race, and Sentencing

The courts treat minority women, especially African American women, more harshly than white women (Agozino, 1997; Bickle & Peterson, 1991; Krohn, Curry, & Nelson-Kilger, 1983; Kruttschnitt, 1981; Steffensmeier, Kramer, et al., 1993). For example, in Florida during 1992 and 1993, black female drug offenders were more often charged by prosecutors as habitual offenders than were white female drug offenders, especially when the court jurisdiction had a high percentage of blacks in the population and there were high rates of drug arrests and violent crime (Crawford, 2000).[55] Prior record, seriousness of the crime, and type of crime did not explain the harsher treatment of black women. In fact, prosecutors most often exercised discretion that resulted in harsher sentences for black women when the offenses were less serious, perhaps because they felt there was less choice when the offense was serious, and thus even white women had to receive harsh sentences.

In some locations, black women pay an even higher race and gender penalty than black men. Again in Florida in 1992 and 1993, habitual offender sentencing resulted in harsher sentencing of black versus white men, but the race-driven severity was greater for black women than black men (Crawford, 2000). In several jurisdictions, the implementation of Florida habitual offender laws opened the door for increased punishment of black women drug offenders. The findings are consistent with theoretical assertions of moral panic about dangerous (i.e., drug-using) minorities, particularly women who break most from what are considered acceptable gender roles, and explain harsh justice system responses (Crawford, 2000, p. 276; Mann, 1995).

An offender's race tempers the benefits to women from familial paternalism. In eight federal courts, the severity of sentencing of women convicted for forgery depended partly on race (Bickle & Peterson, 1991). White women with dependents were treated more leniently than white women without dependents. Black women who were described in presentence reports as providing high levels of emotional support to their children also received more lenient sentences. Whereas white women were sentenced more leniently just by virtue of having dependents, "black women do not benefit from simply occupying this central family role [of having dependents]; they must perform this role well" (Bickle & Peterson, 1991, p. 388). A study of women and men convicted of cocaine offenses showed the same pattern, that white women with children received more lenient sentences, but only black women who had maintained custody of their children, and therefore could be assumed to be good mothers, were sentenced leniently (Flavin, 2001). Black women appear to benefit from familial paternalism only when there is some evidence that they are good mothers, whereas white women seem to benefit from the assumption that they are good mothers regardless of the evidence.

Concluding Comments About Sentencing

Beginning in the 1970s, theorists have repeatedly emphasized that both historically and into the 20th century, sentencing outcomes for women and girls were influenced not only by their offenses and criminal or delinquent histories, but also by the degree to which females' behavior and character were consistent with gender role expectations (Carlen, 1983, 1985, 1998; Heidensohn, 1986, 1995; Kennedy, 1992; Lloyd, 1995; Smart, 1976, 1989, 1992). At different places and times, social control agents have based stepped-up efforts to control and confine on their perceptions that girls are failing to fill gender role expectations. In some instances, the result has been incarceration of girls for behaviors in which boys are expected and allowed to engage.

Counteracting the tendency to punish women who behave inconsistently with gender role expectations, at least at some times and places, females are treated more leniently than males who have committed the same offenses. More research is needed to expose the actual thinking about gender, race, and ethnicity that accounts for the statistical models that are confirmed in quantitative research. Whatever the thinking is, the result is an overrepresentation of especially minority males and then minority females in the justice system and its jails and prisons. This overrepresentation cannot be explained fully by criminal history or current offense.

Correctional and Punitive Responses

Once a person is convicted of a crime and sentenced, gender continues to have its affect on subsequent juvenile or criminal justice system responses. Postsentencing responses are colloquially referred to as *correctional programming*, but in light of the realities of how most offenders spend most of their time in prison or under parole and probation supervision, *punitive programming* is often a more accurate term. Despite the inaccuracy of describing all official postconviction responses as **corrections**, this book does follow the convention, but readers should understand that the terms *corrections* and *correctional* refer to an enterprise, not to the intended or actual effects of situations, regimes, and programs that the correctional enterprise implements. This enterprise consists of both state agencies and facilities and of numerous private businesses that produce and support construction, services, security, and programs.

Gender is relevant to correctional programming in four ways. First, constructions of masculinity and femininity are embedded and encouraged in the practices and interactions within correctional institutions and programs. Second, to the extent that masculinities and femininities have something to do with life choices (including breaking the law) and life chances, desisting from crime involves an offender's revisioning what it is to be a female or a male. Programs and institutions sometimes try to require or encourage offenders to change their gender ideologies and identities, and at other times they reinforce or ignore gender identity. Third, correctional programming and social policy might alter existing gender arrangements through concrete actions such as job creation, giving access to welfare benefits, and providing advocacy services to disadvantaged gender, racial, and ethnic groups. Finally, the gender ideologies of program developers and implementers influence the design and delivery of correctional and punitive experiences.[56]

Practices and Interactions in the Institutions

A unique characteristic of institutional correctional settings for females is the close scrutiny and the persistent attention to changing women and girls so they will conform to rules. Different expectations for males and females were documented in the contemporary disciplinary practices for young offenders in Australia and Germany (Kersten, 1990, p. 856). Fighting among boys, which was more frequent than fighting among girls, was seen as typical masculine aggressive behavior, and thus less often punished. When girls fought, they were seen as unfeminine and, almost by definition, pathological, and they were punished. Similarly, compared to men in Texas prisons, Texas women were more often cited for rules violations, and even though the rules they broke were less serious than rules men broke, women were punished more severely (McClellan, 1994). Women were most often cited for breaking posted rules, like drying undergarments, displaying excessive art work in their cells, or talking in the line of people who were waiting for medication. In the men's prisons, citations were most often for failing to work, and the wardens encouraged informal handling of less serious violations. Staff responded to women based on their perceptions that female inmates are overly expressive and temperamental. In the disparate settings of Australia, Germany, and Texas, females were expected to be more subdued and to follow minor rules more than the males, and if they did not, they were punished.

Gender-Responsive Correctional Programming

The U.S. movement to alter the nature of correctional programs for women and girls has been more high profile than has the movement to keep them out of institutions. FAMM and similar groups have included women in their target group of people to deincarcerate, but the relevance of gender to programming in institutions and in community settings has been emphasized primarily for females.

Because of the efforts of activists, the National Institute of Corrections funded research to assess the circumstances and needs of women offenders (Owen & Bloom, 1995). As a result, in the last decade of the 20th century, many different program models were developed to address women offenders' gender-specific needs (Bloom & Covington, 1998; Bloom, Owen, Covington, & Raeder, 2003). In 1999, the U.S. Office of Justice Programs in the U.S. Department of Justice held a conference to educate key personnel in state correctional departments on women offenders' unique needs (Office of Justice Programs, 1999). During that conference, key points were that prison facilities had been designed without attention to the needs and circumstances of women, and that correctional programs should be "based on supporting women in relationships, providing them with good role models and mentors, helping them work through their problems with sexual abuse and trauma, providing them with the job training and education they need to find productive work, and helping them gain increased feelings of self-esteem" (Office of Justice Programs, 1999, p. 25). At this time, the U.S. National Institute of Corrections supports correctional programming that addresses the special needs of female offenders.

In Canada during the late 20th century, feminists lobbied the government to reinvent prisons so they would empower women offenders (Shaw, 1999). Government and nongovernment studies, reports, and actions led to the abandonment of one old, central facility for federal female prisoners. Contrary to recommendations, a part of that facility still houses women who are seen as high risk. So that women could be closer to their homes, most federally sentenced women now go to one of several regional facilities, including a Healing House for Native American women. Other aspects of the new Canadian prison regimes were the use of therapies and other programming that would address gender oppression, that would provide meaningful choices for women to develop their potentials, and that were related to their cultural and spiritual backgrounds. The programs would emphasize treatment with respect and dignity, a supportive environment, and shared responsibility between community, voluntary organizations, and the women themselves for women's care and development.

In Great Britain, there were efforts to block the rebuilding of old Holloway Prison for women in the 1970s. In the 1980s, a group called Women in Prison began to work against discriminatory practices against women prisoners. They protested the lack of suitable programs and the close disciplinary surveillance and regulation that men in prison did not experience (Carlen & Tchaikovsky, 1996). Although British prisoners are still kept far from their homes, there were some positive changes, specifically improved sanitation and facilities.

Results of Correctional Reform Efforts

In the United States and other countries, there are numerous programs that try to address gender-related needs of women offenders. Some of these programs address women's use of illegal drugs. The programs typically address the connection between gender-related victimization and drug use. Advocates for the programs stress that drugs offer a means of dealing with traumatizing experiences, memories of cruelty, and learned helplessness, and this paves the way to eventual addiction (Ladwig & Andersen, 1989; Vogt, 1998). In other words, drugs are used for self-medication. Since the 1970s, U.S. feminist activists have started women-sensitive programs for addictions and introduced innovative treatment methods into conventional treatment settings (Vogt, 1998, p. 291). Programs typically assist women who have problems resulting from childhood sexual abuse. They also provide women with alternatives for dealing with trauma and with female role models who have overcome problems similar to those of women who have broken the law. Both for drug-oriented and for other correctional programs, there are many examples of the **gender-issues perspective on corrections**, a perspective that focuses on meeting women's and girls' needs.

There are some U.S. programs that try to challenge existing gender arrangements (using the **gender-challenge perspective on corrections**). A practicing therapist described programming to provide a weekly group session with girls who were living in a mixed-sex detention facility (Tuesday, 1998). For at least one and a half hours a week, the program offered girls their own space and place in the facility, which was dominated by programming and activities for boys. The therapists also exposed the girls to ways of understanding everyday disempowering occurrences, for example the girls' giving up each other's friendship to keep relations with males. Girls reproduced their own powerlessness through such interactions. The therapists wrote about the girls' identity:

> [T]hese are young women who do not fit into stereotypical images of femininity. They are aggressive, they are angry, they get in trouble, they run away, they have sex, use drugs, rob, cheat and steal. They do not see themselves as conforming to any of society's expectations of female behavior. This is juxtaposed against their traditional and conservative views of marriage and family. (Tuesday, 1998, p. 134)

Tuesday's description of the girls and of group sessions provides an example of a gender-challenging approach in corrections at the same time that it shows the force of culturally supported gender ideologies and existing gender arrangements. The program operated at the group level, but the institution continued to emphasize the needs of boys. Outside the therapy sessions, neither the girls nor their advocates were successful in clarifying that the girls deserved equitable or specialized resources and attention.

Although programs have shifted to address some gender issues and to a lesser extent to provide *gender challenge* programming, there is evidence that there has not been marked change in the United States (Morash, Bynum, & Koons, 1998) or in other countries (Bertrand, 1999). Four State of Maryland, jail-based therapeutic community programs for women drug users produced mixed results (Bouffard & Taxman, 2000). The programs were implemented in a period when there was explicit recognition in the drug research and treatment literature that treatment activities should address females' experiences with social stigma as drug-using women, as well as women's special self-esteem issues. Female drug users needed help in developing strong, effective social support networks (Bouffard & Taxman, 2000). The programs were implemented differently for women and men. Men's treatment sessions focused on building their motivation and on relapse prevention, and women's sessions focused on spirituality and aftercare planning. Women's sessions neglected many recognized needs, for example for psychological treatment and vocational training, but parenting education was included only for women. Also, men's sessions used more structured therapeutic techniques aimed at helping them change their behavior than did the women's. It is not known how the different program activities and approaches affected outcomes (Bouffard & Taxman, 2000). It is clear, however, that the programs were fashioned based on implicit ideologies and images linked to gender: Only women need parenting education, women must be educated to be good parents, women's multiple and often very practical needs are not the salient issues for treatment (e.g., vocational training, housing, abusive partners), and spirituality helps women, but therapeutic interventions aimed at changing one's own behavior help men. These findings reflect the gender stereotypes embedded within and resulting in correctional programming even after explicit acceptance of the importance of **gender-responsive programs** for women.

Correctional responses often meld new ideas about meeting needs and empowering women with old practices and related gender and racial stereotypes. The mixture is sometimes a result of staff differences. New York State's Bedford Hills prison facility has considerable gender-responsive correctional programming and an established training program for staff to work with women inmates. Still, compared to program staff and inmates who delivered programming, custodial staff were much more likely to apply negative and limiting stereotypes to women offenders (Schram, 1996). Also, for prisons in the United States and Canada:

> para-therapeutic activities and formal therapy abound in the women's prisons of common-law countries, while nothing of the sort is to be seen in continental Europe. Para-therapeutic activities include workshops on anxiety, anger, violence; learning sessions on parental care, budgeting, home economics, etc. as well as A.A. and N.A. group meetings, which keep inmates busy for hours. . . . In Canadian and U.S. prisons for women, phrases like the "need to heal" and concerns about "healing" are key words in the inmates' discourses. Women inmates are often pictured by the therapists as traumatized irresponsible victims, by the mere use of these terms. (Bertrand, 1999, p. 50)

Different from the typical U.S. and Canadian prisons for women, prison schools were active and well attended in Denmark, Norway, England, Scotland, Finland,

and the state of Minnesota. But even in the other European countries, facilities reproduced gender arrangements by making the highest-paying jobs for inmates available only to men. Overall, correctional institutions for women tend to emphasize meeting their emotional needs and preparing them for parental responsibilities, and programs for men address issues of employment and drug addiction.

In both closed and open institutions in Commonwealth and European countries, even institutional and community programs that were explicitly designed to break with old stereotypes of women often inadvertently reproduce these stereotypes through common practices (Bertrand, 1999). In Germany and England, prison nurseries implicitly reinforced the notion that women should be rewarded for fulfilling their role as mothers who remain at home caring for their children. Mothers whose young children lived in prison were provided with better living quarters, were allowed to take their children outside unaccompanied, and were sometimes excused from work and education programs (Bertrand, 1999, p. 55).[57] Bertrand, who conducted the multicountry research with colleagues and students, wrote:

> As we saw, new well equipped training programs in closed prisons (gardening, flower arrangement, silk-flower workshops, parental-care formation—which are nowhere to be seen in men's prisons) were found to be, if possible, more "feminine" and more "outdated" and gendering than the older ones. (Bertrand, 1999, p. 57)

Evidence of repackaged gender stereotypes continues to signal that women's appropriate roles are child care and the creation of beautiful living environments, at the same time that it reinforces masculinist images for males.

In Great Britain, another recent study found that incarcerated women were able to get what they wanted from staff by conforming to stereotypes of femininity, that is, by being passive and dependent (Bosworth, 1999). Although some nontraditional training is available to women incarcerated in the United States, for example in the building and construction trades, on average training programs for women still focus on technical, sales, administration, and service jobs (Lahm, 2000). Many offenders have very limited resources and very restricted ideas about the types of work that women can and should do. For the majority of incarcerated women, contemporary prisons are unlikely to result in empowerment, and if individual needs are met, the emphasis is on those needs that are consistent with the notion that women's worth lies in their capabilities as mothers and, more generally, as helpful and nurturing people.

Canada's reform efforts for women in prison have been exceptional in the extent that they included feminist collectivist and bureaucratic activists in redesigning the entire system (Shaw, 1999). An important part of the Canadian prison reforms was the use of careful assessment of each woman so that she could participate in programs that met her needs and built on her strengths. However, the postreform management practice was to consider needs as indicators of risks (Hannah-Moffat, 1999). Specifically, women who had injured themselves or who had a history of abuse or mental health problems were subjected to required treatment interventions, increased security, and accountability for attending programs, so they could reduce the risks that stemmed from their own backgrounds and circumstances. The transformation of needs into risks was epitomized in what was called an intensive healing program. The intensive healing program was a closed unit with increased restrictions for both high-risk (i.e., violent) and high-needs women. Women with low risk but high need were in settings designed to provide restrictions thought necessary to control violent women. The method of categorizing a woman as "high need" ensured that women from the most disadvantaged community and social groups would be included. For example, belonging to a community and a family that is functioning well is an indicator of low need, but "Aboriginal people [in Canada] do not belong to communities that are functional and healthy" (Monture-Angus, 2000, p. 57). In Canada, what began as a feminist critique of the correctional system's inability to understand and meet women offenders' needs resulted in reproducing the historically rooted, extreme scrutiny of women's backgrounds and personalities, and reacting most coercively to the women who had been most disadvantaged, regardless of any track record of their being violent or in some other way dangerous. The resulting gender programming, marked by scrutiny and control, was at sharp odds with the explicit ideal of bringing resources to women and empowering them.

Also at odds with the intent of reforms, prisoners' failure to use and succeed in programs to meet needs for empowerment was used as the basis for punishing women. Programs did not empower women by providing them with child care, housing, or other concrete resources. One criminologist who studied the reforms wrote that women were responsible for using job preparation programs and then for finding a job, regardless of the job market (Hannah-Moffat & Shaw, 2000, p. 32). Failure to use drug treatment or other types of programs led to labeling as uncooperative and classification at a higher security level, with resulting greater controls and reduced privileges (Hannah-Moffat & Shaw, 2000). Although some women were housed closer to their families after the reforms, the program content did not become empowering as the feminist activists had hoped.

Many of the gender-related needs that are addressed in contemporary correctional programming for females were identified as causes of females' illegal activity in theories that are supported by considerable empirical evidence. For example, childhood sexual abuse sets people on trajectories that include running away in adolescence, using illegal substances to deal with emotional stress, and engaging in prostitution to survive on the streets. However, theoretical explanation goes far beyond identifying the effects of individual traumas and problems. Theories also implicate a broader context and distribution of resources in crime causation, and these levels of influence are part and parcel of the explanation of why some women and girls break the law. The focus on addressing gender-related needs at the individual level leaves the structural and contextual sources of the problems untouched.

Continuing Emphasis on Extreme Punishment

At the same time that there are movements to encourage greater attention to the needs of female offenders, the push to extreme punishment in the United States continues to have an effect. In some states, prison environments have become more controlling and sterile and afford less and less privacy. The style of prison architecture and management for new prisons often makes it difficult if not impossible to create ameliorative environments (Seymour, 1977) where needs-based or even empowering programs might operate. The most extremely punitive prisons, which are large, sterile, and equipped with extensive surveillance technology, are referred to as **supermax prisons**. Supermax prisons have the effect of stopping gendered patterns of behavior that actually benefit women. In a supermax setting, women did not form strong, family-like ties to peers as is common for females in other prison settings (Kruttschnitt, Gartner, & Miller, 2000). Instead, the women were anomic, suspicious, and detached. It may be that women's predispositions and the cottage style of older prison facilities together made their interrelations more positive than peer relations in men's prisons. Or perhaps women's predispositions were overestimated, though this is contradicted by what we know about females' socialization and observations that women offenders in correctional programs are more cohesive and supportive of each other than men in correctional programs.

Consistent with findings about extreme punishment in the United States, in women's prisons in England and Wales, severe methods of punishment, lack of incentives for good behavior, poor staff-inmate relations, inmates' sense of having little autonomy, and inexperienced staff were related to high levels of disciplinary charges against inmates (Mandaraka-Sheppard, 1986). Women who had been in more than one institution varied in their behavior depending on the organization's characteristics. A dynamic that increased serious infractions was labeling women as violent or dangerous. The label resulted in staff expectations that women would be violent and led staff to interpret women's actions with suspicion. In response, women were defiant and were more prone to negative responses, which then, as part of a vicious cycle, resulted in more punishment.

International Perspectives

Aside from work that has been done in the United States, Canada, Great Britain, Australia, and New Zealand, very limited systematic research about the punishment and corrections of women in other countries is available to English-speaking audiences. The United States is different from many other countries in its limited provision of facilities where incarcerated women can remain with their children. In the United States, 11 state correctional departments do provide at least one facility in the state for infants, and some of these provide housing for children up to 18 months old, but most women who give birth in prison or who have very young children cannot have them live in the facility (National Institute of Corrections, 2002). In many other parts of the world, including Asian, African, European, and South American countries, children, often up to the age of 2 and even older, are routinely allowed to live with their incarcerated mothers.[58] For instance, in South Korea, pregnant women are allowed to leave the prison for the birth of their babies, and then on returning, keep the children with them in their small rooms, where several other women often live and assist in caring for the youngsters. Russia

A woman in the Florida State Correctional Institution for women holds her 2-week-old son. A 2-year-old law allows qualified female inmates to keep the children born to them while in prison, if they have a court permission. So far, judges have limited the prison child-rearing program to 18 months.

© Bettmann/CORBIS

recently passed legislation to pardon all mothers with children in prison nurseries (Ferraro & Moe, 2003, p. 9). There are many different reasons that children remain with their mothers, including state reliance on the women to care for their young children and recognition of the importance of mothers and children remaining connected. To the degree that women want to continue their efforts as mothers by keeping their children with them, the separation of mother and child does not have to be a part of the punishment that comes with incarceration.

In a number of countries, women experience particularly harsh punishments. Women trying to survive by escaping economic hardships and critical human rights abuses may be incarcerated in alien countries where they are subjected to extreme forms of physical and sexual abuse as well as fundamental deprivations (Ransley, 1999). A prison in South Africa attempts to break women's identity through constant surveillance and sensory deprivation, and to develop an acceptable feminine identity through "gender-appropriate" work, such as cooking and doll making (Dirsuweit, 1999). These are but two of many examples that could be given of serious human rights violations against incarcerated women in different parts of the world.

Although there is a cross-national theme that ties girls' and women's failure to fit gender norms with punitive responses to the women, there are tremendous variations in these norms as well as in the political circumstances that make some, but not other, behaviors most subject to severe responses by the justice system. For instance, before the collapse of the Eastern Bloc countries, in Poland, socialist ideals

Sixteen women are detained on sentences of at least 5 years in this prison cell in Kabul, Afganistan. Most are guilty of having remarried or run away. Although prison conditions are harsh, the women are allowed to keep their young children with them.

© Frances Keyser/In Visu/CORBIS

resulted in high levels of incarceration of women who committed crimes against the state. Many women were sentenced to prison for relatively minor workplace crime. Imprisonment was a favored response, because prison industry was part of state industry, and therefore prisoners could continue their contributions as workers while they were being resocialized. However, with the collapse of the Soviet Union, states saw their costs rise for assuming care for women's dependents, particular children and the elderly. As a result, sentences were reduced. Economic, political, and ideological forces shape patterns in responses to lawbreakers, making them more or less punitive at a particular time and place.

Individual-Level Explanations of Responses to Lawbreakers

A U.S. national survey of correctional administrators and program directors in the community and in institutions revealed four ways that administrators (e.g., directors and deputy directors in state departments of corrections, wardens and assistant wardens of prisons) conceptualized gender and showed how these conceptualizations were connected to decisions about desirable and appropriate programming (Morash & Robinson, 2002a). Particularly in jails, there were correctional administrators who said there were no differences between female and male offenders (**gender-irrelevant perspective on corrections**), but who held traditional gender stereotypes and promoted them. For example, they involved women exclusively in housekeeping within the institution. For custodial staff and administrators, stereotypes often were negative and were the basis for correctional staff conclusions that women were difficult to oversee (Rasche, 2000). In a drug treatment program that had been developed for men but then implemented in a woman's prison, one researcher observed that administrators and counselors conceptualized women's criminality as rooted in their deviant psychological makeup (McCorkel, 2003). The warden of the prison explained:

> Poor men stick somebody up or sell drugs. To me, as strange as this may sound coming from a warden, that is understandable. I can see how you would make that choice. Women degrade themselves. Selling themselves, you should hear some of the stuff they do. There is no sense of self-respect, of dignity. . . . There is something wrong on the inside that makes an individual take up those kind of behaviors and choices. (McCorkel, 2003, p. 69)

Program staff also defined women's emotionality and connection to other people as deviant, and attempted to change these attributes through therapeutic confrontation and related punishments. At the same time that the program denied gender differences by using the same treatment approach for both women and men, program staff negatively valued women's open expression of feelings and connections to children and other relatives as stereotypically weak and feminine.

A second group of administrators felt that women and men had different program needs, and they emphasized almost exclusively the importance of women's care of their children and other family members. This is the **gender-maintenance perspective on corrections** and the related approach to programming. A third group took a **gender-issues perspective** and valued programs that dealt with a host of individual needs, including emotional problems, education and job preparation, low self-esteem, abuse, and victimization. Needs related to parenting were included in the mix. Programs would help women to identify, fix, or obtain help addressing their problems. The final group, those that had a **gender-challenge perspective**, focused on gender-related disadvantages and favored programs that would challenge gender arrangements, for instance by encouraging girls and women to consider and prepare for nontraditional vocations and to become less dependent on relationships with others.

In the gender-challenge perspective, women's roles as mothers and their needs were not ignored, but consideration was given to inequitable gender arrangements. A correctional administrator with a gender-challenge perspective said, "We also, for example, discuss negotiating sex, which is a really important issue for women in some cultures, particularly Latina." Another said, "The program seeks to develop a stand alone woman, tries to make the women understand they do not need to live in a relationship that is not beneficial to them and helps them recognize and avoid codependency. [This] may not be unique to women but they certainly come from a different angle" (Author's research notes, n.d.). Programs that challenged gender arrangements were intended to increase women's limited power in the workforce, in relationships with men, or, in the second quotation above, with social services.

Offenders Exercising Agency: Personal Resources and Decisions

Organizations of Sex Workers

Sharply contradicting the idea that individuals who work in prostitution are victims of either poverty, exploitation, or prior sexual abuse, in the United States and some other countries, individuals who work as prostitutes have organized in an attempt to change laws and to improve their working conditions. They have promoted the use of the term *sex workers* and have emphasized that they are psychologically healthy, adjusted people with normal needs and aspirations (Weitzer, 1991, p. 26). For example, a group in the United States called COYOTE (Call Off Your Old Tired Ethics) was founded by Margo St. James in 1973. The group works to protect the rights of strippers, phone operators, prostitutes, porn actresses, and other people involved in sex work. COYOTE is a member of the larger North American Task Force on Prostitution, which was founded in 1979 to act as an umbrella organization of groups nationwide. The North American Task Force has the goals to:

1. repeal the existing prostitution laws;

2. ensure the right of prostitutes and other sex workers to bargain with their employers, and when they work for third parties, in order to improve their working conditions;

3. inform the public about a wide range of issues related to prostitution and other forms of sex work;

4. promote the development of support services for sex workers (including HIV/AIDS/STD and violence prevention projects, health and social support services for sex workers . . . ;

5. end the public stigma associated with sex work. (North American Task Force on Prostitution, www.bayswan.org/NTFP.html, accessed July 31, 2004)

Because prostitution is legal in the Netherlands, the local movement focuses on ensuring that legislation has the intended positive effects for sex workers (Mathieu, 2003). Some local movements have had less ambitious goals than the North American Task Force on Prostitution. For example, French prostitutes occupied churches in 1975 to protest police harassment and repression. What all of the prostitutes' movements have are activists who want to influence their own work situations and who are employed in prostitution.

Prostitutes' movements do have a number of difficulties in bringing about change (Mathieu, 2003). Many people who work as prostitutes are not well educated and have limited understanding about how to participate in a political process. They also are ambivalent about whether they want to work as prostitutes; they may have no choice, or they may feel stigmatized. People who work as prostitutes do not come from an actual community, and there is little cohesion between them because they are competing with each other for business. Leaders usually have been people who have more control over their work than people who are working the streets. Margo St. James was unique from most sex workers in that she had a brief involvement in prostitution and had links with the Feminist Movement (Pheterson, 1989, pp. xvii–xx). Although there have been brief alliances between people working as prostitutes and the Feminist Movement, many feminist organizations criticize prostitution as objectifying women and keeping them subordinate. Activist organizations for people who work in the sex trades exist and have in some places developed to have a professional staff. However, by and large they have not achieved their primary goals of decriminalizing prostitution (Mathieu, 2003).

Girls and Women Acting With Agency

At the individual level, even up against the power of incarcerative institutions, girls and women act in their own interest and in accord with their own feelings and identities. During the early 20th century, girls in reform school used a variety of individual and collective resistance methods. In the face of blatant efforts to "reinscribe the girls conscience with sexual purity and modesty," some reform school girls ran away and openly declared their preference for living with older men (T. Myers & Sangster, 2001, p. 674). In an unusual example, when they became aware that being treated as adults in prisons for adult women would result in less oppressive regimes, a group of reform school girls planned and initiated a riot and asked to be transferred to adult institution (T. Myers & Sangster, 2001, p. 683). More usually, women and girls are not bold and strategic when they resist prison regimes, but instead they engage in self-mutilation, other forms of self-destruction, or passive resignation (R. P. Dobash, Dobash, & Gutteridge, 1986, pp. 77–84). There are many examples of girls and women resisting efforts to enforce stereotypical notions of femininity that stress passivity, and historically girls have resisted the sexual purity standard and the related criminalization and punishment of sexual activity.

Control and rehabilitation efforts may have less influence than personal drive and decisions. For girls and women, one of the strongest motivators to stop drug use is pregnancy, which gives women reason to leave lives that are exhausting and emotionally and physically dangerous (Vogt, 1998, p. 287). Formal interventions do not predominate in turning people around from using drugs:

> Many women who live through episodes of drug dependence—some lasting years—mature out naturally, sometimes with the help of professionals, although not necessarily expert drug counselors, but mostly with the help of friends and families. After long years of drug abuse, including prostitution to pay for drugs, many women still have an extended and well-functioning social network on which they can rely when they are ready to give up drugs. In the European countries, unlike alcoholics, women who want to quit do not rely on self-help groups. . . . Rather they activate their own, very private social networks, which often have no relationship at all to self-help organizations. (Vogt, 1998, pp. 286–287)

There is much talk about people "maturing out" of life on the streets and the drug and alcohol use that mark it; but it is just as reasonable to talk about people actually taking control of their actions and just stopping certain behaviors.

At the same time that women can act on their own to stop breaking the law, they can resist efforts to change them through rehabilitative programs. Women in a drug treatment program that emphasized recognition of the severity of their addiction, their emotional well-being, and their skills in parenting reported their discovery of their needs and coping strategies in these areas (P. L. Baker, 2000). The program appeared to have considerable effect on their identity transformation. However, a close look at participants' comments revealed contradictory information. Women did not totally accept the program line about how they were emotionally damaged, severely addicted, and bad parents. They resisted this image of themselves, and it would be expected that this resistance would increase as they distanced themselves from the immediate influence of the program.

Some women offenders also resist their depiction as lacking agency. The bold attempt to infuse Canadian corrections for women with feminist ideas and ideals is summarized in the document *Creating Choices* (Correctional Service Canada, 1990), which was to serve as a blueprint for the new system of justice as the country moved into the 21st century. The document depicted women offenders as dependent on other people and suffering from pathological conditions.[59] Inconsistent with this picture, interviews with Caribbean Canadian women revealed they broke the law to "*avoid* dependency and to provide for the various family members who are in fact *dependent upon them*" (Pollack, 2000, p. 75). One incarcerated woman said:

I am a *very* independent, resourceful person. I will do anything and everything to provide the best for my family. There are certain things I won't do, because that's not me. I'd rather go out and steal a turkey before I'd ask a man to buy me a turkey. Because I'm independent and that's the way I saw my mother. She would rather sacrifice and do it herself, than ask anybody to help her. So, I am set in my ways, kind of, because this is the way I seen it. (Pollack, 2000, p. 76)

Caribbean women actively resisted portrayals of themselves as victims, insisting that they and other Caribbean women in fact committed their offenses for financial gain, not because of being a "drug addict or being sexually molested by our father . . ." (Pollack, 2000, p. 76). They rejected the script that described them as damaged and dependent, and they talked about how they did not want to be on welfare because they would then be relegated to poverty and unable to escape.

Women in contemporary U.S. prisons become involved in litigation, and some small number become "jailhouse lawyers," working on their own cases and offering advice to other women. They complain to staff or to watchdog groups or express themselves artistically. Like incarcerated girls, they form strong friendships to meet their emotional needs. One woman described her choice of friends:

I had a few friends. I mean you need people to talk to or you will go crazy. It's hard to know who to trust, but there was one girl who worked in the library with me. She helped me out a lot. She was real smart and she had been in before and when I would get mad she would calm me down. We would talk and we cried together a lot, but it was cool, we helped each other out. (Pogrebin & Dodge, 2001, p. 533)

Often with the support of some friends, most women do their time purposely with the aim of avoiding trouble. The majority stay away from the mix of risky and self-defeating behaviors that include using drugs, fighting, or getting involved with damaging relationships inside the prison (Owen, 1998).

Extremely oppressive conditions and different culture and circumstances can result in forms of resistance that are not commonly found in U.S. prisons. A case study of a South African prison, which was characterized by constant surveillance, sensory deprivation, and efforts to "break" the identity of inmates, revealed that similar to women who carve out safe places in communities, the women prisoners created special spaces in the institutions where they could support each other, express their sexuality, develop meaningful relationships, and create a life and maintain identity (Dirsuweit, 1999). Despite both open and hidden surveillance, women partitioned off "rooms" with bed sheets and fabric. When systems of communication were threatened, the women rioted. Women refused to work at all because they were not allowed to develop real skills, such as welding, woodwork, and computer literacy. Their acts and threats of defiance were effective because prison officials could not risk complete lack of cooperation.

Constraints on Empowerment

Some proponents of correctional approaches argue that even in the most restrictive environments of a prison, it is possible to create places, sometimes referred to as niches, where interactions are empowering and allow the inmate some agency that can be exercised in some way other than resistance to the immediate confinement. However, the day-to-day routines of life in most prisons are a very strong countervailing force. Women in prison may be treated as children incapable of making decisions; encouraged to highlight domestic skills, such as cleaning and cooking, in their personal development; and treated as though they were psychologically disturbed rather than stressed by real-life realities (Bosworth, 1999). The disempowering stance toward women in prison results from staff assumptions that the women cannot and should not make decisions for themselves and from staff actions that minimize women's perceptions of their own lives and what is best for their futures. It is worth noting that some programs and a few prisons have tried to create empowering environments, but that these efforts touch the lives of a limited number of incarcerated women, usually for only a limited part of each day.

Social Science Considerations of Agency

Social science is implicated in perpetuating the idea that women offenders are relatively helpless, because some theories emphasize the victimization and survivor status of girls and women who break the law. Theories that have the most impact on programs and professional services in prison emphasize the psychological needs of offenders, not the structural and cultural constraints that led to their economic marginalization or abuse. There are, of course, exceptions in some prisons: College courses on gender are taught, battered women's shelters come into the prison to explain the gender oppressions within relationships, and women become legal advocates for themselves and each other. The result is an environment with more complex and inconsistent messages about whether women should and can exercise agency than are found in the free world.

Conclusion

Putting her own work in a broader context, Daly (1989c, p. 29) noted that sentencing disparities revealed relations between family and state. The state, which is represented by the court, is interested in keeping mothers involved in nurturing their children and fathers involved in supporting their families. The state has more capacity to replace income than to assume child-rearing responsibilities, so there is emphasis on keeping mothers at home. The shift in focus that Daly introduced is important. It means that the key research question is not whether particular variables, such as race, class, or gender, predict sentencing outcomes or other types of responses to offenders. The key question is why and how courts and other state entities try to control and shape the family. Decisions about offenders and the programming and punishment provided to them are heavily influenced by notions about good and bad parents, or more generally about good and bad females and males.

Gender combined with race and ethnicity have an important influence on how deeply people who are accused of breaking the law go into the justice system, and ultimately whether they become incarcerated. In recent years, there has been a dramatic increase in the prison population, and very large numbers of African Americans, both women and men, are incarcerated or under probation or parole supervision. Consistent with historical precedent, girls and women who do not live up to expectations of appropriate and desirable behavior for females have been treated most harshly by the justice system. A large portion of the increase in women in prison is due to the severe penalties established for drug-related offenses.

When males behave aggressively, they are judged more harshly if they are black rather than white, and in general males are judged more harshly than are females (Duncan, 1976; Sagar & Schofield, 1980). Despite racial differences in response to males in conflict with the law, and despite clear gender differences in responses, little is known about what goes into thinking about race and gender in making decisions about male offenders.[60] Few people have questioned whether judges and people who prepare presentence investigations fail to see signs of mental illness, indicators of ties to community, or other individual attributes of men that might ameliorate negative views of them as dangerous and in need of containment. Nor have they questioned whether agents of the criminal justice system routinely or consistently take such factors into account as signs that men who break the law might productively, reasonably, or fairly be responded to in some ways other than heightened supervision, surveillance, and lockup. Do assumptions about masculinity, mixed with assumptions about race and ethnicity, influence judges' reasoning to sentence men more or less severely? For both women and men, how does the proportion of minorities in the community influence judges' thinking about sentencing? How does their reasoning relate to the connection of the proportion of minorities in the community to harsh sentences for minority offenders? These questions beg for an answer.

Gender and debates about its relationship to correctional interventions shape the form of programs intended to punish or rehabilitate convicted offenders. In some cases, with no thought, stereotypes attached to females and males are reflected and supported in programs and practices. In other cases, programs have been designed to be sensitive to female offenders' actual needs and circumstances or even to challenge existing gender arrangements. Reform efforts to develop gender-responsive programs for women have not always had their desired results. In some cases, the new programming for women has continued to reinforce images of women offenders as a heterogeneous, powerless, and dependent group. The discourses of psychology and individual empowerment are easier to hear and to apply than ideas about gender inequality and efforts that would actually bring financial and other resources to who need them.

It is sometimes difficult to determine whether prison regimes and other correctional programs reproduce stereotypes or not. There is a dense and unclear intertwining of implicit and explicit gender beliefs and practices in prison and community settings. Prisons meet many women's basic needs as well as their special needs for therapy, medical care, and a safer place to live than where they lived in the community.

To use one prison as an example, the environment at Bedford Hills Correctional facility in New York provides more than a period of "removal" from society. Its many programs and services provide opportunities for women to reinvent and redefine themselves. Prisons provide, for some women offenders, alternative cognitive frameworks that women can use to understand themselves and their lives. For example, in the Family Violence Program at Bedford Hills:

> [W]omen are encouraged to draw connections between their experience in childhood abuse and their destructive and self-destructive behaviors as adults, . . . [and] some friendships give women a chance to address old issues, make connections, and get comfort that helps to heal some of the abuse, emptiness, loneliness, and lack of support they've experienced in the past. (Weston-Henriques & Jones-Brown, 2000, p. 271)

At the same time that prisons provide an opportunity for women to recognize their own gender-related victimization and to thereby become empowered, correctional employees typically act as punitive parents, imposing rules and sanctions. Is there a distinction between meeting women's most basic needs and infantilizing and controlling them in the process of doing so? The answer to this question lies in the way that women in prison experience their own incarceration at a particular moment. It is one thing to be cared for and nurtured back to some essential level of physical and emotional health, but it is another thing to be controlled and supervised beyond that point in the name of treatment.

Key Terms

Corrections

Familial paternalism

Gender-challenge perspective on corrections

Gender-irrelevant perspective on corrections

Gender-issues perspective on corrections

Gender-maintenance perspective on corrections

Gender-responsive programs

Mass incarceration society

Prison industrial complex

Supermax prison

Review and Discussion

1. Based on the theories of crime causation discussed in Chapter 6, is it just for women to be treated more leniently before the courts than are men?

2. For both females and males, what are the types of injustice that result from the influence of gender on responses to illegal behavior?

3. Would it be just to treat females and males in exactly the same way within the criminal justice system? Why?

4. Identify programs described in the literature or in local corrections settings, and classify them as reflecting a gender-irrelevant, gender-relevant, gender-issues, or gender-challenge perspective. Do any of them reflect multiple perspectives?

Web Sites to Explore

Families Against Mandatory Minimums (FAMM) is a group that advocates against legislation that requires long sentences for particular offenses. www.famm.org

The U.S. National Institute of Corrections sponsors a Web site to provide assistance to individuals who are doing research or who are practitioners. The site includes a special section on women offenders. http://nicic.org/CatalogBrowse Page.aspx?txt=women+offender

CHAPTER 8

Advances and Challenges in Understanding Gender, Crime, and Justice

There have been several key advances in understanding gender, crime, and justice. Advances extend beyond a singular focus on girls and women. They include analysis of how beliefs about gender influence the form and implementation of laws, responses to both males and females in the justice system, and why and how boys and men, girls and women break the law. Just as some crimes are influenced by the gender of people who are victimized, hate crimes are influenced by sexual orientation of the victims. A complementary knowledge base is developing to show similarities and differences in the influence of gender and the influence of sexual orientation on crime, victimization, and justice.

There are several ways in which our theories have improved. Globalization increasingly has been highlighted in explanations of the connection of gender to crime and justice. Theory also has been elaborated to describe the multilevel interplay between individuals and contexts where they are situated (i.e., family, neighborhood, organization), and broader social and cultural features of a society. Context is recognized as important to making sense of a person's beliefs and behaviors. Gender, racial, and other inequalities are broad social forces that affect the nature of both contexts and individuals.

Related to gender and other inequities in the United States, girls and women who are Native American, African American, or Hispanic have many more constraints on their exercise of agency and their opportunities for action than do other people. Men who are poor and who are African American, Native American, or Hispanic similarly are highly constrained in making choices. People in more advantaged social locations have more intended effect on their own lives and on laws, criminal justice practices and experiences, and social life. Still, it is misleading to conclude that any group exercises either no or full agency. Complex theories assume agency and change at the same time that they link the individual to both context and broader patterns of social arrangements.

To show advances in understanding crime, gender, and justice, this concluding chapter draws conclusions about the current state of knowledge in sections on globalization, context, intersections, agency and constraints, and complex theory. Areas for linking existing explanations to theories in other disciplines are noted. These sections are followed by consideration of the research approaches that have been especially fruitful and some concluding comments on justice.

Global Perspective and Globalization

To show how the interconnections and inequities between countries are related to patterns and dynamics of crime and victimization, this book considered countries besides the United States. Other countries also were considered to highlight common patterns across countries and unique features within the United States, and to show how U.S. policies and foreign relations have influenced responses to victims and offenders worldwide.

Consideration of multiple countries revealed several ways that globalization affects the connection of gender to crime and justice:

- A combination of (a) inequities between countries, (b) the existence of organized criminal groups motivated to profit from trafficking, (c) a setting where prostitution is tolerated, and (d) customer demand have resulted in enticement and trickery to involve women and children in prostitution away from their places of origin.
- A result of immigration is that people change their ideas about appropriate gender roles within the family. When women become more independent and less traditional in their thinking about division of responsibilities in the family and the freedoms that women should have, some men attack them in an effort to prohibit these changes.
- Because people from different cultures and nations think differently about domestic violence, marriage, and sexual assault, high levels of migration between countries has resulted in victims with unique needs for assistance and help negotiating with the justice system.

In general, global inequities and women's poverty in many different countries place females at risk for victimization and for becoming involved in criminal activities, sometimes against their own will. The Feminist Movement has tried to address inequities and gender-related primary and secondary victimization, and in some settings there is considerable change in gender ideologies and gender arrangements. When women are better off economically and have more political influence, over time they are less victimized and less often in situations where they break the law, for example through prostitution, in order to survive.

Internationally, patriarchal gender arrangements support processes that result in primary and secondary victimization of girls and women. When girls are seen as economic burdens because of their dependent status, they may be abandoned as infants or rushed into marriages with older men. The latter practice creates a power imbalance that supports abuse within marriage. In the United States and other countries for which research is available, crime victims who act inconsistently with gender role expectations are not seen by criminal justice system employees as "real victims" and instead are blamed for their own ill fate. A variety of victimizations result from girls and women's lower status and/or restrictive expectations about how they should be and act. Women who are most protected from abuse are those who have resources, whose work outside the home provides them with supportive networks, and who are well educated. Their protection derives not just from their personal efficacy but also from their collective ability to draw on the support and resources from other people and to influence laws and policies to provide increased protection.

More than any of the other leading industrialized nations, the United States has had a prolonged and continuing policy that emphasizes criminalization, incarceration, and cutbacks in social welfare supports, and this type of policy has had negative results for girls and women (Sudbury, 2002). Compared to both developed and transitional economies, the United States has the highest gender gap in poverty rate and the highest poverty rate for female-headed households. The combined punishment and welfare policies are exemplified by federal efforts to encourage states to implement a lifelong ban on welfare benefits for drug offenders. The United States has influenced other nations in the adoption of its policies, specifically by encouraging allies to wage a war on drugs and to incarcerate the offenders, and by trying

Women who are most protected from abuse are those who have resources, whose work outside the home provides them with supportive networks, and who are well educated.

© Jim Craigmyle/CORBIS

to restrict access to abortion by not funding agencies that support abortion in developing countries. There are criticisms and efforts aimed at softening U.S. policies, but it is unclear when or whether the United States will tailor its policies to be less uniquely punitive. There is a need for continued study to explain the unusual U.S. policies and their particular impacts on racial and ethnic minorities and on women.

The Relevance of Context

The early theories about gender and crime explained victimization and illegal behavior as the results of the victim's or offender's psychological inadequacies. A major advance in criminological theory has been the increased attention to intermediate and macrolevel influences. Macrolevel influences include structural and cultural variations that are relevant to gender. They also include existing economic, welfare, and correctional policies. Intermediate-level contexts include family, neighborhood, and organizational settings. A person's beliefs, decisions, and actions make sense only in relation to some context. The contexts created by families, communities, and organizations, and more widely by the social structure and the media, have been highlighted in theoretical work on gender and crime.

For girls and women, family and community contexts often are characterized by the domination of males and restrictions on females. There are exceptions. For example, girls and boys in egalitarian homes have similar freedoms and restrictions (McCarthy et al., 1999). However, many contemporary girls experience more parental supervision than do their brothers, and male peers resist girls' involvement in breaking the law, in part because many forms of delinquency contradict gender ideologies (Bottcher, 1993). Similarly, women who hustle for illegal earnings on the street are severely constrained by men in the types of crimes they have the opportunity to commit (Maher, 1997). The choices that females and males make about whether and how to break the law are heavily affected by the gender arrangements and expectations in families, communities, and organizations.

For both females and males, the resources that are available to people in their families and communities can restrict the options they have for acting according to particular definitions of masculinity and femininity. When men have very limited resources, their abusive domination over women can be an avenue for accomplishing masculinity (Bourgois, 1996; Messerschmidt, 2000; Schwartz & DeKeseredy 1997; Whaley, 2001). Crime is less readily available to most girls and women as a way to accomplish a version of femininity. Instead, common ideologies about femininity need to be adjusted to fit with illegal activity. In many cases, gender ideologies and responsibilities for children influence females to be less involved than males in serious delinquency and crime.

Organizational context explains reactions to victims and to offenders. However, at the individual level, gender ideologies and stereotypes endure as influences on responses to people who break the law and those who have been victimized. For example, despite numerous reforms and training programs for personnel, the practices and attitudes of criminal justice actors do not always reflect the legal position that domestic violence is a serious crime (Iovanni & Miller, 2001). Some organizations, though, seem to have been considerably changed by the Feminist Movement and the resulting training and laws. For instance, judges in one court saw themselves as championing new laws against domestic violence (Ptacek, 1999). Also, there are correctional programs that purposely challenge gender stereotypes regarding appropriate work for women (Morash & Robinson, 2002a). In the field of organizational psychology, there is theory and research on how organizational change occurs, or why it does not occur (W. French & Bell, 1995; Porras & Robertson, 1992). This literature could profitably be integrated with feminist theory to improve understanding of both consistency and change in gender-related organizational responses to offenders and victims.

Looking at a broader context, a number of theoretical formulations explain how media imagery supports or justifies gender-related (and race-related) violence and negative responses to victims. Postmodern theorists point to the saturation of our daily lives with media that often distort human experience, and some criminological theories have identified the media as a source of ideas and attitudes that can stimulate and incite violence against women. It is commonly assumed that there is cross-national and cross-cultural sharing of media information that supports primary and secondary victimization of women and girls. This assumption requires careful examination. Many people around the world do not have access to international or even local media. Also, media have their effects selectively. Within the field of communications, the concept of *resistant readings* explains how an individual can be exposed to information contradictory to her or his beliefs, but those beliefs can remain unchanged. Consistent with the notion of resistant readings, exposure to local crime news did not affect people's fear of crime, although it did suggest to them that crime was a social problem worthy of attention (Gross & Aday, 2003). There is a need for better understanding of whether and when the media influence people. The stereotypes that are sometimes reinforced through community- and organization-level interactions might also be reinforced by media coverage. It also would be useful to understand the dynamics of resistant reading so that education might be developed to prevent the influence of violence-promoting media messages.

Intersections

At this point, there is considerable theory to link gender inequalities, which are magnified when combined with racial, ethnic, and other status markers, with victimization and crime. Quite a bit is known about the treatment of African Americans in the United States and, more specifically, in the criminal justice system. Although there are racial and ethnic inequalities for Native Americans and Hispanics in the United States, there has been relatively little research on how these differences and related ideologies play out in the justice system or in medical and other organizations that respond to victims and offenders. African Americans, Native Americans, and Hispanics are poorer, more residentially segregated, and more concentrated in poor and crime-ridden areas than are whites and Asians in the United States. One result is much higher levels of victimization, and another is greater risk for involvement in criminal activity. High rates of victimization are further created because racial and ethnic minorities (along with females and gay men) are the targets of hate crimes.

Agents of the criminal justice system repeatedly have been shown to think about black and white people differently. They are less likely to view African American women as legitimate victims of crime, and they are more likely to order harsh punishment for both men and women who are African American. For victims, recent research confirms old findings that black women raped by white men are disadvantaged in getting help in the community, even if that community has ample and well-developed resources for crime victims (R. Campbell, 1998; LaFree, 1989). For women offenders, harsh judgments about character are related to thinking about how good a mother a woman is, and it is more difficult for African American than for white women to establish that they are good mothers. The persistence of bias against African American women shows the importance of ideologies about white women and black women in influencing responses of community and criminal justice agency personnel.

There is a need for better explanations of how the intersection of minority race or ethnicity with being male is connected to criminal justice system responses.[61] The proportion of minorities in a community is related to harsher charges against African American men. Also, African American males are often viewed as highly dangerous and intractable. These factors suggest that judgments about the character

Because of the assumption that African American women are not good mothers, judges tend to sentence them to a term in prison.

© Bill Gentile/CORBIS

of minority men justify harsh criminal justice system responses devoid of any attempts to address or meet special needs. What are the attributions and assumptions about minority men that support this pattern of responses? Are these attributions and assumptions connected to misleading ideologies about masculinity and race or ethnicity? It is known that the attribution of different causes of crime for minority and majority youth can explain harsher judicial response to African American boys (Bridges & Steen, 1998). We need to know more about whether the same thought processes partly explain harsh punishment of minority adults.

Despite the variation that is introduced by race, ethnicity, and immigrant status, there is a persistent consistency across groups and between countries in the types of victimizations that are commonly experienced by girls and women, and in the gender ideologies that influence criminal justice system and other organizations' responses to crime and victimization. For women, motherhood is revered and the label of "bad mother" can lead to harsh punishment. For men, there is a certain acceptance of violence and disregard of relationships with children other than through economic support. Race and immigrant status may intensify the connection of gender to victimization, criminality, and responses of the justice system, but they do not obliterate the relationship.

Agency and Empowerment

Social movement activists stand as examples of individuals who, in groups or as part of organizations, have exercised agency to change laws, responses to victims, and responses to offenders. Theories also have increasingly assumed or even highlighted the agency of victims and offenders. It is recognized that women carve out safe places for themselves and resist everyday violence, offenders are heard saying they have made choices and are not victims, and many people who have been victimized say they are *survivors* to signal that they are not helpless, perpetual victims. Also emphasizing agency, there has been quite a bit of detailed information on the many considerations and circumstances that victims of ongoing violence take into account when they decide on their best course of action.

Even as there is increasing documentation of how women, girls, and other groups act with agency, there is also increasing documentation of the relatively limited capacity of people to chart their own courses and of the many constraints on their doing this. This is particularly the case for women offenders, including those who are and who are not incarcerated (Bosworth, 1996; Maher, 1997). Also, although crime victims resist, legal processes and procedures often silence them and keep them from explaining their own behavior and the context and circumstances of their victimization (Dunn, 2002). Material empowerment, in the form of financial resources through a job or some other source, is critical to domestic violence victims who seek to leave the offender (C. M. Sullivan, 1991). Material resources are also important for women who seek to break with a pattern of criminality (Holtfreter, Reisig, et al., 2002). National and state policies that reduce or eliminate welfare support and access to public housing therefore become implicated in whether people can act with agency. Understanding an individual's exercise of agency requires understanding the distribution of constraints and how this distribution is connected to gender, race, immigrant, and other statuses.

Complex Theories

Throughout this book, macrolevel, intermediate, and individual influences on social life have been described. Immediate contexts that give rise to patterns of crime and victimization are not just the result of the beliefs of people within those contexts, but also are considerably affected by worldwide economic conditions. Because of a weak economy in Puerto Rico, people immigrated to East Harlem, New York (Bourgois, 1996). There, the economic arrangements and opportunities led to women's employment and men's unemployment, and some men came to view violence against women as their primary (and only available) indicator of masculine dominance. Theory has been informed by numerous researchers who have heard the voices of victims, offenders, and criminal justice system personnel. The theorists' recognition of the broader social structure has been critical in adding a standpoint in addition to that taken by the subjects of research. Without the researchers' standpoint, gender and other inequities and differences can remain hidden in studies of individuals and contexts, and the theoretical explanations will be incomplete.

It is quite recently and somewhat minimally that there has been description of how girls and women create innovative gender identities in response to constraints and inequalities in family, neighborhood, and peer groups. This may reflect the fact that illegal activity is rarely a viable way for girls to achieve their femininities, and that barriers to breaking the law may be the reason.

Unlike the notion of femininities, *masculinities* is a lynchpin concept directing attention to the connection of males' individuality to both context and social structure. The interest in masculinities and crime has grown rapidly since 1990 (Alder & Polk, 1996, p. 396). Interest has extended to terrorist groups both inside (e.g., the White Aryan Resistance) and outside (e.g., the Taliban) of the United States. Kimmel (2003) argued that the predominantly male terrorist group members are angered by their fall in influence and economic resources that resulted from the development of a global economy. Members of groups inside the United States feel that they are not granted the influence and the prosperity to which they are entitled. Outside the United States, individuals become involved in terrorist acts where political history makes this a feasible response and a means to express their hate for countries or groups that they feel have infringed on their entitlements (Turk, 2004). In patriarchal societies, for men who feel that their economic status and related gender identity have been challenged, terrorist acts are one solution (Kimmel, 2003). Another is to exert increased control over women in efforts to reassert their prominence in patriarchal arrangements. For example, the Taliban in Afghanistan have prohibited women from exposing any part of their skin, from working outside the home, from venturing out of their homes without a male escort, and from being educated. The explanation of domestic and international terrorism shows the connection between social location, masculinity, and violent and criminal acts.

In work on identity and crime, the individual cannot meaningfully be separated from the context without risk of falling into the old mistake of attributing criminality to one's psychology, in this case gender identity. It would be a mistake to overemphasize creative gender identities that allow girls and women to break the law to the point of downplaying the situations of people who are troubled by their lawbreaking because it does not fit their senses of self. Many prior theories of boys' and men's criminality have been criticized for glorifying breaking the law. People do not always break the law as a way to accomplish masculinity or femininity, and there are compelling complementary and competing explanations for breaking the law. Gender identity, for some people, provides a connection between self, context, and illegal behavior, but a gender identity that supports lawbreaking is not a necessary condition for illegal activity.

Transgressing Academic Fields and Theories Within Fields

The rather small field of criminology and criminal justice would profit from ideas in other fields. For example, there is the interesting finding from psychological research (Silverthorn & Frick, 1999; Silverthorn, Frick, & Reynolds, 2001) that girls with troubled backgrounds do not exhibit antisocial behavior in early childhood, but that they later become involved in patterns of persistent criminal activity. This finding begs for some complementary detailed information about what was happening to these girls during their school years both inside and outside the classroom that might explain this dynamic. Another example is the failure of life course theorists to pay much attention to the considerable data-grounded theorizing about various pathways that girls and women follow into illegal activity (Chesney-Lind, 1983, 1989; Daly, 1992; Erickson et al., 2000; Giordano et al., 2002; E. M. Miller, 1986). The recent discovery (Laub & Sampson, 2003) that men move out of criminality in rather unpredictable ways reaffirms the very early findings in the pathways research that numerous exigencies, including individual choice and motivation, affect women's involvement and persistence in illegal activity. Yet, the life course theorizing seems to be untouched by the pathways work (E. M. Miller, 1986). The life course and pathway perspectives stand as distinct bodies of work, the first allowing some comparison of males with females, usually without much consideration of gendered contexts, the second focusing on girls and women, and emphasizing the relevance of gender identity and gendered contexts. The two approaches are informed by qualitative research, though there is more quantitative work in the life course perspective, and both suggest quantitative models for testing. Both consider the effects of criminal justice system responses on subsequent illegal behavior. Though not fundamentally incompatible with each other, the life course and pathways perspectives are relatively uninformed by each other. In some cases, perspectives are narrowed by academic discipline; in others, by a perspective within a discipline. Also, with some exceptions, people who do not work within feminist perspectives tend to completely ignore feminist theory and research (Daly & Chesney-Lind, 1988).

Gender and Sexual Orientation

At several points, this book has considered sexual orientation. Both women (lesbian and heterosexual) and gay men experience victimization that is related to not being a heterosexual male. They and other groups, for instance racial minorities, are the targets of hate crimes. Also, when they are victimized by sexual assault or domestic violence, agents in the criminal justice system along with other people may interpret their behavior as incongruous with what would be consistent with gender role expectations—with the result that their victimization is not taken seriously and is doubted. Both groups also have struggled to change laws that criminalize their sexual behaviors. Finally, at various times feminist and gay, lesbian and bisexual activists have joined together to address common issues and concerns. By considering the parallels between gender and sexual orientation in relation to victimization and justice system responses, it is possible to see the enforcement of dominant ideologies and arrangements that advantage heterosexual, white males and that disadvantage multiple groups.

Gay and lesbian individuals feel that they are targets of violence because of patriarchy in the United States.

© Ed Kashi/CORBIS

A consideration of sexual orientation not only shows similarities between two groups that are not dominant but also raises questions about the adequacy of feminist theory to explain all forms of violence. Feminist theory emphasizes the connection of patriarchal beliefs and arrangements to violence. Because some women attack women, and gay men attack other men, the power and control linked to patriarchy cannot be the sole explanation of violence within lesbian or gay relationships. This reality underscores the importance of considering multiple oppressions, and of realizing that in certain contexts, patriarchal arrangements are not the immediate explanations for abuse. This line of reasoning can extend to violence in different-sexed relationships. There may be multiple reasons that men attack women, and patriarchy is not always one of the reasons. Patriarchy is one variant of a larger emphasis on power and control in intimate-partner relationships. The dislocation that results from immigration, the isolation that comes when people feel they must hide their lifestyles, and the lack of knowledge and connection to support networks can affect both gay and lesbian and straight people in their intimate relationships. Patriarchal arrangements can produce or exacerbate the disadvantages of a potential victim, but patriarchal arrangements are not the only causes of vulnerability. A consideration of alternative or multilevel causes makes it possible to include people who are not heterosexual in explanations of both violence and responses to victims and offenders.

Research Approaches

Advances in understanding gender, crime, and justice have been pushed forward by researchers using a number of different approaches. Consistent with the nexus of feminist activism with theory development, qualitative research, including research that recognizes and describes the standpoints of both subjects and researchers, has been particularly important in discovering new concepts that are influential in gendered settings and in showing people's agency and the constraints on that agency. Qualitative research also has revealed details of how people make decisions and the ideologies that influence their thinking. When research captures the standpoint of people being studied, it can show limitations on their choices and the constraints on agency that result from gender (Comack, 1993). Quantitative research has provided complementary information by exposing the strength of the connection between influences and outcomes, whether these connections occur in alternative locations, and in some cases by refining conceptualization.

Qualitative Research

For three reasons, qualitative research has been important in the development of theory on gender, victimization, criminality, law, and the justice system. First, qualitative research is well suited to concept identification and refinement.

Concept identification and refinement has been a crucial building block in the many academic fields that had previously ignored gender and the realities of girls' and women's lives. Second, qualitative research allows discovery and description of how contexts are gendered. Interactions within families, communities, and criminal justice agencies provide different experiences and opportunities depending on one's gender. Detailed descriptions are necessary to fully understand the gendered effects of contexts and to understand how those contexts are reproduced and therefore maintained. Third, qualitative research can provide detailed information on individuals' perceptions of their own experiences and settings, their reasoning, and their motivations. Subjects in qualitative research have some voice and can shape discussion to pursue a new topic or provide detailed descriptions and explanations of circumstances, events, and self. Thus, a specific contribution of qualitative research has been to show how people's gender ideologies affect involvement in criminal activity, the law, and responses to victims and offenders.

Quantitative Research

Quantitative research also has resulted in major contributions to theory on gender, crime, and justice. In some cases, discoveries from qualitative research have been studied and refined through subsequent quantitative work. From her qualitative research and observations of prosecutors interacting at their offices, Frohmann (1991) discovered that prosecutors' concerns that a case be winnable led them to discredit some victims' allegations. Subsequent quantitative research findings were consistent with this same dynamic, because blame and believability factors were strong predictors of prosecutors' decisions in another setting (Spohn, Beichner, et al., 2001). In another example, Daly (1994) collected qualitative data from interviews with court personnel. She then confirmed her findings with quantitative research on sentencing. Later, other individuals showed, with quantitative research, that offenders' role in caring for dependents was connected to the severity of sentences, as would be expected from the familial paternalism explanation (Bickle & Peterson, 1991; Daly, 1987b; Flavin, 2001). Research that is connected to observation, interview, and detailed description of both settings and individuals can reveal the effects of gender, race, and other statuses, and can show how that context constrains or enables certain actions. The individual is not lost, for it is possible to discern how she or he reasons and thinks. Yet, the effects of gender arrangements also are apparent. Quantitative research can show that some contextual and individual differences, perhaps in combination, are important in explaining social phenomena of interest. It should be noted, however, that an absence of quantitative evidence does not invalidate the conclusions from qualitative research. It is possible that the observed unfolding of events occurs rarely or only in particular settings, or that it is not possible to capture, in numbers, complex events and their sequencing. Under these conditions, the qualitative evidence of how social phenomena come about is not invalidated by the absence of quantitative confirmation.

Need for Replication

Research designs that address the issue of changes over time and differences between places contribute to understanding the influence (or lack of influence) of local context and the dynamics of change or stability. The relatively few instances of even partial replication of research for different periods are helpful in revealing change or continuity. Bertrand's (1999) assessment of the gendered aspects of correctional programming for women confirmed the suspicion that new approaches are like old wine in new bottles. She and her colleagues found that across different countries, motherhood was idealized in the prison setting and work-related programs reflected common gender stereotypes. The conclusion was the same in research published more than 20 years earlier (Glick & Neto, 1977). Despite exceptions, the relative lack of updated research results in serious gaps in knowledge. For example, it remains unclear whether criminal justice and mental health professionals are basing the placement of girls in secure settings on their sexual activity to the extent that they did in the past. In relation to differences in place, although some researchers use data from multiple sites (e.g., Bertrand, 1999; Farley, Baral, et al., 1998; Frohmann, 1991; Levinson, 1989), few replicate each other's work. (An exception is studies in Australia and the United States that showed that police tended to blame men for their own sexual assault because they assumed that males should be able to defend themselves; see Finn & Stalans, 1997; Stewart & Maddren, 1997). Funding availability and academic rewards and values may be partial explanations for why there is limited replication of studies. Given the decentralization of the U.S. justice, mental health, and other governmental services systems; demographic differences across the country; and changes over time, replication and multisite studies are essential if theory is to reveal either time- and place- specific processes or processes that persist.

At several points in this book, just one or two studies have been cited to support an explanation, and generalizability beyond a particular place and time therefore has been limited. Historical, geographic, and local contexts are important in understanding crime and the criminal justice system. For instance, gender-, ethnic group–, and race-specific networks of people in communities provide very different opportunities for both legal and illegal earnings. Similarly, legal resources for addressing violence against women vary considerably between places. Because of continuous efforts to reform the system (often in incongruent ways) and the fragmentation of criminal justice in the United States, there is a need for research that applies to more than one place and that looks for changes over time. One strategy for doing this is through funding of similar studies at multiple sites. For example, the Minneapolis Domestic Violence research was replicated at five different sites (Buzawa & Buzawa, 2003, pp. 98–104). Although the replications were not exact, the studies together raised doubts that the connection of arrest to deterrence is uniform or simple. Another example is the federally funded Causes and Correlates of Delinquency Program, which examined pathways into delinquency in Denver, Rochester, and Pittsburgh. Despite examples of funded research in more than one site, feminist explanations rarely have been developed through this sort of research. It would be useful to have more research on how gender, race, ethnicity, or combinations of these affect responses to either victims or offenders, and the dynamics of how these effects emerge in different settings. Given the investment in changing laws, policies, and programs with resources from the Violence Against Women Act (VAWA), it would seem to be wise to compare some key places across the country in rigorous research on the contemporary decision-making process. The same is true in regard to gender-responsive programming for girls and women.

Short of funding incentives, it would be possible for collectives of researchers to coordinate their efforts and collect data at multiple sites. This would seem to be consistent with feminist tenets of carrying out research to promote positive changes for disadvantaged gender groups. One might imagine a group of researchers examining women's understanding of whether they have been treated justly as they look back at and try to make sense of a string of police encounters, court appearances, and correctional program experiences. By doing this sort of research in several places, it would become clear whether there are common threads through the experiences, or whether the experiences depend on the local context. Another example of much-needed research is comparison of females' and males' experiences with public defense services, which vary widely across the United States and which might vary according to the gender and the race of the accused. Although the networks of contributors to feminist theory on crime are strong, notably in the professional associations The American Society of Criminology and The Academy of Criminal Justice Sciences, these networks are not typically used to organize research efforts. Instead, the sole researcher or small research team approach is used. The feminist network would usefully be used to support multisite, coordinated research to fill key gaps in understanding gender and crime.

Final Comments on Justice

Justice requires fairly addressing conflicts and inequities between people. In the case of criminal law, conflicts are between individuals and the state, which represents other citizens. In civil law, conflicts are between individuals. Gender inequities in the United States and between and within other nations influence patterns of criminality, patterns of victimization, and the responses of the justice and other systems when crimes have occurred. These inequities are maintained by broad social policies, such as international aid and crime control policy and national welfare, housing, and punishment policy. The inequities also persist in part because they are supported by ideologies and related distributions of opportunities and resources related to gender, race, social class, ethnic, and immigrant status.

At the same time that society-wide inequities persist, the nature of laws and the practices of the criminal justice system have been challenged vigorously, and there has been some change. Notably, in the United States and many other countries, in some places domestic violence is dealt with differently than it was in the past, with the result that many women have additional resources and support when they contend with abuse. Similarly, there is widely publicized recognition by federal agencies, including the National Institute of Corrections, and some state and local entities that correctional programs for women should address gender-specific needs or even empower and equip women to step out of the constraints of traditional gender roles. Challenges to inequities are complemented in governmental jurisdictions where there is growing realization of the financial drain imposed by punitive policies related to crime.

Equivalent Versus Special Treatment Based on Gender

There are alternative viewpoints on whether just criminal justice responses require equivalent responses to females and males. One point of view is that women and girls are not necessarily treated justly if they are treated equivalently to how men and boys are treated (Chesney-Lind & Pollock, 1995). According to this viewpoint, because gender is relevant to the experiences and needs of both crime victims and offenders, fair justice system and legal responses would take gender differences into account, though they would not disadvantage any gender group. For example, correctional programs for women would challenge negative stereotypes about women's capabilities and appropriate activities. In the same vein, when judge and jury ponder how the typical person might act in a given situation, not only the expected actions of the common man but also the expected actions of the common woman would be considered. An impending domestic assault might be assessed quite differently depending on the intended victim's gender. This would be taken into account in making sense of whether the victim acted in a reasonable way. More generally, the application of criminal law would take into account an understanding of how women experience a variety of situations and would not assume that they have the same options or perceptions as do men.

A second point of view on justice and equivalent versus special treatment is that any special consideration of females would not be desirable because it will emphasize their need to be controlled for their own good and their victim status (Nagel & Johnson, 1994). Historically, women's and girls' special treatment in the justice system has not always been to their benefit, for example when they received long indeterminate sentences and men received shorter sentences, or when girls were incarcerated to prevent their sexual activity. An argument against this rationale, however, is that it is not clear why taking the offender's situation into account will necessarily result in her being treated more harshly. Sentences that expose women to programs that empower them, build their resources, or allow them to continue roles as parents or in other positive relationships would seem to promote a positive outcome. Perhaps the important consideration in assessing gender-specific or gender-relevant criminal justice system responses is whether gender-related stereotypes and ideologies that have disadvantaged women in the past can be changed so that special treatment has positive results for them.

Public Policy, Legislation, and Change

Public policies and laws have had inconsistent effects on women's resources and opportunities. In many settings, there have been increased resources to address violence against women. However, women have had their choices limited in states that have developed new restrictions on access to abortion. Across the country, severely penalizing drug-related crime has led to high rates of incarceration. Abused mothers have been held responsible when their children have witnessed the abuse. Additionally, lifetime restrictions on receiving welfare after a drug conviction and no-tolerance policies when any household member is involved in drug or violent crimes have reduced resources for women, especially those who are poor and/or African American, Native American, or Hispanic. As a result of both feminist and conservative political forces and of state and local variation within the United States, women's control of key aspects of their lives varies by place.

Because of larger social forces, the U.S. criminal justice system has limited capacity to ensure justice. There is no doubt that some degree of criminality and victimization is connected to urban poverty, racial segregation, and joblessness (Krivo et al., 1998; Wilson, 1996). Addressing structurally induced inequities that feed illegal behavior would require not just individual help and advocacy for victims and offenders, but also changes in social policies. For example, for women addicted to drugs, a safe environment and support through health and social services outreach might have the benefits of keeping women alive and HIV-negative (Erickson et al., 2000). Explicit purposes of federal welfare policies are to encourage the formation and maintenance of two-parent families and to keep fathers who do not live in the home involved with their children through visitation or joint custody arrangements (Mink, 2001). Most mothers who are not married must work outside the home, but those who are married to a working man do not have this requirement. Justice would require changing these policies so that women who have a child with an abusive male have more opportunity to establish independent living situations and end contact with abusers. In fact, an argument could be made that all women who are in an unhappy marriage should have the opportunity to establish an independent living situation.

It should be recognized that there are approaches to promoting justice outside the agencies of the criminal justice system and apart from changing public policy and legislation. People can promote justice through the groups and the communities they belong to. One result of the Feminist Movement is that in some settings there are new developments in both talk and action as they pertain to gender and crime. For example, in sharp contrast to lingering beliefs that mitigate against taking women's reports of victimization at face value, at least in some settings, contemporary discourse has moved beyond assertions of and reactions to stereotypes about females and males. Specifically relevant to sexual assault, in secondary schools and on college campuses, there is dialogue, often in peer workshops, about the meaning of terms such as *affirmative verbal consent, freely given agreement,* and *sexual communication* (Sanday, 1996, p. 265). A core assumption in such dialogue is that sexual assault victimization does not require that women resist in order for a sexual assault to occur, and that women's sexiness, desire, and silence cannot be translated to a "yes" by men absent conversation that allows women to explicitly state their preferences for or against sexual activity. Also on college campuses, some pro-feminist men have confronted and opposed their male peers in efforts to challenge rape myths and prevent violence against women (Schwartz & DeKeseredy, 1997, p. x). In the college campus examples, the fundamental changes reflected by shifts in dialogue and attitudes toward women transgress the confines of official criminal justice agencies and suggest broad social changes that could reduce the everyday injustices of insults and injuries, many of which do not come to the attention of the justice system or are not the subject of laws.

Conclusion

Justice and injustice are embedded in the broader social structure that creates inequities within and between nations. Justice and injustice are the product of (sometimes contradicting) social movements, organizational practices, and individual patterns of actions and discrete acts. The categorization of something as "just" or "unjust" depends on an individual's standpoint. Thus, whether circumstances or actions are just or not depends on multiple levels of influence, including how each of us sees particular patterns, situations, or events. There are three perspectives on injustice as it pertains to gender and crime. They are the *structural inequality perspective, the human rights perspective*, and the *criminal justice system and law perspective*. For each perspective, activists,' victims,' and offenders' assessments of the achievement of justice can be imagined.

Individuals who are concerned with the **structural inequality perspective on justice**, both within and between nations, see injustice in conditions that promote illegal activity and subsequent responses that then punish it with no attention to the initial causes. From this perspective, persistent pockets of poverty that result in boys' and men's reliance on illegal activity, including violence, to live up to their own images of ideal masculinity can be conceptualized as an injustice. The combination of women's and girls' disadvantaged position in many countries and their extreme poverty in particular countries creates injustice by contributing to trafficking for sexual exploitation or coping by engaging in prostitution. The criminal justice system then magnifies injustice through policies such as mass incarceration of people for a variety of offenses and criminalization of people forced to trade sex for money. For offenders, there is injustice in programs that do not enable people to overcome their economic and other disadvantages, or that even increase these disadvantages.

The **human rights perspective on justice** identifies a wide range of rights that all people have just because they are human beings. In the human rights perspective, violence against females and people who are gay, lesbian, or bisexual is not acceptable. U.S. laws guarantee human rights, and the United Nations and other international bodies, such as the World Court, seek to address human rights violations through sanctions, programs to promote change, and international justice processes. In this perspective, lack of health care, food, and shelter; the use of torture; and poverty are other major justice issues.

The **criminal justice system and law perspective on justice** emphasizes legal rights and the operations, programs, and practices of the juvenile and criminal

A speaker before the 1975 World Conference on International Women told the assembled delegates that the crusade for women's rights is meaningless without a total "transformation of the world economic order." This viewpoint highlights the structural inequality perspective on justice.

© Bettmann/CORBIS

justice systems. From this perspective, there are several improvements in justice for girls and women who are victims and offenders, at least in some locations. For example, the VAWA shifted resources and changed responses to victims of domestic violence and sexual assault. There are increases in the variety and the location of services to support intimate-partner and domestic violence victims. In the Netherlands, prostitutes' collectives and their advocates have had laws reformed so that they are not criminalized, but individuals who exploit them through trafficking or involving minors are apprehended and punished. What is common across the three perspectives is that gender in combination with race, ethnicity, and other location markers continues to have negative effects on girls and women. Efforts to ensure justice are continuous.

Key Terms

Criminal justice system and law perspective on justice

Human rights perspective on justice

Structural inequality perspective on justice

Review and Discussion

1. What are the greatest injustices that are related to gender? How are they related? For example, are they a result of gender arrangements? Are they more often experienced by one gender group?

2. If you could recommend one policy change that the U.S. government could promote to increase justice, what would it be? Justify your choice of this policy change.

3. What are the most effective steps that private citizens, advocates for justice, and the Feminist Movement could take at this time to increase justice for all citizens, both inside and outside the United States?

4. The following question is suitable for a group activity or individual writing. Groups or individuals can assess the adequacy of one type of feminism against the evidence presented in this book. Which of the following feminist perspectives best explains the connection of gender to criminality, victimization, responses to crime and victimization, and the criminal law and its implementation: radical, liberal, socialist, psychoanalytic and gender, multicultural, or global feminism? These terms were defined in the first chapter of the book. Provide research evidence to support your response.

Web Sites to Explore

Resources that can be used to assess justice from a criminal justice system and law perspective are available at www.lib.msu.edu/harris23/crimjust/women.htm

The site www.whrnet.org/ provides comprehensive information and analysis on women's human rights and global issues.

At www.globalpolicy.org/socecon/inequal/indexgen.htm, there are resources for understanding the structural inequalities that affect girls and women worldwide.

Notes

Chapter 1: Tackling Key Questions About Gender, Crime, and Justice

1. Each new key term is marked in bold type and is defined in the index. Key terms are introduced throughout the book.

2. *DeGraffenreid et al. v. General Motors*, 413 F. Supp. 142 (E.D. Mo. 1976).

3. *Moore v. Hughes Helicopter, Inc.*, 708 F. 2d 475 (9th Cir. 1983).

4. Status offenses are behaviors that would not be considered criminal for an adult and include being runaway, use of alcohol, being incorrigible or out of control of parents, and truancy.

5. These data were collected by Merry Morash and Anna Santiago with funding from the Social Science Research Council.

6. This section borrows heavily from fuller descriptions of the types of feminist theory in Daly and Chesney-Lind (1988) and Tong (1998).

Chapter 2: Gender and the Law

1. Another reason for the shift toward criminal apprehension and processing of perpetrators of domestic violence was a widely publicized study that concluded that arrest was a greater deterrent to future violence than was either crisis intervention or therapeutic counseling (L. W. Sherman & Berk, 1984). The New York case was *Bruno v. Codd*, 407 N.Y.S. 2d 165 (App. Div. 1978); the California case was *Scott v. Hart*, U.S. District Court for the Northern District of California, C76–2395. The Torrington case was *Thurman v. City of Torrington*, 595 F. Supp. 1521, 1984.

2. *Navarro v. Block*, 72 F. 3rd 712 (9th Cir. 1995), aff'd. *Fajardo v. County of Los Angeles* (9th Cir. June 3, 1999) 179 F. 3rd 698.

3. *Hakken v. Washtenaw County*, 901 F. Supp. 1245 (E.D. Mich. 1995).

4. In some states, restraining orders can be obtained through the criminal court (Chaudhuri & Daly, 1992, p. 228).

5. *United States v. Morrison*, 529 U.S. 598, 627.

6. FGM is also referred to as *female circumcision*. This is misleading, because particularly the more extreme forms of cutting are not at all analogous to male circumcision.

7. Public Law No. 104–208, Sections 579, 644, 645 passed September 30, 1996.

8. H.R. 1048, passed April 23, 1990.

9. Public Law 103-322, H.R. 3355, 103rd Congress, 2nd session.

10. H.R.1082, 106th Congress, passed March 11, 1999.

11. *Romer v. Evans*, 517 U.S. 620 (1996).

12. *Roe v. Wade* (410 U.S. 113), 1973.

13. The pro-choice activists claimed that 1 million people marched on April 25, 2004. It is not possible to know the exact number of pro-choice and pro-life protesters who were present, but the demonstration was one of the largest in U.S. history.

14. Social Security Act, 42 U.S.C.A. 1396 (2000).

15. *Harris v. McRae*, 448 U.S. 297 (1980); *Webster v. Reproductive Health Services*, 492 U.S. 490, 511 (1989); *Poelker v. Doe*, 432 U.S. 519, 521 (1977).

16. Partial Birth Abortion Ban Act of 2003, S. 3, 108th Congress (2003), enacted as Pub. Law No. 108–105, November 5, 2003.

17. Unborn Victims of Violence Act, U.S. Public Law 108–212, March 25, 2004.

18. *Ferguson v. City of Charleston* (South Carolina), 186 F.3d 469, 476 (4th Cir., 1999).

19. *Ferguson v. City of Charleston*, 532 U.S. 67 (2001).

20. See U.S. Constitution, Art VI, 2; Restatement (Third) of the Foreign Relations Law of the United States, 115 (1987).

21. International Covenant on Civil and Political Rights, opened for signature December 16, 1966, 999 U.N.T.S. 171.

22. Declaration on the Elimination of Violence Against Women, General Assembly Resolution, U.N. General Assembly Official Records, 48th Session, U.N. Doc. A/Res/48/104 (1994).

23. Supreme Court of the United States, John Geddes Lawrence and Tyron Garner, *Petitioners v. Texas*, No. 02–102, June 26, 2003.

Chapter 3: Gender-Related Victimization

1. The NCVS results presented in Table 3.1 through Table 3.3 are based on analysis completed by Merry Morash, Hoan Bui, and Yan Zhang. The analysis was supported by a grant from the American Statistical Association. The incidents considered are all those reported in bounded interviews between 1993 and 1999. Analysis was done to take into account the sampling design and to produce estimates for the population. The data were combined for several years so that there were enough cases in less-populous racial groups (e.g., Asian, Native American).

2. There is limited good evidence of the breakdown in types of hate crimes. Police reports from 17 law enforcement jurisdictions indicate that most (61%) hate crimes that are officially tallied and publicized are motivated by race, and 14% are motivated by religion, 13% by sexual orientation, 11% by ethnicity, and 1% by victim disability. Most involve violence. These figures are from Strom (2001).

3. Countries included in the research included Australia, Austria, Belgium, Canada, the Czech Republic, Denmark, Finland, France, Germany, Hungary, Ireland, Israel, Italy, Luxembourg, the Netherlands, Norway, Poland, Russia, the Slovak Republic, Spain, Sweden, Switzerland, Taiwan, the United Kingdom, and the United States.

4. Similarly, in two Native American communities, women's increased status was connected to increased domestic violence against them (Durst, 1991).

5. Examples are from data collected by Merry Morash and Anna Santiago with funding from the Institute for Social Science Research.

6. The questions and analysis described here were done by Merry Morash, Hoan Bui, and Yan Zhang with support from the National Science Foundation.

7. The Indian Child Welfare Act, Public Law 95-608 (1978), 25 U.S.C. 1901.

8. Current immigration law does stipulate that women who leave a sponsoring husband will not be deported if they have been abused. However, not all women are aware of this, and even if they are aware, they may not have the knowledge and resources to make their case before the courts.

Chapter 4: Social Movements and the Response to Victims of Gender-Related Crime

1. *Manavi* means "primal woman" in Sanskrit.

2. For additional discussion of South Asian women's organizations in the United States and their focus on violence against women, see Abraham (1995).

3. Information on the history of the social movement against violence against gay and lesbian people is taken from Jenness and Broad (1997, pp. 49–73).

Chapter 5: The Influence of Context and Individual Differences on Responses to Gender-Related Victimization

1. When one spouse threatens the other with retracting sponsorship that makes it possible to stay in the United States legally or with reporting irregularities to the Immigration and Naturalization Service, this is called the green card factor.

2. Controversy over the consistency of this finding is found in articles by Bachman (1993, 1998), who has argued that there are no differences in reporting of stranger and nonstranger sexual assaults, and Pollard (1995), who has argued that Bachman's research was flawed.

Chapter 6: Explanations of Illegal Behavior

1. This finding is consistent with research that considered an earlier period (LaFree, 1998; Steffensmeier & Allan, 1996).

2. This view challenges life course theorists' concentration on boys' antisocial behavior (Laub & Sampson, 1993; Moffitt, 1990; Nagin, Farrington, & Moffitt, 1995).

3. See the section on "Child Abuse Through Failure to Protect" in Chapter 2, pp. 51–52.

4. Much of the information in this section is found in Fishbein (2001).

Chapter 7: Gender and Response to Lawbreakers

1. Personal Responsibility and Work Opportunity Reconciliation Act of 1996, Pub. L. No. 104–193.

2. Unfortunately, their analysis did not consider predictors of particular relevance to women (e.g., welfare support) and did not therefore shed light on the drivers of women-specific incarceration rates.

3. Finally, "the concentration of blacks in the population has dramatically opposite effects on the imprisonment of white women and black women, significantly increasing the likelihood

of imprisonment for white women while decreasing the likelihood of imprisonment for black women" (Bridges & Beretta, 1994, p. 173).

4. Supermax prisons are very large prisons that use advanced technologies to monitor and physically control and isolate offenders.

5. Policies have been enacted to restrict public housing for people involved in drug-related offenses or those in the presence of, or associated with, drug users. Federal law has limited the time that a child can remain in foster care; an unintended result is that many women who are incarcerated lose custody of their children permanently.

6. Cain has noted that given the importance of discourse, "It is necessary, therefore, not only to recognize the discourse but also to examine its internal (il)logic, and the ways and sites in which it is deployed. This is the *strategy of deconstruction*" (Cain, 1990, p. 7).

7. Because their full model was not statistically significant, they considered these findings as suggestive.

8. To figure out the influence of gender on sentencing decisions, Daly (1987b) began her work with interviews with 35 officials of a western Massachusetts courthouse. At a later time, these interviews were supplemented with additional data from judges in New York. The interviews were designed to expose how court officials reasoned about the appropriate sentences for both women and men. Findings from the interviews were confirmed with quantitative data on 2,004 defendants prosecuted in a New York City criminal court during 1974–1975 (Daly, 1987a), and later with data on 500 defendants convicted in the King County, Washington, superior court in 1973 (Daly, 1989b).

9. Habitual offender laws make it possible to charge an offender not only with particular crimes, but as a repeat offender who can be penalized more severely than others. In Florida, people are eligible for sentencing under the habitual offender statute under the following conditions: "(1) The inmate's current offense must have been committed after October 1, 1988. (2) The inmate must have at least two prior felony convictions or one prior violent felony conviction. (3) Each prior offense must be unique—meaning that each offense is a separate commitment to the Florida Department of Corrections and is not related to the current offense. (4) The prior offenses must have been committed within five years of the current offense, or the release from the previous sentence" (Crawford, 2000, p. 265).

10. For example, Rafter (1985, p. 234) described how, historically, the discipline of male convicts was shaped by notions about masculinity in addition to ideas about control and labor.

11. In contrast, in the 1990s, a study revealed that at Bedford Hills Correctional Facility in New York, mothers with children in the nursery were expected to participate in work and/or education, but had the added responsibility of arranging for child care for their children and of caring for them before and after work and/or education.

12. A small number of U.S. prisons do provide nurseries for young children, occasional weekend visits, or visits during vacations.

13. The document recognized structural disadvantages, especially for Aboriginal women.

14. Daly's (1987a) work on familial patriarchy is a rare exception to the silence on this topic.

Chapter 8: Advances and Challenges in Understanding Gender, Crime, and Justice

1. As noted in Chapter 7, Rafter (1985, p. 234) does describe how, historically, discipline imposed on male convicts was shaped by notions about masculinity as well as ideas about control and labor.

Glossary

Accomplishing gender entails acting in a way that one defines as feminine or masculine.

Adolescent onset conduct disorder refers to initial involvement in antisocial behaviors during the adolescent years.

Agency is the capacity of a person to act in a self-directed and purposeful way.

Antisocial behavior. See *conduct disorders.*

Backlash is the countermovement against change promoted by a social movement.

Backlash hypothesis refers to the idea that a reduction in women's inequality with men is met with men's efforts to reestablish their dominance through violence against women, for example through rape, domestic violence, or homicide.

A *battered woman who harmed or killed the abuser* typically has little or no criminal record, and has been violently attacked or been threatened with violent attack.

Battered women's syndrome is a condition of being so fearful of being battered again that it is impossible for a woman to take action or leave the abuser.

Benevolent sexist beliefs stereotype females as weak and passive, and therefore in need of men's protection. These stereotypes are seen as reflecting positive qualities.

Blame and believability factors are information about the victim, the offender, and the incident that the prosecutor considers when she or he reasons about whether the jury will believe the victim.

Bureaucratic activists in the Feminist Movement include professionals who were recruited into the U.S. feminist movement from the bureaucracies in which they worked.

Childhood onset conduct disorder refers to antisocial behavior that begins in childhood.

Civil law specifies violations of citizens' rights that are not necessarily in themselves criminal actions and allows victims to take cases to court to obtain economic relief from perpetrators.

Classic rape profile refers to the erroneous assumption that rape typically is perpetrated by a male stranger against a female in an unfamiliar or deserted place, and as resulting in obvious physical injury to the victim.

Collectivist activists in the Feminist Movement typically are younger women who were politically active at the grassroots level and who were recruited into the U.S. Feminist Movement.

Complex posttraumatic syndrome, which can result from repeated victimization, is indicated by long-term changes in how survivors regulate their emotions, self-perceptions, relations with other people, and meanings they attach to actions and events.

Conduct disorders (also referred to as *antisocial behavior*) are indicated by some of a set of aggressive behaviors, including aggression to people and animals (such as bullying or intimidating others and stealing from victims while confronting them), destruction of property, deceitfulness along with lying or stealing, and serious violation of rules set by the family or school.

Coordinated community response involves numerous agencies and programs in a community that plan for and implement a consistent response to one or more types of criminal victimization in order to communicate that victimization is not tolerated and to enhance the assistance that is provided to victims. Medical, business, social welfare, and criminal justice agencies, among others, can be involved.

Corrections refers to an enterprise, not to the intended or actual effects of situations, regimes, and programs that the correctional enterprise implements. This enterprise consists both of state agencies and facilities and of numerous private businesses that produce and support construction, services, security, and programs.

Court talk is about the law, the merits and the realities of a case, and what should be done by the state to and for both the alleged victim and the alleged offender.

Criminal justice refers to the laws that define and prohibit criminal behavior and to the police, court, and corrections agencies that implement the laws.

Criminal justice system and law perspective on justice emphasizes legal rights and the operations, programs, and practices of the juvenile and criminal justice systems.

Criminal law defines violations against the state. A public prosecutor represents the state before the court.

Cultural relativity argument is that behavior should not be criminalized if that behavior is consistent with religious or cultural beliefs held by an individual as a member of a group.

Culture is a set of shared beliefs, values, norms, objects, and creations, found in national, ethnic, and other groups.

Date rape refers to forced sex within a dating relationship.

Discourse includes verbal and written communication that constitutes influential systems of thought and related practice. Postmodernist theory has emphasized that discourses justify and influence how people treat each other, for example, how the criminal justice system treats offenders.

Domestic violence includes violence directed by one member of a household against another.

Dominant refers to the privileged status of people who are a majority and/or who have uniquely ready access to resources, opportunities, and power, and therefore can exert some control over other people.

Dowry burning is a form of wife abuse that involves a husband setting his newly married wife on fire, often with the support of his family, to express dissatisfaction with the dowry provided by the wife's family to the husband's family. It results in death or disfigurement, and it opens the husband's opportunity to seek another wife.

Drug-connected women are women with limited criminal records who broke the law and have used or sold drugs as a result of relationships with a male intimate, children, or their mothers.

Dual arrest refers to domestic violence cases in which both parties are arrested.

The *Duluth model* of coordinated community response to victimization, developed in Minnesota in 1980, created a freestanding organization with responsibilities for promoting cooperation and institutional change in response to domestic violence.

Economically motivated women who break the law typically commit crimes to cope with poverty or out of greed.

Emphasized femininity reflects stereotypical female qualities, such as passivity, dependence, and fragility, and is considered as complementary to the aggressive domination embodied in interactions that reflect *hegemonic masculinity*.

Empowerment is the process of increasing *agency*.

Everyday practices theory explains boys' greater involvement in delinquency than girls' as the result of gender differences in everyday patterns of action and practices, especially in the family and among peers.

Everyday violence refers to fear-promoting experiences and circumstances that influence people to automatically take possible acts of violence into account.

Familial paternalism is judicial concern with the welfare of the family members who were dependent on the defendant.

Female genital mutilation is the surgical removal of the clitoris and/or the labia minora or majora.

Femininities and masculinities are conceptions of what it is to be a girl or boy, or a woman or man.

Feminist empiricism is the application of positivist social science methods to the study of gender-related oppression. An objective of the research is to reduce oppression.

Feminist Movement, also referred to as the *Women's Movement,* is group mobilization in many countries intended to establish gender equality and to address problems that are common to girls and women.

Feminist theory (actually several theories) considers the oppression of girls and women and emphasizes research that will improve the lives of individuals who are oppressed.

Feminization of poverty is a trend beginning at the end of the 20th century in the United States for poverty to be increasingly concentrated among women and the members of households they head.

First wave of the Feminist Movement is social activism to promote the right of women to vote and participate in other aspects of social life, between 1848 and 1919 in the United States.

Fixed identity is a status that sums up the totality of a person's life and personality and that does not change. Some people regard *prostitute* as a fixed identity.

Gender—individual level conceptualization consists of ideas about self and about others, regarding appropriate and expected behaviors connected to femininity and masculinity. These ideas result from interactions with other people, but they also are influenced by education, experience, and self-reflection.

Gender—macrolevel conceptualization consists of patterns of social and economic differences related to whether people are women or men and girls or boys. Specifically, there are gender differences in monetary and other resources, access to different kinds of jobs, and power. The patterns of differences are referred to with different terms, including gender organization, the sex gender system, and gender stratification.

Gender-challenge perspective on corrections focuses on gender-related disadvantages and the need for programs that would challenge gender arrangements, for instance by encouraging girls and women to consider and prepare for nontraditional vocations so as to become less dependent on relationships with others.

Gender definitions. See *gender ideologies.*

Gender definitions theory posits that a combination of gender definitions and ideas that are more or less favorable toward breaking the law explains why boys are more delinquent than are girls, and traditional views of gender are among these definitions.

Gender entrapment involves a woman being lured into a compromising act, and it can result in some women being forced or coerced into crime because of their gender role expectations, violence in intimate relations, and their social location, which limits access to resources.

Gender feminism. See *psychoanalytic and gender feminism.*

Gender harassment is behavior and comments that are directed against a gender group and that create a hostile environment. The legal definition of gender harassment specifies that it interferes with performance in specified settings, such as in the workplace or in educational institutions.

Gender identity is a person's sense of self as a person of a certain gender.

Gender ideologies are images, concepts, assumptions, and beliefs about masculinity and femininity that differ between cultural, national, religious, social class, and other groups. These are also referred to as *gender definitions.*

Gender-irrelevant perspective on corrections does not explicitly acknowledge differences between females and males, but incorporates and promotes implicit traditional gender stereotypes.

Gender-issues perspective on corrections values programs that deal with a host of individual gender-related needs, including emotional problems, education and job preparation, low self-esteem, abuse, and victimization.

Gender-maintenance perspective on corrections explicitly recognizes gender differences, and emphasizes almost exclusively the importance of women's care of their children and other family members.

Gender organization. See *gender—macro level conceptualization.*

Gender-related victimization concerns crime that is concentrated on a particular gender group and often is motivated by the victim's gender.

Gender-responsive programs address offenders' gender-related needs.

Gender role prescriptions are expectations that men and women will hold different kinds of positions in society.

Gender role stereotypes are exaggerated, oversimplified beliefs about appropriate behavior for females and for males that do not allow for individual differences.

Gender roles are constructed notions about the behaviors and characteristics that are natural and appropriate for females and males.

Gender stratification. See *gender—macro level conceptualization.*

Global feminism rejects the idea that the concept of "woman" is invariant and stresses that women who are privileged because of their race or class cannot speak for other groups. Gender oppression is heavily influenced by economic and political conditions that characterize First World, Third World, colonialist, and colonized countries.

Globalization is the influence of population movements and the economic and other interdependencies between nations. Other aspects of globalization, which are not specifically considered in this book, are the exchange of information between nations, the concentration of economic activity among multinational firms, and international trade.

The *green card factor* is when one spouse threatens the other either with retracting the sponsorship that makes it possible to stay in the United States legally or with reporting irregularities to the Immigration and Naturalization Service.

Hate crimes are usually violent and are motivated by hate of an entire group, including those differentiated by race, color, religion, national origin, ethnicity, gender, disability, or sexual orientation.

Hegemonic masculinity is the pattern of gender practice that embodies the currently accepted answer to the problem of legitimacy of patriarchy, which supports the dominant position of men and the subordination of women.

Hooks for change are life events that, in combination with immediate context and a person's inclinations and motivations, influence desistance from patterns of criminal activity.

Hostile masculinity is males' beliefs that masculinity is signified by being dominating and in control, especially of women, and feelings of insecurity and distrust toward women.

Human rights perspective on justice identifies a wide range of rights that all people have simply because they are human beings.

Hypermasculinity is males' acceptance of exaggerated gender roles, including the belief that masculinity is characterized by dominance over women, extreme difference from and hostility toward females, and sexual aggression toward women.

In the lifestyle refers to interconnected circumstances and behaviors of women involved in crime, including prostitution, drug use to handle stress and stigmatization, need for money to support drug dependency, deviant networks, the use of violence to survive on the streets, and the experience of violent victimization.

Intimate-partner violence includes violence directed against a person whom the aggressor is married to, living with, or dating. It also can include violence by a former marital partner or date or a person who was previously cohabitating, including a person who has a child in common with the victim.

Justice requires fairly addressing conflicts and inequities between people.

Learned helplessness is a concept that battered women give up and become helpless, to the point that they cannot stop the abuse or leave the relationship. Over time, the learned helplessness explanation for staying in an abusive relationship became an explanation for being in an abusive relationship in the first place.

Levels of explanation. At the *macro* level, explanatory factors for illegal behavior and responses to it include widespread economic conditions and arrangements, public health and illness, type of government and legal system, and cultural heritage and change. At an *intermediate* level, organizational, community, and family characteristics explain illegal behavior and responses to it. At more *micro* levels, human behavior and social life are seen as products of people's interactions and their individual ideas and characteristics.

Liberal feminism posits that socialization and equitable treatment will reduce or abate gender oppression. The key is to give females and males equal access to education, opportunities, and resources.

Liberation thesis is that the women's movement had loosened gender role prescriptions, and as a result women were becoming more like men in their penchant for competition and in their criminality.

Life course theories attend to the timing and sequencing of potential influences on an individual's aggression, norm-violating behavior, and, more specifically, illegal behavior. A combination of events, context, and characteristics (including age and the related concept of stage in development) ultimately influences whether or not a person breaks the law, continues breaking it, or stops. Key events at particular points in time can start or interrupt a trajectory in a pattern of delinquency or adult offending.

Madonna/whore duality reflects the untenable tendency to categorize women as either totally good or totally bad, and to place them in the "bad" category if they overstep rigid gender role prescriptions.

Mail-order brides are women who immigrate through marriage to a man whom they do not know or barely know.

Mandatory arrest laws and policies require police to arrest a suspect if there is probable cause that domestic violence has occurred.

Masculinities—see *femininities and masculinities.*

Mass incarceration society refers to U.S. policies that result in incarceration of a large proportion of the population.

Missing girls refers to a lower ratio than would be expected between the number of girls and boys in a population, and it results from selective abortion of female fetuses or neglect of girl infants that results in their death.

Morality politics theory includes the proposition that some relatively small but politically active groups in the United States have been able to use the coercive power of the state to force their values on others.

Multicultural feminism rejects the idea that the concept of "woman" is invariant and stresses that women who are privileged because of their race or class cannot speak for other groups. Even within a given country, race, class, sexual orientation, age, and myriad other differences alter the experience of gender-related oppressions.

No drop policies deny the victim the right to drop a charge of domestic violence that is being moved to court by the prosecutor.

Oppositional femininity does not reflect characteristics of *emphasized femininity*, and it includes characteristics of loyalty, bravery, willingness to fight, and fighting ability.

Oppositional masculinity involves explicit resistance and challenges to hegemonic forms of masculinity.

Pathways theory and research has paid attention to the effect of sexual and other victimization and of crime-supporting relationships, especially relationships to men who are intimate partners and/or sexual exploiters, on girls' and women's criminality.

Patriarchy is used to refer to gender arrangements characterized by males' domination of females, but it is important to recognize that there is not one universal form of gender organization that exists through all cultures or historical periods, and that within a historical period or a particular setting, gender inequalities are not experienced equally by all people.

Peacemaking model of justice. See *restorative justice.*

Positivist social science relies on observation and measurement of social reality to build theory, and on deductive reasoning to generate predictive hypotheses that can be tested against factual information. In some cases, theory rather than observation is used to generate hypotheses.

Postmodern social science theory is characterized by a focus on themes that include the impact of the media in shaping different versions of reality, the themes of war and inequity that dominate global politics, the emergence and power of multinational firms, and the role that discourses—notably the discourses of medical, legal, social science, and other experts—have had in altering how people are understood, treated, and managed. The postmodernist epistemological orientation is highly critical of positivist and other methods that oversimplify how and why things happen, because they impose incomplete models of causation that do not capture nonlinear ways in which certain things come about. Like constructionist and standpoint theorists, postmodernists caution that pre-given categories can be misleading.

Postmodern themes include the impact of the media in shaping different versions of reality, the themes of war and inequity that dominate global politics, and the role that discourses—notably the discourses of medical, legal, social science, and other experts—have had in altering how people are understood and responded to.

Posttraumatic stress disorder is a constellation of difficulties that result from victimization or other traumatic experiences. The difficulties include repeated rethinking of the experience of the trauma, avoiding stimuli that are similar to the trauma, a general numbing of responsiveness, and anxiety.

Power control theory links patriarchal family structure to gender differences in delinquency.

Presumptive arrest laws and policies stipulate that in domestic and other intimate-partner violence incidents, police shall make an arrest given probable cause that a crime has occurred.

Prison industry complex includes the many businesses that provide services to build and maintain prisons and support activities within the prison.

Pro-choice position on abortion emphasizes a woman's right to make decisions about her body.

Pro-life position on abortion emphasizes the fetus's right to develop and be born.

Prostitute as sex worker is a conceptualization of people who sell sex for money that emphasizes their free and rational choice of an occupation. This conceptualization is the basis for laws that decriminalize prostitution as long as it is a freely chosen occupation.

Prostitute as victim is a conceptualization of people who sell sex for money that emphasizes that they are victims of their economic circumstances, trafficking and trickery, or prior criminal victimization. This conceptualization is the basis for arguing for laws that criminalize customers and individuals who profit but that decriminalize the activities of the people who actually have sex in exchange for money.

Psychoanalytical and gender feminism highlight the unique and positive psychological makeup of females that orients them to need to love and be loved in close relationships with other people.

Radical feminism stresses that the domination of women, the oldest and most widespread oppression in the world, is rooted in men's needs to control women's sexuality and their potential to reproduce. Change would require overthrowing the existing social structure and obliterating gender differences.

Rape culture is a set of beliefs that support sexual assault.

Rape shield laws limit the admissibility of evidence, in sexual assault cases, concerning the victim's prior sexual activity. Such evidence can be admitted only if its relevance is determined in advance by a judge.

Rape within marriage refers to forced sex between people married to each other.

The *real victim* concerns an idea that people hold about how a victim of crime would present herself or himself and react, and about the typical circumstances of crimes.

Relationship violence extends beyond heterosexual relationships to include violence in relationships between people with the same sex.

Restorative justice and *peacemaking models* of delivering justice eschew the formal court processes and the limits of the law, and instead focus on repairing harms done to the victim and restoring the offender to the community as a contributing and positive force.

Routine oppression is a phrase that has been used to describe the widespread and common occurrence of sexual harassment of women.

Second assault. See *secondary victimization.*

Second rape. See *secondary victimization.*

Second wave of the Feminist Movement is social activism that began in the 1960s to create social change that would improve the situation of girls and women. Activists concentrated on equality in the workplace, the value of women's work in the home, women's right to control their own bodies, and myriad other issues, including the victimization of women and girls.

Secondary victimization is damaging practices that occur when people question the veracity of a victim's account of a crime, discount recent or potential harm to the victim, or blame the victim for instigating the offense. Individuals, organizations, systems of organizations (e.g., the criminal justice system) and communities can produce secondary victimization, which is also called the *second assault* or the *second rape.*

Self-medication refers to the use of illegal drugs to block out confusion, distress, and pain resulting from childhood sexual and other abuse.

Sex is a biological characteristic, with a more or less fixed state (less when people have genitalia that are ambiguous or when they undergo sex-change operations or drug therapies).

Sex gender system. See *gender—macro-level conceptualization.*

Sex tourism involves the availability of children and adults who engage in sex for money with tourists at particular destinations.

Sexual assault refers to the range of sexually aggressive behaviors that people experience as traumatic and assaulting.

Sexual harassment is unwelcome sexual advances or requests for sexual favors. The legal definition of sexual harassment specifies that it interferes with performance in specified settings, such as the workplace or educational institutions.

Sexual orientation motivated crime is stimulated by the offender's hate for all individuals who are gay, lesbian, or bisexual.

Social location is a person's place within existing social arrangements, including the existing gender organization.

Socialist feminism highlights the ways that people are oppressed both because of gender and because of social class; thus, working and lower class females are most disadvantaged. Change requires new gender arrangements and a move away from capitalism toward either socialism or communism.

Stalking is the act of deliberately and repeatedly following or harassing another to create fear in the victim or to coerce him or her into acceding to the wishes of the stalker.

Structural inequality perspective on justice considers within- and between-nation conditions that promote illegal activity and subsequent responses that then punish it with no attention to the initial causes.

Subordinate masculinity is related to subordinate statuses of race, class, and sexual orientation.

Supermax prisons are large, sterile, and equipped with extensive surveillance technology.

Survivors is a term used by people who have lived through their criminal victimization and by their advocates to convey that after victimization, individuals are capable of independence and self-direction.

Take Back the Night initiatives involve people's demonstrations, by marching through areas after dark, that they are reclaiming the areas as safe from rape.

Third wave of the Feminist Movement refers to the period from 1980 to the present during which activists focused heavily on the multiple realities of different groups of women, the inadequacy of dichotomous distinctions between males and females, media distortions of females and males, and technology-aided networking.

Trafficking is the transport of people across local or national borders for the purpose of sexually exploiting them.

Unobtrusive mobilization is criticism and change that is initiated from within traditional organizations and programs.

Variable-driven research involves measurement of social phenomena that are not selected based on any theoretical rationale or meaning. It is also referred to as *empiricist* research.

Victim precipitation is a central concept in theory that explains crime as a rational reaction to the behavior or appearance of the victim.

Violence Against Women Act, passed in 1994, is federal legislation that initially focused on safe streets, safe homes, and civil rights for women. Later, it was extended to cover safe campuses and equal justice for women. The act defined gender-motivated crimes as hate crimes, and it included an amendment to federal civil rights laws giving victims access to civil as well as criminal courts.

The *violent stranger myth* is the belief that most crimes are committed by strangers. A relatively high proportion of crimes against women are committed by a person they know.

Wife abuse reflects women's experience of a range of emotional and physical attacks, including emotional abuse.

Wife battering refers to repeated physical force within a marital relationship.

References

Abraham, M. (1995). Ethnicity, gender, and marital violence: South Asian women's organizations in the United States. *Gender & Society, 9,* 450–468.

Abrams, D., Viki, G. T., Masser, B. M., & Bohner, G. (2003). Perceptions of stranger and acquaintance rape: The role of benevolent and hostile sexism in victim blame and rape proclivity. *Journal of Personality and Social Psychology, 84*(1), 111–125.

Abrams, L. S. (2000). Guardians of virtue: The social reformers and the "girl problem," 1890–1920. *Social Service Review, 74*(3), 436–452.

Acoca, L. (1998). Outside/Inside: The violation of American girls at home, on the streets, and in the juvenile justice system. *Crime & Delinquency, 44*(4), 561–589.

Acoca, L. (1999). Investing in girls: A 21st century challenge. *Juvenile Justice, 6,* 3–13.

Acoca, L., & Austin, J. (1996). *The hidden crisis: Women in prison.* San Francisco: National Council on Crime and Delinquency.

Adedoyin, M., & Adegoke, A. A. (1995). Teenage prostitution—child abuse: A survey of the Ilorin situation. *African Journal of Medicine and Medical Sciences, 24*(1), 27–31.

Adler, F. (1975). *Sisters in crime.* New York: McGraw-Hill.

Agozino, B. (1997). *Black women and the criminal justice system.* Aldershot, UK: Ashgate.

Aker, J. (1989). The problem with patriarchy. *Sociology, 23,* 235–240.

Albonetti, C. A. (1997). Sentencing under the federal sentencing guidelines: Effects of defendant characteristics, guilty pleas, and departures on sentence outcomes for drug offenses, 1991–1992. *Law & Society Review, 31,* 789–819.

Alder, C. M., & Polk, K. (1996). Masculinity and child homicide. *British Journal of Criminology, 36*(3), 396–411.

Allen, H. (1987). *Justice unbalanced: Gender, psychiatry, and judicial decisions.* Milton Keynes, UK: Open University Press.

Allen, N. E. (2001). *Coordinating councils as vehicles for achieving a coordinated community response to domestic violence: An examination of the correlates of council effectiveness.* Unpublished doctoral dissertation, Michigan State University, East Lansing, MI.

Amato, P. R., & Booth, A. (1997). *Generation at risk: Growing up in the era of family upheaval.* Cambridge, MA: Harvard University Press.

American Bar Association and National Bar Association. (2001). *Justice by gender: The lack of appropriate prevention, diversion and treatment alternatives for girls in the justice system.* Washington, DC: Author.

American Psychological Association. (1998). *Hate crimes today: An age-old foe in modern dress.* Washington, DC: Author. Retrieved July 10, 2004, from www.apa.org/pubinfo/hate

Amir, M. (1971). *Patterns in forcible rape.* Chicago: University of Chicago Press.

Amnesty International. (1999). *"Not part of my sentence": Violations of the human rights of women in custody.* Retrieved from http://nicic.org/Library/015028

Anderson, M. (1988). *Thinking about women: Sociological perspectives on sex and gender.* New York: Macmillan.

Anderson, M., & Hill Collins, P. (1998). *Race, class and gender: An anthology.* Belmont, CA: Wadsworth.

Annie E. Casey Foundation. (1999). *Kids count data book.* Baltimore, MD: Author.

Arizpe, L. (1999). Freedom to create: Women's agenda for cyberspace. In W. Harcourt (Ed.), *Women@Internet: Creating new cultures in cyberspace* (pp. xii–xvi). London: Zed.

Arnold, F., Kishor, S., & Roy, T. K. (2002). Sex-selective abortions in India. *Population and Development Review, 28*(4), 759–785.

Arnold, R. (1990). Women of color: Processes of victimization and criminalization of black women. *Social Justice, 17*(3), 153–156.

Arnot, M. L., & Usborne, C. (1999). Why gender and crime? Aspects of an international debate. In M. L. Arnot & C. Usborne (Eds.), *Gender and crime in modern Europe* (pp. 1–43). London: UCL Press.

Bachman, R. (1993). Predicting the reporting of rape victimizations: Have reforms made a difference? *Criminal Justice and Behavior, 20,* 254–270.

Bachman, R. (1998). The factors related to rape reporting behavior and arrest: New evidence from the national crime survey. *Criminal Justice and Behavior, 25,* 8–29.

Bachman, R., & Paternoster, R. (1993). A contemporary look at the effects of rape law reform: How far have we really come? *Journal of Criminal Law and Criminology, 84*(3), 554–574.

Baily, W. C. (1999). The socioeconomic status of women and patterns of forcible rape for major U.S. cities. *Sociological Focus, 32,* 43–63.

Baird, I. C. (2000). Violence against women: Looking behind the mask of incarcerated batterers. In T. J. Sork, V.L. Chapman, & R. St. Clair (Eds.), *Proceedings of the 41st Annual Adult Education Research Conference* (pp. 21–25). Vancouver: University of British Columbia.

Baker, K. A., & Dwairy, M. (2003). Cultural norms versus state law in treating incest: A suggested model for Arab families. *Child Abuse and Neglect, 27*(1), 109–123.

Baker, P. L. (2000). I didn't know: Discoveries and identity transformations of women addicts in treatment. *Journal of Drug Issues, 30,* 863–880.

Baldry, A. C. (1996). Rape victims' risk of secondary victimization by police officers. *Issues in Criminological and Legal Psychology, 25,* 65–68.

Baldwin, M. A. (1992). Split at the root: Prostitution and feminist discourses of law reform. *Yale Journal of Law and Feminism, 5,* 47–120.

Balgopal, P. R. (1988). Social networks and Asian Indian families. In C. Jacobs & D. D. Bowles (Eds.), *Ethnicity and race* (pp. 18–33). Silver Spring, MD: NASW Press.

Balough, D. W., Kite, M. E., Pickel, K. L., Canel, D., & Schroeder, J. (2003). The effects of delayed report and motive for reporting on perceptions of sexual harassment. *Sex Roles, 48,* 337–348.

Banerjee, P. (1996, March 1). Bride burning and dowry deaths in India: Gruesome and escalating violence on women. *MANAVI Newsletter,* pp. 1–5.

Bank, L. (1994). Angry men and working women: Gender, violence and economic change in Qwaqua in the 1980s. *African Studies, 53*(1), 89–114.

Banks, T., & Dabbs, J. M. (1996). Salivary testosterone and cortisol in a delinquent and violent urban subculture. *Journal of Social Psychology, 136,* 49–56.

Baradaren-Robison, S. (2003). Tipping the balance in favor of justice: Due process and the Thirteenth and Nineteenth Amendments in child removal from battered mothers. *Brigham Young University Law Review, 1,* 227–263.

Baron, L. S., & Straus, M. A. (1987). Four theories of rape: A macrosociological analysis. *Social Problems, 34,* 467–489.

Barry, K. (1995). *The prostitution of sexuality: The global exploitation of women.* New York: New York University Press.

Bartollas, C. (1993). Little girls grown up: The perils of institutionalization. In C. Culliver (Ed.), *Female criminality: The state of the art* (pp. 469–482). New York: Garland.

Baskin, D. R., & Sommers, I. B. (1998). *Causalities of community disorder: Women's careers in violent crime.* Boulder, CO: Westview.

Bauer, H. M., Rodriguez, M. A., Quiroga, S. S., & Flores-Ortiz, Y. G. (2000). Barriers to health care for abused Latina and Asian immigrant women. *Journal of Health Care for the Poor and Underserved, 11,* 33–44.

Baumgartner, M. P. (1993). Violent networks: The origins and management of domestic conflict. In R. B. Felson & J. Tedeschi (Eds.), *Violence and aggression: The social interactionist approach* (pp. 209–231). Washington, DC: American Psychological Association.

Beaton, A. M., Tougas, F., & Joly, S. (1997). Neosexism among male managers: Is it a matter of numbers? *Journal of Applied Social Psychology, 26,* 2189–2203.

Becket, C., & Macey, M. (2001). Race, gender and sexuality: The oppression of multiculturalism. *Women's Studies International Forum, 24,* 309–319.

Beckett, K. (1966). Culture and politics of signification: The case of child sexual abuse. *Social Problems, 43,* 57–75.

Beckett, K., & Western, B. (2001). Governing social marginality: Welfare, incarceration, and the transformation of state policy. *Punishment and Society, 3*(1), 43–59.

Belknap, J. (1990). Police training in domestic violence: Perceptions of training and knowledge of the law. *American Journal of Criminal Justice, 16*(2), 248–264.

Belknap, J. (2001). *The invisible woman* (2nd ed.). Belmont, CA: Wadsworth.

Belknap, J., & Hartman, J. (2000). *Police responses to woman battering: Victim advocates' reports.* Bicester, Oxfordshire, UK: AB Academic.

Belknap, J., & Holsinger, K. (1998). An overview of delinquent girls: How theory and practice have failed and the need for innovative changes. In R. T. Zaplin (Ed.), *Female offenders: Critical perspectives and effective interventions* (pp. 31–64). Gaithersburg, MD: Aspen.

Bell, I. P. (1984). The double standard: Age. In J. Freeman (Ed.), *Women: A feminist perspective* (pp. 256–263). Palo Alto, CA: Mayfield.

Benedict, H. (1992). *Virgin or vamp: How the press covers sex crimes.* New York: Oxford University Press.

Berenbaum, S. A., & Resnick, S. M. (1997). Early androgen effects on aggression in children and adults with congenital adrenal hyperplasia. *Psychoneuroendocrinology, 22,* 505–515.

Berger, R. J., Neuman, W. L., & Searles, P. (1994). The impact of rape law reform: An aggregate analysis of police reports and arrests. *Criminal Justice Review, 19*(1), 1–23.

Bertrand, M. A. (1999). Incarceration as a gendering strategy. *Canadian Journal of Law and Society, 14*(1), 47–59.

Best, C. L., Dansky, B. S., & Kilpatrick, D. G. (1992). Medical students' attitudes about female rape victims. *Journal of Interpersonal Violence, 7,* 175–188.

Best, J. (1999). *Random violence.* Berkeley: University of California Press.

Beyer, M. (2000, Summer). Immaturity, culpability, and competence in juveniles: A study of 17 cases. *Criminal Justice,* pp. 27ff.

Bickle, G. S., & Peterson, R. D. (1991). The impact of gender-based family roles on criminal sentencing. *Social Problems, 38*(3), 372–394.

Bindman, J. (1997). *Redefining prostitution as sex work on the international agenda.* Retrieved March 10, 2005, from www.walnet.org/csis/papers/redefining.html

Black, H. C. (1968). *Black's law dictionary* (4th ed. rev.). St. Paul, MN: West.

Blackwell, B. S. (2000). Perceived sanction threats, gender, and crime: A test and elaboration of power-control theory. *Criminology, 38,* 439–488.

Blackwell, B. S., & Reed, M. D. (2003). Power-control as a between- and within-family model: Reconsidering the unit of analysis. *Journal of Youth and Adolescence, 32,* 385–400.

Blackwell, B. S., & Vaughn, M. S. (2003). Police civil liability for inappropriate response to domestic assault victims. *Journal of Criminal Justice, 31*(2), 129–146.

Block, C. B., & Block, R. (1993). *Street gang crime in Chicago.* Washington, DC: National Institute of Justice, Office of Justice Programs.

Bloom, B., & Covington, S. S. (1998, November). *Gender-specific programming for female offenders: What is it and why is it important?* Paper presented at the 50th annual meeting of the American Society of Criminology, Washington, DC.

Bloom, B., Owen, B., Covington, S. S., & Raeder, M. S. (2003). *Gender-responsive strategies: Research, practice, and guiding principles for women offenders.* Washington DC: National Institute of Justice.

Blumstein, A., & Beck, A. J. (1999). Population growth in U.S. prisons, 1980–1996. In M. Tonry (Ed.), *Prisons* (pp. 17–61). Chicago: University of Chicago Press.

Boonstra, H., & Sonfield, A. (2000). Rights without access: Revisiting public funding of abortion for poor women. *Guttmacher Report on Public Policy, 3*(2). Retrieved July 10, 2004, from www.agi-usa.org/pubs/journals/gr030208.html

Boswell, A. A., & Spade, J. Z. (1996). Fraternities and collegiate rape culture: Why are some fraternities more dangerous places for women? *Gender & Society, 10,* 133–147.

Bosworth, M. (1996). Resistance and compliance in women's prisons: Towards a critique of legitimacy. *Critical Criminology, 7*(2), 5–19.

Bosworth, M. (1999). *Confining femininity: A history of gender, power and imprisonment.* New York: Fordham University.

Bottcher, J. (1993). *Dimensions of gender and delinquent behavior: An analysis of qualitative data on incarcerated youths and their siblings in Greater Sacramento.* Sacramento: Research Division, California Department of the Youth Authority.

Bottcher, J. (2001). Social practices of gender: How gender relates to delinquency in the everyday lives of high-risk youths. *Criminology: An Interdisciplinary Journal, 39*(4), 893–932.

Bouffard, J. A., & Taxman, F. S. (2000). Client gender and the implementation of jail-based therapeutic community programs. *Journal of Drug Issues, 30*(4), 881–900.

Bourgois, P. (1996). In search of masculinity: Violence, respect and sexuality among Puerto Rican crack dealers in East Harlem. *British Journal of Criminology, 36*(3), 412–427.

Box, S. (1983). *Power, crime and mystification.* London: Tavistock.

Boyer, D., Chapman, L., & Marshall, B. (1993). *Survival sex in King County: Helping women out* (Report submitted to King County Women's Advisory Board). Seattle, WA: Northwest Resource Associates.

Braithwaite, J., & Daly, K. (1994). Masculinities, violence and communitarian control. In E. A. Stanko (Ed.), *Just boys doing business? Men, masculinities and crime* (pp. 188–213). London: Routledge.

Brems, C., & Wagner, P. (1994). Blame of victim and perpetrator in rape versus theft. *Journal of Social Psychology, 134*(3), 363–374.

Bridges, G. S., & Beretta, G. (1994). Gender, race, and social control: Toward an understanding of sex disparities in imprisonment. In G. S. Bridges & M. A. Byers (Eds.), *Inequality, crime, and social control* (pp. 158–175). Boulder, CO: Westview.

Bridges, G. S., & Steen, S. (1998). Racial disparities in official assessments of juvenile offenders: Attributional stereotypes as mediating mechanisms. *American Sociological Review, 63*(4), 554–570.

Brown, L. M., & Gilligan, C. (1993). Meeting at the crossroads: Women's psychology and girls' development. *Feminism and Psychology, 3*, 11–35.

Browne, A. (1987). *When battered women kill.* New York: Free Press.

Browne, A., & Finkelhor, D. (1976). Impact of child sexual abuse: A review of the research. *Psychological Bulletin, 99*(1), 66–77.

Browne, A., & Williams, K. R. (1989). Exploring the effect of resource availability and the likelihood of female-perpetrated homicides. *Law & Society Review, 23*, 75–118.

Bufkin, J. L. (1996). Toward an understanding of bias crimes and bias groups: A theory of masculinity and power. *Dissertation Abstracts International, 57*(8-A), 3689.

Bui, H. N. (2001). Domestic violence victims' behavior in favor of prosecution: Effects of gender relations. *Women and Criminal Justice, 12*(4), 51–76.

Bui, H. N. (2004). *In the adopted land: Abused immigrant women and the criminal justice system.* Westport, CT: Praeger.

Bureau of Justice Statistics. (2002, November 21). *Homicide trends in the U.S.: Intimate homicide.* Washington, DC: Author. Retrieved July 10, 2004, from www.ojp.usdoj.gov/bjs/homicide/intimates.htm

Burnham, L. (2001). Welfare reform, family hardship, and women of color. *Annals of the American Academy of Political and Social Science, 577*, 38–48.

Burt, M. R., Zweig, J. M., Schlichter, K., Kamya, S., Katz, B., & Miller, N. (2000). *2000 report: Evaluation of the STOP formula grants to combat violence against women.* Washington, DC: Urban Institute.

Bush, D. M. (1992). Women's movements and state policy reform aimed at domestic violence against women: A comparison of the consequences of movement mobilization in the U.S. and India. *Gender & Society, 6*(4), 587–608.

Butler, S. (1982). Incest: Whose reality, whose theory? In B. R. Price & N. Sokoloff (Eds.), *The criminal justice system and women* (pp. 323–334). New York: Clark Boardman.

Buzawa, E. S., & Austin, T. (1993). Determining police response to domestic violence victims. *American Behavioral Scientist, 36*(5), 596–609.

Buzawa, E. S., & Buzawa, C. G. (2003). *Domestic violence: The criminal justice system response.* Thousand Oaks, CA: Sage.

Caetano, R., Schafer, J., Clark, C. L., Cunradi, C. B., & Raspberry, K. (2000). Intimate partner violence, acculturation, and alcohol consumption among Hispanic couples in the United States. *Journal of Interpersonal Violence, 15*, 30–45.

Cain, M. (Ed.). (1989). *Growing up good: Policing the behavior of girls in Europe.* London: Sage.

Cain, M. (1990). Towards transgression: New directions in feminist criminology. *International Journal of the Sociology of Law, 18*(1), 1–18.

Campbell, A. (1990). The invisibility of the female delinquent peer group. *Women and Criminal Justice, 2*(1), 41–62.

Campbell, A. (1991). *The girls in the gang.* Cambridge, MA: Basil Blackwell.

Campbell, J. (1992). If I can't have you, no one can. In J. Radford & D.E.H. Russell (Eds.), *Femicide: The politics of woman killing* (pp. 99–113). New York: Twayne.

Campbell, J., Rose, L., Kub, J., & Nedd, D. (1994). Battered women's experiences in emergency room departments: Need for appropriate policy and procedures. *Journal of Interpersonal Violence, 13,* 743–762.

Campbell, R. (1998). The community response to rape: Victims' experiences with the legal, medical, and mental health systems. *American Journal of Community Psychology, 26*(3), 355–379.

Campbell, R., & Ahrens, C. E. (1998). Innovative community services for rape victims: An application of multiple case study methodology. *American Journal of Community Psychology, 26,* 537–571.

Campbell, R., Baker, C. K., & Mazurek T. L. (1998). Remaining radical? Organizational predictors of rape crisis centers' social change initiatives. *American Journal of Community Psychology, 26,* 457–483.

Campbell, R., & Johnson, C. R. (1997). Police officers' perceptions of rape: Is there consistency between state law and individual beliefs? *Journal of Interpersonal Violence, 12,* 255–274.

Campbell, R., & Raja, S. (1999). Secondary victimization of rape victims: Insights from mental health professionals who treat survivors of violence. *Violence and Victims, 14*(2), 261–275.

Campbell, R., Sefl, T., Barnes, H. E., Ahrens, C. E., Wasco, S. M., & Zaragoza-Diesfeld, Y. (1999). Community services for rape survivors: Enhancing psychological well-being or increasing trauma? *Journal of Consulting and Clinical Psychology, 67,* 847–858.

Campbell, R., Wasco, S. M., Ahrens, C. E., Sefl, T., & Barnes, H. E. (2001). Preventing the "second rape": Rape survivors' experiences with community service providers. *Journal of Interpersonal Violence, 16,* 1239–1255.

Candib, L. M. (1999). Incest and other harms to daughters across cultures: Maternal complicity and patriarchal power. *Women's Studies International Forum, 22*(2), 185–201.

Caputi, J. (1992). To acknowledge and heal: 20 years of feminist thought and activism on sexual violence. In C. Kramarae & D. Spender (Eds.), *The knowledge explosion: Generations of feminist scholarship* (pp. 340–352). New York: Teachers College Press.

Caringella-MacDonald, S., & Humphries, D. (1998). Guest editors' introduction. *Violence Against Women, 4,* 3–9.

Carlen, P. (1983). *Criminal women: Autobiographical accounts.* Cambridge, UK: Polity Press.

Carlen, P. (1985). *Criminal women.* Cambridge, UK: Polity Press.

Carlen, P. (1998). *Title sledgehammer: Women's imprisonment at the millennium.* Houndmills, Basingstoke, Hampshire, UK: Macmillan.

Carlen, P., & Tchaikovsky, C. (1996). Women's imprisonment at the end of the twentieth century: Legitimacy, realities and utopias. In R. Matthews & P. Francis (Eds.), *Prisons 2000: An international perspective on the current state and future of imprisonment* (pp. 201–208). London: Macmillan.

Caron, S. L., &. Carter, D. B. (1997). The relationships among sex role orientation, egalitarianism, attitudes toward sexuality, and attitudes toward violence against women. *Journal of Social Psychology, 137*(5), 568–587.

Carrington, K. (1993). *Offending girls: Sex, youth and justice.* St. Leonards, Australia: Allen & Unwin.

Cassidy, L., & Hurell, R. M. (1995). The influence of victim's attire on adolescents' judgments of date rape. *Adolescence, 30,* 319–324.

Cauffman, E., Feldman, S., Waterman J., & Steiner, H. (1998). Post-traumatic stress disorder among female juvenile offenders. *Journal of the American Academy of Child and Adolescent Psychiatry, 37,* 1209–1216.

Cernkovich, S. A., & Giordano, P. C. (1987). Family relationships and delinquency. *Criminology, 25,* 295–321.

Charlesworth, H. (1998). The mid-life crisis of the universal declaration of human rights. *Washington and Lee Law Review, 55,* 781–796.

Chattopadhyay, M., Bandyopadhyay, S., & Duttagupta, C. (1994). Biosocial factors influencing women to become prostitutes in India. *Social Biology, 41*(3–4), 252–259.

Chaudhuri, M., & Daly, K. (1992). Do restraining orders help? Battered women's experience with male violence and legal process. In E. S. Buzawa & C. Buzawa (Eds.), *Domestic violence: The changing criminal justice response* (2nd ed., pp. 227–252). Westport, CT: Auburn House.

Chesney-Lind, M. (1973). Judicial enforcement of the female sex role: The family court and the female delinquent. *Issues in Criminology, 8,* 51–69.

Chesney-Lind, M. (1977). Judicial paternalism and the female status offender: Training women to know their place. *Crime & Delinquency, 23*(2), 121–130.

Chesney-Lind, M. (1983). *Girls and violence: An exploration of the gender gap in serious delinquent behavior.* Report for Youth Development and Research Center, School of Social Work, University of Hawaii–Manoa.

Chesney-Lind, M. (1989). Girls' crime and woman's place: Toward a feminist model of female delinquency. *Crime & Delinquency, 35*(1), 5–29.

Chesney-Lind, M. (1997). *The female offender: Girls, women and crime.* Thousand Oaks, CA: Sage.

Chesney-Lind, M. (2001). Girls, violence and delinquency. In S. O. White (Ed.), *Handbook of youth and justice* (pp. 135–158). New York: Kluwer Academic/Plenum.

Chesney-Lind, M. (2002). Criminalizing victimization: The unintended consequences of pro-arrest policies for girls and women. *Criminology & Public Policy, 2*(1), 81–90.

Chesney-Lind, M., & Hagedorn, J. M. (1999). Historical perspectives. In M. Chesney-Lind & J. M. Hagedorn (Eds.), *Female gangs in America* (pp. 6–9). Chicago: Lake View Press.

Chesney-Lind, M., & Okamoto, S. (2001). Gender matters: Patterns in girl's delinquency and gender responsive programming. *Journal of Forensic Psychology Practice, 1,* 1–28.

Chesney-Lind, M., & Paramore, V. V. (2002). Are girls getting more violent? Exploring juvenile robbery trends. *Journal of Contemporary Criminal Justice, 17*(2), 142–166.

Chesney-Lind, M., & Pollock, J. M. (1995). Women's prisons: Equality with a vengeance. In A. V. Merlo & J. M. Pollock (Eds.), *Women, law and social control* (pp. 155–175). Boston: Allyn & Bacon.

Chesney-Lind, M., & Rodriguez, N. (1983). Women under lock and key: A view from the inside. *The Prison Journal, 63*(2), 47–65.

Chesney-Lind, M., & Shelden, R. G. (1997). *Girls, delinquency, and juvenile justice.* Pacific Grove, CA: Brooks/Cole.

Clark, S. J., Burt, M. R., Schulte, M. M., & Maguire, K. (1996). *Coordinated community responses to domestic violence in six communities: Beyond the justice system.* Final report to the U.S. Department of Health and Human Services by the Urban Institute, Washington, DC.

Cobble, D. S. (2004). *The other women's movement: Workplace justice and social rights in modern America.* Princeton, NJ: Princeton University Press.

Cohn, Y. (1970). Criteria for the probation officer's recommendation to the juvenile court judge. In P. G. Garabedian & D. C. Gibbons (Eds.), *Becoming delinquent* (pp.190–206). Chicago: Aldine.

Coker, D. (1999). Enhancing autonomy for battered women: Lessons from Navajo Peacemaking. *UCLA Law Review, 47*(1), 1–111.

Coleman, C., & Moynihan, J. (1996). *Understanding the crime data: Haunted by the dark figure.* Buckingham, UK: Open University Press.

Collins, J. M., & Collins, M. D. (1999, August). *Female frauds in the corporate suite: Biodata and personality predictors.* Paper presented at the annual conference of the American Psychological Association, Boston.

Collins, M. (1992). The gay-bashers. In G. M. Herek & K. Berrill (Eds.), *Hate crimes: Confronting violence against lesbians and gay men* (pp. 191–200). Newbury Park, CA: Sage.

Collins, P. H. (1990). *Black feminist thought: Knowledge, consciousness, and the politics of empowerment.* Boston: Unwin Hyman.

Collison, M. (1996). In search of the high life: Drugs, crime, masculinities and consumption. *British Journal of Criminology, 36*(3), 428–444.

Comack, E. (1993). Producing feminist knowledge: Lessons from women in trouble. *Theoretical Criminology, 3*(3), 287–306.

Comstock, G. (1991). *Violence against lesbians and gay men.* New York: Columbia University Press.

Connell, R. W. (1995). *Masculinities.* Cambridge, UK: Polity Press.

Consalvo, M. (1998). "3 shot dead in courthouse": Examining news coverage of domestic violence and mail-order brides. *Women's Studies in Communications, 21*(2), 188–211.

Conway, A., & Bogdan, C. (1977). Sexual delinquency: The persistence of a double standard. *Crime & Delinquency, 23,* 131–135.

Correctional Service Canada. (1990). *Creating choices: The report of the Task Force on Federally Sentenced Women.* Ottawa: Author.

Coulter, M. L., Kuehnle, K., Byers, R., & Alfonso, M. (1999). Police-reporting behavior and victim-police interactions as described by women in a domestic violence shelter. *Journal of Interpersonal Violence, 14,* 1290–1298.

Cowie, J., Cowie, V., & Slater, E. (1968). *Delinquency in girls.* London: Heineman.

Crawford, C. (2000). Gender, race, and habitual offender sentencing in Florida. *Criminology, 38*(1), 263–280.

Crenshaw, K. (1989). Demarginalizing the intersection of race and sex: A black feminist critique of antidiscrimination doctrine, feminist theory and antiracist politics. *University of Chicago Legal Forum, 14,* 139–167.

Crick, N. R., & Collins, W. A. (2002). Relational aggression and victimization in young adults' romantic relationships: Associations with perceptions of parent, peer, and romantic relationship quality. *Social Development, 11,* 69–86.

Crick, N. R., & Grotpeter, J. K. (1995). Relational aggression, gender, and social-psychological adjustment. *Child Development, 66,* 710–722.

Crimmins, S. M., Langley, S. C., Brownstein, H. H., & Spunt, B. (1997). Convicted women who have killed children: A self-psychological perspective. *Journal of Interpersonal Violence, 12,* 49–69.

Cruz, J. M., & Firestone, M. J. (1998). Exploring violence and abuse in gay male relationships. *Violence and Victims, 13,* 159–173.

Currie, E. (1998). *Crime and punishment in America.* New York: Holt.

Dabbs, J. M., & Hargrove, M. F. (1997). Age, testosterone, and behavior among female prison inmates. *Psychosomatic Medicine, 59,* 477–480.

Dabbs, J. M., Ruback, R. B., Frady, R. L., Hopper, C. H., & Sgoutas, D. S. (1988). Saliva testosterone and criminal violence among women. *Personality and Individual Differences, 9,* 269–275.

Daly, K. (1987a). Discrimination in the criminal courts: Family, gender, and the problem of equal treatment. *Social Forces, 66*(1), 153–175.

Daly, K. (1987b). Structure and practice of familial-based justice in a criminal court. *Law and Society Review, 21*(2), 267–290.

Daly, K. (1989a). Gender and varieties of white-collar crime. *Criminology, 27*(4), 769–797.

Daly, K. (1989b). Neither conflict nor labeling nor paternalism will suffice. *Crime & Delinquency, 35*(1), 136–168.

Daly, K. (1989c). Rethinking judicial paternalism: Gender, work-family relations, and sentencing. *Gender & Society, 3*(1), 9–36.

Daly, K. (1992). Women's pathways to felony court: Feminist theories of lawbreaking and problems of representation. *Southern California Review of Law and Women's Studies, 2*(1), 11–52.

Daly, K. (1994). *Gender, crime, and punishment.* New Haven, CT: Yale University Press.

Daly, K., & Chesney-Lind, M. (1988). Feminism and criminology. *Justice Quarterly, 5*(4), 497–535.

Das Gupta, M., Zhenghua, J., Bohua, L., Zhenming, X., Chung, W., & Hwa-Ok, B. (2003). Why is son preference so persistent in East and South Asia? A cross-country study of China, India and the Republic of Korea. *Journal of Development Studies, 40*(2), 153–197.

Dasgupta, S. D. (1998). Women's realities: Defining violence against women by immigration, race and class. In R. K. Bergen (Ed.), *Issues in intimate violence* (pp. 209–219). Thousand Oaks, CA: Sage.

Datesman, S. K., & Scarpitti, F. R. (1977). Unequal protection for males and females in the juvenile court. In T. N. Ferdinand (Ed.), *Juvenile delinquency: Little brother grows up* (pp. 59–77). Beverly Hills, CA: Sage.

Datesman, S. K., & Scarpitti, F. R. (1980). *Women, crime and justice.* New York: Oxford University Press.

D'Augelli, A. R., & Grossman, A. H. (2001). Disclosure of sexual orientation, victimization, and mental health among lesbian, gay, and bisexual older adults. *Journal of Interpersonal Violence, 16*, 1008–1027.

Davidson, J.O.C. (1998). *Prostitution, power and freedom.* Ann Arbor: University of Michigan Press.

Davies, M. (1994). *Violence and women.* Atlantic Highlands, NJ: Zed.

Davis, A. Y. (1978). Rape, racism and the capitalist setting. *Black Scholar, 9*(7), 24–30.

Day, K. (1999). Embassies and sanctuaries: Women's experiences of race and fear in public space. *Environment and Planning, 17*, 307–328.

De Judicibus, M., & McCabe, M. P. (2001). Blaming the target of sexual harassment: Impact of gender role, sexist attitudes, and work role. *Sex Roles, 44*, 401–417.

Dean, L., Wu, S., & Martin, J. L. (1992). Trends in violence and discrimination against gay men in New York City: 1984 to 1990. In G. M. Herek & K. T. Berrill (Eds.), *Hate crimes: Confronting violence against lesbians and gay men* (pp. 46–64). Newbury Park, CA: Sage.

Deflem, M. (1998). The boundaries of abortion law: Systems theory from Parsons to Luhmann and Habermas. *Social Forces, 76*(3), 775–818.

DeKeseredy, W. S. (1988). *Women abuse in dating relationships: The role of male peer support.* Toronto: Canadian Scholars' Press.

DeKeseredy, W. S., Alvi, S., Schwartz, M. D., & Perry, B. (1999). Violence against and the harassment of women in Canadian public housing: An exploratory study. *Canadian Review of Sociology and Anthropology, 36*, 499–516.

DeKeseredy, W. S., & Kelly, K. (1993). Woman abuse in university and college dating relationships: The contribution of the ideology of familial patriarchy. *Journal of Human Justice, 4*, 25–52.

DeKeseredy, W. S., Saunders, D. G., Schwartz, M. D., & Alvi, S. (1997). Meanings and motives for women's use of violence in Canadian college dating relationship: Results from a national survey. *Sociological Spectrum, 17*(2), 199–222.

del Frate, A. A. (1995). *Women's victimisation in developing countries.* Rome: United Nations Interregional Crime and Justice Research Institute.

Dell, C. A, & Boe, R (1997). *Female young offenders in Canada: Recent trends.* Ottawa: Canada Correctional Service.

Denfield, R. (1996). *The new Victorians: A young woman's challenge to the old feminist order.* New York: Warner Books.

Dirsuweit, T. (1999). Carceral spaces in South Africa: A case study of institutional power, sexuality and transgression in a women's prison. *Geoforum, 30,* 71–83.

Dobash, R. E., & Dobash, R. (1979). *Violence against wives: A case against patriarchy.* New York: Free Press.

Dobash, R. E., & Dobash, R. P. (1992). *Women, violence, and social change.* London: Routledge.

Dobash, R. P., Dobash, R. E., & Gutteridge, S. (1986). *The imprisonment of women.* New York: Basil Blackwell.

Dobash, R. P., Dobash, R. E., Wilson, M., & Daly, M. (1992). The myth of sexual symmetry in marital violence. *Social Problems, 39*(1), 71–91.

Downes, D. (1999). The macho penal economy: Mass incarceration in the United States—A European perspective. *Punishment and Society, 3*(1), 61–80.

Drieschner, K., & Lange, A. (1999). A review of cognitive factors in the etiology of rape: Theories, empirical studies, and implications. *Clinical Psychology Review, 19*(1), 57–77.

Du Mont, J., Miller, K. L., & Myhr, T. L. (2003). The role of "real rape" and "real victim" stereotypes in the police reporting practices of sexually assaulted women. *Violence Against Women, 9,* 466–486.

Du Mont, J., & Myhr, T. L. (2000). So few convictions: The role of client-related characteristics in the legal processing of sexual assaults. *Violence Against Women, 6,* 1109–1136.

Duchesne, D. (1997). *Street prostitution in Canada* (Juristat Service Bulletin 17, No. 2). Ottawa, Canadian Center of Justice Statistics.

Duffy, A. (1996). Bad girls in hard times: Canadian female juvenile offenders. In G. M. O'Bireck (Ed.), *Not a kid anymore: Canadian youth, crime, and subcultures* (pp. 203–220). Scarborough, Ontario: Nelson Canada.

Dugan, L., Rosenfeld, R., & Nagin, D. S. (2003). Exposure reduction or retaliation? The effects of domestic violence resources on intimate-partner homicide. *Law and Society Review, 37,* 169–198.

Duncan, B. L. (1976). Differential social perception and attribution of intergroup violence: Testing the lower limits of stereotyping of blacks. *Journal of Personality and Social Psychology, 34,* 590–598.

Dunn, J. L. (2002). *Courting disaster: Intimate stalking, culture, and criminal justice.* New York: Aldine de Gruyter.

Duran, E., Duran, B., Woodis, W., & Woodis, P. (1998). A postcolonial perspective on domestic violence in Indian country. In R. Carillo & J. Tello (Eds.), *Family violence and men of color: Healing the wounded male spirit* (pp. 95–113). New York: Springer.

Durst, D. (1991). Conjugal violence: Changing attitudes in two northern Native communities. *Community Mental Health Journal, 27,* 359–373.

Dutton, D. G. (1994). Patriarchy and wife assault: The ecological fallacy. *Violence and Victims, 9,* 167–182.

Dutton, M. A. (1996). Battered women's strategic response to violence: The role of context. In J. L. Edleson & Z. C. Eisikovits (Eds.), *Future interventions with battered women and their families* (pp. 105–124). Thousand Oaks, CA: Sage.

Eaton, M. (1986). *Justice for women? Family, court, and social control.* Milton Keynes, UK: Open University Press.

Eaton, M. (1994). The question of bail: Magistrates' responses to applications for bail on behalf of men and women defendants. In N. Lacey (Ed.), *Criminal justice* (pp. 134–150). New York: Oxford University Press.

Edin, K., & Lein, L. (1997). Work, welfare, and single mothers' economic survival strategies. *American Sociological Review, 62,* 253–266.

Edwards, S. S. (1989). *Policing "domestic" violence: Women, the law and the state.* Newbury Park, CA: Sage.

Eichler, M. (1988). *Nonsexist research methods.* Boston: Allen & Unwin.

Elliott, D. S., Huizinga, D., & Menard, S. (1989). *Multiple problem youth: Delinquency, substance abuse, and mental health problems.* New York: Springer-Verlag.

Enos, V. P. (1996). Prosecuting battered mothers: State laws' failure to protect battered women and abused children. *Harvard Women's Law Journal, 19,* 229–268.

Erez, E., & Belknap, J. (1998). In their own words: Battered women's assessment of the criminal processing system's response. *Violence Against Women, 13,* 251–268.

Erez, E., & King, T. A. (2000). Patriarchal terrorism or common couple violence: Attorneys' views of prosecuting and defending woman batterers. In E. Erez & T. A. King (Eds.), *Domestic violence: Global responses* (pp. 207–226). Bicester, Oxfordshire, UK: AB Academic.

Erickson, P. G., Butters, J., McGillicuddy, P., & Hallgren, A. (2000). Crack and prostitution: Gender, myths, and experiences. *Journal of Drug Issues, 30*(4), 767–788.

Ernst, J. L., Katzive, L., & Smock, E. (2004). The global pattern of U.S. initiatives curtailing women's reproductive rights: A perspective on the increasingly anti-choice mosaic. *University of Pennsylvania Journal of Constitutional Law, 6,* 752–795.

European Parliament. (n.d.). *A summary of the prostitution regulations in the EU member states.* Retrieved April 1, 2004, from www.europarl.eu.int/hearings/20040119/femm/document1_en.pdf

Evans, J. H. (2003). Have Americans' attitudes become more polarized? *Social Science Quarterly, 84*(1), 71–90.

Fairchild, E., & Dammer, H. R. (2001). *Comparative criminal justice systems.* Belmont, CA: Wadsworth.

Farley, M., Baral, I., Kiremire, M., & Sezgin, U. (1998). Prostitution in five countries: Violence and post-traumatic stress disorder. *Feminism and Psychology, 8*(4), 405–426.

Farley, M., & Kelly, V. (2000). Prostitution: A critical review of the medical and social sciences literature. *Women & Criminal Justice, 11*(4), 29–64.

Fegan, E. V. (1996). Fathers, foetuses and abortion decision-making: The reproduction of maternal ideology in Canadian judicial discourse. *Social & Legal Studies, 5,* 75–93.

Feinman, C. (1973). Sex-role stereotypes and justice for women. In K. W. Burkhart (Ed.), *Women and crime in America* (pp. 387–390). Garden City, NY: Doubleday.

Feinman, C. (1986). *Women in the criminal justice system.* New York: Praeger.

Feinman, C. (1985). Criminal codes, criminal justice and female offenders: New Jersey as a case study. In I. L. Moyer (Ed.), *The changing roles of women in the criminal justice system: Offenders, victims, and professionals* (pp. 30–40). Prospect Heights, IL: Waveland Press.

Feldblum, C. (2001). Gay rights and the Rehnquist court: A mixed bag since the heady days of *Romer v. Evans. Gay and Lesbian Review, 8,* 11–15.

Felson, R. B., Messner, S. F., & Hoskin, A. (1999). The victim-offender relationship and calling the police in assaults. *Criminology, 37*(4), 931–946.

Ferraro, K. J. (1993). Cops, courts and woman battering. In P. B. Bart & E. G. Moran (Eds.), *Violence against women: The bloody footprints* (pp. 165–177). Newbury Park, CA: Sage.

Ferraro, K. J., & Moe, A. M. (2003). Mothering, crime, and incarceration. *Journal of Contemporary Ethnography, 32*(1), 9–40.

Ferree, M. M., & Hess, B. B. (1987). Introduction. In B. B. Hess & M. M. Ferree (Eds.), *Analyzing gender: A handbook of social science research* (pp. 9–30). Newbury Park, CA: Sage.

Ferree, M. M., & Hess, B. B. (1995). *Controversy and coalition.* New York: Routledge.

Figueira-McDonough, J. (1985). Gender differences in informal processing: A look at charge bargaining and sentence reduction in Washington, D.C. *Journal of Research in Crime and Delinquency, 22*(2), 101–133.

Filax, G. (2003). Queer invisibility: The case of Ellen, Michel, and Oscar. In S. Books (Ed.), *Invisible children in the society and its schools* (pp. 147–169). Mahwah, NJ: Erlbaum.

Findlen, B. (Ed.). (1995). *Listen up: Voices from the next feminist generation.* Seattle, WA: Seal Press.

Finkelhor, D. (1982). Sexual abuse: A sociological perspective. *Child Abuse and Neglect, 6,* 95–102.

Finkelhor, D. (1990). Early and long-term effects of child sexual abuse: An update. *Professional Psychology: Research and Practice, 21,* 325–330.

Finkelhor, D., & Ormrod, R. (1999, November). Reporting crimes against juveniles. *OJJDP Juvenile Justice Bulletin,* pp. 1–7.

Finkelson, L., & Oswalt, R. (1995) College date rape—Incidence and reporting. *Psychological Reports, 77,* 526.

Finn, M. A., & Stalans, L. J. (1997). The influence of gender and mental state on police decisions in domestic assault cases. *Criminal Justice and Behavior, 24,* 157–176.

Fischer, G. J. (1986). College student attitudes toward forcible rape: I. Cognitive predictors. *Archive of Sexual Behavior, 15,* 457–466.

Fishbein, D. (2001). *Biobehavioral perspectives in criminology.* Belmont, CA: Wadsworth.

Fisher, B. S., Daigle, L. E., Cullen, F. T., & Turner, M. G. (2003). Reporting sexual victimization to the police and others: Results from a national-level study of college women. *Criminal Justice and Behavior, 30*(1), 6–38.

Flavin, J. (2001). Of punishment and parenthood: Family-based social control and the sentencing of black drug offenders. *Gender & Society, 15*(4), 611–633.

Fleischman, J. (1989). *Street prostitution: Assessing the impact of the law—synthesis report.* Ottawa, Ontario, Canada: Department of Justice.

Ford, H. H., Schindler, C. B. & Medway, F. J. (2001). School professionals' attributions of blame for child sexual abuse. *Journal of School Psychology, 39*(1), 25–44.

Fox, J. A., & Zawitz, M. W. (2003). *Homicide trends in the United States: 2000 update.* Washington, DC: Bureau of Justice Statistics.

Franklin, K. (1997). Hate crime or rite of passage? Assailant motivations in antigay violence. *Dissertations Abstracts International, B57–12.* (UMI No. 9511399)

Frazier, P. A., & Haney, B. (1996). Sexual assault cases in the legal system: Police, prosecutor, and victim perspectives. *Law and Human Behavior, 20,* 607–628.

Freedman, E. B. (1981). *Their sisters' keepers: Women's prison reform in America, 1830–1930.* Ann Arbor: University of Michigan Press.

Freedman, E. B. (1987). "Uncontrolled desires": The response to the sexual psychopath, 1920–1960. *Journal of American History, 74*(1), 83–106.

Freeman, C. (2001). Is local:global as feminine:masculine? Rethinking the gender of globalization. *Signs: Journal of Women in Culture and Society, 26*(4), 1007–1037.

French, M. (1977). *The women's room.* New York: Jove.

French, W., & Bell, C. (1995). *Organizational development.* Englewood Cliffs, NJ: Prentice Hall.

Freud, S. (1933). *New introductory lectures on psychoanalysis.* New York: Norton.

Freud, S. (1966). "Civilized" sexual morality and modern nervous illness. *Civilization, society and religion* (Penguin Freud Library, Vol. 12). Harmondsworth, UK: Penguin.

Frohmann, L. (1991). Discrediting victims' allegations of sexual assault: Prosecutorial accounts of case rejections. *Social Problems, 38*(2), 213–226.

Frohmann, L. (1997). Convictability and discordant locales: Reproducing race, class, and gender ideologies in prosecutorial decision making. *Law and Society Review, 31*(3), 531–555.

Furstenberg, F. F., Jr. (1976). *Unplanned parenthood: Social consequences of teenage childbearing.* New York: Free Press.

Fusilli, N. (2002). New York state of mind: Rape and mens rea. *St. John's Law Review, 76,* 603–630.

Garland, D. (1999). Introduction: The meaning of mass imprisonment. *Punishment and Society, 3*(1), 5–7.

Garofalo, R., Wolf, R. C., Wissow, L. S., Woods, W. R., & Goodman, E. (1999). Sexual orientation and risk of suicide attempts among a representative sample of youth. *Archives of Pediatrics and Adolescent Medicine, 153*(5), 487–493.

Garrison, E. K. (2000). U.S. feminism—Grrrl style! Youth (sub) cultures and the technologics of the third wave. *Feminist Studies, 26,*141–170.

Gartner, R., Baker, K., & Pampel, F. C. (1990). Gender stratification and the gender gap in homicide victimization. *Social Problems, 37*(4), 593–612.

Gartner, R., & Macmillan, R. (1995). The effect of victim-offender relationship on reporting crimes of violence against women. *Canadian Journal of Criminology, 37*(3), 393–415.

Gartner, R., & McCarthy, B. (1991). The social distribution of femicide in urban Canada, 1921–1988. *Law and Society Review, 25*(2), 287–311.

Gavey, N., Florence, J., Pezaro, S., & Tan, J. (1990). Mother-blaming, the perfect alibi: Family therapy and the mothers of incest survivors. *Journal of Feminist Family Therapy, 2,* 1–25.

Gelsthorpe, L. (1992). Social inquiry reports: Race and gender considerations. *Research Bulletin, 32,* 17–22.

General Accounting Office. (1999). *Women in prison: Sexual misconduct by correctional staff.* Washington, DC: Author.

Gerbert, B., Johnston, K., Caspers, N., Bleecker, T., Woods, A., & Rosenbaum, A. (1996). Experiences of battered women in health care settings: A qualitative study. *Women and Health, 24,* 1–17.

Gere, A. R., & Robbins, S. R. (1996). Gendered: Turn of the century African-American and European-American club literacy in black and white women's printed texts. *Signs: Journal of Women in Culture and Society, 21*(3), 643–678.

Gibbons, D. C. (1970). *Delinquent behavior.* Englewood Cliffs, NJ: Prentice Hall.

Gilchrist, E., Bannister, J., Ditton, J., & Farrall, S. (1998). Women and the "fear of crime": Challenging the accepted stereotype. *British Journal of Criminology, 38,* 283–299.

Gilligan, C. (1982). *In a different voice: Psychological theory and women's development.* Cambridge, MA: Harvard University Press.

Giobbe, E. (1991). Prostitution: Buying the right to rape. In A. W. Burgess (Ed.), *Rape and sexual assault III: A research handbook* (pp. 143–160). New York: Garland Press.

Giobbe, E., Harrigan, M., Ryan, J., & Gamache, D. (1990). *Prostitution: A matter of violence against women.* Minneapolis, MN: Whisper.

Giordano, P. C., Cernkovich, S. A., & Rudolph, J. L. (2002). Gender, crime, and desistance: Toward a theory of cognitive transformation. *American Journal of Sociology, 107,* 990–1064.

Giorgio, G. (2002). Speaking silence: Definitional dialogues in abusive lesbian research. *Violence Against Women, 8,* 1233–1259.

Girshick, L. B. (2002a). No sugar, no spice: Reflections on woman-to-woman sexual violence. *Violence Against Women, 8,* 1500–1530.

Girshick, L. B. (2002b). *Woman-to-woman sexual violence: Does she call it rape?* Boston: Northeastern University Press.

Glick, R. M., & Neto, V. V. (1977). National study of women's correctional programs. Washington, DC: Government Printing Office.

Glover v. Johnson, 478 F.Supp. 1075, E.D. Mich. (1979).

Gondolf, E. W., & Fisher, E. R. (1988). *Battered women as survivors.* Lexington, MA: Lexington Books.

Gondolf, E. W., Fisher, E., & McFerron, J. R. (1988). Racial differences among shelter residents: A comparison of Anglo, Black and Hispanic battered women. *Journal of Family Violence, 3*(1), 39–51.

Goode, W. J. (1969). Violence among intimates. In D. J. Mulvihill, M. M. Tumin, & L. A. Curtis (Eds.). *Crimes of violence* (pp. 941–977). Washington, DC: Government Printing Office.

Goodey, J. (1997). Boys don't cry: Masculinities, fear of crime and fearlessness. *British Journal of Criminology, 37,* 401–418.

Gordon, A. F. (1999). Globalism and the prison industrial complex: An interview with Angela Davis. *Race & Class, 2/3,* 145–169.

Gordon, M., & Riger, S. (1989). *The female fear.* New York: Free Press.

Gorham, D. (1978). The "maiden tribute of modern Babylon" re-examined: Child prostitution and the idea of childhood in late-Victorian England. *Victorian Studies, 21*(3), 353–369.

Gorlick, S. (1991). Contradictions of feminist methodology. *Gender & Society, 5,* 459–477.

Gover, A. R., MacDonald, J. M., & Alpert, G. P. (2003). Combatting domestic violence: Findings from an evaluation of a local domestic violence court. *Criminology and Public Policy, 3,* 109–122.

Gramache, D., & Asmus, M. (1999). Enhancing networking among service providers. In M. F. Shepard & E. Pence (Eds.), *Coordinating community response to domestic violence: Lessons from Duluth and beyond* (pp. 65–88). Thousand Oaks, CA: Sage.

Grasmick, H. G., Hagan, J., Blackwell, B. S., & Arneclev, B. J. (1996). Risk preferences and patriarchy: Extending power-control theory. *Social Forces, 75*(1), 177–199.

Greenberg, D. F., & West, V. (2001). State prison populations and their growth, 1971–1991. *Criminology: An Interdisciplinary Journal, 39,* 615–654.

Greenfeld, L. A., Rand, M. R., Craven, D., Klaus, P. A., Perkins, C. A., Ringel, C., et al. (1998). *Violence by intimates: Analysis of data on crimes by current or former spouses, boyfriends, and girlfriends.* Washington, DC: Government Printing Office.

Gross, K., & Aday, S. (2003). The scary world in your living room and neighborhood: Local broadcast news, neighborhood crime rates, and personal experience to test agenda setting and cultivation. *Journal of Communications, 53,* 411–426.

Groth, A. N., & Burgess, A. W. (1977). Rape: A sexual deviation. *American Journal of Orthopsychiatry, 47,* 400–406.

Guba, E. G., & Lincoln, Y. S. (1994). Competing paradigms in qualitative research. In N. K. Denzin & Y. S. Lincoln (Eds.), *Handbook of qualitative research* (pp. 105–117). Thousand Oaks, CA: Sage.

Guterman, N. B. (2001). *Stopping child maltreatment before it starts: Emerging horizons in early home visitation services.* Thousand Oaks, CA: Sage.

Gutheil, T. G., & Avery, N. C. (1977). Multiple overt incest as family defense against loss. *Family Process, 16,* 105–116.

Hagan, J., Gillis, A. R., & Simpson, J. (1985). The class structure of gender and delinquency: Toward a power-control theory of common delinquent behavior. *American Journal of Sociology, 90,* 1151–1178.

Hagan, J. (with J. Simpson & A. R. Gillis). (1988). Feminist scholarship, relational and instrumental control, and a power-control theory of gender and delinquency. *British Journal of Sociology, 39*(3), 301–336.

Hagedorn, J. (1988). *People and folks: Gangs, crime and the underclass in a rustbelt city.* Chicago: Lake View Press.

Hagedorn, J., M., & Devitt, M. L. (1999). Fighting female: The social construction of female gangs. In J. Hagedorn (Ed.), *Female gangs in America* (pp. 256–276). Chicago: Lake View Press.

Hahn, N. F. (1980). Too dumb to know better: Cacogenic family studies and the criminology of women. *Criminology, 18,* 3–25.

Haj Yahia, M. M. (2002). Attitudes of Arab women toward different patterns of coping with wife abuse. *Journal of Interpersonal Violence, 17,* 721–745.

Hamby, S. L. (1997). Responses to partner violence: Moving away from deficit models. *Journal of Family Psychology, 11*(3), 339–350.

Hamby, S. L. (2000). The importance of community in a feminist analysis of domestic violence among American Indians. *American Journal of Community Psychology, 28*(5), 649–669.

Hampton, R. L. (1987). *Violence in the black family.* Lexington, MA: D. C. Heath.

Hannah-Moffat, K. (1999). Moral agent or actuarial subject: Risk and Canadian women's imprisonment. *Theoretical Criminology, 3*(1), 71–94.

Hannah-Moffat, K., & Shaw, M. (Eds.). (2000). *An ideal prison? Critical essays on women's imprisonment in Canada.* Halifax, Nova Scotia, Canada: Fernwood.

Hannon, L., & Defronzo, J. (1998). The truly disadvantaged, public assistance, and crime. *Social Problems, 45*(3), 383–392.

Hanson, R. F., Resnick, H. S., Saunders, B. E., Kilpatrick, D. G., & Best, C. (1999). Factors related to the reporting of childhood rape. *Child Abuse and Neglect, 23,* 559–569.

Harding, S. (1990). Feminism, science, and the anti-enlightenment critiques. In L. J. Nicholson (Ed.), *Feminism/postmodernism* (pp. 49–82). London: Routledge.

Harker, L., & Keltner, D. (2001). Expressions of positive emotion in women's college yearbook pictures and their relationship to personality and life outcomes across adulthood. *Journal of Personality and Social Psychology, 80,* 112–124.

Harrell, A., & Smith, B. (1996). Effects of restraining orders on domestic violence victims. In E. Buzawa & C. Buzawa (Eds.), *Domestic violence: The changing criminal justice response* (2nd ed., pp. 227–252). Westport, CT: Auburn House.

Harris, L., & Associates (1997). *The Commonwealth Fund survey of the health of adolescent girls.* New York: Commonwealth Fund.

Harris, L. H., & Paltrow, L. (2003). The status of pregnant women and fetuses in the US criminal law. *Medical Student Journal of the American Medical Association, 289,* 1697–1699.

Harstock, N. (1987). The feminist standpoint: Developing a ground for a specifically feminist historical materialism. In S. Harding (Ed.), *Feminism and methodology* (pp. 57–180). Milton Keynes, UK: Open University Press.

Hart, E. L. (1995, March). *Coordinated community approaches to domestic violence.* Paper presented at the National Institute of Justice's Strategic Planning Workshop on Violence Against Women, Washington, DC.

Hartley, C. C. (2001). "He said, she said": The defense attack of credibility in domestic violence felony trials. *Violence Against Women, 7,* 510–544.

Hashima, P. Y., & Finkelhor, D. (1999). Violent victimization of youth versus adults in the national crime victimization survey. *Journal of Interpersonal Violence, 14,* 799–820.

Hausbeck, K., & Brents, B. G. (2000). Inside Nevada's brothel industry. In R. Weitzer (Ed.), *Sex for sale: Prostitution, pornography, and the sex industry* (pp. 217–243). London: Routledge.

Haviland, M., Frye, V., Rajah, V., Thukral, J., & Trinity, M. (2001). *The Family Protection and Domestic Violence Intervention Act of 1995: Examining the effects of mandatory arrest in New York City.* New York: Family Violence Project, Urban Justice Center.

Hawthorne, S., & Klein, R. (Eds.). (1999). *Cyberfeminism: Connectivity, critique and creativity.* Melbourne, Australia: Spiniflex.

Healey, K., Smith, C., & O'Sullivan, K. C. (1998). *Batterer intervention: Program approaches and criminal justice strategies.* Washington, DC: Department of Justice.

Heather, D. (2000). The influence of presentence reports on sentencing in a district court in New Zealand. *Australian and New Zealand Journal of Criminology, 33*(1), 91–106.

Heidensohn, F. (1986). Models of justice: Portia or Peresphone? Some thoughts on equality, fairness and gender in the field of criminal justice. *International Journal of the Sociology of the Law, 14,* 287–298.

Heidensohn, F. (1995). *Women and crime.* Washington Square, NY: New York University Press.

Heimer, K. (2000). Changes in the gender gap in crime and women's economic marginalization. In G. LaFree (Ed.), *From the nature of crime: Continuity and change; criminal justice 2000* (Vol. 1, pp. 427–483). Washington DC: National Institute of Justice.

Heimer, K., & DeCoster, S. (1999). The gendering of violent delinquency. *Criminology, 27*(2), 277–313.

Heimer, K., Unal, H., & DeCoster, S. (2000). *Opening the black box: The social psychology of gender and delinquency.* Paper presented at the annual meeting of the American Society of Criminology, Toronto.

Heise, L. L., Pitanguy, J., & Germain, A. (1994). *Violence against women: The hidden health burden.* Washington, DC: World Bank.

Hennington, C., Hughes, J. N., Cavell, T. A., & Thompson, B. (1998). The role of relational aggression in identifying aggressive boys and girls. *Journal of School Psychology, 36,* 457–477.

Herek, G. M., Gillis, J. R., & Cogan, J. C. (1999). Psychological sequelae of hate-crime victimization among lesbian, gay, and bisexual adults. *Journal of Consulting and Clinical Psychology, 67*(6), 945–951.

Herek, G. M., Gillis, J. R., Cogan, J. C., & Glunt, E. K. (1997). Hate crime victimization among lesbian, gay, and bisexual adults: Prevalence, psychological correlates, and methodological issues. *Journal of Interpersonal Violence, 12,* 195–215.

Herman, J. L. (1992). *Trauma and recovery.* New York: Basic Books.

Herman, J. L., & Hirschman, L. (1981). *Father-daughter incest.* Cambridge, MA: Harvard University Press.

Heywood, L., & Drake, J. (1997). *Third wave agenda: Being feminist, doing feminism.* Minneapolis: University of Minnesota Press.

Hochschild, A., & Manchung, A. (1989). *The second shift: Working parents and the revolution at home.* New York: Viking Penguin.

Hoigard, C., & Finstad, L. (1992). *Backstreets: Prostitution, money, and love.* University Park: Pennsylvania State University Press.

Holmstrom, L. L., & Burgess, A. W. (1978). *The victim of rape: Institutional reactions.* New York: John Wiley.

Holmstrom, L. L., & Burgess, A. W. (1983). Rape and everyday life. *Society, 20*(5), 33–40.

Holtfreter, K., & Morash, M. (2001, March). *Criminogenic needs among women offenders and implications for correctional programming.* Paper presented at the Academy of Criminal Justice Sciences, Washington, DC.

Holtfreter, K., Reisig, M. D., & Morash, M. (2002, March). *Risk, poverty, and recidivism among women offenders.* Paper presented at the 39th annual meeting of the Academy of Criminal Justice Sciences, Anaheim, CA.

hooks, b. (1981). *Ain't I a woman: Black women and feminism.* Boston: South End Press.

Hopkins, S. (1999). A discussion of the legal aspects of female genital mutilation. *Journal of Advanced Nursing, 30*(4), 926–933.

Horowitz, C. R., & Jackson, C. (1997). Female "circumcision": African women confront American medicine. *Journal of General Internal Medicine, 12*(8), 491–499.

Hughes, D. M. (2000). The "Natasha" trade: The transnational shadow market of trafficking in women. *Journal of International Affairs, 53*(2), 625–651.

Hughes, D. M. (2001, January). The Natasha trade: Transnational sex trafficking. *National Institute of Justice Journal,* pp. 8–15.

Ignasi, P.I.A. (1993). *The dark side of the moon: Life conditions of the prostitutes in Asturias.* Barcelona, Spain: University of Barcelona.

Iovanni, L., & Miller, S. L. (2001). Criminal justice system responses to domestic violence: Law enforcement and the courts. In C. M. Renzetti, J. L. Edleson, & R. K. Bergen (Eds.), *Sourcebook on violence against women* (pp. 303–327). Thousand Oaks, CA: Sage.

Jablow, P. M. (2000). Victims of abuse and discrimination: Protecting battered homosexuals under domestic violence legislation. *Hofstra Law Review, 28,* 1095–1145.

Jacobs, J. B., & Potter, K. (1998). *Hate crimes: Criminal law and identity politics.* New York: Oxford University Press.

Jargowsky, P. (1997). *Poverty and place: Ghettos, barrios, and the American city.* New York: Russell Sage.

Jenness, V., & Broad, K. (1997). *Hate crimes: New social movements and the politics of violence.* New York: Aldine de Gruyter.

Jensen, I. W., & Gutek, B. A. (1982). Attributions and assignment of responsibility in sexual harassment. *Journal of Social Issues, 38,* 55–74.

Johnson, M. P., & Ferraro, K. J. (2000). Research on domestic violence in the 1990s: Making distinctions. *Journal of Marriage and the Family, 62,* 948–963.

Jones, L., & Finkelhor, D. (2001). *The decline in child abuse cases.* Washington, DC: Office of Juvenile Justice and Delinquency Prevention.

Jones, W. K., Smith, J., Kieke, B., Jr., & Wilcox, L. (1997). Female genital mutilation/female circumcision: Who is at risk in the U.S.? *Public Health Report, 112*(5), 368–377.

Jordan, J. (2001). Women, rape and the police reporting process. *British Journal of Criminology, 41,* 679–706.

Jos, P. H., Perlmutter, M., & Marshall, M. F. (2003). Substance abuse during pregnancy: Clinical and public health approaches. *Journal of Law, Medicine and Ethics, 31,* 340–360.

Kahn, S. (1999). Through a window darkly: Men who sell sex to men in India and Bangladesh. In P. Aggleton (Ed.), *Men who sell sex: International perspectives on male prostitution and AIDS* (pp. 195–212). London: UCL Press.

Kane, R. (1999). Patterns of arrest in domestic violence encounters: Identifying a police decision-making model. *Journal of Criminal Justice, 27,* 65–80.

Kane, R. (2000). Police responses to restraining orders in domestic violence incidents: Identifying the custody-threshold thesis. *Criminal Justice and Behavior, 27*(5), 561–580.

Kanin, E. J. (1985). Date rapists: Differential sexual socialization and relative deprivation. *Archives of Sexual Behavior, 14*(3), 218–232.

Kanuha, Y. (1996). Domestic violence, racism, and the battered women's movement in the United States. In J. L. Edleson & Z. C. Eisikovits (Eds.), *Future interventions with battered women and their families* (pp. 34–50). Thousand Oaks, CA: Sage.

Karan, A., Keilitz, S. L., & Denaro, S. (1999). Domestic violence courts: What are they and how should we manage them? *Juvenile and Family Court Journal, 50,* 75–86.

Karl, H. R., Gizzarelli, R., & Scott, H. (1994). The attitudes of incest offenders: Sexual entitlement and acceptance of sex with children. *Criminal Justice and Behavior, 21,* 187–202.

Kelly, L. (1987). The continuum of sexual violence. In J. Hanmer & M. Maynard (Eds.), *Women, violence and social control* (pp. 46–60). Atlantic Heights, NJ: Humanities Press.

Kelly, L. (1988). *Surviving sexual violence.* Minneapolis: University of Minneapolis Press.

Kennedy, H. (1992). *Eve was framed: Women and British justice.* London: Vintage.

Kenny, D. J., & Reuland, M. (2002). Public order policing: A national survey of abortion-related conflict. *Journal of Criminal Justice, 30,* 355–368.

Kenworthy, T. (1999, Nov. 3). Jury to weigh motives in gay killing. *Washington Post,* p. A3.

Kersten, J. (1990). A gender specific look at patterns of violence in juvenile institutions: Or are girls really "more difficult to handle"? *International Journal of Sociology of the Law, 18,* 473–493.

Kessler, S., & McKenna, W. (1978). *Gender: An ethnomethodological approach.* New York: John Wiley & Sons.

Kimmel, M. S. (2003). Globalization and its mal(e)contents: The gendered moral and political economy of terrorism. *International Sociology, 18,* 603–620.

Kirkpatrick, C., & Kanin, E. (1957). Male sex aggression on a university campus. *American Sociological Review, 22,* 52–58.

Kirkwood, C. (1993). *Leaving abusive partners.* London: Sage.

Klein, D. (1973). The etiology of female crime: A review of the literature. *Crime and Social Justice: Issues in Criminology, 8,* 3–30.

Klein, D. (1981). Violence against women: Some considerations regarding its causes and its elimination. *Crime & Delinquency, 27*(1), 64–80.

Klein, D. (1982). The dark side of marriage: Battered wives and the domination of women. In N. H. Rafter & E. A. Stanko (Eds.), *Judge, lawyer, victim, thief: Women, gender roles and criminal justice* (pp. 83–110). Boston: Northeastern University Press.

Koenig, D. M., & Askin, K. D. (2000). International criminal law and the international criminal court statute: Crimes against women. In K. D. Askin & D. M. Koenig (Eds.), *Women and international human rights law* (Vol. 2, pp. 3–29). New York: Transnational Press.

Koester, S., & Schwartz, J. (1993). Crack, gangs, sex and powerlessness: A view from Denver. In M. A. Ratner (Ed.), *Crack pipe as pimp: An ethnographic investigation of sex-for-crack exchanges* (pp. 187–203). New York: Lexington Books.

Kohn, L. P., & Wilson, M. (1995). Social support networks in the African American family: Utility for culturally compatible intervention. In M. Wilson (Ed.), *African American family life: Its structural and ecological aspects* (pp. 35–58). San Francisco: Jossey-Bass.

Kojima, Y. (2001). In the business of cultural reproduction: Theoretical implications of the mail-order bride phenomenon. *Women's Studies International Forum, 24*(2), 199–210.

Konopka, G. (1966). *The adolescent girl in conflict.* Englewood Cliffs, NJ: Prentice Hall.

Konradi, A. (1996). Preparing to testify: Rape survivors negotiating the criminal justice process. *Gender & Society, 10,* 404–452.

Koons-Witt, B. (2000, November). *Gender and justice: The role of gender in sentencing decisions in the state of Minnesota, pre- and post-sentencing guidelines.* Paper presented at the American Society of Criminology, San Francisco.

Koss, M. P. (1988). Hidden rape: Sexual aggression and victimization in a national sample in higher education. In A. W. Burgess (Ed.), *Rape and sexual assault* (pp. 3–25). New York: Garland.

Koss, M. P. (1989). Hidden rape: Sexual aggression and victimization in a national sample of students in higher education. In M. A. Pirog-Good & J. E. Stets (Eds.), *Violence in dating relationships* (Vol. 2, pp. 3–25). Westport, CT: Praeger.

Koss, M. P. (1993). Rape: Scope, impact, interventions and public policy responses. *American Psychologist, 10,* 1062–1070.

Koss, M. P., Gidycz, C. A., & Wisniewski, N. (1987). The scope of rape: Incidence and prevalence of sexual aggression and victimization in a national sample of higher education students. *Journal of Counseling and Clinical Psychology, 55,* 162–170.

Koss, M. P., Leonard, K. E., Beezley, D., & Oros, C. (1985). Nonstranger sexual aggression: A discriminant analysis of the psychological characteristics of undetected offenders. *Sex Roles, 12,* 981–992.

Krahe, B. (1998). Sexual aggression among adolescents: Prevalence and predictors in a German sample. *Psychology of Women Quarterly, 22,* 537–554.

Kramer, J. H., & Ulmer, J. T. (1996). Sentencing disparity and departures from guidelines. *Justice Quarterly, 13,* 81–105.

Krishnan, S., Baig-Amin, M., Gilbert, L., El-Bassel, N., & Waters, A. (1998). Lifting the veil of secrecy: Domestic violence against South Asian women in the United States. In S. Das Gupta (Ed.), *A patchwork shawl: Chronicles of South Asian womanhood in America* (pp. 145–159). New Brunswick, NJ: Rutgers University Press.

Krivo, L., Peterson, R., Rizzo, H., & Reynolds, J. (1998). Race, segregation, and the concentration of disadvantage: 1980–1990. *Social Problems, 45,* 61–80.

Krohn, M., Curry, J. P., & Nelson-Kilger, S. (1983). "Is chivalry dead?" An analysis of changes in police dispositions of males and females. *Criminology, 21,* 417–437.

Kruttschnitt, C. (1981). Social status and the sentences of female offenders. *Law and Society Review, 15*(2), 247–265.

Kruttschnitt, C. (1995). Violence by and against women: A comparative and cross-national analysis source. In R. B. Ruback & N. A. Weiner (Eds.), *Interpersonal violent behaviors: Social and cultural aspects* (pp. 89–108). New York: Springer.

Kruttschnitt, C. (1996). Contributions of quantitative methods to the study of gender and crime, or bootstrapping our way into the theoretical thicket. *Journal of Quantitative Criminology, 12*(2), 135–161.

Kruttschnitt, C. (2001). Gender and violence. In C. M. Renzetti & L. Goodstein (Eds.), *Women, crime and criminal justice* (pp. 77–92). Los Angeles: Roxbury.

Kruttschnitt, C., Gartner, R., & Miller, A. (2000). Doing her own time? Women's responses to prison in the context of the old and the new penology. *Criminology, 38,* 681–718.

Kurz, D. (1987). Emergency department responses to battered women: Resistance to medicalization. *Social Problems, 34*(1), 69–81.

Ladwig, G. B., & Anderson, M. D. (1989). Substance abuse in women: Relationship between chemical dependency of women and past reports of physical and/or sexual abuse. *International Journal of the Addictions, 24,* 739–754.

LaFramboise, T. D., Choney, S. B., James, A., & Running Wolf, P. (1995). American Indian women and psychology. In H. Landrine (Ed.), *Bringing cultural diversity to feminist psychology: Theory, research and practice* (pp. 197–239). Washington, DC: American Psychological Association.

LaFree, G. (1981). Official reactions to social problems: Police decisions in sexual assault cases. *Social Problems, 28,* 582–594.

LaFree, G. (1989). *Rape and criminal justice: The social construction of sexual assault.* Belmont, CA: Wadsworth.

LaFree, G. (1998). *Losing legitimacy: Street crime and the decline of social institutions in America.* Boulder, CO: Westview.

Lahm, K. F. (2000). Equal or equitable: An exploration of educational and vocational program availability for male and female offenders. *Federal Probation, 64*(2), 39–46.

Laidler, K. J., & Hunt, G. (2001). Accomplishing femininity among the girls in the gang. *British Journal of Criminology, 41,* 656–678.

Lamb, S. (1999). Constructing the victim: Popular images and lasting labels. In S. Lamb (Ed.), *New versions of victims: Feminists struggle with the concept* (pp. 108–138). New York: New York University Press.

Lambda Legal Defense and Education Fund. (2001). *Nebraska's highest court unanimously holds sheriff accountable for Brandon Teena's death.* Retrieved March 15, 2005, from www.lambdalegal.org/cgi-bin/iowa/news/press.html?record=825

Landau, T. C. (2000). Women's experiences with mandatory charging for wife assault in Ontario, Canada: A case against the prosecution. In E. Erez & T. A. King (Eds.), *Domestic violence: Global responses* (pp. 141–157). Bicester, Oxfordshire, UK: AB Academic.

Laster, K., & Douglas, R. (2000). Treating spousal violence "differently." In E. Erez & T. A. King (Eds.), *Domestic violence: Global responses* (pp. 115–139). Bicester, Oxfordshire, UK: AB Academic.

Latham, M. (2001). Deregulation and emergency contraception: A way forward for women's health care? *Feminist Legal Studies, 9*(3), 221–246.

Laub, J. H., & Sampson, R. J. (1993). Turning points in the life course: Why change matters to the study of crime. *Criminology, 31*(3), 301–325.

Laub, J. H., & Sampson, R. J. (2003). *Shared beginnings, divergent lives.* Cambridge, MA: Harvard University Press.

Lazarus-Black, M. (2000). Law and the pragmatics of inclusion: Governing domestic violence in Trinidad and Tobago. *American Ethnologist, 28*(2), 388–416.

Lea, S., Auburn, T., & Kibblewhite, K. (1999). Working with sex offenders: The perceptions and experiences of professionals and paraprofessionals. *International Journal of Offender Therapy and Comparative Criminology, 43*(1), 103–119.

Lee, E. (2001). Reinventing abortion as a social problem: "Postabortion syndrome" in the United States and Britain. In J. Best (Ed.), *How claims spread: Cross-national diffusion of social problems* (pp. 39–68). New York: Aldine de Gruyter.

Leidholdt, D. (1991). Prostitution: A violation of women's human rights. *Cardozo Women's Law Journal, 1,* 133–147.

Leonard, E. (1982). *Women, crime and society: A critique of criminology theory.* New York: Longman.

Letellier, P. (1994). Gay and bisexual male domestic violence victimization: Challenges to feminist theory and responses to violence. *Violence and Victims, 9,* 95–105.

Levinson, D. (1989). *Family violence in cross-cultural perspective.* Newbury Park, CA: Sage.

Lewis, R., Dobash, R. P., Dobash, R. E., & Cavanagh, K. (2000). Protection, prevention, rehabilitation or justice? Women's use of the law to challenge domestic violence. In E. Erez & T. A. King (Eds.), *Domestic violence: Global responses* (pp. 179–205). Bicester, Oxfordshire, UK: AB Academic.

Li, J., & Lavely, W. (2003). Village context, women's status, and son preference among rural Chinese women. *Rural Sociology, 68*(1), 87–106.

Lillich, R. B. (1992). The role of domestic courts in enforcing international human rights law. In H. Hannum (Ed.), *Guide to international human rights practice* (2nd ed., pp. 228–246). Philadelphia: University of Pennsylvania Press.

Lloyd, A. (1995). *Doubly deviant, doubly damned.* New York: Penguin Books.

Lombroso, C. (1920). *The female offender* [Translation]. New York: Applegate.

Lorber, J. (1994). *Paradoxes of gender.* New Haven, CT: Yale University Press.

Loseke, D. R. (1991). Reply to Murray Straus: Readings on "discipline and deviance." *Social Problems, 38*(2), 133–154.

Loseke, D. R., & Cahil, S. E. (1984). The social construction of deviance: Experts on battered women. *Social Problems, 31,* 296–309.

Lott, B., & Bullock, H. E. (2001). Who are the poor? *Journal of Social Issues, 57*(2), 189–206.

Lowman, J. (in press). Prostitution law reform in Canada. In T. Shiibashi (Ed.), *An anthology celebrating the fiftieth anniversary of the institute of comparative law.* Chuo University, Japan.

Lowney, K. S., & Best, J. (1995). Stalking strangers and lovers: Changing media typifications of a new crime problem. In J. Best (Ed.), *Images of issues: Typifying contemporary social problems* (pp. 33–57). New York: Aldine de Gruyter.

Luke, N. (2003). Age and economic asymmetries in the sexual relationships of adolescent girls in sub-Saharan Africa. *Studies in Family Planning, 34*(2), 67–86.

Luker, K. (1984). *Abortion and the politics of motherhood.* Berkeley: University of California Press.

Mac An Ghaill, M. (1994). *The making of men.* Buckingham, UK: Open University Press.

MacDonald, J. M., & Chesney-Lind, M. (2001). Gender bias and juvenile justice revisited: A multiyear analysis. *Crime and Delinquency, 47,* 173–195.

Macmillan, R., & Gartner, R. (1999). When she brings home the bacon: Labor-force participation and the risk of spousal violence against women. *Journal of Marriage and the Family, 61*(4), 947–958.

Madigan, L., & Gamble, N. (1991). *The second rape: Society's continued betrayal of the victim.* New York: Lexington Books.

Madriz, E. I. (1997). Images of criminals and victims: A study on women's fear and social control. *Gender & Society, 11*(3), 342–356.

Maguire, K., & Pastore, A. L. (Eds.). (1997). *Sourcebook of criminal justice statistics, 1996.* Washington, DC: Bureau of Justice Statistics.

Maher, L. (1997). *Sexed work: Gender, race, and resistance in a Brooklyn drug market.* New York: Oxford University Press.

Mahoney, M. (1991). Legal images of battered women: Redefining the issue of separation. *Michigan Law Review, 90,* 2–94.

Makepeace, J. M. (1981). Courtship violence among college students. *Family Relations, 30*(1), 97–102.

Malamuth, N. M., Addison, T., & Koss, M. (2000). Pornography and sexual aggression: Are there reliable effects and can we understand them? *Annual Review of Sex Research, 11,* 26–91.

Malamuth, N. M., Scokloski, R. J., Koss, M. P., & Tanaka, J. S. (1991). Characteristics of aggressors against women: Testing a model using a national sample of college students. *Journal of Consulting and Clinical Psychology, 59,* 670–681.

Mama, A. (1989). *The hidden struggle: Statutory and voluntary sector responses to violence against black women in the home.* London: London Race and Housing Unit.

Mancuso, R. F., & Miller, B. A. (2000). Crime and punishment in the lives of women alcohol and other drug (AOD) users: Exploring the gender, lifestyle, and legal issues. In C. M. Renzetti & L. Goodstein (Eds.), *Women, crime, and criminal justice* (pp. 93–110). Los Angeles: Roxbury.

Mandaraka-Sheppard, A. (1986). *The dynamics of aggression in women's prisons in England and Wales.* London: Gower.

Mann, C. R. (1995). Women of color and the criminal justice system. In B. R. Price & N. Sokoloff (Eds.), *The criminal justice system and women: Offenders, victims, and workers* (pp. 118–135). New York: McGraw-Hill.

Marin, A. J., & Guadagno, R. E. (1999). Perceptions of sexual harassment victims as a function of labeling and reporting. *Sex Roles, 41,* 921–940.

Martin, D. (1982). Battered women: Society's problem. In J. R. Chapman & M. Gates (Eds.), *The criminal justice system and women* (pp. 263–290). Beverly Hills, CA: Sage.

Martin, D. I., & Mosher, J. E. (1995). Unkept promises: Experiences of immigrant women with the neo-criminalization of wife abuse. *Canadian Journal of Women and the Law, 8,* 3–44.

Martin, M. E. (1997). Double your trouble: Dual arrest in family violence. *Journal of Family Violence, 12*(2), 139–157.

Martin, P. Y., & Powell, M. (1995). Accounting for the "second assault": Legal organizations' framing of rape victims. *Law and Social Inquiry, 19,* 853–890.

Mason, K. O. (1987). The impact of women's social position on fertility in developing countries. *Sociological Forum, 2,* 718–741.

Mathieu, L. (2003). The emergence and uncertain outcomes of prostitutes' social movements. *European Journal of Women's Studies, 10,* 29–50.

Matsoesian, G. M. (1993). *Reproducing rape: Domination through talk in the courtroom.* Chicago: University of Chicago Press.

Matsoesian, G. M. (2001). *Law and the language of identity: Discourse in the William Kennedy Smith rape trial.* Oxford, UK: Oxford University Press.

Mauer, M., & Chesney-Lind, M. (Eds.). (2002). *Invisible punishment: The collateral consequences of mass imprisonment.* Washington, DC: Sentencing Project.

Mayer, J. (1994). *Girls in the Maryland juvenile justice system: Findings of the Female Population Taskforce.* Presentation to the Gender Specific Services Training Group, Minneapolis, MN.

Mazumdar, R. (1998). Marital rape: Some ethical and cultural considerations. In S. D. Dasgupta (Ed.), *A patchwork shawl: Chronicles of South Asian women in America* (pp. 129–144). New Brunswick, NJ: Rutgers University Press.

Mazur, A., & Booth, A. (1998). Testosterone and dominance in men. *Behavior and Brain Sciences, 21,* 353–363.

McCarthy, B., Hagan, J., & Woodward, T. S. (1999). In the company of women: Structure and agency in a revised power-control theory of gender and delinquency. *Criminology, 37,* 761–788.

McClellan, D. S. (1994). Disparity in the discipline of male and female inmates in Texas prisons. *Women and Criminal Justice, 5*(2), 71–97.

McCorkel, J. A. (2003). Embodied surveillance and the gendering of punishment. *Journal of Contemporary Ethnography, 32,* 31–76.

McKeganey, N., & Barnard, M. (1996). *Sex work on the streets: Prostitutes and their clients.* Milton Keynes, UK: Open University Press.

McKinley-Floyd, L. A. (1998). The impact of values on the selection of philanthropic clubs by elite African American women: An historical perspective. *Psychology and Marketing, 15*(2), 145–161.

McMaster, L. E., Connolly, J., Pepler, D., & Craig, W. M. (2002). Peer to peer sexual harassment in early adolescence: A developmental perspective. *Development and Psychopathology, 14,* 91–105.

McNeely, R. L., & Robinson-Simpson, G. (1987). The truth about domestic violence: A falsely framed issue. *Social Work, 32,* 485–490.

Mechanic, M. B., Uhlmansiek, M. H., Weaver, T. L., & Resick, P. A. (2000). The impact of severe stalking experienced by acutely battered women: An examination of violence, psychological symptoms and strategic responding. *Violence and Victims, 15*(4), 443–458.

Meier, E. (2002). Child rape in South Africa. *Pediatric Nursing, 28*(5), 532–536.

Meis Knupfer, A. (1996). *Toward a tenderer humanity and a nobler womanhood: African American women's clubs in turn-of-the-century Chicago.* New York: New York University Press.

Merry, S. (1995). Wife battering and the ambiguities of rights. In A. Sarat & T. Kearns (Eds.), *Identities, politics, and rights* (pp. 271–307). Ann Arbor: University of Michigan Press.

Messerschmidt, J. W. (1986). *Capitalism, patriarchy, and crime: Toward a socialist feminist criminology.* Totowa, NJ: Rowman and Littlefield.

Messerschmidt, J. (1987). Feminism, criminology and the rise of the female sex "delinquent," 1880–1930: The role and sentencing of women in drug trafficking crime. *Contemporary Crises, 11*(3), 243–264.

Messerschmidt, J. W. (1999). Making bodies matter: Adolescent masculinities, the body, and varieties of violence. *Theoretical Criminology, 3,* 197–220.

Messerschmidt, J. W. (2000). *Nine lives: Adolescent masculinities, the body, and violence.* Boulder, CO: Westview.

Messito, C. M. (1997–1998). Regulating rites: Legal responses to female genital mutilation in the West. *Public Interest, 16,* 33–77.

Metcalf, A. (1976). From schoolgirl to mother: The effects of education on Navajo women. *Social Problems, 23,* 535–544.

Meyers, M. (1997). *News coverage of violence against women.* Thousand Oaks, CA: Sage.

Mignon, S., & Holmes, W. (1995). Police response to mandatory arrest laws. *Crime & Delinquency, 32,* 308–324.

Miller, B. D. (2001). Female-selective abortion in Asia: Patterns, policies, and debates. *American Anthropologist, 103,* 1083–1095.

Miller, E. M. (1986). *Street woman.* Philadelphia: Temple University Press.

Miller, J. (1995). Gender and power on the streets: Street prostitution in the era of crack cocaine. *Journal of Contemporary Ethnography, 23,* 427–452.

Miller, J. (2002). Violence and coercion in Sri Lanka's commercial sex industry: Intersections of gender, sexuality, culture, and the law. *Violence Against Women, 8,* 1044–1073.

Miller, S. L. (2001). The paradox of women arrested for domestic violence: Criminal justice professionals and service providers respond. *Violence Against Women, 7,* 1339–1376.

Mills, E. A. (1982). One hundred years of fear: Rape and the medical profession. In N. H. Rafter & E. A. Stanko (Eds.), *Judge, lawyer, victim, thief: Women, gender roles and criminal justice* (pp. 29–62). Boston: Northeastern University Press.

Milton, C. H., Pierce, C., Lyons, M., & Hippenstead, B. (1977). *Little sisters and the law.* Washington, DC: Office of Juvenile Justice and Delinquency Prevention.

Mink, G. (2001). Violating women: Rights abuses in the welfare police state. *Annals of the American Academy of Political and Social Science, 577,* 79–93.

Moffitt, T. E. (1990). Juvenile delinquency and attention deficit disorder: Boys' developmental trajectories from age 3 to age 15. *Child Development, 61,* 893–910.

Moffitt, T. E., & Caspi, A. (1999). *Findings about partner violence from the Dunedin Multidisciplinary Health and Development Study.* Washington, DC: National Institute of Justice.

Moffitt, T. E., Caspi, A., Rutter, M., & Silva, P. A. (2001). *Sex differences in antisocial behavior.* Cambridge UK: Cambridge University Press.

Monture-Angus, P. (2000). Aboriginal women and correctional practice: Reflections on the task force on federally sentenced women. In K. Hannah-Moffat & M. Shaw (Eds.), *An ideal prison? Critical essays on women's imprisonment in Canada* (pp. 52–60). Halifax, Nova Scotia, Canada: Fernwood.

Moore, G. (1992). Structural determinants of men's and women's personal networks. *American Sociological Review, 55,* 726–735.

Moore, J. (1991). *Going down to the barrio: Homeboys and homegirls in change.* Philadelphia: Temple University Press.

Moore, S.A.D. (2003). Understanding the connection between domestic violence, crime, and poverty: How welfare reform may keep battered women from leaving abusive relationships. *Texas Journal of Women and the Law, 12,* 451–484.

Morash, M., & Bui, H. (2002). *Interim report: Vietnamese-American women and wife abuse.* East Lansing: Michigan State University, School of Criminal Justice.

Morash, M., Bui, H., & Santiago, A. (2000). Culture-specific gender ideology and wife abuse in Mexican-descent families. *International Review of Victimology, 7*(1–3), 67–91.

Morash, M., Bynum, T., & Koons, B. A. (1998). *Women offenders: Programming needs and promising approaches.* Washington, DC: National Institute of Justice.

Morash, M., & Chesney-Lind, M. (1991). A reformulation and partial test of the power control theory of delinquency. *Justice Quarterly, 8*(3), 347–377.

Morash, M., Holtfreter, K., & Reisig, M. (2002, November). *A comparison of the characteristics and outcomes of gender-responsive and traditional programs for women offenders.* Paper presented at the 54th annual meeting of the American Society of Criminology, Chicago.

Morash, M., & Robinson, A. L. (2002a). Correctional administrators' perspectives on gender arrangements and family-related programming for women offenders. *Marriage and the Family Review, 32*(3–4), 83–109.

Morash, M., & Robinson, A. L. (2002b). The nexus of community policing and domestic violence. In M. Morash & J. K. Ford (Eds.), *The move to community policing: Making change happen* (pp. 180–203). Thousand Oaks, CA: Sage.

Morash, M., & Rucker, L. (1990). A critical look at the idea of boot camp as a correctional reform. *Crime & Delinquency, 36,* 204–222.

Morash, M., & Schram, P. J. (2002). *The prison experience: Special issues of Women in prison.* Prospect Heights, IL: Waveland.

Morse, E. V., Simon, P. M., & Burchfiel, K. E. (1999). Social environment and male sex work in the United States. In P. Aggleton (Ed.), *Men who sell sex: International perspectives on male prostitution and AIDS* (pp. 83–101). London: UCL Press.

Mosher, D. L., & Sirkin, M. (1984). Measuring a macho personality constellation. *Journal of Research in Personality, 18,* 150–163.

Moulds, E. F. (1980). Chivalry and paternalism: Disparities of treatment in the criminal justice system. In S. K. Datesman & F. R. Scarpitti (Eds.), *Women, crime, and justice* (pp. 277–299). New York: Oxford University Press.

Moya, E. A. de M., & Garcia, R. (1999). Three decades of male sex work in Santo Domingo. In P. Aggleton (Ed.), *Men who sell sex: International perspectives on male prostitution and AIDS* (pp. 27–139). London: UCL Press.

Murnen, S. K. (2000). Gender and the use of sexually degrading language. *Psychology of Women Quarterly, 24,* 319–327.

Murnen, S. K., Wright, C., & Kaluzny, G. (2002). If "boys will be boys," then girls will be victims? A meta-analytic review of the research that relates masculine ideology to sexual aggression. *Sex Roles, 46,* 359–375.

Murphy, C. M., Musser, P. H., & Maton, K. I. (1998). Coordinated community intervention for domestic abusers: Intervention system involvement and criminal recidivism. *Journal of Family Violence, 13*(2), 263–284.

Myers, J. B. (1994). *The backlash: Child protection under fire.* Thousand Oaks, CA: Sage.

Myers, T., & Sangster, J. (2001). Retorts, runaways and riots: Patterns of resistance in Canadian reform schools for girls. *Journal of Social History, 34,* 660–697.

Naffine, N. (1987). *Female crime: The construction of women in criminology.* Winchester, MA: Allen & Unwin.

Nagel, I. H., & Johnson, B. L. (1994). Role of gender in a structured sentencing system: Equal treatment, policy choices, and the sentencing of female offenders under the United States sentencing guidelines. *Journal of Criminal Law and Criminology, 85,* 181–222.

Nagin, D. S., Farrington, D. P., & Moffitt, T. (1995). Life-course trajectories of different types of offenders. *Criminology, 33*(1), 111–138.

Naples, N. A. (2003). Deconstructing and locating survivor discourse: Dynamics of narrative, empowerment, and resistance for survivors of childhood sexual abuse. *Signs: Journal of Women in Culture and Society, 28*(4), 1151–1185.

National Institute of Corrections. (2002). *Services for families of prison inmates.* Longmont, CO: National Institute of Corrections Information Center.

Naylor, B. (2001). Reporting violence in the British print media: Gendered stories. *Howard Journal of Criminal Justice, 40,* 180–194.

Nearpass, G. R. (2003). Comment: The overlooked constitutional objection and practical concerns to penalty-enhancement provisions of hate crime legislation. *Albany Law Review, 66,* 547–572.

Nencel, L. (2001). *Ethnography and prostitution in Peru.* London: Pluto Press.

Newman, K. S. (1999). *No shame in my game: The working poor in the inner city.* New York: Knopf and the Russell Sage Foundation.

Nossiff, R. (1998). Discourse, party, and policy: The case of abortion, 1965–1972. *Policy Studies Journal, 26*(2), 244–256.

O'Connor, R. E., & Berkman, M. B. (1995). Religious determinants of state abortion policy. *Social Science Quarterly, 76,* 447–459.

O'Dell, L. (1997). Child sexual abuse and the academic construction of symptomatologies. *Feminism and Psychology, 7,* 334–339.

Odem, M. E. (1995). *Delinquent daughters: Protecting and policing adolescent female sexuality in the United States, 1885–1920.* Chapel Hill: University of North Carolina Press.

Office of Justice Programs. (1999). *Conference proceedings: National symposium on women offenders.* Washington, DC: Author.

Oleson, V. (1994). Feminisms and models of qualitative research. In N. K. Denzin & Y. S. Lincoln (Eds.), *Handbook of qualitative research* (pp. 158–174). Thousand Oaks, CA: Sage.

Oppenlander, N. (1982). Coping or copping out. *Criminology, 20*(3–4), 449–465.

Osgood, D. W., Johnston, L. D., O'Malley, P. M., & Bachman, J. G. (1988). The generality of deviance in late adolescence and early adulthood. *American Sociological Review, 53*(1), 81–93.

Otis, M. D., & Skinner, W. F. (1996). The prevalence of victimization and its effect on mental well-being among lesbian and gay people. *Journal of Homosexuality, 30*(3), 93–121.

Owen, B. (1998). *"In the mix": Struggle and survival in a women's prison.* Albany: State University of New York Press.

Owen, B., & Bloom, B. (1995). Profiling women prisoners: Findings from national surveys and a California sample. *The Prison Journal, 75*(2), 165–185.

Padilla, F. (1992). *The gang as an American enterprise.* New Brunswick, NJ: Rutgers University Press.

Pain, R. H. (1997). Social geographies of women's fear of crime. *Transactions of the Institute of British Geographers, 22,* 231–244.

Pain, R. (2001). Gender, race, age and fear in the city. *Urban Studies, 38,* 899–913.

Paradise, J. E. (2001). Current concepts in preventing sexual abuse. *Current Opinion in Pediatrics, 13*(5), 402–407.

Patai, D., & Koertge, N. (1994). *Professing feminism.* New York: Basic Books.

Pearce, D. M. (1989). *The feminization of poverty: A second look.* Washington, DC: Institute for Women's Policy Research.

Pearson, P. (1997). *When she was bad: Violent women and the myth of innocence.* Toronto: Random House.

Pence, E., & McMahon, M. (1997). *Coordinated community response to domestic violence.* Duluth, MN: National Training Project.

Pence, E. L., & Shepard, M. F. (1999). An introduction: Developing a coordinated community response. In M. F. Shepard & E. Pence (Eds.), *Coordinating community response to domestic violence: Lessons from Duluth and beyond* (pp. 3–23). Thousand Oaks, CA: Sage.

Perry, B. (2001). *In the name of hate: Understanding hate crime.* New York: Routledge.

Petersilia, J. (1993). The influence of research on policing. In R. G. Dunham & G. P. Alpert (Eds.), *Critical issues in policing: Contemporary readings* (pp. 220–236). Prospect Heights, IL: Waveland.

Peterson, J., Zong, X., & Jones-DeWeever, A. (2002). *Life after welfare reform: Low-income single parent families, pre- and post-TANF* (IWPR Publication No. D446). Washington, DC: Institute for Women's Policy Research.

Pheterson, G. (Ed.). (1989). *A vindication of the rights of whores.* Seattle, WA: Seal Press.

Phillips, L. M. (1999). Recasting consent: Agency and victimization in adult-teen relationships. In S. Lamb (Ed.), *New versions of victims: Feminists struggle with the concept* (pp. 108–138). New York: New York University Press.

Phoenix, J. (2002). Youth prostitution policy reform: New discourse, same old story. In P. Carlen (Ed.), *Women and punishment: The struggle for justice* (pp. 67–93). Portland, OR: Willan.

Pierce, M. C., & Harris, R. J. (1993). The effect of provocation, race, and injury description on men's and women's perceptions of a wife-battering incident. *Journal of Applied Social Psychology, 23,* 767–790.

Pilkington, N. W., & D'Augelli, A. R. (1995). Victimization of lesbian, gay, and bisexual youth in community settings. *Journal of Community Psychology, 23,* 33–56.

Pinn, V. W., & Chunko, M. T. (1997). The diverse face of violence: Minority women and domestic abuse. *Academic Medicine, 72*(1), S65–S71.

Pino, R., & Meier, F. (1999). Gender differences in rape reporting. *Sex Roles, 40,* 979–990.

Pitts, V. L., & Schwartz, M. D. (1993). Promoting self-blame in hidden rape cases. *Humanity and Society, 17,* 383–398.

Pleck, E. H. (1987). *Domestic tyranny: The making of social policy against family violence from colonial times to the present.* New York: Oxford University Press.

Plummer, C. (2001). Prevention of child sexual abuse: A survey of 87 programs. *Violence and Victims, 16,* 575–588.

Pogrebin, M. R., & Dodge, M. (2001). Women's accounts of their prison experiences: A retrospective view of their subjective realities. *Journal of Criminal Justice, 29,* 531–541.

Polk, K. (1994). Masculinity, honour, and homicide. In T. Newburn & E. A. Stanko (Eds.), *Just boys doing business? Men, masculinities and crime* (pp. 166–188). London: Routledge.

Pollack, S. (2000). Dependency discourse as social control. In K. Hannah-Moffat & M. Shaw (Eds.), *The ideal prison? Critical essays on women's imprisonment in Canada* (pp. 72–81). Halifax, Nova Scotia, Canada: Fernwood.

Pollak, O. (1950). *The criminality of women.* Philadelphia: University of Pennsylvania Press.

Pollard, P. (1995). Rape reporting as a function of victim-offender relationships: A critique of the lack of effect reported by Bachman. *Criminal Justice and Behavior, 22,* 74–80.

Porras, J. I., & Robertson. P. J. (1992). Organizational development: Theory, practice, and research. In M. Dunnette & L. M. Hough (Eds.), *Handbook of industrial and organizational psychology* (pp. 760–797). Palo Alto, CA: Consulting Psychologists Press.

Portillo, E. L. (1999). Women, men and gangs: The social construction of gender in the Barrio. In M. Chesney-Lind & J. Hagedorn (Eds.), *Female gangs in America* (pp. 232–244). Chicago: Lakeview Press.

Posner, R. A., & Silbaugh, K. B. (1996). *A guide to America's sex laws.* Chicago: University of Chicago Press.

Poupart, L. M. (2002). Social justice. *Social Justice, 29*(1/2), 144–159.

Preisser, A. B. (1999). Domestic violence in South Asian communities in America: Advocacy and intervention. *Violence Against Women, 5,* 684–699.

Presser, L., & Gaarder, E. (2000). Can restorative justice reduce battering? Some preliminary considerations. *Social Justice, 27,* 175–195.

Pressman, S. (2002). Explaining the gender poverty gap in developed and transitional economies. *Journal of Economic Issues, 36*(1), 17–40.

Proctor, B. D., & Dalaker, J. (2003). Poverty in the United States: 2002. *Current population reports.* Washington, DC: U.S. Census Bureau.

Ptacek, J. (1988). The clinical literature on men who batter: A review and critique. In G. T. Hotaling, D. Finkelhor, J. Kirkpatrick, & M. Straus (Eds.), *Family abuse and its consequences: New directions in research* (pp. 149–162). Newbury Park, CA: Sage.

Ptacek, J. (1999). *Battered women in the courtroom: The power of judicial responses.* Boston: Northeastern University Press.

Quicker, J. (1999). Black female gangs in Philadelphia. In M. Chesney-Lind & J. M. Hagedorn (Eds.), *Female gangs in America* (pp. 48–56). Chicago: Lakeview Press.

Quisumbing, A. R., Haddad, L., & Peña, C. (2001). Are women overrepresented among the poor? An analysis of poverty in 10 developing countries. *Journal of Development Economics, 66*(1), 225–269.

Radford, J., & Stanko, E. (1996). Violence against women and children: The contradictions of crime control under patriarchy. In M. Hester, L. Kelly, & J. Radford (Eds.), *Women, violence and male power* (pp. 65–80). Philadelphia: Open University Press.

Rafter, N. H. (1985). *Partial justice: Women in state prisons, 1800–1935.* Boston: Northeastern University Press.

Rafter, N. H. (1990). *Partial justice: Women, prisons, and social control.* New Brunswick, NJ: Transaction.

Rafter, N. H., & Stanko, E. A. (1982). Introduction. In N. H. Rafter & E. A. Stanko (Eds.), *Judge, lawyer, victim, thief: Women, gender roles, and criminal justice* (pp. 1–28). Boston: Northeastern University Press.

Ransley, C. (1999). Unheard voices: Burmese women in immigration detention in Thailand. In S. Cook & S. Davies (Eds.), *Harsh punishment: International experiences of women's imprisonment* (pp. 172–188). Boston: Northeastern University Press.

Rasche, C. E. (1974). The female offender as an object of criminological research. *Criminal Justice and Behavior, 1,* 301–319.

Rasche, C. (2000). The dislike of female offenders among correctional officers: Need for special training. In R. Muraskin (Ed.), *It's a crime: Women and justice* (3rd ed., pp. 237–252). Upper Saddle River, NJ: Prentice Hall.

Ratnapala, N. (1999). Male sex work in Sri Lanka. In P. Aggleton (Ed.), *Men who sell sex: International perspectives on male prostitution and AIDS* (pp. 213–221). London: UCL Press.

Raymond, J. G., & Hughes, D. M. (2001). *Sex trafficking of women in the United States: International and domestic trends.* North Amherst, MA: Coalition Against Trafficking in Women.

Reinelt, C. (1994). Moving on to the terrain of the state: The politics of battered women's shelters in Texas. In M. M. Ferree & P. Y. Martin (Eds.), *Feminist organizations: Harvest of the new women's movement* (pp. 84–104). Philadelphia: Temple University Press.

Rennison, C. M. (2001). *Intimate partner violence and age of victim, 1993–99.* Washington, DC: Bureau of Justice Statistics.

Rennison, C. (2002). *Rape and sexual assault: Reporting to police and medical attention, 1992–2000.* Washington, DC: Bureau of Justice Statistics.

Rennison, C. M. (2003). *Intimate partner violence: 1993–2001.* Washington, DC: Bureau of Justice Statistics.

Rennison, C. M., & Welchans, S. (2000). *Intimate partner violence.* Washington, DC: Bureau of Justice Statistics.

Renzetti, C. M. (1992). *Violent betrayal: Partner abuse in lesbian relationships.* Newbury Park, CA: Sage.

Rice, M. (1990). Challenging orthodoxies in feminist theory: A black feminist critique. In L. Gelsthorpe & A. Morris (Eds.), *Feminist perspectives in criminology* (pp. 57–69). Buckingham, UK: Open University Press.

Richie, B. E. (1996). *Compelled to crime: The gender entrapment of battered black women.* New York: Routledge.

Rigakos, G. (1997). Situational determinants of police responses to civil and criminal injunctions for battered women. *Violence Against Women, 3,* 204–216.

Risley-Curtiss, C., & Heffernan, K. (2003). Gender biases in child welfare. *Affilia, 18*(4), 395–410.

Ristock, J. L. (1991). Understanding violence in lesbian relationships: An examination of misogyny and homophobia. In S. Kirby, D. Daniels, K. McKenna, M. Pojol, & M. Valiquette (Eds.), *Women changing academe: The proceedings of the 1990 Canadian Women's Studies Conference* (pp. 113–121). Winnipeg: Sororal.

Ristock, J. L. (2003). Exploring dynamics of abusive lesbian relationships: Preliminary analysis of a multisite, qualitative study. *American Journal of Community Psychology, 31*(3/4), 329–341.

Roberts, D. E. (1993). Motherhood and crime. *Iowa Law Review, 95,* 95–141.

Roberts, J. V. (1992). Reforming rape laws: Effects of legislative change in Canada. *Law and Human Behavior, 16,* 555–573.

Robinson, R. (1990). *Violations of girlhood: A qualitative study of female delinquents and children in need of services in Massachusetts.* Unpublished doctoral dissertation, Brandeis University.

Roh, J., & Haider-Markel, D. P. (2003). All politics is not local: National forces in state abortion initiatives. *Social Science Quarterly, 84*(1), 15–31.

Roiphe, K. (1993, June 13). Rape hype betrays feminism: Date rape's other victim. *New York Times Magazine.* pp. 26–30, 40, 68.

Romenesko, K., & Miller, E. M. (1989). The second step in double jeopardy: Appropriating the labor of female street hustlers. *Crime & Delinquency, 35,* 109–135.

Rose, V. M. (1977). Rape as a social problem: A byproduct of the feminist movement. *Social Problems, 25,* 79–85.

Rosen, R. (1982). *The lost sisterhood: Prostitution in America, 1900–1918.* Baltimore, MD: Johns Hopkins University Press.

Rothbaum, B. O., Foa, E. B., Riggs, D. S., Murdock, T., & Walsh, W. (1992). A prospective examination of post traumatic stress disorder in rape victims. *Journal of Traumatic Stress, 5,* 455–475.

Royal College of General Practitioners. (2003, May). *Female genital mutilation* (Statement Number 3). Retrieved from www.rcog.org.uk/resources/Public/RCOG_Statement_No3.pdf

Ruback, R. B., Menard, K. S., Outlaw, M. S., & Shaffer, J. N. (1999). Normative advice to campus crime victims: Effects of gender, age, and alcohol. *Violence and Victims, 14,* 381–396.

Rush, F. (1990). *The best kept secret: Sexual abuse of children.* Englewood Cliffs, NJ: Prentice Hall.

Rys, G. S., & Bear, G. G. (1997). Relational aggression and peer relations: Gender and developmental issues. *Merrill-Palmer Quarterly, 43,* 87–106.

Sacks, K. B. (1988). *Caring by the hour: Women, work and organizing at Duke Medical Center.* Urbana: University of Illinois Press.

Sagar, H. A., & Schofield, J. W. (1980). Racial and behavioral cues in black and white children's perceptions of ambiguously aggressive acts. *Journal of Personality and Social Psychology, 39,* 590–598.

Sanday, P. R. (1981). *Female power and male dominance: On the origins of sexual inequality.* Cambridge, UK: Cambridge University Press.

Sanday, P. R. (1986). *Divine hunger: Cannibalism as a cultural system.* Cambridge, UK: Cambridge University Press.

Sanday, P. R. (1990). *Fraternity gang rape: Sex, brotherhood, and privilege on campus.* New York: New York University Press.

Sanday, P. R. (1996). *A woman scorned: Acquaintance rape on trial.* New York: Doubleday.

Santiago, A. M., & Morash, M. (1994). Strategies for serving Latina battered women. In J. A. Garber & R. S. Turner (Eds.), *Urban affairs annual review: Vol. 42. Gender in urban research* (pp. 219–235). Thousand Oaks, CA: Sage.

Sarri, R. (1976). Juvenile law: How it penalizes females. In L. Crites (Ed.), *The female offender* (pp. 67–87). Lexington, MA: Lexington Books.

Saunders, D. G. (1986). When battered women use violence: Husband-abuse or self-defense? *Victims and Violence, 1*(1), 47–60.

Schaffner, L. (1999). Violence and female delinquency: Gender transgressions and gender invisibility. *Berkeley Women's Law Journal, 14,* 40–65.

Scharf, M. P. (1997). *Balkan justice: The story behind the first international war crimes tribunal since Nuremberg.* Durham, NC: Carolina Academic Press.

Schechter, S. (1982). *Women and male violence.* Boston: South End Press.

Schifter, J., & Aggleton, P. (1999). Cacherismo in a San Jose brothel: Aspects of male sex work in Costa Rica. In P. Aggleton (Ed.), *Men who sell sex: International perspectives on male prostitution and AIDS* (pp. 141–158). London: UCL Press.

Schilt, K. (2003). "A little too ironic": The appropriation and packaging of Riot Grrrl politics by mainstream female musicians. *Popular Music and Society, 26,* 5–16.

Schlesinger, P., Dobash, R. E., Dobash, R. P., & Weaver, C. K. (1992). *Women viewing violence.* London: British Film Institute.

Schlossman, S., & Wallach. S. (1978). The crime of precocious sexuality: Female juvenile delinquency in the Progressive Era. *Harvard Educational Review, 48*(1), 65–93.

Schmitt, F. E., & Martin, P. Y. (1999). Unobtrusive mobilization by an institutionalized rape crisis center: "All we do comes from victims." *Gender & Society, 13*(3), 364–384.

Schneider, E. M. (1992). Particularity and generality: Challenges of feminist theory and practice in work on woman-abuse. *New York University Law Review, 67,* 520–568.

Schneider, E. M. (2000). *Battered women and the laws.* New Haven, CT: Yale University Press.

Schram, P. J. (1996). *The link between stereotype attitudes and behavioral intentions among female inmates, correctional officers, and program staff.* Unpublished doctoral dissertation, Michigan State University, Department of Criminal Justice.

Schrom Dye, N. (1980). *As equals and as sisters: Feminism, the labor movement, and the Women's Trade Union League of New York.* Columbia: University of Missouri Press.

Schulhofer, S. J. (1998). *Unwanted sex: The culture of intimidation and the failure of law.* Cambridge, MA: Harvard University Press.

Schwartz, M. D., & DeKesseredy, W. S. (1997). *Sexual assault on the college campus: The role of male peer support.* Thousand Oaks, CA: Sage.

Schwendinger, J. R., & Schwendinger, H. (1983). *Rape and inequality.* Beverly Hills, CA: Sage.

Scraton, P. (1990). Scientific knowledge or masculine discourses? Challenging patriarchy in criminology. In L. Gelsthorpe & A. Morris (Eds.), *Feminist perspectives in criminology* (pp. 10–25). Buckingham, UK: Open University Press.

Scully, D., & Marolla, J. (1985). Riding the bull at Gilley's: Convicted rapists describe the rewards of rape. *Social Problems, 32*(3), 251–263.

Selo, E. (1976). The cottage dwellers: Boys and girls in training school. In L. Crites (Ed.), *The female offender* (pp. 149–171). Lexington, MA: Lexington Books.

Senate Committee on the Judiciary. Report on the Violence Against Women Act of 1993, S. Rep. No. 103–138, 103rd Congress, 1st Sess. (1993), p. 42.

The Sentencing Project. (2005). *Life sentences: Denying welfare benefits to women convicted of drug offenses.* Washington, DC: The Sentencing Project. (Available at www.sentencingproject.org/pdfs/9088smy.pdf)

Seyers, M. A., & Edleson, J. L. (1992). The combined effects of coordinated criminal justice intervention in women abuse. *Journal of Interpersonal Violence, 7,* 490–502.

Seymour, J. (1977). Niches in prison. In H. Toch (Ed.), *Living in prison: The ecology of survival* (pp. 179–205). New York: Free Press.

Shainess, N. (1984). *Sweet suffering: Woman as victim.* New York: Pocket Books.

Shaw, M. (1999). Is there a feminist future for women's prisons? In R. Matthews & P. Francis *Prisons 2000* (pp. 179–200). London: Macmillan.

Shelton, D. (2000). The human rights of women in the jurisprudence of permanent international tribunals. In K. D. Askin & D. M. Koenig (Eds.), *Women and international human rights law* (Vol. 2, pp. 31–50). New York: Transnational.

Sherman, F. T. (2001). Effective advocacy strategies for girls: Promoting justice in an unjust system. *PLI litigation and administrative practice: Criminal Law and Urban Problems Course Handbook Series, 187,* 157–172.

Sherman, L. W., & Berk, R. A. (1984). The specific deterrent effects of arrest for domestic assault. *American Sociological Review, 49*(2), 261–272.

Sherman, L. W., Schmidt, J. D., Rogan, D. P., Smith, D. A., Gartin, P. R., Cohn, E. G., et al. (1992). The variable effects of arrest on criminal careers: The Milwaukee domestic violence experiment. *Journal of Criminal Law and Criminology, 83,* 137–169.

Silbert, M. H., & Pines, A. M. (1993). Making violence sexy: Feminist views on pornography. In D.E.H. Russell (Ed.), *Making violence sexy: Feminist views on pornography* (pp. 113–119). New York: Teachers College Press.

Silverthorn, P., & Frick, P. J. (1999). Developmental pathways to antisocial behavior: The delayed-onset pathway in girls. *Development and Psychopathology, 11,* 101–126.

Silverthorn, P., Frick, P. J., & Reynolds, R. (2001). Timing of onset and correlates of severe conduct problems in adjudicated girls and boys. *Journal of Psychopathology and Behavioral Assessment, 23*(3), 171–181.

Simkins, S., & Katz, S. (2002). Criminalizing abused girls. *Violence Against Women, 8,* 1474–1499.

Simmons, R. (2002). *Odd girl out: The hidden culture of aggression in girls.* Orlando, FL: Harcourt.

Simmons, R. G., & Blyth, D. A. (1987). *Moving into adolescence: The impact of pubertal change and school context.* New York: Aldine de Gruyter.

Simon, R. (1975). *Women and crime.* Lexington, MA: Lexington Books.

Simonson, K., & Subich, L. M. (1999). Rape perceptions as a function of gender-role traditionality and victim-perpetrator association. *Sex Roles, 40,* 617–634.

Simpson, A. R. (2001). *Raising teens: A synthesis of research and a foundation for action.* Cambridge, MA: Harvard School of Public Health, Center for Health Communication.

Skolnik, L., & Bootinand, J. (1999). Traffic in women in Asia-Pacific. *Forum for Applied Research and Public Policy, 14*(1), 76–81.

Sloan, L. M. (1995). Revictimization by polygraph: The practice of polygraphy survivors of sexual assault. *Medicine and Law, 14,* 255–267.

Smart, C. (1976). *Women, crime, and criminology.* London: Routledge & Kegan Paul.

Smart, C. (1989). *Sociology of law and crime: Feminism and the power of law.* London: Routledge.

Smart, C. (1992). *Regulating womanhood.* London & New York: Routledge.

Smart, C. (1995). *Law, crime and sexuality: Essays in feminism.* London: Sage.

Smith, D. A., & Klein, J. R. (1984). Police control of interpersonal disputes. *Social Problems, 31,* 468–481.

Smith, D. W., Letourneau, E. J., Saunders, B. E., Kilpatrick, D. G., Resnick, H. S., & Best, C. L. (2000). Delay in disclosure of childhood rape: Results from a national survey. *Child Abuse & Neglect, 24*(2), 273–287.

Smith, J. D., & Mancoske, R. J. (1999). Contributing issues to violence among gay male couples. In J. C. McClennen & J. Gunther (Eds.), *A professional guide to understanding gay and lesbian domestic violence: Understanding practice interventions* (pp. 257–276). Lewiston, NY: Edwin Mellen Press.

Smith, M. D. (1990). Patriarchal ideology and wife beating: A test of a feminist hypothesis. *Violence and Victims, 5*(4), 257–273.

Snyder, H. N. (2000). *Sexual assault of young children as reported to law enforcement: Victim, incident and offender characteristics.* Washington, DC: Bureau of Justice Statistics.

Snyder, H. N., & Sickmund, M. (1999). *Juvenile offenders and victims: 1999 national report* (NCJ 178257). Washington, DC: U.S. Department of Justice, Office of Justice Programs, Office of Juvenile Justice and Delinquency Prevention. [Also available on the World Wide Web: www. ncjrs.org/html/ojjdp/nationalreport99/toc.html]

Spears, J. W., & Spohn, C. C. (1996). The genuine victim and prosecutors' charging decisions in sexual assault cases. *American Journal of Criminal Justice, 20*(2), 183–205.

Spender, D. (1995). *Nattering on the net: Women, power and cyberspace.* Melbourne: Spiniflex.

Spohn, C., & Beichner, D. (2000). Is preferential treatment of female offenders a thing of the past? A multisite study of gender, race, and imprisonment. *Criminal Justice Policy Review, 11*(2), 149–184.

Spohn, C., Beichner, D., & Davis-Frenzel, E. (2001). Prosecutorial justifications for sexual assault case rejection: Guarding the "gateway to justice." *Social Problems, 48*(2), 206–236.

Spohn, C., & Holleran, D. (2000). The imprisonment penalty paid by young, unemployed black and Hispanic male offenders. *Criminology, 38*(1), 281–306.

Spohn, C., & Horney, J. (1990). The case of unrealistic expectations: The impact of rape reform legislation in Illinois. *Criminal Justice Policy Review, 4*(1), 1–18.

Spohn, C., & Horney, J. (1992). *Rape law reform: A grassroots revolution and its impact.* New York: Plenum.

Spohn, C., & Horney, J. (1993). Rape law reform and the effect of victim characteristics on case processing. *Journal of Quantitative Criminology, 9*(4), 383–409.

Spohn, C., & Horney, J. (1996). The impact of rape law reform on the processing of simple and aggravated rape cases. *Journal of Criminal Law and Criminology, 86*(3), 861–884.

Staggenborg, S. (1991). *The pro-choice movement.* New York: Oxford University Press.

Stalins, L. J., & Finn, M. A. (1995). How novice and experienced officers interpret wife assaults: Normative and efficiency frames. *Law and Society Review, 29,* 287–321.

Stanko, E. (1990). *Everyday violence: How women and men experience sexual and physical danger.* London: Pandora.

Stanko, E. A. (1995). Women, crime, and fear. *Annals of the American Academy of Political and Social Science, 539,* 46–58.

Stanko, E. A., & Hobdell, K. (1993). Assault on men: Masculinity and male victimisation. *British Journal of Criminology, 33,* 400–415.

Stark, E., & Flitcraft, A. H. (1988). Women and children at risk: A feminist perspective on child abuse. *International Journal of Health Services, 18,* 97–110.

Steffensmeier, D., & Allan, E. (1996). Gender and crime: Toward a gendered theory of female offending. *Annual Review of Sociology, 22,* 459–487.

Steffensmeier, D., & Haynie, D. (2000). Gender, structural disadvantage, and urban crime: Do macrosocial variables also explain female offending rates? *Criminology, 38*(2), 403–438.

Steffensmeier, D., Kramer, J., & Streifel, C. (1993). Gender and imprisonment decisions. *Criminology, 31,* 411–446.

Steffensmeier, D., & Streifel, C. (1992). Time series analysis of the female percentage of arrests for property crimes, 1960–1985: A test of alternative explanations. *Justice Quarterly, 9*(1), 77–104.

Steffensmeier, D., Ulmer, J., & Kramer, J. (1998). The interaction of race, gender, and age in criminal sentencing: The punishment cost of being young, black, and male. *Criminology, 36*(4), 763–798.

Steinman, M. (1990). Lowering recidivism among men who batter women. *Journal of Police Science and Administration, 17,* 124–132.

Steinmetz, S. K., & Lucca, J. S. (1988). Husband battering. In V. B. Van Hasselt, R. L. Morrison, A. S. Bellack, & M. Hersen (Eds.), *Handbook of family violence* (pp. 233–236). New York: Plenum.

Stephens, B. J., & Sinden, P. G. (2000). Victims' voices. *Journal of Interpersonal Violence, 15,* 534–547.

Stewart, A., & Maddren, K. (1997). Police officers' judgments of blame in family violence: The impact of gender and alcohol. *Sex Roles, 37,* 921–933.

Stith, S. M. (1990). Police response to domestic violence: The influence of individual and familial factors. *Violence Against Women, 5,* 37–49.

Stockdale, M. S., Visio, M., & Batra, L. (1999). The sexual harassment of men: Evidence for a broader theory of sexual harassment and sex discrimination. *Psychology, Public Policy, and Law, 5,* 630–664.

Stone, A. E., & Fialk, R. J. (1997). Criminalizing the exposure of children to family violence: Breaking the cycle of abuse. *Harvard Women's Law Journal, 20,* 205–227.

Strang, H., & Braithwaite, J. (Eds.). (2002). *Restorative justice and family violence.* Cambridge, UK: Cambridge University Press.

Straus, M. (1980). The marriage license as a hitting license: Evidence from popular culture, law and social science. In M. A. Straus & G. T. Hotaling (Eds.), *The social causes of husband-wife violence* (pp. 39–50). Minneapolis: University of Minnesota Press.

Straus, M. A. (1993). Physical assault by wives: A major social problem. In R. J. Gelles & D. R. Loseke (Eds.), *Current controversies on family violence* (pp. 67–97). Newbury Park, CA: Sage.

Straus, M. A., & Gelles, R. (1990). *Physical violence in American families.* New Brunswick, NJ: Transaction.

Strauss, A., & Corbin, J. (1990). *Basics of qualitative research: Grounded theory procedures and techniques.* Thousand Oaks, CA: Sage.

Strom, K. J. (2001). *Hate crimes reported in NIBRS, 1997–99.* Washington, DC: Bureau of Justice Statistics.

Strossen, N. (1996). A feminist critique of "the" feminist critique of pornography. In D. K. Weisberg (Ed.), *Applications of feminist legal theory to women's lives* (pp. 131–149). Philadelphia: Temple University Press.

Struckman-Johnson, C. J., & Struckman-Johnson, D. L. (2000). Sexual coercion rates in seven Midwestern prison facilities for men. *The Prison Journal, 80*(4), 379–390.

Struckman-Johnson, C. J., Struckman-Johnson, D. L., Rucker, L., Bumby, K., & Donaldson, S. (1996). Sexual coercion reported by men and women in prison. *Journal of Sex Research, 33,* 67–76.

Sudbury, J. (2002). Celling black bodies: Black women in the global prison industrial complex. *Feminist Review, 70,* 57–74.

Sullivan, C. M. (1991). Battered women as active helpseekers. *Violence Update, 1*(12), 1, 8, 10.

Sullivan, C. M., & Bybee, D. I. (1999). Reducing violence using community-based services for battered women and their children. *Journal of Consulting and Clinical Psychology, 67*(1), 43–53.

Sullivan, C. M., Tan, C., Basta, J., Rumptz, M., & Davidson, W. S., II. (1992). An advocacy intervention program for women with abusive partners: Initial evaluation. *American Journal of Community Psychology, 20*(3), 309–332.

Sullivan, M. L. (1989). *Getting paid: Youth crime and work in the inner city.* Ithaca, NY: Cornell University Press.

Sutherland, E. H. (1924). *Criminology.* Philadelphia: Lippincott.

Swanson, L., & Biaggio, M. K. (1985). Therapeutic perspectives on father-daughter incest. *American Journal of Psychiatry, 142,* 667–674.

Swartz, J., Martinovich, Z., & Goldstein, P. (2003). An analysis of the criminogenic effects of terminating the supplemental security income program for drug addiction and alcoholism. *Contemporary Drug Problems, 30,* 391–424.

Taylor, U. Y. (1998). Making waves: The theory and practice of black feminism. *The Black Scholar, 28,* 18–28.

Temin, C. E. (1980). Discriminatory sentencing of women offenders: The argument for ERA in a nutshell. In S. K. Datesman & F. R. Scarpitti (Eds.), *Women, crime, and justice* (pp. 255–276). New York: Oxford University Press.

Temkin, J. (1997). Plus ça change: Reporting rape in the 1990s. *British Journal of Criminology, 37*(4), 507–528.

Terr, L. C. (1991). Childhood traumas: An outline and overview. *American Journal of Psychiatry, 148,* 10–20.

Terry, R. M. (1970). Discrimination in the handling of juvenile offenders by social control agencies. In P. G. Garabedian & D. C. Gibbons (Eds.), *Becoming delinquent* (pp. 78–92). Chicago: Aldine Press.

Thomas, W. I. (1923). *The unadjusted girl.* New York: Harper & Row.

Thornton, A. (1989). Changing attitudes toward family issues in the United States. *Journal of Marriage and the Family, 51,* 873–894.

Thrasher, F. M. (1927). *The gang.* Chicago: University of Chicago Press.

Thurman v. City of Torrington, 5595 F. Supp., D. Conn. 1521 (1984).

Tierney, K. J. (1982). The battered women movement and the creation of the wife beating problem. *Social Problems, 29*(3), 207-220.

Tjaden, P., & Thoennes, N. (1998). *Prevalence, incidence, and consequences of violence against women: Findings from the National Violence Against Women Survey.* Washington, DC: National Institute of Justice and Center for Disease Control and Prevention.

Tjaden, P., & Thoennes, N. (2000a). *Extent, nature, and consequences of intimate partner violence: Findings from the National Violence Against Women Survey* (National Institute of Justice and the Centers for Disease Control and Prevention). Washington, DC: Government Printing Office.

Tjaden, P., & Thoennes, N. (2000b). The role of stalking in domestic violence crime reports generated by the Colorado Springs Police Department. *Violence and Victims, 15*(4), 427–441.

Tong, R. P. (1984). *Women, sex, and the law.* Totowa, NJ: Rowman & Allenheld.

Tong, R. P. (1998). *Feminist thought: A more comprehensive introduction.* Boulder, CO: Westview.

Trepper, T. S., & Barrett, M. J. (1989). *Systemic treatment of incest: A therapeutic handbook.* New York: Brunner/Mazel.

Tuesday, V. J. (1998). Girls in jail. *Women & Therapy, 21*(1), 127–139.

Turk, A. T. (2004). Sociology of terrorism. *Annual Review of Sociology* (pp. 271–286). Palo Alto, CA: Annual Reviews.

Turrell, S. C. (2000). A descriptive analysis of same-sex relationship violence for a diverse sample. *Journal of Family Violence, 15,* 281–293.

Twenge, J. M. (1997). Attitudes toward women 1970–1995: A meta-analysis. *Psychology of Women Quarterly 21,* 35–51.

Uggen, C., & Kruttschnitt, C. (1998). Crime in the breaking: Gender differences in desistance. *Law and Society Review, 32*(2), 339–366.

Underwood, M. K. (2003). *Social aggression among girls.* New York: Guilford.

Underwood, M. K. (2004). Glares of contempt, eye rolls of disgust and turning away to exclude: Non-verbal forms of social aggression among girls. *Feminism and Psychology, 14,* 371–375.

U.S. Department of Health and Human Services. (2001). *Youth violence: A report of the Surgeon General.* Rockville, MD: U.S. Department of Health and Human Services, Centers for Disease Control and Prevention, National Center for Injury Prevention and Control; Substance Abuse and Mental Health Services Administration, Center for Mental Health Services; and National Institutes of Health and Mental Health.

Vance, C. S. (1984). *Pleasure and danger: Exploring female sexuality.* Boston: Routledge and Kegan Paul.

Vedder, C. B., & Sommerville, D. B. (1970). *The delinquent girl.* Springfield, IL: Charles C Thomas.

Venkatesh, S. A. (1998). Gender and outlaw capitalism: A historical account of the Black Sisters United "girl gang." *Signs: Journal of Women in Culture and Society, 23*(3), 683–709.

Vicinus, M. (1973). *Suffer and be still.* Bloomington: Indiana University Press.

Viki, G. T., & Abrams, D. (2002). But she was unfaithful: Benevolent sexism and reactions to rape victims who violate traditional gender role expectations. *Sex Roles, 47,* 289–293.

Violence Against Women Grants Office. (1998). *Stalking and domestic violence in the U.S.* Washington, DC: Office of Justice Programs.

Visher, C. (1983). Gender, police arrest decisions and notions of chivalry. *Criminology, 21,* 5–27.

Vogt, I. (1998). Gender and drug treatment systems. In H. Klingemann & G. Hunt (Eds.), *Drug treatment systems in an international perspective: Drugs, demons, and delinquents* (pp. 281–297). Thousand Oaks, CA: Sage.

Vrettos, T. M. (2002). Victimizing the victim: Evicting domestic violence victims from public housing based on the zero tolerance policy. *Cardozo Women's Law Journal, 9,* 97–130.

Waldo, C. R., Hesson-McInnis, M. S., & D'Augelli, A. R. (1998). Antecedents and consequences of victimization of lesbian, gay, and bisexual young people: A structural model comparing rural university and urban samples. *American Journal of Community Psychology, 26*(2), 307–334.

Walker, A. (1992). *Possessing the secret of joy.* New York: Harcourt Brace Jovanovich.

Walker, L.E.A. (1984). *The battered woman syndrome.* New York: Springer.

Walker, R. (Ed.). (1995). *To be real: Telling the truth and changing the face of feminism.* New York: Anchor Books.

Walker, S. J. (2001). *The meaning of consent: College women's and men's experiences with nonviolent sexual coercion.* Unpublished doctoral dissertation, Austin, University of Texas, Department of Sciences and Engineering.

Walkowitz, J. R. (1980). *Prostitution and Victorian society: Women, class, and the state.* Cambridge, UK: Cambridge University Press.

Walter, N. (1999). *The new feminism.* London: Virago.

Wan, A. M. (2000). Battered women in the restraining order process: Observations on a court advocacy program. *Violence Against Women, 6,* 606–632.

Washington, P. A. (1999). Second assault of male survivors of sexual violence: Ways in which survivors of sexual assault are revictimized by society. *Journal of Interpersonal Violence, 14,* 713–730.

Wattenberg, E. (1985). In a different light: A feminist perspective on the role of mothers in father-daughter incest. *Child Welfare, 64,* 203–211.

Websdale, N. (1999). *Understanding domestic homicide.* Boston: Northeastern University Press.

Weiner, M. H. (2003). The potential and challenges of transnational litigation for feminists concerned about domestic violence here and abroad. *American University Journal of Gender, Social Policy & the Law, 11,* 749–800.

Weis, K., & Borges, S. (1973). Victimology and rape: The case of the legitimate victim. *Issues in Criminology, 8,* 71–115.

Weis, K., & Borges, S. (1977). Victimology and rape: The case of the legitimate victim. In D. R. Nass (Ed.), *The rape victim* (pp. 35–75). Dubuque, IA: Kendall/Hunt.

Weissman, D. M. (2001). Gender-based violence as judicial anomaly: Between "the truly national and the truly local." *Boston College Law Review, 42,* 1081–1159.

Weitzer, R. (1991). Prostitutes' rights in the United States: The failure of a movement. *The Sociological Quarterly, 32,* 23–41.

Weldon, S. L. (2002). *Protest, policy, and the problem of violence against women: A cross-national comparison.* Pittsburgh, PA: University of Pittsburgh Press.

West, C. M., Kantor, G. K., & Jasinski, J. L. (1998). Sociodemographic predictors and cultural barriers to help-seeking behavior by Latina and Anglo American battered women. *Violence and Victims, 13*(4), 361–375.

West, C., & Zimmerman, D. H. (1987). Doing gender. *Gender and Society, 1,* 125–151.

West, J. (2000). Prostitution: Collectives and the politics of regulation. *Gender, Work and Organization, 7*(2), 106–118.

Weston-Henriques, Z., & Jones-Brown, D. D. (2000). Prisons as "safe havens" for African-American women. In M. W. Markowitz & D. D. Jones-Brown (Eds.), *The system in black and white: Exploring the connections between race, crime and justice* (pp. 267–273). Westport, CT: Praeger.

Whaley, R. B. (2001). The paradoxical relationship between gender inequality and rape: Toward a refined theory. *Gender & Society, 15,* 531–555.

Whetstone, T. S. (2001). Measuring the impact of a domestic violence coordinated response team. *Policing: An International Journal of Police Strategies & Management, 24*(3), 371–398.

White, J. W., & Humphrey, J. A. (1991). Young people's attitudes towards acquaintance rape. In A. Parrot & L. Bechhofer (Eds.), *Acquaintance rape: The hidden crime* (pp. 43–56). New York: John Wiley.

Whitley, B. E., Jr. (2001). Gender-role variables and attitudes toward homosexuality. *Sex Roles, 45,* 691–721.

Widom, C. S. (1996). Childhood sexual abuse and its criminal consequences. *Society, 33,* 47–53.

Wilkie, M. (1993). *Sentencing women: Pre-sentence reports and constructions of female offenders.* Nedland: University of Western Australia Crime Research Center.

Williams, J. A. (2003). The "pitiless double abuse" of battered mothers. *American University Journal of Gender, Social Policy & the Law, 11,* 523–531.

Wilson, W. J. (1996). *When work disappears: The world of the new urban poor.* New York: Knopf.

Winter, B. (1994). Women, the law, and cultural relativism in France: The case of excision. *Signs: Journal of Women in Culture and Society, 19,* 939–974.

Wolfgang, M. E., Thornberry, T. P., & Figlio, R. (1987). *From boy to man: From delinquency to crime.* Chicago: University of Chicago Press.

Women, Law and Development International. (1997). *Women's human rights step by step.* Washington, DC: Women, Law and Development International.

Wood, K., Maforah, F., & Jewkes, R. (1998). "He forced me to love him": Putting violence on adolescent sexual health agendas. *Social Science and Medicine, 47*(2), 233–242.

World Health Organization. (2000). *Breaking the silence on violence and HIV* (Fact Sheet 49). Washington, DC: Author.

Worrall, A. (1989). *Nondescript women.* London: Routledge.

Yazzie, R. (1994). Life comes from it: Navajo justice. *Context: A Quarterly of Human Sustainable Culture, 38,* 29–31.

Yllo, K. (1983). Sexual equality and violence against wives in American states. *Journal of Comparative Family Studies, 14,* 67–86.

Yllo, K., & Straus, M. A. (1984). The impact of structural inequality and sexist family norms on rates of wife beating. *Journal of International and Comparative Social Welfare, 1,* 16–29.

Yoshioka, M. R., Gilbert, L., & El-Bassel, N. (2003). Social support and disclosure of abuse: Comparing South Asian, African American, and Hispanic battered women. *Journal of Family Violence, 18*(3), 171–180.

Younglove, J. A., Kerr, M. G., & Vitello, C. J. (2002). Law enforcement officers' perceptions of same sex domestic violence reason for cautious optimism. *Journal of Interpersonal Violence, 17,* 760–772.

Zahn-Waxler, C. (1993). Warriors and worriers: Gender and psychopathology. *Development and Psychopathology, 5,* 79–90.

Zahn-Waxler, C. (2000). The development of empathy, guilt, and internalization of distress. In R. Davidson (Ed.), *Anxiety, depression, and emotion: Wisconsin symposium on emotion* (Vol. 2, pp. 222–265). New York: Oxford University Press.

Zald, M., & Useem, B. (1987). Movement and countermovement interactions: Mobilization, tactics, and state involvement. In M. N. Zald & J. D. McCarthy (Eds.), *Social movements in an organizational society* (pp. 247–272). New Brunswick, NJ: Transaction.

Zatz, N. D. (1997). Sex work/sex act. *Signs: Journal of Women in Culture and Society, 22*(2), 277–308.

Zellerer, E. (1999). Restorative justice in indigenous communities: Critical issues in confronting violence against women. *International Review of Victimology, 6,* 345–368.

Zion, J., & Zion, E. B. (1996). "Hazho' Sokee"—Stay together nicely: Domestic violence under Navajo common law. In M. O. Nielsen & R. A. Silverman (Eds.), *Native Americans, crime, and justice* (pp. 96–113). Boulder, CO: Westview.

Index

About the Author

Merry Morash is Professor at the Michigan State University School of Criminal Justice, where she served as director from 1991 to 2001. She also is founder, director, and faculty instructor of the Michigan Victim Assistance Academy, which provides education for individuals who work with crime victims; director of the Michigan Regional Community Policing Institute; secretary of the Michigan DARE (Drug and Alcohol Abuse Resistance Education) Advisory Board. Her primary research emphasis is on gender and crime, and current research is on domestic violence among Asian Americans and gender-responsive programming for women offenders. She also has done extensive research on women in policing and is currently engaged in research to follow up on women who participated in a study nearly a decade ago. She recently served on the Domestic Violence Homicide Prevention Task Force, which was chaired by Michigan's lieutenant governor, and on the Advisory Board for the Michigan Judicial Institute bench book to assist judges in their work with crime victims. She is a member of the Girls Study Group, which, with the support of the U.S. Office of Juvenile Justice and Delinquency Prevention, is assembling state-of-the-art knowledge on the causes of and effective responses to girls who break the law. She is coauthor of the textbook *Juvenile Delinquency: Concepts and Control* and co-editor of *The Move to Community Policing: Making Change Happen*, and she has written and published extensively on women as offenders, police officers, and crime victims. Additional publications focus on assessment and implementation of criminal justice policy and juvenile delinquency programming and causation.